MW01054201

AFRICAN AMERICAN LITERATURE
IN TRANSITION, 1960–1970

This volume considers innovations, transitions, and traditions in both familiar and unfamiliar texts and moments in 1960s African American literature and culture. It interrogates declarations of race, authenticity, personal and collective empowerment, political action, and aesthetics within this key decade. It is divided into three sections. The first section engages poetry and music as pivotal cultural forms in 1960s literary transitions. The second section explains how literature, culture, and politics intersect to offer a blueprint for revolution within and beyond the United States. The final section addresses literary and cultural moments that are lesser-known in the canon of African American literature and culture. This book presents the 1960s as a unique moment of commitment to art, when "Black" became a political identity, one in which racial social justice became inseparable from aesthetic practice.

SHELLY EVERSLEY teaches literature, feminism, and Black studies at Baruch College, The City University of New York, where she is Chair of the Black and Latinx Studies Department. Her research and publishing specializes in African American literature and culture as well as in feminist studies, and she is founder of equalityarchive.com.

AFRICAN AMERICAN LITERATURE IN TRANSITION

Editor Joycelyn K. Moody, The University of Texas at San Antonio

Associate Editor Cassander Smith, The University of Alabama

Across 17 authoritative volumes and featuring over 200 of today's foremost literary critics and social historians, African American Literature in Transition offers a critical and comprehensive revisionary analysis of creative expression by people of African descent. Reading transtemporally from the origins of "African American literature" by the first peoples calling themselves "African Americans," this series foregrounds change, and examines pivotal moments, years, decades, and centuries in African American literature and culture. While collectively analyzing both far-reaching and flash-forward transitions within four centuries, the multi-volume series replaces conventional historical periodization in African American scholastic and literary anthologies with a framework that contextualizes shifts, changes, and transformations in African American literature, culture, politics, and history.

Books in the series

African American Literature in Transition, 1800–1830 edited by
JASMINE NICHOLE COBB

African American Literature in Transition, 1830–1850 edited by
BENJAMIN FAGAN

African American Literature in Transition, 1850–1865 edited by
TERESA ZACKODNIK

African American Literature in Transition, 1865–1880 edited by
ERIC GARDNER

African American Literature in Transition, 1900–1910 edited by
SHIRLEY MOODY-TURNER

African American Literature in Transition, 1920–1930 edited by
MIRIAM THAGGERT AND RACHEL FAREBROTHER

African American Literature in Transition 1930–1940 edited by
EVE DUNBAR AND AYESHA K. HARDISON

African American Literature in Transition, 1960–1970 edited by
SHELLY EVERSLEY

AFRICAN AMERICAN LITERATURE IN TRANSITION, 1960–1970

Black Art, Politics, and Aesthetics

EDITED BY

SHELLY EVERSLEY

Baruch College, The City University of New York

CAMBRIDGE
UNIVERSITY PRESS

CAMBRIDGE
UNIVERSITY PRESS

University Printing House, Cambridge CB2 8BS, United Kingdom

One Liberty Plaza, 20th Floor, New York, NY 10006, USA

477 Williamstown Road, Port Melbourne, VIC 3207, Australia

314–321, 3rd Floor, Plot 3, Splendor Forum, Jasola District Centre,
New Delhi – 110025, India

103 Penang Road, #05–06/07, Visioncrest Commercial, Singapore 238467

Cambridge University Press is part of the University of Cambridge.

It furthers the University's mission by disseminating knowledge in the pursuit of
education, learning, and research at the highest international levels of excellence.

www.cambridge.org
Information on this title: www.cambridge.org/9781108422932
DOI: 10.1017/9781108386043

© Cambridge University Press 2022

This publication is in copyright. Subject to statutory exception
and to the provisions of relevant collective licensing agreements,
no reproduction of any part may take place without the written
permission of Cambridge University Press.

First published 2022

A catalogue record for this publication is available from the British Library.

ISBN 978-1-108-42293-2 Hardback

Cambridge University Press has no responsibility for the persistence or accuracy of
URLs for external or third-party internet websites referred to in this publication
and does not guarantee that any content on such websites is, or will remain,
accurate or appropriate.

Contents

Contributors

GERSHUN AVILEZ, University of Maryland.

SHELLY EVERSLEY, Baruch College, The City University of New York.

PHILLIP BRIAN HARPER, The Andrew W. Mellon Foundation and New
York University (Emeritus).

PATRICIA HERRERA, University of Richmond.

CHERYL HIGASHIDA, University of Colorado at Boulder.

KEITH D. LEONARD, American University.

KELLY M. NIMS, Hunter College, The City University of New York.

ERIC PORTER, University of California, Santa Cruz.

DERIK SMITH, Claremont McKenna College.

PAUL C. TAYLOR, Vanderbilt University.

DAGMAWI WOUBSHET, University of Pennsylvania.

Preface
African American Literature in Transition
Joycelyn K. Moody, General Editor

When I accepted the invitation to act as Series Editor for African American Literature in Transition, Barack Obama had several months more to serve as President of the United States. The United States was in a time of tremendous transition, we knew, but the extent of the impact of the coming election and its outcomes on the lives of African Americans, we had yet to learn. In the years since, dozens of today's foremost literary critics and social historians have traced across this authoritative multi-volume series revisionary analyses of creative expression by peoples of the African diaspora. Reading transtemporally, African American Literature in Transition foregrounds change, and examines pivotal moments and eras in African American history and historiography, literature and culture, art and ideology. The contributors explore four centuries of far-reaching as well as flash-forward transitions, to replace conventional literary periodization with a framework that contextualizes shifts, changes, and transformations affecting African American people.

Taken singly or together, the more than 200 chapters of the series provide not customary synopses of African American literature but unprecedented, detailed analyses – each expansive, in-depth, engaging. Every contributor finds their perfect pitch. Where contributors are musicians, then, to quote John Lovell, Jr.'s *Black Song: The Forge and the Flame*, "music raise[s] both performer and audience far above routine emotion; the elderly throw away their sticks and dance."

The central aim of African American Literature in Transition is to reorient readers' expectations of the literary critical and appreciative experience. The series emphasizes the importance of reading intertextually, transhistorically, and interdisciplinarily. In this way, we foster readers' comprehension of ways in which legal cases such as the *Dred Scott* Decision and *Plessy* v. *Ferguson*, for example, were forecast in David Walker's 1829 *Appeal to the Colored Citizens of the World* and have reappeared in *Solitary: My Story of Transformation and Hope*, by Albert

Woodfox (2019). Truly distinctive, African American Literature in Transition offers rich demonstrations of how to read Black creative expression as a sequence of shifting contexts and dynamic landscapes.

I offer sincere gratitude to Ray Ryan at Cambridge University Press for selecting me to spearhead this project, and to Cassander Smith for seeing it through with me. I am grateful to Edgar Mendez and Cambridge interns Caitlin Gallagher and Rebecca Rom-Frank. I appreciate the enthusiastic support of my family, friends, and colleagues over the years: especially Lorraine Martínez, Roxanne Donovan, Kimberly Blockett, Barbara Neely, Cynthia Lockett, Rhonda Gonzales, T. Jackie Cuevas, and Howard Rambsy II. Colleen J. McElroy and my uncles Charles and Glenn inspire me in ways they cannot imagine. My son and my parents influence everything I undertake. To the African American Literature in Transition volume editors and contributors: your dedication to tracing transitions with me made all the difference.

Acknowledgments

Today it feels like the violent conflicts of the 1960s, that escalated each year as the decade progressed, have deepened and emerged in twenty-first-century hyper-drive. It is impossible to ignore how the violence piling up in this contemporary moment brings with it so many echoes of the past.

As I write these acknowledgments, a pandemic has caused the whole world to stop. Sickness, death, isolation, and the visible and global signs of structural inequalities have been laid bare. In the United States, an election with unprecedented voter participation has revealed a nation horribly divided by antagonisms about race, immigration, the police, civil rights, gender identity and equity, climate change, education, and the very notion of democracy itself. People are marching in the streets – most are hoping for more justice in a world in which so many can't breathe. And in this, there is hope. The people marching and voting and writing and making music, art, and poems recall a spirit of survival and resistance that can energize a new transition. Maybe this time, we will learn the lessons the past offers to us.

I offer my deepest thanks to the authors who contributed to the making of this book. It has been my honor to collaborate with them. They are all Black, Indigenous, and people of color (BIPOC) – scholars, writers, teachers, and community members whose generosity and intellectual rigor are an inspiration. Alex Polish has been a kind and patient editor whose organizational brilliance has been essential to getting this project across the finish line. And Joycelyn Moody! As the General Editor of this ambitious series, her vision, her leadership, and her incredible commitment model how African American literature and culture is indeed central to U.S. self-understanding. As a scholar, teacher, and friend she has taught me so much about how to be an ethical person in this complicated world. Thank you, Joycelyn.

Many thanks to Cambridge University Press for its investment in this project, especially to Ray Ryan and Edgar Mendez.

Chronology

1960   The Greensboro Four begin the Sit-in Movement at F. W. Woolworth department store in Greensboro, North Carolina.
The Student Nonviolent Coordinating Committee (SNCC) is established in Raleigh, North Carolina.
President Dwight D. Eisenhower signs the Civil Rights Act of 1960.
Ruby Bridges integrates William Frantz Elementary School in New Orleans, Louisiana.
Gwendolyn Brooks publishes *The Bean Eaters*.
Miles Davis records *Sketches of Spain*.
John Coltrane and Don Cherry collaborate on the album *The Avant-Garde*.
Ornette Colemen records *Free Jazz*.
John Coltrane records *My Favorite Things*.
The Federal Drug Administration approves "The Pill," giving women more control over their reproductive rights.

1961   Nina Simone releases *Forbidden Fruit*.
The Freedom Rides are organized by the Congress of Racial Equality (CORE).
John F. Kennedy becomes the first Catholic President of the United States.
Richard Wright's *Eight Men* is published posthumously.
Lorraine Hansberry's *A Raisin in the Sun* is produced as a film (dir. Daniel Petrie).
Bay of Pigs coup attempt against Cuba fails.
The Berlin Wall is completed.

1962   Representatives from SNCC, CORE, and the National Association for the Advancement of Colored People (NAACP) form the Council of Federated Organizations (COFO).

Robert Hayden publishes *A Ballad of Remembrance*.

U.S. Department of Defense orders full integration of military reserve units, except the National Guard.

Fannie Lou Hamer attempts to register to vote in Indianola, Mississippi.

James Meredith is barred from enrolling at the University of Mississippi.

James Baldwin publishes *Another Country*.

Bob Thompson paints *Tree*.

1963   Watts Towers Art Center is established in Los Angeles.

Martin Luther King completes "Letter from a Birmingham Jail."

James Baldwin organizes a meeting with Black leaders and Attorney General Robert F. Kennedy to discuss race relations.

Medgar Evers, NAACP field secretary, is assassinated in Jackson, Mississippi.

March on Washington for Jobs and Freedom draws millions from international cities; Martin Luther King, Jr. delivers "I Have a Dream" speech.

Charles Mingus records *The Black Saint and Sinner Lady*.

James Baldwin publishes *The Fire Next Time*.

LeRoi Jones publishes *Blues People: Negro Music in White America*.

Romare Bearden and Hale Woodruff establish Spiral artists collective in Harlem.

16th Street Baptist Church in Birmingham, Alabama, is bombed.

President John F. Kennedy is assassinated in Texas; Lyndon B. Johnson becomes President of the United States.

Nina Simone releases *Nina's Choice*.

1964   The 24th Amendment to the U.S. Constitution abolishing poll taxes for federal elections is ratified.

Freedom Summer movement for voter education and registration begins in Mississippi.

Nelson Mandela begins a life sentence in a South African prison.

Bloody Tuesday: peaceful marchers are beaten, arrested, and tear-gassed in Tuscaloosa, Alabama.

James Chaney, Andrew Goodman, and Michael "Mickey" Schwerner, Mississippi civil rights workers, are abducted and murdered in Neshoba County, Mississippi.
Black Like Me is released as a film (dir. Carl Lerner).
Nothing But a Man is released as a film (dir. Michael Roemer).
John Coltrane records *A Love Supreme.*
Organization of Afro-American Unity (OAAU) is established by Malcolm X.
President Lyndon B. Johnson signs the Civil Rights Act of 1964.
Martin Luther King, Jr., becomes the youngest person to receive the Nobel Peace Prize.

1965   Malcolm X is assassinated.
Civil Rights Movement organizes Selma to Montgomery March.
Equal Employment Opportunity Commission (EEOC) begins operations.
President Lyndon B. Johnson signs the Voting Rights Act of 1965.
Uprising begins in the Watts neighborhood of Los Angeles.
The Black Arts Repertory Theater/School (BART/S) opens in Harlem.
Dudley Randall establishes the Broadside Press in Detroit.
LeRoi Jones performs "Black Art" for Sonny Murray's album, *Sonny's Time Now*; Jones' "The Revolutionary Theater" appears in the *Liberator* (July).
Nina Simone releases *I Put a Spell on You.*
LeRoi Jones' "A Poem for Black Hearts" is published in *Negro Digest* (September).
James Baldwin publishes *Going to Meet the Man.*
Alex Haley publishes *Autobiography of Malcolm X.*
John Coltrane records *Ascension.*
Spiral artists' collective exhibits "First Group Show: Works in Black and White" in New York.
Weusi Art Collective is formed in Harlem.

1966   The Black Panther Party is established in Oakland, California, by Huey P. Newton and Bobby Seale.
Duke Ellington receives the Presidential Medal of Honor.
Langston Hughes publishes *Simple's Uncle Sam.*
The First Black Writers' Conference, organized by John Oliver Killens, takes place at Fisk University in Nashville, Tennessee.

Barbara Jordan becomes the first African American woman elected to the Texas Senate.

Jimi Hendrix releases "Hey Joe."

A Black Arts Convention convenes in Detroit.

John T. Biggers paints *Shotgun, Third Ward #1*.

Maulana Karenga creates Kwanzaa, the first pan-African non-religious holiday.

1967   Martin Luther King, Jr., delivers "Beyond Vietnam" speech.

Long, Hot Summer of 1967 includes the largest and deadliest uprisings in Newark, New Jersey, and Detroit, Michigan.

Jimi Hendrix releases "Purple Haze" and albums *Are You Experienced*, and *Axis: Bold as Love*.

U.S. Supreme Court declares state laws prohibiting interracial marriage unconstitutional, in *Loving v. Virginia*.

Thurgood Marshall becomes the first African American justice on the U.S. Supreme Court.

Lester Bowie forms the Art Ensemble of Chicago.

Faith Ringgold paints *American People Series #18: The Flag Is Bleeding*.

John Coltrane dies aged forty.

Sidney Poitier stars in *In the Heat of the Night* (dir. Norman Jewison).

Haki Madhubuti establishes the Third World Press in Chicago.

John A. Williams publishes *The Man Who Cried I Am*.

Romare Bearden completes his mixed media collage, *La Primavera*.

Wall of Respect mural by the Visual Arts Workshop of the Organization of Black American Culture (OBAC) exhibited in Chicago.

Nina Simone releases *High Priestess of Soul* and *Nina Simone Sings the Blues*.

1968   Orangeburg Massacre occurs during university protest in South Carolina.

Memphis Sanitation strike begins.

Martin Luther King, Jr., is assassinated in Memphis, Tennessee.

Uprisings begin in Chicago, Washington, DC, Louisville, Kansas City, and more than 150 cities in response to the assassination of Martin Luther King, Jr.

The Poor People's Campaign encampment begins at the National Mall in Washington, DC.

Aretha Franklin releases *Aretha Now* and *Lady Soul*.
Student occupation protests take place in Paris, France.
Jimi Hendrix releases *Electric Ladyland*.
Poet Henry Dumas is killed by New York City transit police officer.
Black Fire! An Anthology of Afro-American Writing, edited by Amiri Baraka and Larry Neal, is published.
Nikki Giovanni publishes *Black Feeling/Black Talk*.
LeRoi Jones changes his name to Imamu Amiri Baraka, and establishes Spirit House in Newark, New Jersey.
AfriCOBRA (African Commune of Bad Relevant Artists) is formed in Chicago.
Vincent D. Smith paints *Do-Rag Brother*.
Chester Himes' *If He Hollers Let Him Go* is released as a film (dir. Charles Martin).
James Brown's "I'm Black and I'm Proud" tops the pop music charts.
Suzanne Jackson opens Gallery 32 in Los Angeles.
Elizabeth Catlett makes *Black Unity* sculpture to honor Olympic medalists.
The Studio Museum in Harlem opens.
Nikki Giovanni publishes *Black Judgement*.

1969   Black Panther Bobby Seale is tried for conspiracy in federal court.
Police raid the home of Chicago Black Panther Party Chairman Fred Hampton and kill him and Mark Clark.
Broadside Press publishes *For Malcolm: Poems on the Life and Death of Malcolm X*, edited by Dudley Randall and Margaret Burroughs.
Jayne Cortez publishes *Pisstained Stairs and the Monkey Man's Wares*.
James Alan McPherson publishes *Hue and Cry: Stories*.
Sam Greenlee publishes *The Spook Who Sat by the Door*.
Carolyn Rodgers publishes "Black Poetry – Where Its At" in *Negro Digest* (September).
Aretha Franklin releases *Once in a Lifetime* and *Soul '69*.
The United States establishes a lottery system for the military draft.
Woodstock Music Festival takes place in New York.

Ebony magazine publishes a special issue titled "The Black Revolution."

Richard M. Nixon becomes President of the United States.

Marie Johnson-Calloway completes the collage *Witch Doctor 1*.

Gordan Parks' *The Learning Tree* is released as a film (dir. Gordon Parks).

Uprising at the Stonewall Inn, a gay club in New York City, ensues.

Introduction
Black Art in Transition

Shelly Eversley

For African American writers and artists, the 1960s was an era of empowerment and polarization, optimism and disillusion. They met this epochal
moment in history with a renewed commitment to art, when "Black" was
not only beautiful but also a political identity, one in which racial justice
became inseparable from aesthetic practice. Even as the "New America"
inaugurated by President John F. Kennedy and continued by President
Lyndon B. Johnson's "Great Society" promised a new frontier, one in
which the United States would be the first to land a man on the moon
while it also achieved some of the most ambitious civil rights legislation
in the twentieth century, equal opportunity in a "post-racial" America
seemed unlikely.

The decade also witnessed incredible moments of violence such as brutal
police responses to peaceful protests by students and citizens, violence
at the Democratic National Convention, attacks against churches and
children, uprisings in cities, and the assassinations of President Kennedy,
Robert F. Kennedy, Medgar Evers, Malcolm X, and the recent Nobel
Laureate Martin Luther King, Jr. Many lost hope in a new America. These
political disappointments and social paradoxes also signaled a necessary
transformation in culture.

*African American Literature in Transition, 1960–1970: Black Art, Politics,
and Aesthetics* takes seriously this notion of transition, particularly as it
informs literature and culture as important indications of the era's zeitgeist,
and it offers an exciting account of the period for a new generation of
readers. For instance, Gwendolyn Brooks (who, in 1950, was the first
African American to win a Pulitzer Prize), published her last book with
a mainstream, white press in 1968. This book of poems, *In the Mecca*,
signaled a significant shift in Brooks' work as well as in the history of
African American literature. Toni Cade Bambara's assessment of her career
in *The New York Times* characterizes this turn: "something happened
to Brooks, something most certainly in evidence in *In the Mecca* and

I

subsequent works – a new movement and energy, intensity, richness, power of statement and a new stripped lean, compressed style. A change of style prompted by a change of mind."[1]

This shift – this "change of mind" – was her now explicit conscious commitment to her racial, social, and political identity as the subject and the inspiration for her writing. In this transition, Brooks had become a *Black* poet as she shed the highly celebrated yet problematic integrationist distinction of being a "real poet," one whose writing was no more "Negro poetry" than, as Robert Frost wrote, "white poetry."

Brooks' attendance at the Second Black Writers' Conference (1967), held at Fisk University, had formally prompted this transition. In her autobiography, she writes that the conference was transformational: "*I* had never been, before, in the general presence of such insouciance, such live firmness, such confident vigor, such determination to mold or carve something DEFINITE."[2] While there, she met a host of younger poets – among them Dudley Randall, whose aesthetics were a politics of Blackness, an attentiveness to the specific social, historical, and political conditions of African Americans that he and other younger poets understood were inseparable from the project of poetry. Their passion moved Brooks. Randall and fellow poet and arts activist Margaret Burroughs had announced their intention to publish a poetry anthology to honor Malcolm X, whose 1965 assassination was another definitive turning point in 1960s Black culture. Brooks' poem, "Malcolm X," which opened their anthology, proclaims:

> We gasped. We saw the maleness.
> The maleness raking out and making guttural the air
> And pushing us to walls.
>
> And in a soft fundamental hour
> A sorcery devout and vertical
> Beguiled the world.
>
> He opened us –
> Who was a key.
>
> Who was a man.[3]

The *For Malcolm* anthology appeared in 1969, soon after Randall had launched Broadside Press in Detroit. Brooks' poem celebrates Malcolm's Black pride – a maleness, a manhood – that stood for many as defiance to an emasculating racism that had been pervasive within a 1960s culture of televised anti-Black violence that seemed to persist with seeming impunity.

The "man" Brooks celebrated in her poem claimed for himself and for Black people a humanity that America's long history of apartheid had sought to deny.

Like the range of poets in the anthology – among them Mari Evans, Ted Joans, Robert Hayden, Clarence Major, Margaret Walker, LeRoi Jones, Etheridge Knight, and Sonia Sanchez – Malcolm X was an inspired symbol for a new, Black consciousness. For instance, in his 1965 eulogy for Malcolm, Ossie Davis proclaims: "Malcolm was our manhood, our living black manhood. This was his meaning to his people. And, in honoring him, we honor the best in ourselves."[4]

Of course, Malcolm had also experienced his own transitions. In *The Autobiography of Malcolm X*, which he authored with Alex Haley and which was published the same year as his murder, Malcolm explains his turn away from a criminal to a religious life, guided by Elijah Muhammad and the Nation of Islam. Malcolm's break with Muhammad and with the Nation coincided with his *hajj* in 1964. During his Muslim pilgrimage to Mecca, Malcolm describes his own personal discovery of a freedom unbound by race or nationality:

> There were tens of thousands of pilgrims, from all over the world. They were of all colors, from blue-eyed blonds to black-skinned Africans. But we were all participating in the same ritual, displaying a spirit of unity and brother-hood that my experiences in America had led me to believe never could exist between the white and the non-white ... You may be shocked by these words coming from me ... what I have seen, and experienced, has forced me to *rearrange* much of my thought-patterns previously held, and to *toss aside* some of my previous conclusions ... We were *truly* all the same (brothers) – because their belief in one God ... I could see from this, that perhaps if white America could accept the Oneness of God, then perhaps too, they could accept *in reality* the Oneness of Man.[5]

This epiphany shows Malcolm at the height of his spiritual and political consciousness, when he understood Black freedom struggles as crucially global and coalitional. He then formed the Organization of Afro-American Unity (OAAU), modeled on the Organization of African Unity (OAU), and designed to support Black human rights all over the world. Months before his death, Malcolm appeared in a television interview announcing his desire to work alongside any organization or person genuinely commit-ted to justice for oppressed people, and it is this man who the poets in *For Malcolm* celebrated as "the best in ourselves." Malcolm and Martin Luther King, Jr., had met only once, also in 1964. In February 1965, Malcolm went to Selma and met with Coretta Scott King while her husband was in jail.

Malcolm and Martin were on a path to collaboration, but Malcolm was murdered later that month, on February 21.

In the same year as *For Malcolm*, Brooks published a short book of poems, *Riot* (1969), with Broadside Press. It chronicles the uprisings in Chicago after Martin Luther King's murder; its title poem in three parts begins with a quote from King, *"A riot is the language of the unheard."*[6] Here, Brooks acknowledges the uprisings in Black communities across the nation as the result of the country's disregard for racial justice. Formally, the collection makes a turn toward assemblage. Its first page is black, with a white-lettered epigram: "[I]t would be a terrible thing for Chicago if this black fountain of life should erupt," it begins, announcing a Black eruption that is both political and creative.

The next page of *Riot* is white. This time, it features an image by Jeff Donaldson, founding artist of the collective AfriCOBRA,[7] whose painting of young Black people shows one of them grasping an African-inspired sculpture pressed against the glass, as if the sculpture, and the person, will smash through it. *Riot*'s content framed by a graphic, mixed-media design visualizes Brooks' transition from mainstream publishing to a new allegiance with smaller, Black presses like Broadside and Chicago's Third World Press. In this moment, the well-established Brooks welcomed young Black creatives into her home, sponsored poetry competitions in schools, traveled to Africa, and began wearing an Afro. This turn toward independent African American publishing houses and their commitment to Black communities as the decisive audiences represents an important resurgence and survival of Black print culture despite the censorship and surveillance that sought to disable it. It is another example of the formal and institutional shifts taking place in the history of the 1960s that would inform transitions in African American literature and culture.

Similarly, Martin Luther King's 1968 murder – inspiring, for example, the "high priestess of soul," Nina Simone, to ask: "what will happen now that the King of Love is dead?" – can be read as the signal apocalypse James Baldwin forewarned of in *The Fire Next Time* (1963). The hope expressed in Baldwin's essays about the transformational power of love, changes into disappointment and disillusionment by the end of the decade. Following King's faith and commitment to nonviolence, Baldwin metaphorizes the country's legal and cultural endorsements of racism as a moral failure, one with apocalyptic consequences. His solution in 1963 was love. Baldwin argues that love can overcome the fearful thinking and behaviors that cause so many to cling to an ethically untenable status quo. He writes that we must, "like lovers, insist on, or create, the consciousness of others . . . we may be able, handful that we are, to end the racial nightmare, and achieve our country, and change the history of the world."[8]

Although Baldwin had spent much of the previous decade abroad, he returned to the United States because he felt compelled to be present for what he hoped would be a long overdue turn to racial justice and love. The same year as his *The Fire Next Time*, he joined his peers at the historic March on Washington for Jobs and Freedom. [9] Here, King delivered his "I Have a Dream" speech to an interracial, intergenerational group of 250,000 people surrounding the Lincoln Memorial to support a message of love, community, and social justice. Its political platform included meaningful legislation, including laws to prohibit employment discrimination and a national minimum wage. Millions also watched and listened to King's speech on television and radio, including via the Voice of America, which translated the speech into thirty-six languages and rebroadcast it globally.

The moment thus symbolized a beacon for equality and change not only in the United States but also abroad where so many people sought to end colonialism, apartheid, and economic injustice. Televised documentary evidence of white police and white citizens attacking peaceful protesters prompted public indignation and calls for legislative action, and it mobilized students of all races to organize in the service of African Americans' civil rights, including the right to vote and to fair housing. In this moment, it seemed as if love and justice would prevail over hatred and fear.

In the following summer of 1964, more than 1,000 college students, mostly white, arrived in Mississippi to join the mostly Black Student Nonviolent Coordinating Committee's (SNCC) Freedom Summer project.[10] Their threefold mission was to secure Black voters' registration inside a state vehemently opposed to Black civil rights; to build "freedom schools" that would provide literacy and history education that the state had denied its Black citizens, even as it required them to "qualify" to vote; and to form a parallel Mississippi Freedom Democratic delegation that would challenge the all-white delegation that would represent the state of Mississippi at the Democratic National Convention that would take place later that year.

They understood that the right to vote was a critical remedy to the state's systematic assault against African Americans, who in Mississippi consisted of more than a third of the population, yet less than 7 percent of its registered voters. That Freedom Summer coalition of students worked alongside Black Mississippians who had been denied voter registration by means of subjective literacy tests, economic reprisals, and physical violence.

One local activist, Fannie Lou Hamer, a sharecropper who summoned up the courage to speak about the numerous assaults and threats against her as she sought her constitutional right to vote, empowered her similarly threatened peers to claim their rights as citizens. Freedom Summer was the most violent in the already violent history of the state. The Ku Klux Klan along with police and other state and local authorities launched vicious attacks against the students and activists:

- ° 1,062 people were arrested under false pretenses
- ° 80 Freedom Summer workers were assaulted
- ° 37 churches were bombed or burned
- ° 30 homes and businesses belonging to African Americans were bombed or burned
- ° 7 or more people were murdered, including James Chaney, Andrew Goodman, and Michael Schwerner[11]

And while FBI investigators searched for Chaney, Goodman, and Schwerner, they also found the bodies of eight African Americans – one boy and seven men – whose corpses were hidden in rivers and swamps throughout the state.

The violence continued and the transformational power of love seemed to wane. Students and citizens were continually attacked and murdered; inspirational leaders were assassinated. Major events such as these define the decade, marking personal and political tensions that also signal important examples of the transitions in African American literature and culture. Mid-decade – after the bombing that killed four girls at Sunday school and after Malcolm X's murder – LeRoi Jones published his elegy for Malcolm, "A Poem for Black Hearts," as well as "Black Art" (1965). Together, these poems signaled his move away from Greenwich Village and the downtown poetry scene associated with New York's mostly white avant-garde.

Now uptown and in Harlem, Jones founded the Black Arts Repertory Theater/School (BART/S) and in 1968 changed his name to Amiri Baraka. His name change, his poems, and his move to Harlem, the iconic capital of African American culture, mark an inaugural moment for a new Black Aesthetic, and for the Black Arts Movement. The spirit of Black empowerment, now less interested in interracial collaboration, appeared in community centers and artist collectives across the United States.

For instance, the Watts Towers Arts Center opened in Los Angeles in 1963; in Detroit, artists and activists convened a Black Arts Convention (1966); in New York, Spiral, an artists' collective was established; and in Los Angeles, Maulana Karenga created the first pan-African non-religious holiday, Kwanzaa (1966). Jazz musician Lester Bowie formed the Art Ensemble of Chicago (1967) and Arthur Mitchell created the Dance Theater of Harlem (1968). In these and other examples, such as in the AfriCOBRA collective, culture became a cause for avant-garde art, civil rights activism, and a defiance of white hegemony. In the 1960s, African American creatives had created a counterculture.

Indicative of the defiance of a generation of Black artists whose creativity announced a radical break with the status quo, Jones/Baraka's poem "Black Art" signaled the emergence of a new, and confrontational, political aesthetic:

> Poems are bullshit unless they are
> teeth or trees or lemons piled
> on a step.[12]

His pronouncement offers a poetic grounded in a wholly touchable, tangible form. The poem's title claims a racial art – a "black imagination" – that recalls a long tradition of aesthetic manifestos and radical declarations of independence. Here, the speaker announces a logic that, without concrete manifestations, "poems are bullshit":

> ... We want live
> words of the hip world live flesh &
> coursing blood. Hearts Brains
> Soul splintering fire. We want poems
> like fists beating niggers out of Jocks
> or dagger poems in the slimy bellies
> of the owner-jews. Black poems ...
> ...
> Assassin poems, Poems that shoot
> guns. Poems that wrestle cops into alleys
> and take their weapons leaving them dead   (ll. 9–15, 20–23)

The poem's claims to a tangibility and a seemingly indiscriminate violence assert a departure from nonviolence; it is a "Black" poem, one that has agency as well as the power and the ability to kill.

Baraka was not alone in this aesthetic turn. As part of the Black Arts/ Black Aesthetic movement of the later 1960s and 1970s, poems like "Black Art" called for confrontation, a radical break with the psychic and material conditions that undermine the full agency of Black people in the United States. Its aesthetic of resistance echoes Frantz Fanon's embrace of a psychological freedom from colonial thinking, and it more immediately reflects a vision of empowerment that is more popularly associated with Malcolm X and with Black nationalism.

In *Black Fire: An Anthology of Afro-American Writing* (1968), which Jones/Baraka edited in collaboration with Larry Neal, they insist this aesthetic turn is more than symbolic, that it would "destroy the double consciousness – the tension that is in the souls of black folk."[13] Their Black Aesthetic manifesto defies the very condition W. E. B. Du Bois called "the problem of the twentieth century," one in which segregation and the color line had been previously characterized as "the Negro Problem."[14] Jones/Baraka and Neal's *Black Fire* understands Black freedom as unconcerned with the values – or the feelings – of the (white) status quo. Instead, it celebrated fearlessness in Black art and Black identity.

And while performance is crucial to poetry, the performance of confrontation is crucial to a Black Aesthetic resistance to an institutional and cultural anti-Blackness. It refuses the violence of racial subjection while it also claims Blackness as African American creative power. For instance, in the same period, Nikki Giovanni, another Black Aesthetic poet, invites polarization in the service of Black freedom, such as in her "The True Import of Black vs. Negro (For Peppe, Who will Ultimately Judge Our Efforts)" (1968):

> Nigger
> Can you kill
> Can you kill
> Can a nigger kill
> Can a nigger kill a honkie
> Can a nigger kill the Man[15]

This ritual demonstration of confrontational anger is an articulation of defiance and rebellion. The poem's title reflects another transition, one that establishes an opposition between "Black" and "Negro," Black and white, to suggest that any liberal notion of progress gained by nonviolence or negotiation is untenable and impossible. For Giovanni, like Baraka whose 1969 *Black Magic* book cover featured a white voodoo doll pierced with pins, oppressive ways of being and thinking must be eradicated. In her poem, the act of murder, to "kill," is to destroy a racist, anti-Black social order.

Similarly, Baraka's commitment to the "revolutionary" value of the performative should "function like an incendiary pencil." He argues: "it should stagger through our universe correcting, insulting, preaching, spitting craziness."[16] More recently, Phillip Brian Harper has argued this kind of poetic performance depicts an example of fearlessness in the face of oppression. He writes that this type of confrontation achieves "maximum impact in a context in which [the poems] are understood as being *heard* directly by whites and over*heard* by blacks."[17]

The notion is that these incendiary poems are a direct address to whites, who as "the Man" represent an oppressive status quo, and they suggest an important instance of chiasmus in which the Black person now looks at the white person with contempt. This reversal inverts the logic of double consciousness, so that the problem of the color line is now "The White Problem."

Like Giovanni's poem, Baraka's "Black Art" announces an uncompromised pro-Blackness, and it invites listeners to choose a side. The speaker announces a collectivity, a "we," who have precise tastes and clear perspectives distinct from the "cops," "jews," "niggers," "Jocks," "wops" (l. 24), and "girdlemamma mulatta bitches" (l. 16). One compelling feature of this racialized confrontation is that it occurs precisely at the moment when the potential for racial justice and love seems lost in the face of such virulent anti-Black violence.

Rather than embrace the promise of an aesthetic, social, and political integration, Baraka's earlier works published under the name LeRoi Jones suggest the poet who publishes "Black Art" insists on a creativity in which Black difference is its most distinct feature. It conceptualizes the era's political aesthetic of empowered outrage. And given Jones' long-established position in New York's avant-garde scene, "Black Art" is the signal emergence of a new poet, Amiri Baraka, and the disappearance of LeRoi Jones. Like Jones/Baraka's only novel, the experimental *The System of Dante's Hell*, also published in 1965, the poem depicts a creative logic in which art becomes the originary site of a decisively Black political consciousness.

Jones/Baraka makes a clear connection between the enraged semantic turn in his writing and the resistance to anti-Black violence so prevalent in the 1960s. For instance, in his 1963 essay on nonviolence, he writes: "[t]here is a war going on now in the United States ... in that war, four Negro children were blown to bits while they were learning to pray."[18] His opening invites anger and the radicalization of a political consciousness that ultimately transforms LeRoi Jones into Amiri Baraka.

His characterization of the white supremacist slaughter of children engaged in Sunday school activities not only justifies his outrage against the violence perpetuated against African Americans with impunity, but also questions the value of nonviolence when, from his perspective, Black people are under attack. He continues "What Does Nonviolence Mean?" with a list of "terroristic tactics": "The leader of the Jackson, Mississippi,

NAACP . . . was assassinated in front of his home. Police dogs, fire hoses, blackjacks, have been used on Negroes, trying to reinforce a simple and brutal social repression." In this, Jones/Baraka refers to the assassination of Medgar Evers, a nonviolent civil rights activist, who was killed in his driveway while his wife and children were inside their home. And as the decade continues, this list of terrorist acts against Black people grows exponentially – water hoses, fire bombs, and more deaths continued to demean African American life.

In 1966, police shot and killed Matthew Johnson in the impoverished Hunters Point neighborhood of San Francisco. Johnson was sixteen years old, unarmed, and Black. Johnson's community erupted in protest, prompting the governor to impose martial law. Incidents like these took place across the United States and throughout the decade. In 1964, an off-duty police officer shot and killed a fifteen-year-old African American boy, prompting uprisings in Harlem, Brooklyn's Bedford-Stuyvesant neighborhood, Rochester, NY, and in three cities in New Jersey.

Aggressive police actions against unarmed African Americans and their allies signaled the era's mood of unrest and polarization. In Tuscaloosa, Alabama, African Americans who attempted to walk from the First African Baptist Church to the County Courthouse to protest segregated drinking fountains and bathrooms, were beaten, tear-gassed, and arrested by an angry mob of whites and white police. This incident, known as "Bloody Tuesday" (June 9, 1964), resembles another event, "Bloody Sunday" (March 7, 1965), when nonviolent activists sought to challenge American apartheid and claim their constitutional right to vote by marching from Selma to Montgomery, Alabama. State troopers and county posse men (some of whom were known members of the KKK) attacked the peaceful protesters with billy clubs and tear gas.

Weeks later, 25,000 people arrived safely in Montgomery to support voting rights for Black Americans – they, along with Martin Luther King, were protected by federally commanded National Guard troops, FBI agents, and federal marshals.[19] The violence that commonly met peaceful protests prompted another approach to Black social justice. Two years after the Freedom Summer, Black students in the SNCC made their own turn when the committee's newly elected chair, Stokely Carmichael, began to voice his loss of faith in nonviolent political action. Carmichael helped transform the SNCC into a more radical organization, and during a voters' rights speech in Mississippi, he declared: "[w]e been saying 'freedom' for six years . . . what we are going to start saying now is 'Black Power.'"[20]

The slogan "Black Power" became a rallying call for a younger generation of activists, including among them anti-imperialists in Africa and anticolonialists in the Caribbean, who were dissatisfied with the slow progress of social justice. The influence of this phrase is particularly noteworthy because of the separate, simultaneous rise of the Black Panther Party for Self Defense in Oakland, California, led by Huey P. Newton and Bobby Seale.

More readily known as the Black Panther Party (BPP), the organization's genesis stemmed from the police killing of Matthew Johnson, the teenager shot by police in San Francisco. The BPP's early activities were primarily concerned with monitoring police activities in Black communities. They claimed a constitutional right to bear arms as a means of self-defense against unnecessary and unjust police violence. And on May 2, 1967, thirty-two fully armed Black women and men met Ronald Reagan, the new governor of California, at the state capital, where Bobby Seale announced, to "The American people in general and black people in particular," that the "racist power structure" had continued to disempower Black people despite the fact that African Americans had "begged, prayed, petition, and demonstrated" in their calls for justice. In his rejection of nonviolent protest, he declared: "[t]he time has come for black people to arm themselves against this terror before it's too late."[21] He and his peers then entered the state capital. In response to this moment of empowered Black defiance, the California legislature drafted and passed the Mulford Act, making it illegal to carry loaded weapons in public.[22]

The Black Panther Party was deeply committed to a larger Black freedom movement; in a platform they called the Ten-Point Program, they emphasized Black pride, community control, equal employment and housing opportunities, and freedom from government harassment and police brutality. They launched several community service programs including free breakfasts for school children and free health clinics.

By 1968, the Black Panther Party was run mostly by women and it had thousands of members and hundreds of branches across the United States.[23] Its organization and its resistance to institutionalized racism inspired racial justice activism and alliances among, for example, the American Indian Movement, Asian Americans' "Yellow Power" movement, and El Movimiento, a Mexican American social justice movement.[24] As their popularity grew, their justice efforts made them targets of a secret federal counterintelligence program, COINTELPRO, in which the FBI sought to undermine community programs, exploit rivalries, and enlist informants who could provide information that would help neutralize the Black Panther Party.[25]

In one egregious instance, the FBI assisted an early morning police raid on the Chicago apartment of BPP chair Fred Hampton, who along with his pregnant girlfriend and associates were asleep inside. The police fired almost one hundred bullets into the apartment, killing Hampton, Mark Clark, and critically injuring four others. Hampton was twenty-one years old.[26]

It is within this context of real and highly publicized anti-Black violence that artists and writers developed their craft to offer jarring, countercultural depictions of the "brutal social repression" they understood as the primary goal of the violence against Black American persons. Baraka, for instance, interprets this anti-Black violence as a failure of imagination – and this failure is the failure to conceive Black humanity. In another direct address to liberal whites, he also offers a sobering aside: "(During slavery a liberal, or a moderate, was a man who didn't want the slaves beaten. But he was not asking that they be freed.)"[27] This jolting indictment of the ethical failures of liberalism is yet another invitation for a radical transformation of thought into action.

For this cohort of Black Arts/Black Aesthetic artists and writers, any commitment that art can change the world must be provocative and political. When Baraka writes: "Art is method. And art, 'like any ashtray or senator,' remains in the world. Wittgenstein said ethics and aesthetics are one. I believe this," he challenges the longstanding theory of tension between art and politics.[28] His provocation returns to the opening lines of "Black Art": "Poems are bullshit unless they are/teeth or trees or lemons piled/on a step," and it characterizes the concrete manifestation of ethics as art.

For Baraka, poetics is politics, and Black literature is an act of resistance. In this aesthetic vision, both poetry and protest create tangible results. This political investment conceives of the imagination, of creativity, as the architect of revolution, so that "imagination ... is all possibility ... Possibility is what moves us."[29]

This interest in the possibility imagination affords suggests two significant implications for literature and politics in the American milieu of 1960s African American literature and culture. First, it signals a self-consciousness about the function of African American creative projects. Rather than support the idea that, with integration, African American literature and culture is no longer necessary nor legitimate, it posits African American creative endeavors as crucial to racial justice issues that remain insidious even after so many civil rights victories. Second, the framing of imagination as particularly "Black" describes a shift away from identity as race to identity as affect. In other words, the Black revolutionary community Baraka and his peers imagine is primarily organized by feeling, not skin color. The implication in this turn is agency.

Here, Blackness is a deliberate choice, one that mobilizes outrage to realize the complete rights of Black personhood. It also celebrates Blackness – skin, hair, and culture – as beautiful. The phrase "Black is beautiful" became popular in the 1960s; recently, philosopher Paul C. Taylor theorized "Black is beautiful" as a heterogeneous position deeply linked to an ocular regime that fails to see Blackness, or one that recognizes it as "ugly," unworthy of aesthetic consideration.[30]

In this decade, "Negro" became an outmoded term to describe people of African descent; 1960s literature, culture, and politics created the transition from "Negro" to "Black," now a signifier for an identity informed by a political and ideological position of defiance and self-love. Gwendolyn Brooks' Afro hairstyle, dashikis and black leather fashions, and James Brown's song "Say it Loud – I'm Black and I'm Proud" (1968) are examples of this shift toward an empowered Blackness celebrated in popular culture. *African American Literature in Transition, 1960–1970*, embraces the very notion of African American literature and culture as both the subject and the agent of change. And change is coalitional.

Noliwe M. Rooks points out that in 1968 when San Francisco State College established the nation's first Black studies department, "white students joined with Asian students, Latino students, American Indian students and black students to found the field. The battle they waged was multiracial, seeing black studies as the first step in the wider-ranging agenda for educational, economic, and social economy."[31] Within twelve months of the founding of the department at San Francisco State, at least 200 new Black studies programs were set to begin. By 1971, the Ford Foundation had become one of the largest supporters of this new field.

The coalitional investment in Black studies facilitated an important shift in higher education, one that redefined the concept of opportunity, access, and equity in institutions that educate the nation. Besides formalizing the need for investments in welcoming Black students, Black faculty, and their creative and intellectual work, these coalitional activisms also facilitated the rise of women's studies, as well as Latinx, Asian American, Native American, and queer studies.

This moment of coalitional justice activities not only informs the literary and cultural collectives that emerged in the 1960s, but it also reflects the political and social movements that shaped them. For instance, Martin

Luther King's increasing concern about U.S. military involvement in Vietnam, intersects with his longstanding interest in economic justice for African Americans, while also signaling his emerging commitments to anticolonialism.

In 1967, a year before his assassination, King collaborated with an interfaith group of clergy to promote peace and to denounce a "deadly Western arrogance" that he understood as the result of U.S. colonial practices. In his "Beyond Vietnam" speech, King argued that the United States had rendered "peaceful revolution impossible by refusing to give up the privileges and pleasures that come from immense profits of overseas investments."[32] Before his death, Malcolm X also denounced the war. In 1967, 64 percent of all eligible African Americans were drafted to fight in Vietnam, while only 31 percent of eligible whites were compelled to serve. The casualty rates of Black soldiers was also disproportionally high – Black soldiers were killed in Vietnam two times more than white soldiers. As a consequence, civil rights, antiwar, and anticolonial movements were intersectional. The postwar baby boom had resulted in an unprecedented population increase in the United States, so that during the 1960s young people represented a major population demographic.

Their shared commitment to justice and to "counterculture" deeply influenced the era. And when the FDA approved the birth control pill in 1960, heterosexually active women achieved autonomy over their bodies and their life choices. This new freedom enabled more women to attend college, develop their careers, and importantly, advocate for equality.[33] Their activisms launched Second-wave feminism.

Each chapter in *African American Literature in Transition, 1960–1970*, which is organized in three sections, situates its subjects in history, in relation to the larger aesthetic and political contexts, and in conversation with recent developments in contemporary criticism. This approach affords the reader a critical frame for the power and the influence of African American literature and culture: it extends beyond the boundaries of African American concerns to reveal the undeniable intersections between feminism and art, anticolonialism and popular culture, civil rights and aesthetic experiments, the community and the artist, literature and film, politics and music, love and revolution, as well as between philosophy and social justice.

This book invites an alternative view of periodization by organizing chapters on literature and culture that engage with the period diachronically and within multiple modes and genres, adding texture to the familiar critical and historical timeline. Among its many interventions, it considers innovations, transitions, and traditions within both familiar and unfamiliar texts and moments in 1960s African American literature and culture, to interrogate declarations of race, authenticity, personal and collective empowerment, political action, and aesthetics.

At the same time, however, experimentation, now a challenge to convention and a call for new ways of being and thinking, became an often overlooked, yet common artistic practice in which many forms of the avant-garde – free jazz, poetry, film, art collectives, and the novel – exposed the potentials and the contradictions that offer new kinds of evaluations and investigations of the 1960s and its influences on the decades that follow.

In "The Society of Umbra and the Coming of the Black Aesthetic," Keith D. Leonard explores the layers of influence that inform 1960s Black poetics, particularly how the writers of the Umbra Writers Workshop engaged with the better-known white poets identified with New York City's Lower East Side and adapted from another art form – Abstract Expressionism in one case, bebop and free jazz in the other. He details how Umbra's improvisational composition strategies demonstrate a vision that idiosyncratically unites the aesthetic and cultural implications of the full New York art scene, in order to orient discussions of the militant politics of the Black Arts Movement. His essay invites readers to recognize a fuller sense of how bohemian artistry served Black nationalist politics with integrity.

Similarly, Eric Porter's "Reconsidering 'the Revolution in Music'" engages jazz and the avant-garde as important indicators of the era's cultural transitions. His essay revisits Frank Kofsky's influential work on the relationship between "free jazz" and 1960s political struggle by offering closer readings of archival interviews of jazz musicians, such as John Coltrane, Elvin Jones, and McCoy Tyner, who were featured in the published work. Porter argues that the archive reveals a more sophisticated, collective analysis of jazz aesthetics and the complicated social and political context than what Kofsky apparently explains.

Poetry maintained a central position in 1960s Black literary and cultural transitions. Derik Smith in his chapter, "Robert Hayden, the Black Arts Movement, and the Politics of Aesthetic Distance," challenges the ways in which critical conceptions of African American poetry of the period often pit Hayden against radical poets of the Black Arts Movement (BAM) in conveniently antagonistic terms – as combatants locked in battle over the meaning of "the Black Aesthetic" during those years that we have come to

call the "Black Arts era." He contends that partisan arguments about
Hayden's ideological and aesthetic disputes with 1960s peers tend to
obscure the fact that Hayden and his apparent rivals confronted a similar
set of mid-century problematics. He posits that the terrain of recent Black
poetry has been prominently shaped by the differing ways in which
Hayden and his BAM contemporaries responded to the same questions
of class and aesthetics.

In her reading of another BAM poet in "Breathing: Sonia Sanchez's Call
to Coalition Building," Patricia Herrera contends that the practice of
diaspora in Sanchez's poetry and plays – such as *The Bronx Is Next*
(1968) – illuminate the ways her work as a feminist figure in the Black Arts
Movement creates fusions between Latinx and African American cultures
and produces a literary and cultural zone that indicates early notions of
Afro-Latinidad. Herrera argues that Sanchez's writing in multiple modalities signals a Third World feminist perspective that also creates
a transnational discourse between African American and Latinx communities to demonstrate a global African American literary expression.

In the next section, engaging the intersection between literature, culture,
and politics, Dagmawi Woubshet's "The Rights of Black Love" reads
James Baldwin's changing perspective on the power and potential of love
from his *The Fire Next Time* (1963) to *No Name in the Street* (1972).
Woubshet traces Baldwin's shifting views through a historical contextual-
ization of 1960s hope and devastation which he reads as not only pivotal to
Baldwin's life and writing, but also crucial to shifts in American life and
letters.

Paul C. Taylor's "Albert Murray Beyond Plight and Blight" offers
a critical rebuke to Murray's landmark collection of integrationist essays,
The Omni-Americans (1970), to invite new considerations of the debates
that shaped 1960s tensions between nationalists and integrationists, offering an incisive critique of Murray's encounters with the theory and practice
of Black aesthetics.

In "Espionage and Paths of Black Radicalism," GerShun Avilez
reads Sam Greenlee's novel *The Spook Who Sat by the Door* as a rich
opportunity to engage with how art represents and interrogates Black
radicalism. He explains how espionage in the novel becomes a metaphor
for Black freedom practices and their cultivation of Black radical personhood. The novel's Black CIA agent/spy is also an outlaw, working
undercover as a double agent in the service of a Black revolution in the
United States. This chapter not only rejects the binary logic that positions integrationist against Black Power strategies, but it also points to

understanding the era's increasingly versatile thinking about Black revolution.

In "The Necessary Violence of Frantz Fanon and Malcolm X in Global Black Revolution," Kelly M. Nims argues that global Black freedoms must confront the violent histories in the making of the United States and its colonial allies. Her detailed assessment explains how Malcolm's and Fanon's turns toward violence are grounded in the shared legacies of the American Revolution and global imperialism. She argues that this violence is cathartic; it offers pleasure and empowerment for Black persons ultimately unbound by national borders.

In the final section, Phillip Brian Harper's "Meanwhile, Back on the Homefront" illuminates an alternative 1960s African American cultural domain within which relatively private modes of communal self-care at once counterbalanced, complemented, and underwrote the public engagement that might otherwise seem to constitute the totality of Black cultural activity during the period. Harper's chapter offers a fresh reading of Vincent O. Carter's posthumously published 1960s novel, *Such Sweet Thunder* (2003), that, in its time, did not seem to "protest enough." He posits the novel as indicative of a shadow realm, whose very obscurity perpetuates and questions the predominance of protest as the definitive impression of the era.

Cheryl Higashida's "*Radio Free Dixie,* Black Arts Radio, and African American Women's Activism" makes visible the often overlooked politics and activisms of women of color. Her chapter describes how exiled African American revolutionaries Robert and Mabel Williams' weekly English language radio program, broadcast from Havana, Cuba between 1962 and 1966, became a key vehicle of political revolution and youth culture across the globe. She argues that *Radio Free Dixie* contributes signally to transnational and hemispheric histories of civil rights and Black Power as a vehicle for forging connections with Fidel Castro, Kwame Nkrumah, and Mao Zedong, and for inspiring the Deacons for Defense and Justice, the Revolutionary Action Movement, and the Black Panther Party. The central claim of her chapter is that the medium as well as content of *Radio Free Dixie* shaped as well as transmitted key elements of Black culture in transition in the 1960s: a shift from Cold War liberalism to race radicalism, and from a focus on domestic rights to human rights and internationalism.

Indeed, 1960s Black literature and culture inspire personal investment in public and political change. These diverse communities of Black people and their allies across race and nation felt outrage toward systems that create hierarchies of personhood; and, together, they imagined solutions that could change not only the social and political landscapes of the United States, but also the world. In this way, the kinds of collaborations, coalitions, and cultural transitions emerging in this decade would become important models for the social justice movements that defined the activisms of the 1970s and beyond.

Notes

1. Bambara (1973).
2. Brooks (1972), 85.
3. Brooks (1969a), 3, ll. 5–13. Extract reprinted by consent of Brooks Permissions.
4. Davis (1969), 121.
5. Malcolm X (1965), 390–92.
6. Brooks (1969b); original italics.
7. AfriCOBRA (African Commune of Bad Relevant Artists), was an artists' collective established in Chicago in 1968. Their mission was "to encapsulate the quintessential features of African-American consciousness and world view as reflected in real time 1968 terms," since for them, the "South and West sides of the city were alive in 1968 with the energy of social change and upheaval . . . In the arts, Black identity and Black is beautiful were watchwords that bound many individuals into a collective force that began many journeys toward rediscovering our ancestral heritage, toward capturing the electricity of the present, and toward unlocking the keys to survival in the future." http://afri cobra.com/Introduction.html [accessed September 23, 2021].
8. Baldwin (1992 [1963]), 105.
9. Among these were: Josephine Baker, Harry Belafonte, Sammy Davis, Jr., Ruby Dee, Dick Gregory, Lena Horne, Mahalia Jackson, Rosa Parks, and Jackie Robinson. Celebrity allies and friends included Joan Baez, Marlon Brando, Bob Dylan, James Garner, Charlton Heston, Rita Moreno, and Joanne Woodward.
10. While the project's conception originated with SNCC, a coalition of Mississippi civil rights organizations managed the massive effort under the umbrella Council of Federated Organizations (COFO).
11. See McAdam (1988) and Nelson (2016).
12. Baraka (1979), 121, ll. 1–3.
13. Jones and Neal (1968), 656.
14. Du Bois (1999).
15. Giovanni (2007 [1968]), 19.
16. Jones (1966a), 212, 211.
17. Harper (1993), 247.
18. Jones (1966b), 133.
19. See Branch (2007).

20. See "Student Nonviolent Coordinating Committee (SNCC)" (2019).
21. Seale (1968).
22. See Randolph (2016), 1.
23. See Cleaver (2001), 123–27.
24. See Ogbar (2001), 29–38, and Gómez-Quiñones and Vasquez (2014).
25. Churchill and Wall (2001).
26. Haas (2011).
27. Jones (1966b), 135.
28. Jones (1966a), 212.
29. Ibid., 213.
30. See Taylor (2016).
31. Rooks (2006).
32. King (2002), 146, 153.
33. "The Pill" (N.d). equalityarchive.com/history/the-pill/ [accessed October 17, 2019].

References

Baldwin, J. 1992 [1963]. *The Fire Next Time*. New York: Vintage.

Bambara, T. C. 1973, January 7. "Report From Part One." *The New York Times*.

Baraka, A. (L. Jones). 1979. "Black Art." In *Transbluesency: Selected Poetry of Amiri Baraka/LeRoi Jones, 1961–1995*, 121. New York: William Morrow.

Branch, T. 2007. *At Canaan's Edge: America in the King Years, 1965–68*. New York: Simon & Schuster.

Brooks, G. 1969a. "Malcolm X (For Dudley Randall)." In *For Malcolm: Poems on the Life and the Death of Malcolm X*, ed. D. Randall and M. G. Burroughs, 3. Detroit: Broadside Press.

1969b. *Riot*. Detroit: Broadside Press.

1972. *Report From Part One*. Detroit: Broadside Press.

Churchill, W., and J. V. Wall. 2001. *Agents of Repression: The FBI's Secret Wars Against the Black Panther Party and the American Indian Movement*. 2nd ed. Boston, MA: South End Press.

Cleaver, K. N. 2001. "Women, Power, and Revolution." In *Liberation, Imagination, and the Black Panther Party: A New Look at the Panthers and their Legacy*, ed. K. Cleaver and G. Katsiaficas, 123–27. New York: Routledge.

Davis, O. 1969. "Eulogy of Malcolm X: 'Our Black Manhood . . . Our Black Shining Prince! . . .'" In *For Malcolm: Poems on the Life and the Death of Malcolm X*, ed. D. Randall and M. G. Burroughs, 121. Detroit: Broadside Press.

Du Bois, W. E. B. 1999. *The Souls of Black Folk*. New York: W. W. Norton & Co.

Giovanni, N. 2007 [1968]. "The True Import of Present Dialogue, Black vs. Negro." In *The Collected Poetry of Nikki Giovanni, 1968–1998*, ed. V. C. Fowler, 19–20. New York: William Morrow.

Gómez-Quiñones, J., and I. Vásquez. 2014. *Making Aztlán: Ideology and Culture of the Chicana and Chicano Movement, 1966–1977*. Albuquerque: University of New Mexico Press.

Haas, J. 2011. *The Assassination of Fred Hampton: How the FBI and the Chicago Police Murdered a Black Panther*. Chicago, IL: Lawrence Hill Books.

Harper, P. B. 1993. "Nationalism and Social Division in Black Arts Poetry of the 1960s." *Critical Inquiry* 19.2 (Winter): 234–55.

Jones, L. 1966a. "The Revolutionary Theater." In *Home: Social Essays*, 210–15. New York: William Morrow.

　　1966b. "What Does Nonviolence Mean?" In *Home: Social Essays*, 133–55. New York: William Morrow.

Jones, L., and L. Neal. 1968. "And Shine Swam On." In *Black Fire: An Anthology of African American Writing*, ed. L. Jones and L. Neal, 656. New York: William Morrow.

King, M. L., Jr. 2002. "Beyond Vietnam." In *A Call to Conscience: The Landmark Speeches of Dr. Martin Luther King, Jr.*, ed. C. Carson and K. Shepard, 133–64. New York: Grand Central Publishing.

Malcolm X. 1965. *The Autobiography of Malcolm X: As Told to Alex Haley*. New York: Ballantine.

McAdam, D. 1988. *Freedom Summer*. New York: Oxford University Press.

Nelson, S. 2016. *Devils Walking: Klan Murders Along the Mississippi in the 1960s*. Baton Rouge: Louisiana State University Press.

Ogbar, J. O. G. 2001. "Yellow Power: The Formation of Asian-American Nationalism in the Age of Black Power, 1966–1975." *Souls* 3.3 (Summer): 29–38.

Randall D., and M. G. Burroughs, eds. 1969. *For Malcolm: Poems on the Life and the Death of Malcolm X*. Detroit: Broadside Press.

Randolph, P. 2016, July 17. "Madravenspeak: The Second Amendment: Looking into the Mirror of Cultural Psychosis." *UWIRE Text*, 1.

Rooks, N. M. 2006, February 10. "The Beginnings of Black Studies." *Chronicle of Higher Education*. www.chronicle.com/article/the-beginnings-of-black-studies/ [accessed October 17, 2019].

Seale, B. 1968, April 16. "Speech Delivered at the Kaleidoscope Theater." https:// americanradioworks.publicradio.org/features/blackspeach/bseale.html [accessed June 16, 2019].

　"Student Nonviolent Coordinating Committee (SNCC)." 2019. The Martin Luther King, Jr. Research and Education Institute. https://kinginstitute .stanford.edu/encyclopedia/student-nonviolent-coordinating-committee-sncc [accessed June 16, 2019].

Taylor, P. C. 2016. *Black Is Beautiful: A Philosophy of Black Aesthetics*. Hoboken, NJ: John Wiley & Sons.

Poetry and Music

CHAPTER I

The Society of Umbra and the Coming of the Black Aesthetic

Keith D. Leonard

The Black Arts Movement – that flourishing of Black nationalist radical politics and poetics of the late 1960s – was an avant-garde movement. This statement should be uncontroversial, but the avant-garde is too fully associated with white American artists and the Black Arts Movement too fully understood in terms of its own rejection of whiteness for this insight to be seen. Yet the movement's avant-garde heritage is apparent even in the common parallel of its nationalist emergence to the transformation of bohemian avant-gardist poet and critic LeRoi Jones into Black nationalist Amiri Baraka, one of the Black Arts Movement's first key spokespersons.

The parallel derives from Jones' conversion from the bohemianism of his early career to the cultural nationalism in the middle that reputedly started when he met several political radicals and activist artists in Cuba in July 1960. Those artists forced him to confront the limitations of the nonconformist withdrawal he pursued in New York City's Lower East Side with fellow Beat-type avant-gardists who understood such non-participation to be substantive resistance, and who imagined that their bohemia constituted an interracial haven conducive to interracial sexual relations and to the validating effects of innovative jazz, despite only oblique engagement with race politics. Jones apparently felt the limits of this idealism when, for example, Mexican poet Jaime Shelley declared: "In that ugliness you live in, you want to cultivate your soul? Well, we've got millions of starving people to feed, and that moves me enough to make poems out of."[1] The assassination of Malcolm X in 1965 confirmed for Jones that his capacity to serve the cultural and political interests of starving Black people was compromised by his engagement with a bohemia that he now considered to be the limited province of apolitical white artists. He subsequently divorced his Jewish wife Hettie, so the story goes, and moved uptown to Harlem to become Amiri Baraka, leading lion of the new movement for Black self-determination, and founder of the Black Arts

Repertory Theater/School (BART/S), one of the movement's originating institutions.

African American artists and intellectuals as disparate as Larry Neal, Nikki Giovanni, Don L. Lee, Gwendolyn Brooks, Hoyt Fuller, Carolyn Rodgers, and Sonia Sanchez followed Jones into Harlems of their own, both literal and figurative, sometimes likewise adopting Africanized names as a measure of their political conversion. Together, they built what they declared to be *the* "Black Aesthetic," an ostensibly singular and "radical reordering of the western cultural aesthetic"[2] keyed to calling a Black audience to nationalist revolution through a turn to Black vernacular cultural traditions, improvisational performative practices inspired by jazz, and innovative revisions of Standard English syntax in the interest of remaking the Black mind.

What is striking about this powerful and apt legend is that its terms of conversion ultimately reveal how fully Jones' Harlem and its Black Aesthetic absorbed and adapted key features of the bohemian withdrawal it disparaged. For example, Jones' collaboration with Hettie Cohen, with whom he published the journal *Yugen: A New Consciousness in Arts and Letters*, a central Lower East Side literary organ, initiated the call for a new artistic consciousness upon which he would elaborate in Harlem as a call for a new racial artistic consciousness. The partnership with Hettie Cohen – who was an accomplished writer, critic, and respected Lower East Side denizen in her own right – thus served as a key foundation of Jones' commitment to collaboration and institution-building in order to provide a space for nonconformist writers, in the case of *Yugen* for the Beats and the Black Mountain School poets, among others. Moreover, in the techniques of the writers the Joneses published in *Yugen*, one finds analogous commitments to performative improvisation, syntactical complexity, ironic critique of bourgeois norms, and a claim among some that innovative artistry could remake the mind. While it would be foolish to claim that Jones/Baraka's Black Aesthetic depended on these white writers, it would be accurate to say that what Jones did when he became Baraka was not to reject bohemia entirely, but rather to test the viability of these bohemian social and aesthetic practices for conveying Black experience and serving racial justice politics, and to revise them accordingly.

There were of course substantive breaks between bohemia and Black nationalism, as is plain in the geography of New York's avant-garde scenes. But from *Yugen* to BART/S, Jones/Baraka pursued and enhanced a Black bohemian aesthetics that was neither simply a mimicry of the white withdrawal that Jones and his critics in Cuba rejected, nor any complicitous cultural appropriation of Black culture as "cool" defiance like that enacted by such white bohemians as the Beats. One can see this alignment of bohemia and Blackness in the first lines of Baraka's well-known 1966 manifesto poem, "Black Art," as in: "Fuck poems / And they are useful, would they shoot / Come at you . . ."[3] In such bohemian moves that passed his Black political litmus test, Jones aligned sexual license with immediate and concrete poetic effect, both of which presaged Black liberation. In the coming of the Black Aesthetic, this alignment became a key means by which African American artists in the Lower East Side – Jones was not the only one – defined the identity, community, and aesthetic ideals that could characterize a distinctive Black art created by a distinctively Black artist and that could serve that liberation. Ultimately, this constitution of a radical Black artistic posture in and through bohemian withdrawal is the pursuit that made the Black Aesthetic and the Black Arts Movement so powerful.

Assessing the full force of *the* Black Aesthetic thus requires recognizing its roots in the bohemian avant-garde of Lower Manhattan, and the best means to assess this neglected transition is to attend not to Jones and other more famous members of the movement in Harlem but to the Society of Umbra, an informal constellation of mostly Black male writers and jazz musicians formed in 1962. Attending to their collaboration with each other and with white members of the group in the Lower East Side illuminates how several aspects of the eventual Black Aesthetic that Jones exemplifies derived from collating the strands of Black politics of self-determination on the one hand with bohemian-inflected social nonconformity and artistic innovation on the other. As Jones had done before his famed conversion, Calvin Hernton, David Henderson, and Lorenzo Thomas, the three Umbra poets discussed here, embraced the key bohemian principles that social withdrawal and nonconformity were acts of resistance, and that the immediacy of aesthetic experience – rather than the bourgeois norms of traditional lyricism or certain conventional kinds of political protest – conveyed a radical vibrancy of the countercultural soul resistant to both bourgeois and racist hegemonies.

These Umbra poets were as invested in social and sexual license and kinds of withdrawal from social conformity as their white peers, then, but they posited the racialized geography of New York City and its attendant specter of interracial sexuality and assimilation as generative of a Black, potentially revolutionary nonconformity in resistance to that bohemia. Because nonconformity was their starting point, Umbra's emergent Black aesthetic was less exclusively about fidelity to Black vernacular cultural forms and presumed political positions in absolute resistance to cultural whiteness, as Jones/Baraka's became at first in 1965. It was more about unpacking and deconstructing limiting modes of thought about Black subjectivity, including some within Black vernacular culture, in order to liberate this desire for potentially revolutionary self-awareness from the cultural forms that circumscribed it. Indeed, their aesthetic practices and community formation led quite directly to the better-known, more explicitly nationalist Black Aesthetic, since several Umbra poets literally followed Baraka to Harlem in 1965 to help found and build BART/S. What Umbra exemplifies, then, is how the Black Aesthetic depends upon the many means by which African American poets rendered the disorienting and alienating experiences and ethos of Black life during the Civil Rights Movement era that so motivated the Cuban radicals in verse forms engaged with both the affirming practices and rituals of Black cultural heritage and with the countercultural aestheticism of Lower Manhattan. This combination became the heart of the Black Aesthetic, adapting the "bohemian" dissident desire in the Black soul into trans-formative art.

Histories of both the avant-garde and of the Black Aesthetic, singular, have until recently neglected this generative aesthetic and political overlap between bohemia and Black nationalism, and therefore have neglected the Society of Umbra. This was in large part because of the legacy of simple opposition that literary criticism has inherited either from the New Criticism and its assertion of an allegedly apolitical modernist lineage, or from the Black Arts Movement's self-characterization as utterly separate from and defiant of that lineage. Such histories of the avant-garde as Marjorie Perloff's (1996) or Daniel Kane's (2003) do not do full justice to the African American presences in famous avant-garde movements in New York City, though Jones and Umbra and others were an undeniable and integral part, and only recently has work in African American studies by James Smethurst, Margo Natalie Crawford, Daniel Widener, David Grundy, and others attended to the full context of the Black Arts Movement revolt outside of Harlem.

Instead of conceding too much to the privileging of white poets in defining New York avant-gardes, or conceding too much to the Harlem Black Arts Movement's own casting of previous generations of Black artists outside of certain urban centers as not revolutionary enough, readers should follow Grundy, Aldon Nielsen, Anthony Reed, Evie Shockley, and Timothy Yu, among others, in emphasizing and illuminating the intricate interdependence between race and the avant-garde, to borrow

Yu's title. The path these scholars chart leads to such groups as Umbra because their compass points to different terms of political integrity and aesthetic innovation at play in the development of racial avant-gardes in general and *the* Black Aesthetic in particular, notions that combined the nationalism Black radicals created and the bohemianism that helped to create them.

These scholars clarify how the dissident individualist desire (often portrayed as libido) usually attributed only to (white) bohemianism translated well, at least aesthetically, into the collective impulses of ethnic cultural self-determination. To the extent that the poets of Umbra had a common aesthetic, then, that sensibility predicated Black self-determination precisely on how such "bohemian" or "avant-garde" gestures of social removal, and what might be called avant-garde aesthetics of emotional immediacy. Abstraction, and deformation of conventional form and discourse, could do more than protest alone to liberate new ways of imagining Blackness from the forms of the existing hegemony. Jones' transformation does exemplify key features of the emergence of the Black Arts Movement and its Black Aesthetic, then, but only when considered as an aspect of both Jones' and the Umbra poets' reformation of bohemia in a Black image. Since the Lower East Side avant-garde and its bohemian self-cultivation were not so fully white in the first place, being avant-garde bohemians for Umbra poets (and for Jones) is different than one might think, and Blacker.

The Society of Umbra thus fomented the coming of the Black Aesthetic by translating the principles of its bohemian formation on the Lower East Side into an aesthetic sensibility of Black self-determination. This translation is as clear from how the group came into being as from the development of each writer's artistic sensibilities. The primary founder of Umbra, Tom Dent, born in New Orleans, came to New York City in 1959 after two years in the army and, before that, study at Morehouse College and Syracuse University. He came to Harlem because he wanted to be a writer but "[c]ertainly I had no concept of what it meant to be a black writer."[4] In pursuing this dream, Dent was withdrawing from the bourgeois life he had enjoyed as the son of Albert W. Dent, president of Dillard University, a historically Black university in New Orleans, and Ernestine Jessie Covington Dent, a concert pianist. While working at the *New York Age*, a Black weekly newspaper, and then at the NAACP Legal Defense Fund, Dent met and read with a number of Black writers in Harlem, eventually calling some of them together on the Lower East Side after moving there in 1962. In describing that group, Dent declared "the essential quality of Umbra as a search, quest – many individual quests woven together."[5]

That shared quest seems to have been precisely each member's pursuit of an answer to Dent's animating question, which is also a central question of the "Black Aesthetic" – what does it mean to be a Black writer?[6] Dent affirmed that the group's unity derived not from a single shared answer to this question but from shared social and aesthetic dissidence, what Nielsen called "a positive assertion of cultural blackness" that was "never totalizing" and that was tied to "a specifically African-American variant of the traditionally bohemian desire to stick it to the bourgeoisie."[7] Dent described this black bohemian sensibility as "a deep cynicism not only toward white America but towards its potential for redemption as a nation of justice for black people and others who were not white."[8] Not strictly bohemian withdrawal, therefore, this posture nonetheless has meaningful analogies with the Beat sensibility that, as Maria Damon described it, imagined that "the only revolutionary alternatives [to the collapse of the socialist left] rested with what we now call 'lifestyle,' a depoliticized revolution against engagement itself" which consisted of "dissent by 'dropping out,' a kind of passive resistance to the military-industrial complex that increasingly came to define the discourse of the public sphere."[9] Cultivating the soul here was a secular religion urging the redemption of the bourgeois nation, or at least the validation of the dissident's personally redemptive resistance through nonengagement against its corrupting force.

But for Dent, and by extension for Umbra, the African American variant of bohemianism drove them toward the proactive resolution of that discontent available in racial self-determination. According to Dent, there was "a growing sense of alienation from the white literary world," that

> was not a negative development born of rejection by the white literary establishment, but a healthy development in the sense that the only way we could say certain things as black artists – the things that needed saying – was to recognize that we constituted a separate world and that this world, propelling itself on the cultural integrity of black people in America, was as distinct with its own value system from the main body of American literature as black culture is distinct from whatever mishmash of advertisement majority American culture represents.[10]

Not satisfied with his version of a conventional bohemian critique of U.S. culture as consumerist commercialism, Dent articulates the quasi-nationalist motivation of Umbra that emerged from and resolved the limitations of this original bohemian posture.

Theirs was a sense that Black literary culture had its "own value system" alongside of, as well as in resistance to, both mainstream literary culture *and* its (white) countercultures. This value system grafted the priorities of Civil Rights Movement pursuits of self-determination onto the initial withdrawal of the bohemian, so that "sticking it to the bourgeoisie" came also to include "sticking it" to "the man." Dent's example of this grafting was his participation in On Guard for Freedom, formed by Calvin Hicks in 1960. This organization of artists and intellectuals actively protested the invasion of Cuba now known as the Bay of Pigs, and offered support to Congolese liberation leader Patrice Lumumba, among other activism. The group also cultivated such intellectual work as the seeds for Harold Cruse's famous *The Crisis of the Negro Intellectual* (1967). Says Dent: "I found the radicalism, projection of pan-Africanism, and comradeship with writers and other artists ... invigorating."[11] He thus saw withdrawal as the initial gesture of a positive racial self-cultivation predicated on the "integrity" of a pan-African Black culture, and on the linking of civil disobedience to mutual intellectual support and artistic production, a "dropping out" of the mainstream and eventually out of white countercultures in order to begin "dropping in" to urgent Black social movements. Here is a solid foundation for any "Black aesthetic."

That both the Society of Umbra and On Guard for Freedom emerged on the Lower East Side of New York City rather than in Harlem should lead scholars to "deterritorialize" bohemia and its avant-gardism, as Nielsen (1992) might have put it. Umbra's presence on the Lower East Side, and even its interracial character, challenges the notion that the avant-garde there was geographically, culturally, and conceptually the preexisting province only of well-known white artists. Instead, as Dent noted: "before the hippies, and before the Mafia moved in, the Lower East Side was an interesting place." It was comprised of "many ethnic groups, especially Eastern European and Jewish, but by the Sixties it had become substantially Puerto Rican, with an increasing population of blacks."[12] In other words, the Lower East Side art scene was only *becoming* white (and apparently less interesting) at the time even as the neighborhood was becoming Blacker. Hernton similarly noted that he arrived with "an influx of young new-generation artists and artist types, beatniks and later on hippies, including a great many poets and writers."[13]

Born in Chattanooga, Tennessee, and raised primarily by his grandmother, Hernton joined this influx after a BA in Sociology at Talladega College and an MA at Howard University, eventually becoming as well known for his sociology – primarily through his groundbreaking book, *Sex and Racism in America* (1965), about how sexual desire informs race politics – as for his verse. Hernton claims to have found one of the spaces created by these Lower East Side writers, the café Les Deux Mégots, by accident. Because of that discovery, before joining Umbra, Hernton was reading and socializing with the likes of "Ginsberg, Gregory Corso, Joel Oppenheimer, Jack Kerouac, Ed Sanders, and others," the very leaders of the white New York avant-garde. "But very few blacks were there," he added, "often I was the only one."[14] Still, just as Nielsen traces how African American modernist poet Melvin B. Tolson claimed to change modernism's cultural territory by locating its origins in African rather than in European sources, readers of Umbra can "deterritorialize" this Lower East Side avant-gardism by recognizing that Black writers were co-generators of its mapping rather than merely inheritors.

The Umbra poets' engagement with white bohemia was thus generative because that bohemia was both a space of liberation and a space from which to liberate oneself. Most Umbra writers engaged productively with white writers, from communist literati Art Berger, who was in the group and who touted Umbra poets in the journal *Mainstream*, a literary vehicle of the Communist Party, to Umbra's celebrated improvisational readings at some of the well-known New York venues dominated by white poets. Thus, when Lorenzo Thomas was brought to Umbra by Henderson from a writers' group that was "made up mostly of garment workers led by the Belgian unionist leather worker Henri Percikow," what united them was the linking of socially radical ideals about society and racial identity with innovative practices of literary art and literary community, practices that, like Beat bohemianism and Frank O'Hara's or John Ashbery's aestheticism, positioned them outside of (Black) bourgeois norms.[15] Thomas spoke often of how his status as an immigrant from Panama, and his eventual loss of Spanish, his native tongue, determined a relation to language (he was often beaten up as a kid for talking "funny") and to society predicated on his always being an outsider looking in. According to Hernton, confronting bourgeois norms from such an ambivalently willful outsider position – from their version of bohemia, complete with white lovers for some – facilitated the group's originating Black aesthetic: "Umbra was my introduction to the Black Arts Movement; it turned me into viewing reality through a black lens."[16] Indeed, says Dent, "[r]eally, we went through every crisis, every form of confrontation over direction, every emotional attitude that black cultural groups went through during the Sixties and Seventies."[17] And they did so while remaining geographically and culturally in the belly of the bohemian beast.

In seeking to carve out a space for itself both within and against (white) bohemia, Umbra writers began to articulate some of the terms and practices of racial self-determination that were to become central to the Black Aesthetic. The Society's magazine declared in its first issue in 1963 that their journal "is not another haphazard 'little literary' publication. *UMBRA* has a definite orientation: (1) the experience of being Negro, especially in America; and (2) that quality of human awareness often termed 'social consciousness.'" Carefully and even cynically distinguishing their resistance to the normative from the by-then clichéd language of literary revolt in (white) "little magazines," the editors declared: "We will not print trash, no matter how relevantly it deals with race, a social issue, or anything else," concluding that, in resisting the claim to be a "self-deemed radical," the journal was "as radical as society demands the truth to be."

Touting a countercultural truth, this statement does not therefore merely elevate aesthetics over politics in the way that the Cuban radicals implied. Rather, it distinguishes the group's social orientation from what they understood to be the falsely radical aestheticist principles of most (white) little magazines, while also insisting that their "social consciousness" required a rigorous aestheticism committed more to "truth" than to political rhetoric or political critique alone. This attempt to navigate between literary "quality" on the one hand and "that quality of human awareness often termed 'social consciousness'" on the other, meaningfully resembles Hoyt Fuller's claim in "Towards a Black Aesthetic," for example, that

> Just as black intellectuals have rejected the NAACP, on the one hand, and the two major political parties, on the other, and gone off in search of new and more effective means and methods of seizing power, so revolutionary black writers have turned their backs on the old "certainties" and struck out in new, if uncharted, directions. They have begun the journey toward a black aesthetic.[18]

Umbra's artists' statement would thus have been as at home in an issue of *Yugen* as it would have been next to Fuller's essay, as it appeared in Addison Gayle's edited manifesto of the movement, *The Black Aesthetic* (1971). The radicalism of truth is a bohemian principle, and when it was wedded to a rejection of the "old certainties" of modernist poetics and gradualist race politics, it became a feature of "viewing reality through a black lens."

That the Society went through every conflict or crisis over direction as any other African American group at the time, as Dent put it, is clear given how Umbra came to an end. The members most committed to cultural nationalist positions had wanted to publish a Ray Durem poem that was "derogatory to President [John F.] Kennedy and to his children" in an issue of *Umbra* that would have been released (too) soon after the assassination of the president.[19] The editorial decision by Henderson and others not to publish the poem sharpened oppositions that had been manifest in the group before. Says Michel Oren: "a faction including Ishmael Reed, Rolland Snellings (Askia M. Touré), Albert Haynes, and the Patterson brothers . . . who were considered the strongest cultural nationalists in the group vehemently protested the decision." This conflict led to debates through which "ideological positions as well as individual stances became more clearly defined."[20] Still, as Oren makes clear, it is impossible to identify whether it was this editorial decision alone, the allegedly violent kidnapping of Norman Pritchard to get *Umbra*'s checkbook that ensued, or the violence against Dent, allegedly by the Mafia, at a March 1965 poetry reading at Le Metro coffeehouse, that caused the final split. Consequently, the dispersal of the group reveals just how Umbra's quest to define what it means to be a Black artist was intertwined with its generative investment in its bohemianism, and how that investment paid off in a countercultural Blackness questing for new literary and political territory.

That their adventures produced a version of *the* Black Aesthetic can be seen quite clearly in key terms and practices of the group as exemplified by Thomas, Henderson, and Hernton. Careful analysis of key poems produces the proof that is in the pudding. Each of these poets wrote important poems in which resolving the ostensible discrepancy between sexual license and Black radical politics, soul cultivation and collective action, was portrayed as the enabling primal scene of both their artistic nonconformity and Black political radicalism.

A good example is Thomas' poem "The Unnatural Life" from the "Early Crimes, 1963–1966" section of *The Bathers* (1981).[21] The poem's epigraph from the Martiniquan Négritude poet, Aimé Césaire, sets this primal scene well: "*What I am is a man alone imprisoned in white* [original italics]." This epigraph implies the strict whiteness of the poetic culture of the United States in general and the Lower East Side in particular, and the isolation of the Black poet within it, but it does not rail against the imprisonment as one might expect from a Black Aesthetic in the making.

Instead, the poem seeks to characterize the consciousness – the "soul" – of that lone, alienated Black individual who is the poem's ostensible speaker, in order to imagine how to pursue from that incarceration the Black Aesthetic radicalism the speaker and poet both prize. The poem does so in part by locating this generative scene of confrontation in a resolutely local and ordinary New York venue, the "Crown Delicatessen." This ordinariness nonetheless becomes the means through which to confront and to contend with the cultural norms such ordinariness implies and masks.

In characterizing the emotional effects of this imprisonment in white, the poem unearths in the negative, and in the abstract, the potentially revolutionary, liberating dissident desire beneath that mask of ordinary, alienated interracial love. The poem does so by disemboweling its own conventional poetic approach to both the love and the politics of a self-doubting revolutionary, in the process critiquing various romantic love conventions common to Western poetry and art in order to skewer the conventions of bohemia's countercultural interracial sexuality. It does so less by defining the experiences of its speaker than by holding up its own conventions for examination and critique as part of what contributes to that speaker's isolation. Because it is "my lucky day," for example, the speaker is glad that "you" are not there, though he can see the shadow of the peach tree, mentioned twice in the poem, that "spreads on the white house / Behind your house It is a simplified heart sketched / Like a delicate jacket, its nude design / Reflecting the pack of cigarets in the pocket" (ll. 17–19). Though the speaker is not encountering the "you," presumably a white lover whose "happy face" he sees "in every blond table," he strains to connect associations from the "nude" shadow of a peach tree on an intervening house to the "you." The shadow on an intervening house suggests the distance between them, since the tree itself is no more in view than the house of the beloved, or the beloved herself. All is merely shadow.

Not just about the absent lover one finds in many love poems, though, these gestures also point toward the *impossibility* of the absent lover. The shadow's meaning as a heart is clearly only projected, a subjective and self-serving imagining of the lovelorn speaker that emphasizes how so many love-poetry gestures are similarly self-serving. Indeed, comparisons of a tree's shadow to the nude that one often finds in classical love paintings is no more indicative of "true" love than the claim that the naked "design" of the tree's shadow "reflects" – as in a mirror – the "cigarets in the pocket." The inadequacy of these images to secure the presence of the "you" reminds us that the "you," while potentially referring to an actual alienated lover, consists of yet another figure, another conventional component of the ideal love poem to which the speaker seems to lack access. In this way, the poem peels open a layer of the onion of love poetry conventions to expose the political anxiety of such (interracial) love, and the inadequacy of conventional verse to ease that anxiety.

Acknowledging the inadequacy of conventional notions of deep, trans-
parent, and transcendent poetic meaning, this poem similarly unpacks the
inadequacy of certain models of radical racial politics. The result is the
implication that desire itself – not any particular object – is the most radical
feature of consciousness and is thus the foundation of Black political
dissidence. In the "plot" of the poem, the speaker is "translating / 'Two
or Three Chants' by Leopold Senghor and / Thinking about the coming
revolution." In addition:

> My copy of Muhammad Speaks covers the table and the wind, and
> The door hanging open, frightened because I am here
> That I might forget these young delusions of love, afraid
> As I emerge from my fashionable jacket my brain turns
> Black and hateful Like a beast, your color rising in my nose
> And you are raped and murdered in the usual manner.   (ll. 25–30)

The speaker is ineffectively seeking to reconcile the ideals of revolution that
are operative in the opposed sensibilities of the credited founder of the
Négritude movement, Léopold Senghor, with his integrationist impulses,
on one hand, and the Nation of Islam's separatist newsletter on the other,
with additional reference to the idea later crystallized in Eldridge Cleaver's
Soul on Ice (1968) that the raping of white women was a revolutionary act.
None of these options satisfies, especially in the light (or the shadow) cast
by Nation of Islam theology through its paper "covering."

How does the translation of an African poet who translates African
heritage into European aesthetics measure up to Elijah Muhammad's
separatist dictates, any more than having a white lover or raping her? In
addition, if the "you" includes an ostensible white reader, "our" absence –
that hypothetical reader's nonrecognition of the speaker – confirms just
how fragile is this potential revolutionary meaning. It may be that no one
but the speaker is attending to his pitiful self-doubt, let alone moved by it to
any action. So how revolutionary could his poetry be? After all, despite its
syntactical irregularities, the poem invites this far-too-convenient and simple an answer to the question of what it means to be a Black writer, namely
that if you associate with white women and/or are too literary, you are
neither revolutionary nor genuinely Black. In such a posture resides both
the justification for unfair judgments of Black literature as too narrowly
political by white critics, and the tendency in the Black Arts Movement to
identify bohemian or bourgeois Black writers as not radical enough.

The poem uses these multiple modes of Black politics to critique each
other in order to push the reader past the limits of these postures and their

limiting languages into a model of potentially radical meaning-making through desire and affect that, though not explicitly radical in its politics, comes to be what ultimately underwrites the Black Art Movement's political aesthetic. This shift includes the sense of what a poem is supposed to be and do. In an interview with Charles Rowell, Thomas declared that he thought "of poetry as performance, and one studies one's craft for the purpose of being able to perform well . . . It's like music in that the practice and artifact are the same thing."[22] This model of poetry as simultaneous practice and artifact motivated both the performance poets of the later Black Arts Movement like Baraka, Giovanni, and Sanchez, and the earlier Objectivists, Beats, and some of the New York School, with whom Umbra poets also variously and directly engaged.

This performativity should be read not just as a reference to reading the poem aloud, as it was for someone like Sanchez, but also in the bohemian sense that language, when arranged in innovative ways on a page, can *act* on and as consciousness. This notion of performance thus clarifies the implications of Thomas' version of the surrealism of Césaire evoked in the epigraph. Césaire declared in an interview with René Depestre that surrealism "was a weapon that exploded the French language. It shook up absolutely everything. This was very important because the traditional forms – burdensome, overused forms – were crushing me." He added: "I felt that beneath the social being would be found a profound being, over whom all sorts of ancestral layers and alluviums had been deposited."[23] At the heart of such surrealist "revolt," following André Breton, is the attention to the "hyper-reality" available at the intersection of the conscious and the subconscious, with each supplying what the other lacks, and with that hyper-reality being the profoundest aspect of human reality defiant of the hierarchies of the lesser social realm. Thomas evokes just such a surrealistic self-consciousness as an empowering alternative to the conventional terms of Black radical politics and their relation to a conventional and domineering white liberalism.

In this framework, Thomas' bohemian aestheticism, ambivalence, and surrealism become a substantively Afrocentric pursuit of the most profound, and thus the most defiant, "being" buried under convention. Hence, for example, the phrasing about the Nation of Islam newspaper covering the door does more than merely suggest the wind blowing through an open door and disturbing a newspaper. The lines also evoke how comprehensive and potentially stifling the Nation of Islam ideology is, covering the spirit evoked by the wind in those same traditions of classical paintings as the nude in love, and darkening the door of other possibilities.

Either the darkened door or *Muhammad Speaks* is "frightened" because the
speaker is at a place of potential surrealistic compromise of himself. Indeed,
the speaker is oddly afraid that, by coming to the delicatessen, he will forget
his "young delusions of love," though he is worried for the wrong reasons.

The deli motivates surrealistic memory by placing the speaker's picture
in the "cheap frame" celebrating a local hero, perhaps by seeing his
reflection in the glass in front of the photo, just as it also evokes the
"you" in the diner's first dollar also framed on the wall, perhaps a hint of
a sense of exploitation or prostitution. What needs to be forgotten, then, is
not the delusion of love, but the speaker's "fashionable jacket," which
renders revolution a style one can wear, making such fashion a set of
conventions not unlike the various figures in love poetry that the poem
ironizes. In these terms, both interracial love and bohemian or Black
nationalist fashion are fads, so that the jacket evokes image as cover, just
as the newspaper did, and either fashionably unfashionable bohemian garb
or Black Panther spectacle constitute something inauthentic ("unnatural")
to the persona's possible revolt. The conscious and subconscious meet
and are perhaps liberated in these odd images, as the surrealist manifestos
suggest, evoking some other mode of perceiving and inhabiting reality.
Delusions of love become the more powerful revolutionary possibility here
because those delusions indicate the refusal of desire or consciousness to
conform to the common-sense rationality of (poetic) "form" and conventional avenues for its expression. Thus desire resists the rationality that has
allowed itself to be aligned entirely with social convention and social
hierarchy. Real radicalism requires getting "under" that cover to reveal
desire's defiant operation, the sense that the yearning to exist and to love
(oneself) constitutes a defining feature of Black radicalism.

Black radical selfhood thus comes to function in an avant-garde way
as what in another context Nathaniel Mackey (1993) aptly called
a "discrepant engagement." Mackey claims that the experimental writer,
whether Black or white, self-consciously and actively pushes the limits of
poetic language and form in order to liberate imaginative and social
possibility from those bounds through non-traditional aesthetic techniques that work against their own rules in order to explore and explode
discrepancies in the social norms they enact. Using Mackey's lens, one
can recognize how, instead of relying on the presumption that realist
aesthetics could adequately capture the reality of some singular thing
called "Black experience" and therefore subtend protest, as some Black
Arts theorists proposed, these Umbra poets understood Black radicalism,
aesthetic and social, as discrepancy.

Their shared surrealism thus purposefully confounded realism, acknowledging as it does, to borrow a formulation from Phillip Brian Harper, that "[representation] necessarily exists *at a remove from* even those real-world phenomena its resemblance to which is its most notable trait [original emphasis]," and that we should "understand this removal as a mode of *abstraction*, understanding the word in its most basic etymological sense to mean simply a state of *withdrawal* from some originary point."[24] Umbra writers explored and exploited this *necessary* remove of abstraction by enacting a principle of poetic composition in which, in Terence Diggory's words about the white New York avant-garde practice of the time, "the present fact of the poem, or its 'surface,' was itself the scene of experience. The self that mattered was the one coming into being through the act of writing, and history was the succession of immediate moments in which the poem was written or read."[25]

Poem as practice and artifact exists in abstraction from the Black self it wants to reveal, to which Thomas' poem adds a model of "history" in which, in his words: "The concept of the poem functioning as a political entity – as rhetoric to be acted upon – was and is a mistaken notion. The poem creating consciousness which will then inspire people to act, is valid."[26] "Creating consciousness" extends the notion of Black self created "on" the "surface" of the poem in the "act of writing" to include a readerly "history" more fully tied than Diggory suggests to social history, in this case to the creation of the sensibility or desire for the revolutionary subjectivity defiant of the hegemonic racial discourse of 1960s liberalism and gradualism. Hence the purposefully false note of the last line of the poem: "I should never have moved into your neighborhood!"

Clearly the note of regret rings true with how some of these downtown Black radicals – presumably including Thomas himself – felt about being on the Lower East Side instead of in Harlem. However, such regret depends too much on superficial fashion and accepts the validity of the segregationist notion that leads to white flight. By turning this language against such whiteness, the poem implies that revolutionary Blackness obtains in the pursuit of kinds of self-recognition and autonomy facilitated by how that Blackness refuses to sit still for its poetic portrait, with the revolutionary poem working through conventionalized rhetoric to trace and enact that movement of Black desire. Blackness thus becomes moving shadow and more than shadow, the umbra that is the substance of the Blackness that casts it.

Umbra poets thus aptly named themselves, for it is in the shadows of convention, in the shades of emotion, and at the edges of poetic language, that a genuine and defiant Black self – and the writer who conveys it – can be found. David Henderson offers a more conventionally affirming version of these shades in his meditation on his ambivalent straddling of the two geographical poles of the New York avant-garde scenes. Perhaps the truest bohemian of Umbra, Henderson studied writing, communications, and Eastern cultures at Bronx Community College, Hunter College, and the New School for Social Research without every finishing a degree, and came to be the longest-standing Black denizen of the Lower East Side bohemia, being involved in the scene for over forty years. He also wrote a biography of Jimi Hendrix, that was more poetic meditation than historical rendering, and sang on songs with pioneering Afrofuturist Sun Ra as well as with jazz musicians Ornette Coleman (saxophone), David Murray (saxophone), and Butch Morris (cornet), and started his involvement in Umbra by bunking on the couches of people like his mentor, Hernton.

It makes sense then, that in "Downtown-Boy Uptown," the first poem in his chapbook *Felix of the Silent Forest* (1967), Henderson turns the racial anxieties of bohemian Blackness even more fully into the root of potentially radicalizing Black beauty. The poem opens by identifying the tensions in sensibility between a "Downtown-boy uptown" and an "Uptown-boy uptown," with the speaker acknowledging that he contains both. In a poem that uses the word "complicity" twice, Henderson rewrites this manifestation of double consciousness – that famous Du Boisian formulation of a divided Black consciousness – into a generative tension that makes possible the integrity of an innovative Black poetic creativity: "*Long has it been that I've mirrored / My entrances through silk screen.*"[27]

A version of W. E. B. Du Bois' veil, the silk screen here constitutes a multicolored fabric lens or distortion or even funhouse mirror, a way to mask as artistic pursuit whatever aspects of selfhood that motivated the speaker's move to the "wrong slum" of the Lower East Side. At the same time, the line resists the claim to mimesis that would suggest that art – or even a mirror – could offer an accurate reflection of the speaker in the first place. The necessary distortions of art make perceiving an authentic self a dubious and largely inaccessible possibility, thereby diminishing the force of a simplistic notion of complicity. Thus, the first stanza of the poem identifies shared and mutually generative complicities in both geographies: "Downtown-boy uptown / Affecting complicity of a Ghetto / and a sub-renascent culture. / Uptown-boy uptown for graces loomed to love." The uptown boy uptown has graces – personal and artistic – that are woven to the love of the place and the people, including "Pudgy," the love interest of the poem, while the downtown "boy" uptown has a more readily visible complicity, namely a pretense to "belonging" in Harlem. While claiming greater authenticity as uptown boy, then, the speaker has nonetheless "long" "walked these de-eternal streets / Seeking a suffice or a number to start my count," seeking an origin for his belonging. He has apparently failed to find full belonging in the unromanticized, time-bound real life of that geography. But in failing to find his "count," he still finds the beauty of the inscrutable: "Trampling Trapezium to tapering hourglass / Behind the melting sun." Whether uptown or downtown, the Black artist is launched from this anxiety.

As in "The Unnatural Life," ambivalence becomes aesthetically product-ive dissent, a means to liberate Blackness from various aesthetic and therefore social bounds. For example, the poem suggests that romance with a Black woman, often rendered in the late-1960s authenticating discourse of the "black queen" in a national family, can function as a kind of complicity rather than affirmation or liberation. The poem concludes that Pudgy, a skinny Black woman who is affirmatively "mis-named" in a Black tradition of purposeful paradox, has a real but limited kind of advantage over the speaker in her integrity for staying uptown:

> You know.
> You are not stupid, Pudgy.
> You look for nothing of a Sun where you live,
> Hourglass is intrinsic . . . where you live.
> The regeneration in your womb is not of my body.
> You have started your count.
> I cannot.

The speaker does not have the biological capacity to carry a posterity in his body, and has lost touch with "de-eternal" time, which is the real-life time outside of art – the time of lifecycles and reproduction – from which the speaker seems to think his surrealistic art may be a distraction.

These lines reflect upon a line earlier in the poem in which the speaker describes the put-on authenticity with which he courted her: "My 140th St. gait varied from my downtown one. / I changed my speed and form for lack of a better tongue." Having no verbal game, the speaker walks Black to get her attention. The relationship between real-life, "de-eternal" time and the time of the literary becomes an anxious but productive discrepancy, one product of which is the realization that neither time can be limited or determined by the other. That realization allows for both to have a kind of legitimacy buttressed anxiously in the relationship each has to the other.

In this way, the poem seeks to resist the exploitation of desire both by bourgeois consumerist norms in "de-eternal" social time, and by any conventionalized protocols of both bohemian and Black nationalist cultural and political revolts in the ostensibly "eternal" time of art. In particular, the speaker rejects exploitation of heterosexual love that his relationship with Pudgy invites, resisting the idea of self-affirming and therefore self-indulgent artistic representation comprised by a heteronormative model of Black authenticity rooted in family and progeny.

What the poem valorizes instead is the surreal, self-contradicting multiplicity of Blackness that is, to reiterate Nielsen's point, "never totalizing" because it derives from ethos and practices, not particular forms or conventions. The last stanza of the poem's first section makes this point clear: "Then was, love you, Pudgy: / Thin young woman with a fat black name. / It is the nature of our paradox that has us / Look to the wrong convex." "[O]ur paradox" of Blackness derives from looking to the "wrong" convex, as if there could be a correct one, and as if there could be no correct concave. Blackness is creative desire, then, countercultural resistance to conformity, staking its claims on a willful and self-affirming countercultural "wrongness" that reveals the invalidity of binary opposition, residing instead in the multiplicity of simultaneously "right" and "wrong" concaves and convexes. This expression of cultural Blackness is neither merely oppositional to whiteness nor even dialectical with it, then, but a curved contradiction that is productive of a lovely Black woman's name and thus an aspect of affirmed and affirming sense of self located in ever-changing but socially grounded cultural practices rather than in mythical pregnancy.

The poem thus ambivalently validates Black nationalism by expanding it into bohemia: "Pudgy: your Mama always said Black man / Must stay in his own balancing cup. / Roach on kneebone I always agreed." Here the agreement is rendered as provisional or even conditional, facilitated by the "roach," its marijuana-induced ease, and genteel politeness. Thus, as the speaker resists the guilt that binary thought fosters, the poem makes this guilt – like his anxiety about time – productive of beauty. He writes: "Did this Tragedian kiss you in anticipation / Of blood-gush separating from your black mirror?" Sexual desire seems to liberate one from gazing narcissistically in the mirror for some reflection of a singular Black aesthetic, turning one instead toward a kind of mutuality whose nonbinary logic beautifies the distortions of art into its own kind of authentic experience of self.

This point is obliquely confirmed when the speaker declares: "If I desire to thrust once more, If I scamper to embrace / Our tragedy in my oblique arms! .... / Nevermind." Never mind a lament for a lost authenticity allegedly remedied by sexual encounter. Never mind an attempt to make tragic racial alienation poetic, offering yet another narrative of Black pain resiliently overcome. Such gestures are outmoded, from "a long gone epoch," the speaker avers, and thus unworthy of the poetry he would write now, as it is also unworthy of Pudgy's ostensible geographical and cultural authenticity that would be marred in his inadequate representation. The poem thus accepts the lived value of these codes of authenticity while rejecting their limiting and limited poetic value. One can live a kind of authenticity but to represent it may be to exploit it.

What Henderson is suggesting is that Black bohemianism offers an empowering resistance to aesthetic exploitation implicit even in some Black literary affirmation that then produces a surrealistic liberatory self-constitution. Here is part of what it can mean to be a Black writer, in other words, one working to be free of exploitation or appropriation. The second poem in the chapbook, "So We Went to Harlem," makes explicit this resistance to artistic self-prostitution, implying a proleptic critique of the tyrannical singularity of *the* Black Aesthetic. Reminiscent of Langston Hughes and William Carlos Williams in its use of a quasi-objective, non-narrative language, and similar to Frank O'Hara in its ostensibly autobiographical commitment to the ordinary, the poem condemns the image of Harlem cultivated by white (*and* Black) bohemia: "we went to Harlem, / The many-fabled letter-men – two black, one white – / Went to Harlem to screw broads."

> So we arrived in Harlem:
> Up and down 125th Street
>   126th Street
>   127th Street
>   128th, 129th ... *up and down*
> – *Lookin' for a good boys?*
>   up and down
> – *Eight dollahs all you need. Any broad you want!*
>   up and down
> – *What's happenin' fellas?*
>   up and down
> – *Hey!*
>   (I ask white Richard if he likes any
>   Special one. He doesn't know.)
>   up and down
> – *What's your name sweetheart.*
>   up and down

BABY! HONEY! SWEETHEART! LOVER!

up

BROADS – ASSES – BUTTER – BROWN – HEAVEN!
the sweeter the berry –

down

Across and below ... *across and below*

Any reader of Williams' *Paterson* will recognize echoes of the passage of Paterson "walking" through the park. One can also recognize Hughes' use of overheard conversations in italics and the found language of neon signs to punctuate his portraits of Harlem and Paris cabarets in such poems as *Montage of a Dream Deferred*. A multifaceted tradition is evoked here, one that resists white supremacist and nationalist cultural boundaries to locate in its border crossings the liberating and potentially revolutionary desire that resists exploitation.

In addition to evoking geographical movement, the "up and down" offers clear sexual innuendo through which the "prostitution" is made explicit. By the end of the poem "white Richard" gets no sex, and has had his money taken by a Black sex worker, with the poem implying that "David" and "Calvin" – presumably Henderson and Hernton – have set him up to fail in this way to wreak vengeance on his (and their own) bohemian sensibility. But that revenge equally exploits Harlem and therefore redounds back to them. Hernton makes a similar point in "Ballad of a Young Jacklegged Poet," in which he critiques the poet as an itinerant jack-of-all trades whose aesthetic vision is tied more to *ideas* of poetic Blackness rather than to immediate experience: "Wake up O jacklegged poet," "wake up out of Central Park – / Wash your face in fountain water" and "walk defiantly / Through streets of Harlem Town."[28] Going to New York City in a fit of bohemian withdrawal implied by sleeping in the park guarantees nothing authentic to the downtown Black poet, nor one from the South, the alleged source of all authentic Blackness, nor even to one raised uptown, unless one is washed of preconceived notions and firmly planted in a reality that one acknowledges one cannot represent fully. Indeed, no poem or aesthetic is free from the prostitution of its material. The poem's integrity must lie in part in how it resists that prostitution through its unification of practice and product, its commitment to immediacy in these cases through Blackened surrealism.

Crucially, all of this surrealistic self-constitution in Umbra's verse touts its ultimate and ideal implication that it is part and particle of a collective and ongoing communal revolutionary fervor. In his poem "Jitterbugging in the

Streets," first published in that defining Black Arts anthology, *Black Fire* (1968), Hernton makes this connection clear. The poem is based upon the protests and violence in the streets, from nonviolent civil disobedience to so-called race riots, but rather than merely celebrating, beautifying, or critiquing those events, the poem respectfully gathers and projects the revolutionary desire buried in these chaotic times, what Anthony Reed (2014) describes as the "future anterior" of "freedom time" in his scholarly book of that name.

This gesture of prolepsis is facilitated by the reference to the jitterbug, a kind of swing dance from the 1920s and 1930s that was related to the Black-inspired Lindy-hop, and that garnered a new cultural life as its name came to be attributed to Black dance more broadly in the 1960s. The violence of the riots may not be the fullest manifestation of the revolutionary desire, the "profound being" these Black bohemians seek, but those uprisings are certainly an enabling discrepancy, the opening of the blank space through which that desire can dance. The poem opens: "There will be no Holy Savior crying out this year," because

> The only Messiah we will see this year is a gunned down man
>   staggering to and fro
>   through the wilderness of the screaming ghetto
> Blotted out by soap opera housewives in the television afternoons
>   exchanging gossip vomited up from cesspools
>   of plastic lives
> Talking themselves[29]

The Savior will be, paradoxically enough, the death of a man in the ghetto whose violent demise will be ignored by the bourgeoisie and the "plastic lives" they lead that leave them only "Talking themselves." He will die for the sins of those who ignore him but will save those in the screaming ghetto by unleashing or expressing a largely unnamed force that is their inchoate response to ongoing racist violence, the force that will become revolutionary desire. Its appearance is foreshadowed in a disparaging line of dialogue attributed in the poem to those who live plastic lives: "Niggers will do anything!" Indeed.

Black desire will reject the conventional morality upon which the plastic people base their critique of the alleged lack of restraint among Black people, even as that assertion justifies the unrestrained violence of the white supremacist state. Of course, that lack of restraint does indeed come from the Black community's collective, if intermittent, lack of respect for the bourgeois norms implied in the statement, but that lack of respect is precisely the point. As much of the four-page poem chronicles the forces both within and without the Black community that lead to and endorse the violence, and though it does at times betray doubts about the coming of this revolution ("And long as the sun rises in the East / Niggers, in dingy fish-n-chip and bar-b-q joints, / Will be doing business as usual – "), the poem locates the savior in the collective action that is to come from that very impulse, disparaged though it may be. This violence and all its systemic and systematic oppressions will not ultimately stand because, ultimately, "Niggers will do anything" in the name of the dissidence that will liberate.

Enacting the role of the jazz griot that Jean-Philippe Marcoux (2012) describes so well, the poet of "Jitterbugging in the Streets" frames poetic experience not only as the creation of individual consciousness that Thomas describes, but also as the enactment in a minor key of the collective dissidence now and to come. The poem concludes with the following description of the coming apocalypse:

TERROR stalks the Black Nation
A Genocide so blatant
Black men and women die in the gutters as if they were reptiles
And every third child will do the dope addict nod in the whore-scented night
    before the fire this time
And Fourth-of July comes with the blasting bullet in the mind of a black man
Against which no great white father, no social worker, no psychothanatopsis
Will nail ninety-nine *theses* to no door:
        Jitterbugging
        in
            the streets![30]

Independence Day will happen when the bullet no longer hits the body but explodes in the mind, the abstracted violence of the transformation of consciousness. It will be as transformative as the emergence of the Protestant Church, but it will not be announced, nor will it be prevented. It will happen in the streets. And of course, jitterbugging was a dance craze, and the idea of dancing in the streets evokes the transformation of the 1964 song of that name, by Martha and the Vandellas, from a summer fun song to a civil rights protest song. As Marcoux observes, the ritual function of even popular, apolitical soul music and its associated dances constitutes both communal affirmation and the foundation of cultural resistance.

Verse participates in this transformation, not by calling for it directly but by becoming an instance of the deranging reconfiguration of conventional language and thought through puns, associative logic, irony, and the warped syntax of these long lines. Clearly, for these poets, the opposition between surface and depth that animates the white New York School poets described so well by Diggory does not hold as firmly. The constitution of Blackness as this desire for revolution-to-come constitutes the ultimate introspection, an inward-turning or depth facilitated by resisting the conventional and even bohemian poetic trappings of that introspection, surface *as* depth. People starving is enough to make poems out of, but so too is people thinking, coming to awareness merely by inhabiting the violence of their cultural moment. Herein lies the coming of the Black Aesthetic.

Amiri Baraka's oft-cited (perhaps over-cited) manifesto poem, "Black Art," which was first published in *The Liberator* in 1966, was thus calling for the very kinds of poems that had already been written by the poets of Umbra. Baraka's poem opens, as mentioned, with a declaration of the value of immediate experience: "Poems are bullshit unless they are / teeth or trees or lemons piled / on a step." Rather than abstract, self-indulgent introspection, poems need to be real things, fully engaged with the material world, less psychological depth and more immediate political surface. It then calls for "Assassin poems, Poems that shoot / guns" and that wrestle cops and disarm them as literally as poems can. This "surface" includes transcription of the sound effects of the machine gun the poem is supposed to be: "rrrrrrrrrrrrrrrr / rrrrrrrrrrrrrrrr ... tuhtuhtuhtuhtuhtuhtuhtuhtuh-tuh /... rrrrrrrrrrrrrrrr ...." And it ends with a call for poems that view reality through a Black lens:

> Let Black people understand
> that they are the lovers and the sons
> of warriors and sons
> of warriors Are poems & poets &
> all the loveliness here in the world
>
> We want a black poem. And a
> Black World.
> Let the world be a Black Poem
> And Let All Black People Speak This Poem
> Silently
> or LOUD[31]

In order for Black people to be poems, they simply need to *be*. But Thomas, Henderson, and Hernton would add, and Jones/Baraka would agree, that they need to be liberated from convention in order most fully to inhabit that being and its beauty. And while Umbra poets portray that liberation in terms less literally violent than Baraka's, their work portrays transformations of consciousness as radical. Black people being a poem for Umbra meant being the embodiment of an uncontainable desire for revolution-to-come, one that diminishes or even dismantles other aspects of conventional, bourgeois Black life.

This is the beautiful shadow that Umbra has cast. And they have cast that shadow through their foundational role in the emergence of a New York poetic aesthetic, their turning of the clash between bohemia and Blackness into the generation of a verse that enacted the poetry of Black people. The point of acknowledging the centrality of Umbra is thus not to diminish the significance of Baraka for the Black Arts Movement, because he remains, and should remain, perhaps the key figure of the famous New York instance of the movement.

But one must expand the story of the emergence the movement's aesthetic in New York City, and of what has come to be called the "historic" avant-garde, to include this complicated model of Black bohemian introspection. They are perhaps a signal example of Shockley's prescient observation that the fundamental premise of Black aesthetics, plural, is "the subjectivity of the African American writer – that is, the subjectivity produced by the experience of identifying or being interpolated as 'black' in the United States – actively working out a poetics in the context of a racist society."[32] This broad but precise definition allows for a useful challenge to the singularity that *the* Black Aesthetic claimed for itself in *Black Fire* and *The Black Aesthetic*, among other key documents, by illuminating how its founding premise necessitates multiplicity.

The Black Aesthetic comes only from the amalgamation of each writer's individual engagement with the desire, discrepancy, and integrity of the revolutionary consciousness to come; in other words, each quest to define what it means to be a Black writer; each Umbra poet's multifaceted portrait of the "subjectivity" of the African American writers as this uncontainable desire for a revolution-to-be. Acknowledging Umbra in this way recuperates the power and value of an innovative mode of poetic introspection called the avant-garde for producing its alleged opposite, the radical poetics and politics of the 1960s.

Notes

1. Baraka (1999b), 147.
2. Neal (1968), 29.
3. Baraka (1999a), 219.

4. Dent (1980), 105.
5. Ibid., 105.
6. Ibid.
7. Nielsen (1997), 125, 99.
8. Dent (1980), 105.
9. Damon (2015), 170.
10. Dent (1980), 107.
11. Ibid., 10.
12. Ibid., 105.
13. Hernton (1993), 580.
14. Ibid., 579.
15. Oren (1986), 183.
16. Hernton (1993), 580.
17. Dent (1980), 105.
18. Fuller (2014), 151.
19. Oren (1986), 181.
20. Ibid., 182.
21. Thomas (1981), 17.
22. Rowell (1981), 24.
23. Depestre (1967), 26.
24. Harper (2015), 19.
25. Diggory (2009), 167.
26. Rowell (1981), 25.
27. Henderson (1967), n.p.
28. Hernton (1976), 13.
29. Ibid., 83.
30. Ibid., 87.
31. Baraka (1999a), 219.
32. Shockley (2011), 9.

Bibliography

Allen, D., ed. 1960. *The New American Poetry, 1945–1960*. New York: Grove Press.

Baraka, A. 1999a. "Black Art." In *The Leroi Jones/Amiri Baraka Reader*, ed. W. J. Harris, 219. New York: Basic Books.

1999b. "Cuba Libre." In *The Leroi Jones/Amiri Baraka Reader*, ed. W. J. Harris, 125–60. New York: Basic Books.

Benston, K. 2000. *Performing Blackness: Enactments of African American Modernism*. London and New York: Routledge, 2000.

Bürger, P. 1984. *Theory of the Avant-Garde*. Minneapolis: University of Minnesota Press.

Cleaver, E. 1968. *Soul on Ice*. New York: Ramparts Press, Inc.

Collins, L. G., and M. Crawford, eds. 2006. *New Thoughts on the Black Arts Movement*. New Brunswick, NJ: Rutgers University Press.

Crawford, M. N. 2017. *Black Post-Blackness: The Black Arts Movement and Twenty-First-Century Aesthetics*. Champaign, IL: University of Illinois Press.

Damon, M. 2015. "Beat Poetry: HeavenHell USA, 1846–1965." In *The Cambridge Companion to Modern American Poetry*, ed. W. Kalaidjian, 167–79. Cambridge University Press.

Dent, T. 1980. "Umbra Days." *Black American Literature Forum* 14.3: 105–8.

Depestre, R. 1967. "An Interview with Aimé Césaire." In *Poesias*, 25–31. Havana: Casa de las Américas.

Diggory, T. 2009. *Encyclopedia of the New York School Poets*. New York: Facts On File.

Fuller, H. 2014. "Towards a Black Aesthetic." In *SOS – Calling All Black People: A Black Arts Movement Reader*, ed. J. H. Bracey, S. Sanchez, and J. Smethurst, 151–56. Amhurst: University of Massachusetts Press.

Gates, H. L., Jr. 1987. "'What's Love Got to Do With It?': Critical Theory, Integrity, and the Black Idiom." *New Literary History* 18.2: 345–62.

   1988. *The Signifying Monkey: A Theory of African-American Literary Criticism*. New York: Oxford University Press.

Gayle, A., ed. 1971. *The Black Aesthetic*. New York: Doubleday.

Giovanni, N. 2003. *The Collected Poetry of Nikki Giovanni, 1968–1998*, ed. V. C. Fowler. New York: William Morrow.

Grundy, D. 2019. *A Black Arts Poetry Machine: Amira Baraka and the Umbra Poets*. London: Bloomsbury Publishing.

Harper, P. B. 2015. *Abstractionist Aesthetics: Artistic Form and Social Critique in African American Culture*. New York University Press.

Henderson, D. 1967. *Felix of the Silent Forest*. New York: Poet's Press.

Hernton, C. 1976. *Medicine Man: Collected Poems*. Berkeley, CA: Reed, Cannon & Johnson.

   1993. "Umbra: A Personal Recounting." *African American Review* 27.4: 579–83.

Hughes, L. 2001. *Montage of a Dream Deferred*. In *The Collected Works of Langston Hughes, Vol. III: The Poems, 1951–1967*, ed. A. Rampersad. Columbia: University of Missouri Press.

Jackson, V. 2005. *Dickinson's Misery: A Theory of Lyric Reading*. Princeton University Press.

Jones, L., and L. Neal, eds. 1968. *Black Fire: An Anthology of African American Writing*. New York: William Morrow.

Kane, D. 2003. *All Poets Welcome: The Lower East Side Poetry Scene in the 1960s*. Berkeley: University of California Press.

Mackey, N. 1993. *Discrepant Engagement: Dissonance, Cross-Culturality, and Experimental Writing*. Tuscaloosa: University of Alabama Press.

Marcoux, J-P. 2012. *Jazz Griots: Music as History in the 1960s African American Poem*. Lanham, MD: Lexington Books.

Neal, L. 1968. "The Black Arts Movement." *The Drama Review* 12.4: 28–39.

Nielsen, A. L. 1992. "Melvin B. Tolson and the Deterritorialization of Modernism." *African American Review* 26.2: 241–55.

   1997. *Black Chant: Languages of African-American Postmodernism*. Cambridge University Press.

Oren, M. 1986. "The Umbra Poets' Workshop, 1962–1965: Some Socio-Literary Puzzles." In *Studies in Black American Literature, Vol. II: Belief vs. Theory in Black American Literary Criticism*, ed. J. Weixlmann and C. J. Fontenot, 177–222. Greenwood, FL: Penkevill Publishing Company.

Perloff, M. 1996. *The Dance of the Intellect: Studies in the Poetry of the Pound Tradition*. Evanston, IL: Northwestern University Press.

Reed, A. 2014. *Freedom Time: The Poetics and Politics of Black Experimental Writing*. Baltimore, MD: Johns Hopkins University Press.

Rowell, C. 1981. "Between the Comedy of Matters and the Ritual Workings of Man." *Callaloo* 11/13: 19–35.

Shockley, E. 2011. *Renegade Poetics: Black Aesthetics and Formal Innovation*. University of Iowa Press.

Smethurst, J. 2005. *The Black Arts Movement: Literary Nationalism in the 1960s and 1970s*. Chapel Hill: University of North Carolina Press.

Thomas, L. 1978. "The Shadow World: New York's Umbra Workshop and Origins of the Black Arts Movement." *Callaloo* 4: 53–72.

1981. *The Bathers*. New York: I. Reed Books.

Widener, D. 2010. *Black Arts West: Culture and Struggle in Postwar Los Angeles*. Durham, NC: Duke University Press.

Yu, T. 2009. *Race and the Avant-Garde: Experimental and Asian American Poetry Since 1965*. Stanford University Press.

CHAPTER 2

Robert Hayden, the Black Arts Movement, and the Politics of Aesthetic Distance

Derik Smith

Langston Hughes once said to me, "Boy, you colleged!"

Robert Hayden

Robert Hayden is rarely considered in appraisals of the most significant developments in African American poetics of the 1960s. Although his career approached its crescendo in the later part of the decade, his poetry is often associated with earlier literary periods. For example, *The Norton Anthology of African American Literature* (2004) situates his work in the era of "Realism, Naturalism, Modernism" which it dates from 1940 to 1960. Similarly, *The Riverside Anthology of the African American Literary Tradition* (1998) places Hayden in a sub-section titled "Voices of African American Tradition and Modernism" contained within a section spanning 1945 to 1960.

No major anthology of African American literature groups Hayden into a historical period beginning after 1960. Yet many of Hayden's celebrated poems – like the anthology staple "Those Winter Sundays" – were not published until after 1960, and the contours of his literary reputation were forged in the middle of the decade. Anthologists, doing the necessarily frustrating work of periodization, distance Hayden from the 1960s because his political aesthetic contrasts so sharply with that of the primary cultural force of the decade, the Black Arts Movement (BAM). While the poetry of the BAM was often Dionysian, vernacular-based, performance-oriented, and invested in the politics of identity, Hayden's 1960s poetry was Apollonian, "writerly," interiorizing, and universalist. However contrastive, these dissimilar poetics represent responses to *problematiques* that confronted African American literary artists in the middle of the twentieth century.

Perhaps chief among the dilemmas facing the African American poet in the 1960s was the question of audience; specifically: How would the culturally elite artist-intellectual position her/himself in relation to the Black folk masses? While BAM-associated figures like Amiri Baraka, Nikki Giovanni, and the Last Poets responded with a populist art modeled on the rhetorical aesthetics of the Black preacher, Hayden refined an erudite and elliptical poetics that drew inspiration from Black folk culture, but was particularly suited for study and appreciation in academic contexts.

Crucially, Hayden honed the perspective of the poet-observer, always creating a modicum of *aesthetic distance* that separated his poetic personae and the folk figures that populated his work. If BAM poets sought to meld with the masses, vanishing the cultural, social, and economic capital that may have distinguished them from workaday Black folk, Hayden often used his poetry to study the paradoxical quality of his relation to under-capitalized, hard-laboring kith and kin that were "remotely near" to him.

Delineating these differences is critical for a charting of the African American poetic tradition that reaches a significant point of furcation in the 1960s, after which it sorts into distinct, equally rich modes: stage-based and vernacular-heavy spoken word and hip-hop on the one hand, and page-based literary poetry on the other. While BAM aesthetic innovation and sensibility gave life to the former, Hayden did Promethean work for the latter – in the 1960s he was a fire-keeper, maintaining and further kindling the light of a "writerly" Black poetic tradition, even as BAM innovators of the era attacked that tradition, deeming it a failure.

In important work on African American women writers of the nine-teenth and twentieth centuries, Harryette Mullen has called attention to a "writerly" tradition of African American literature that has been under-appreciated in the years since prominent theorists like Henry Louis Gates, Jr., and Houston Baker focused scholarship on Black "speakerly texts" that obtain operative energy from "speech-based poetics or the trope of orality."[1] Mullen points out that, since the 1980s, the critical search for "speakerly" elements of African American literature has tended to margin-alize a tradition of "writerly" texts, which "draw more on the culture of books, writing and print than they do on the culture of orality."[2]

Although the distinction between writerly and speakerly texts is not always clear, Hayden's 1960s poetry appears unabashedly writerly when juxtaposed to much of the art associated with the BAM. Hayden's erudite diction, ellipticism, and reverent engagement with the plenitude of literary tradition was anomalous in the BAM context, which was enlivened by the belief that literature could be a "collective ritual" enacted by textual acts meant to bring on the "psychological liberation" of the Black masses.[3]

Leading poet-theorists of the BAM like Larry Neal, held that this liberation required a deliberate expurgation of the writerly impulse that had generated the wan literature of the "Negro" bourgeoisie.

Strong commitment to liberatory, ritualistic art, and class-inflected suspicion of the bookish tradition of "Negro" literature gave rise to a poetics that thrived on what Stephen Henderson would call the "living speech of the Black community."[4] The speech referenced by Henderson was primarily the vernacular language of Black urbanites who, by the middle decades of the twentieth century, outnumbered their rural counterparts.

For adamant theorists like Neal, the writerly tradition of "Negro" literature was not sufficiently guided by the culture of orality associated with these Black masses, and was thus a "failure" – a symptom of the "Negro" bourgeoisie's desire to gain "acceptance on the white man's terms."[5] As Neal framed it, the new literature of the 1960s was not to be a "case of our elite addressing another elite";[6] instead, it became a project in which culturally capitalized artist intellectuals crafted speakerly texts shaped by oral idiom and consciously oriented toward the Black masses. Among other things, the new poetics asked the artist to do away with estranging language and allusion, while fusing with the Black community by way of what Henderson once called "Soul talk."[7]

Hayden's reflexive resistance to these political-aesthetic impulses registered in his notable stand during the 1966 Fisk Writers' conference. In one of the most often remembered episodes of the literary 1960s, Hayden voiced particular opposition to the expectation that literary intellectuals give elevated attention to the cultural comfort of an intended audience. Commentators have frequently keyed on Hayden's rejection of the "black poet" label and portrayed him as an embattled artist, perilously clinging to a universalism that compelled him to self-identify as a "poet," without racial qualification. But at the Fisk conference, Hayden's stand was as much about audience as it was self-identification; which is to say, when Hayden eschewed the "black poet" designation he was not just quarreling about the semantics of artistic identity. More tangibly, he was making a claim about the artist's relation to a Black audience that, in the 1960s, was especially honored and valorized in the poetic work of an emergent Black cultural elite.

The issue of audience was central to Hayden's remarks during the proceedings of the Fisk conference. In the pages of *Negro Digest*, the reporting of David Llorens portrays Hayden as an exasperated conference participant – a lonely opponent of the new aesthetic that emphasized racial particularism, and the necessity of art that, before all else, addressed itself to Black people. At one point in his article, Llorens quotes Hayden in a moment of frustration: "Let's quit saying we're black writers writing to black folks – it has been give an importance it should not have."[8] Embedded in Hayden's insistence is a discomfort with the growing assumption that a special connection – or nearness – between Black writers and audience ought to be discernible in Black literary production.

While theorists of the BAM wanted a quasi-participatory art modeled on pre-modern, non-Western forms of ritual communion wherein the artist was figured as "a kind of priest, a black magician" among his people,[9] Hayden was committed to an aesthetic model in which the poet remained *productively* distanced from the folk figures that populated his work. Although he was no less invested in representations of Black life than the younger poets of the 1960s, Hayden was far more circumspect about asserting an easy contiguity between himself and the folk masses that were both the imagined audience and central characters of BAM-era poetry.

Aesthetic Distance, *For Malcolm*

Anthologies of the era furnish many examples of BAM-associated poets using vernacular orality to draw near to a folk audience in need of "psychological liberation." For instance, the important 1969 collection, *For Malcolm: Poems on the Life and the Death of Malcolm X*, is in one sense a catalogue of verse featuring the speakerly flourishes of artist-intellectuals asserting allegiance to the slain leader while also aligning themselves with the Black masses.

But this key BAM-era anthology, which was collaboratively conceived by publisher-poets Dudley Randall and Margaret Burroughs in the midst of the 1966 Fisk conference, also included Hayden's poem, "El Hajj Malik El-Shabazz." Howard Rambsy II has noted that Hayden's inclusion in *For Malcolm* and other important anthologies associated with the BAM troubles any simplifying literary history that would exclude Hayden from discussions of "black arts discourse."[10] Indeed, considering Hayden as a full participant in the discourse of the era significantly widens scholarly conceptions of Black poetics of the 1960s.

In *For Malcolm*, Hayden's contribution offers a stark contrast to so many of the other anthologized poems, in which poets employ vernacular shibboleths, familial language, and collective pronouns to link themselves in community with both Malcolm and his folk admirers. In this context, Hayden's poem is distinctive, operating by way of a writerly voice that is

distanced from a mass audience, and that approaches Malcolm as respectful observer rather than hagiographer.

While most of the anthology pieces construct a figure of first-name
familiarity or a familial – "Brother Malcolm" – intimacy, Hayden's "El-
Hajj Malik El-Shabazz" begins with the less familiar name that Malcolm
took in the final months of life, after his 1964 pilgrimage to Mecca.
Introduced via the Arabic title, Hayden's Malcolm becomes a somewhat
estranged figure, not immediately accessed by the "black folks" (or others)
in the poem's audience. Moreover, in using the title to foreground
Malcolm in his post-pilgrimage period, Hayden calls to mind the political
and ethical complexities that must have presented themselves to Malcolm
after he was affected by the universalist ethic of orthodox Islam, or what
Malcolm himself described as the "spirit of true brotherhood as it is
practiced by people of all colors and races here in this ancient holy land."[11]

By immediately evoking the phase of Malcolm's life in which he
modulated the rhetoric of racial particularism that is associated with his
Nation of Islam period, Hayden's poem opens with a subtle indication that
it is not meant to have exclusivist or primary resonance for a Black readership. As the poem concludes, it seems to fully endorse an understanding of
Malcolm that deemphasizes his role as a Black leader while celebrating his
recognition of an Allah, enfolding "all colors and races." After chronicling
Malcolm's several life transformations – as they are presented in his
Autobiography – the poem ends with an image of Malcolm on pilgrimage.
The penultimate sentence reads: "He fell upon his face before / Allah the
raceless in whose blazing Oneness all / were one."[12]

If the title of Hayden's poem distances Malcolm from Black audiences
unfamiliar with the contours of his life after his ministry in the Nation
of Islam, the subtitle of the poem filters perceptions of Malcolm through
the plenitude of the literary tradition. Prefacing the poetic biography is
the subtitle "O masks and metamorphoses of Ahab, Native Son." While
reference to Richard Wright's mainstay of the African American literary
tradition is a writerly gesture that draws on "the culture of books" to
deepen the poem's implication, by likening Malcolm to Ahab, Hayden's
subtitle builds upon the defamiliarizing foundation of the poem's title to
fully push its subject into Western grand narratives. Hayden provocatively
affiliates Malcolm with both the biblical King Ahab, and Herman
Melville's famous antihero – flawed pillar characters of a European-
American cultural canon. The poet associates these fallible leaders with
Malcolm in his iconic Nation of Islam period, when "He X'd his name,
became *his people's* anger, / exhorted them to vengeance for *their* past."[13]

In *For Malcolm*, the narratorial distance between Hayden's speaker and Malcolm's "people" is anomalous, as is the critique of the racial particularism of the most iconic phase of Malcolm's life. The critique is registered by way of subtle allusion: "Rejecting Ahab, he was of Ahab's tribe. / 'Strike through the mask!'" (15). Here, Hayden links Malcolm to the King of Israel who, because of his idolatry, brings a curse upon himself and his descendants. Then, transcribing the most recognizable words of Melville's Ahab, Hayden suggests that, like the monomaniacal captain, Malcolm in his X manifestation offered profound exhortation, albeit in a doomed campaign against a mythic, malevolent whiteness.

Hayden's avoidance of a hagiographic representation of Malcolm and his non-aligned relation to Malcolm's "people" do not merely reflect the conservative values of a middle-class integrationist writer. These positions are more productively understood as the expression of an aesthetic ideal, which held that the artistic representation of experience was most effective when the artist achieved a kind of detachment from represented experience. In the early twentieth century, Edward Bullough seminally described the ideal of aesthetic distance as something more complex and involved than the depersonalization of artistic subject matter. "Distance," wrote Bullough, "does not imply an impersonal, purely intellectually interested relation of such a kind. On the contrary, it describes a personal relation, often highly emotionally coloured, but of a peculiar character. Its peculiarity lies in that the personal character of the relation has been, so to speak, filtered."[14]

African American literary artists of the nineteenth and twentieth centuries were, for the most part, attentive to this ideal. Up until the 1960s, culturally capitalized Black writers were manifestly conscious of their own double-consciousness – aware of their liminal status at the border between a Black folk world enlivened by oral culture, and a bourgeois American world associated with the culture of literacy. Writers straddled this border – Janus faced – attempting to transubstantiate the world of Black orality into the world of literary formations.

In the 1920s, Alain Locke would bid writers to *lift* "the folk gift to the altitude of art," and implicitly assert a cultural hierarchy that BAM poets in particular sought to dismantle.[15] By the 1960s, many Black poets were beginning to conceive of the "folk gift" of song and vernacular language as the very highest form of artistic expression. Thus, many learned poet-intellectuals eschewed literary idiom, took cues from Black musicians, and favored a colloquial tongue that was borrowed from the street corners of the Northern city.

If the artful deployment of "soul talk" was a distinguishing component of what Stephen Henderson (1973) would call the "New Black Poetry," Etheridge Knight ranks among its most thoughtful practitioners. Two of his three contributions to *For Malcolm* exemplify a speakerly Black Arts-era poetics that contrasts sharply with Hayden's aesthetic of distance. In "It Was a Funky Deal," for example, Knight relies on the vernacular of the moment to produce a text that elegizes Malcolm, but also emphasizes the poet-speaker's close connection to the lumpen Black masses. While the title of Hayden's "El-Hajj Malik El-Shabazz" served to disorient readers, the title of Knight's poem welcomes a readership weaned on the Black vernacular.

Recapitulating Malcolm's efforts to connect with, what he called, "the little man in the street" through appeal to the parlance and cadences of the Black masses,[16] Knight offers a conceptually traditional elegiac poem, but suffuses it with colloquial idiom. The funky declarative sentence that acts as the title of the poem is also its refrain, appearing five times in the seventeen-line elegy. And the sense that the poem doubles as urban exchange is deepened by the deployment of vernacular passwords like "jive," "cat," and "man."[17]

Knight's appeal to a register of language that might attract a Black audience is not simply superficial stylization; indeed, in "It Was a Funky Deal" Malcolm's success in connecting with the Black street – the way he "pulled . . . coats" – is precisely what allows him to live on in the hearts and minds of those who survive him. Addressing the spirit of the slain leader, Knight's poetic persona affirms: "You reached the wild guys / like me" (21). But here it is important to note that the enjambment in the sentence asserting Malcolm's charismatic reach elicits a consideration of the relation between the lumpen "wild guys" and the poet-speaker. Even as Knight insists on his oneness with masculine urban outsiders, his line-break begs readers to note the novelty of the idea that the poet and the wild guy are one in the same.

The unlikely alignment of the literary poet and the urban folk figure was an essential gambit of the powerful strand of Black Arts-era poetry that relied upon vernacular orality. While Hayden carried on a tradition that observed and acknowledged a distance between the Black literary artist and the most dispossessed of Black folk, the BAM political aesthetic encouraged the disappearance of this distance – even when lived experience would seem to militate against it. A poet like Knight, who lived through poverty and addiction and wrote his *For Malcolm* poems while in prison, could credibly use vernacular language and explicit declaration to group himself with the economically and culturally marginalized; but far more culturally capitalized Black poets of the 1960s were also linking themselves to Black experience in the lower reaches of the American class and social structure.

For example, Ted Joans was probably among the most bohemian, cosmopolitan, and artistically versatile poets of the Black Arts era; but his contributions to the *For Malcolm* anthology – pointedly titled "My Ace of Spades" and "True Blues for a Dues Payer" – are laced in the idiom of the Black American everyman. Joans moved in the same circles as leaders of a mid-century international avant-garde, like Salvadore Dalí, Aimé Césaire, and André Breton, and when he sent his poems to the editors of the anthology he was living in Guelmim, Morocco; yet, in those poems, Joans constructed poetic personae that used vernacular language to instantiate strong identification with Black American street brothers. When his speaker in "My Ace of Spades" declares "Malcolm X tol' it lak it DAMN SHO' IS!!,"[18] Joans positions himself squarely among Malcolm's people, and concomitantly severs himself from "those black blue bloods / who attend the White House policy lunch." In fact, in "True Blues for a Dues Payer," the speaker wishes that it was "black blue bloods" who had been assassinated, rather than Malcolm.

Even when culturally accomplished, highly educated poets of the 1960s did not dramatize connection to the Black masses through literary approximations of folk orality, they renounced association with "black blue bloods." *For Malcolm* furnishes evidence of prodigiously talented artists rejecting any elite affiliation: Margaret Walker and Gwendolyn Brooks – certainly among the most esteemed and recognized Black poets of the era – employ poetic personae that are at one with a Black proletariat class that Walker's poem, "For Malcolm X," characterizes as "[h]ating white devils and black bourgeoisie."[19] Collective pronouns and adjectives "us," "we," and "our" serve to group together the speakers of Brooks' and Walker's poems with Malcolmites described by Walker as "gambling sons and hooked children and bowery bums."[20] In their seemingly identical response to Malcolm's murder, Walker's speaker is amalgamated into the experience of sufferers at the bottom of the American ethnic and social hierarchy, and confidently addresses the fallen hero on behalf of the indigent class evoked earlier in the poem: "Our blood and water pour from your flowing wounds."[21]

Black Cleaving in the 1960s

If the poetry of *For Malcolm* and other anthologies of the late 1960s dramatizes a general desire to disappear life experience that might separate

the Black literary class from "wild guys" and "bowery bums," this represents the influence of a collectivism inherent to the politics of Black
nationalism, and the apparent rejection of key elements of older models
of racial uplift. At the beginning of the twentieth century, when
W. E. B. Du Bois proposed that Black progress would be achieved through
the leadership of the "Talented Tenth" of the race prepared to "guide the
Mass," he concretized an intraracial division of labor that valorized a Black
intellectual and cultural "aristocracy" while castigating the benighted,
immoral poor.[22]

But, by the time of Du Bois' passing in 1963, the new leaders of a Black
literary aristocracy were resonating with the nationalism articulated by
Malcolm X; and by the end of the decade they were producing a poetics
that in both form and content effectively turned the "Talented Tenth"
model on its head: Many of the most accomplished literary artists of the
late 1960s wrote poems that valorized (what some have euphemistically
called) the untalented nine-tenths, while castigating immoral "black blue
bloods."

In 1967, Gwendolyn Brooks would write that the poetics of the "New
Black" seemed to shout: "Up against the wall, white man!"[23] But vehe-
mence of interracial oppositionalism was only one element of the new
poetics. Almost equally important was an intensification of the rhetoric
around intraracial politics. In the months leading up to and following
the assassination of Martin Luther King, Jr., Black poetics was infused
with strategically efficient dichotomies, which sorted Black people into
class-inflected categories populated by imagined working-class and poor
nationalists – or potential nationalists – on the one hand, and elitist
integrationists or accommodationists on the other.

While poets who wanted to draw near to and celebrate the vernacular
culture of the folk masses did so by saturating poems in Black orality and
asserting oneness with folk figures, they also sought to sever themselves
from upwardly mobile stock characters like the "girdlemamma mulatto
bitches" and "slick halfwhite / Politicians" who are the primary villains in
Amiri Baraka's 1969 *ars poetica*, "Black Art."[24]

These sacrificial effigies have strayed too far from the fold of proper
Blackness and their punishment in art helped establish and police the
boundaries of an imagined Black nationalist collective. A pithy example
of this policing of transgressive Blackness is witnessed in Reginald Lockett's
poem "Die Black Pervert," collected in the pivotal 1968 anthology, *Black
Fire*. Lockett's poem condenses homosexuality, Europhilia, and economic
wherewithal into a single Black figure worthy of death, extermination.

Concocting this medley of damnable qualities in the vessel of one character, "Die Black Pervert" succinctly suggests the anxieties produced by the 1960s destabilization of categories of gender, sexuality, race, and class. It also gives much credence to the work of critics like Amy Ongiri, who underscore the importance of class identity in Black cultural production of the 1960s. Ongiri points out that: "Although heteronormative hypermasculinity is widely on display throughout *Black Fire*, as is 'anti-white' performativity, it is definitely tension over intragroup class divisions and possibilities for class ascendancy that most consistently permeates the anthology and much of Black Arts writing."[25]

While the violently exclusionary rhetoric of Lockett's style of BAM poetry seemed to demarcate the ideological and lifestyle expectations of proper Black nationalist subjectivity, it also widened the distance between the poet speaker and the degraded scapegoat. Critics like Phillip Brian Harper have convincingly argued that Black Arts poetry offered only limited forms of racial solidarity, because poems thematically similar to "Die Black Pervert" and "Black Art" were dependent on the degradation and expulsion of certain types of Black people – namely "black blue bloods" and queer folk. But it should be noted that this poetry of persecution also declared the bona fides of poet-intellectuals who wanted to destroy any trace of connection to an elite (and effete) status that might complicate their averred nearness to Black folk without much social standing, economic capital, or formal education.

In some of his earliest work, published in the 1930s and 1940s, Hayden had experimented with versions of the vernacular language and racial solidarity manifestos that grew popular among Black poets in the 1960s. These early poems by Hayden – with suggestive titles like "Ole Jim Crow," "Shine, Mister?," and "These Are My People" – bore the ideological and aesthetic imprint of the socialist realism that was advocated by the Communist Party of the USA, and which became important to African American letters of the Great Depression era.

While they were not as rhetorically militant as many Black Arts-era poems, nor marked by anxiety about intraracial class divisions, they carried in them the stirrings of artistic impulses that were fine-tuned by poets like Langston Hughes and Margaret Walker and then amplified in Black poetry of the 1960s. But, although Hayden began his career by sometimes inhabiting the vernacular voice of the folk and advocating for forms of political solidarity, he was also already working with the high culture technique that would eventually become an essential aspect of his poetic reputation. By the late 1940s, Hayden had shifted into a type of modernist

register that privileged erudite, allusive language, elliptical form and introspective investigation of "universal" themes like history, faith, and the
powers and limitations of art itself.

Coming under the influence of the English poet W. H. Auden and the
religious, existential sway of the Bahá'í Faith, during the middle decades of
the twentieth century Hayden cultivated a distinctive body of work that
differed markedly from the more populist and "New Negro"-like verse
gathered in his 1940 collection, *Heart-Shape in the Dust*. He would eventually come to regard the works in *Heart-Shape* as "prentice pieces," and
hope that all copies of it would be destroyed.[26]

Some of Hayden's most important readers – like his critical-biographer,
John Hatcher – have followed the poet's cue and separated *Heart-Shape*
from the rest of Hayden's corpus, regarding it as rather derivative protest
poetry, imitative of verse produced by Harlem Renaissance lynchpins like
Hughes. But other scholars have gestured toward the relation between
Hayden's earliest published work and the poetic ethos he was firmly
establishing in the 1960s, and which brought him into apparent conflict
with advocates of the new Black aesthetic during the 1966 Fisk conference.
James Smethurst, for example, has positioned Hayden in the literary
landscape of the Old Left-era through an analysis of the poet's use of
"low" folk and "high" literary forms. Smethurst (1999) argues that the
competitive interplay between folk and literary voices in Hayden's early
work expresses suspicion of an aesthetic stance that would posit an easy
alignment of the experience of the artist-intellectual and the Black folk
community.

In the stanzas of a blues ballad like "Bacchanale," a youthful Hayden
enters fully into the dialect-governed consciousness of the Black laborer
who is "Gonna git high, / High's a Georgia pine" because the "Factory
closed this mawnin" and he "Done drawed that last full pay."[27] But in the
imagist poem "Old Woman with Violets" Hayden offers an alternative
take on the condition of the folk figure:

> Quiet and alone she stands
> Within the whirling market-place.
> Holding the spring in winter hands
> And April's shadow in her face.[28]

The short piece issues from the contemplative distance observed by
a speaker who seeks to create a literary painting of the folk subject, rather
than an authentic-seeming persona poem narrated from the bottom of the
class structure. Noting contrastive representations like this, Smethurst

contends that in *Heart-Shape* Hayden's forays into imagism and Anglo-American modernism represent a conscious effort to move beyond the more populist brand of Black poetics that Hughes honed in the 1920s and 1930s.

Rather than focusing on Hayden's mimicry of Hughes' innovative blues poems, Smethurst calls attention to the distanced vantage point and modernist method of some of the folk-life poems in *Heart-Shape*, to suggest that Hayden's effort actually "critiques Hughes's work with its implicit insistence that Hughes's location of the narratorial consciousness-poet as an insider (or potential insider) is simplistic and in fact is a capitulation to an oppressive race identity imposed on African Americans."[29]

Smethurst concludes his brief but generative reading of Hayden's first volume by mentioning that later in his career the poet would create a significant body of work committed to the exploration of "the alienation of the African-American narratorial consciousness-poet from ... African-American communities, experiences, heroes and so on."[30] This undeveloped assessment of Hayden's mature career is certainly corroborated by the poet's late 1960s contribution to the *For Malcolm* anthology, which – as argued above – displays some degree of "alienation" from the adopted patron-saint of BAM-era poetics and from a generalized Black community. But the simple fact of Hayden's participation in *For Malcolm*, and his poem's studied engagement with Malcolm's life, indicates that the poet's alienation was not imbued with disaffection, hostility, or stark isolation.

From his earliest writings in the 1930s up until his death in 1980, Hayden's poems never scorned or scolded the Black "communities, experiences, heroes and so on" that were their primary subjects. Although Hayden was beset by a self-pronounced "sense of alienation nothing could alter,"[31] what Smethurst calls, "the narratorial consciousness-poet" associated with Hayden can only be described as one characterized by *loving* alienation.[32] Indeed, the contranymic quality of the word "cleaved" best describes Hayden's seemingly paradoxical relation to the Black folk world from which he emerged and about which he wrote about with a paradigm-forging force throughout his maturity.

If Hayden's late 1960s poem about Malcolm X offers distanced writerly appraisal of the Black Power hero, poems he published in the early and mid-1960s represent some of Hayden's first fully developed explorations of his cleaved relation to the lower-class matrix of his boyhood and youth. After Hayden had achieved considerable literary success, making the journey from Depression-era destitution in Detroit's Paradise Valley neighborhood to middle-class stability in 1970s Ann Arbor, he would often remind interlocutors of his hardscrabble beginnings: "My family was poor, hardworking, with no education . . . my roots are really very deep in what I like to call Afro-American folk life."[33]

In explicating his art, Hayden would evoke his familiarity with "slum life," with "dilapidated" housing;[34] and he would lightly admonish interviewers, reminding them that he "grew up in the ghetto,"[35] the adopted son of a "coal-wagon driver."[36] Hayden's endeavors to produce this kind of extra-poetic autobiography were likely brought on by the worry that his sartorial choices and personal demeanor, coupled to his neo-modernist art, might obscure his folk "roots." (Some sense of Hayden's high-culture presence might be achieved by conjuring a plausible scene in which he is puffing on his tobacco pipe while asserting his "predilection for the folk idiom," and his wife, Erma – a Julliard-trained pianist – plays a Brahms concerto for ambience.[37])

Certainly, there were aspects of Hayden's affect that might have prompted observers to count him among the Black aristocracy that, by the end of the 1960s, had come under withering attack in BAM poetry. But it was precisely the tension between Hayden's deep affinity for the accoutrements of high-culture expressivity and his deep familiarity with a lower-class folk world that gave life to some of his signature 1960s poetry.

In "Those Winter Sundays" and the lesser-known "Electrical Storm," Hayden takes on a *problematique* that was sidestepped by the great majority of BAM-era poets who, following a logic of racial solidarity politics, produced work in which the culturally capitalized artist-intellectual melded with the Black masses. Partly because of his refusal to conduct racial solidarity politics through art, Hayden was able to carve out a distinctive poetic space that implicitly acknowledged what Harper has aptly described as "the inexorable social processes" that inevitably distance the Black artist-intellectual from the Black majority. While poets described by Harper as "Black Aestheticians" sought to cover over the "attenuation" of their "*organic* connection to the life of the folk" – an attenuation brought on "by virtue of their increasing engagement with the *traditional* (Euro-American) categories of intellectual endeavor" – Hayden often created poetic personae that called attention to that attenuation.[38]

His "Electrical Storm," first published in *Selected Poems* of 1966, considers the mixed allegiances of the Black intellectual, whose induction into the epistemologies of Western modernity necessarily distance him from folk origins. The storm that brings down electrical wires, and represents mortal danger to the speaker, is a kind of objective correlative for the internal turbulence experienced by the Black intellectual weaned in the bosom of folk wisdom and superstition, but indelibly shaped by formal schooling. The dissonant comingling of the speaker's dual inheritances is the poem's underlying motif, suggested by both narrative and linguistic register. Hayden abuts erudite lexicon and folk vernacular to demonstrate the wide range of his speaker's cultural experience, but also to bring on the sense of self-division that is central to the poem. It opens with colloquialism and high culture poetic register, and with biblical allusion:

> God's angry with the world again,
> The grey neglected ones would say;
> He don't like ugly.
> Have mercy, Lord, they prayed,
> seeing the lightning's
> Mene Mene Tekel,
> hearing the preaching thunder's deep
> Upharsin.[39]

The poem's interpretive keys are suggested by the Aramaic words borrowed from Daniel, chapter 5. These words have long been invested with foreboding because in their original context they constitute the "handwriting on the wall" that portends the fall of the Babylonian king, Belshazzar. The "grey neglected ones" who articulate vernacular wisdom – God "don't like ugly" – interpret the poem's storm as an ominous message from Divinity, like the message that appears on the wall in the palace of Belshazzar, who has turned away from the Old Testament God. But for Hayden's speaker, the cause of the storm is not simply reducible to the will of an angry deity.

Schooled in rationality and scientism, the speaker attributes the storm to atmospheric shifts and finds himself distanced from the folk knowledge, and the folk, of his youth. Hayden indicates the centrality of this division in the speaker by breaking up the four Aramaic terms of the message written on Belshazzar's wall. "Upharsin," which translates as "divided," is separated from the terms of its original context by the poet's own language, and stands significantly alone on its line.

But the speaker's division from his folk context is no clean severance; the "colleged" consciousness of the poem cannot dismiss the vernacular voices of his past:

> I huddled too, when a boy,
> mindful of things they'd told me
> God was bound to make me answer for.
> But later I was colleged (as they said)
> and learned that it was not celestial ire
> (Beware the infidels, my son)

but pressure systems,
colliding massive energies
that make a storm.
Well for us. . . .⁴⁰

Although the educated speaker would interpret the storm as meteorological event rather than divine portent, he cannot fully untether himself from the religiosity and social ethos of the folk. By curating splinters of the folk voice, Hayden does not simply demonstrate his affinity for the materials of a Black vernacular tradition.

The fragmented appearances of the folk voice in the poem are intrusions into the erudite consciousness of the poet-speaker, who attempts to bracket the folk voice – keeping it sequestered from the "colleged" voice that guides the poem. But if the stanza quoted above suggests that the poet appealed to parenthetical constructions to distinguish folk consciousness and colleged consciousness, the ambiguous identity of the speaking voice in the stanza's last line: "Well for us. . . . " – offered without parenthetical qualifications – indicates the difficulty of hermetically separating these aspects, or "massive energies," that circulate within the Black artist-intellectual. For Hayden, high- and low-culture epistemologies, secular and religious belief systems, colleged and folk voices are not easily divided; instead, they collide – such that his speaker cannot be fully included or excluded from the Black folk collective that is evoked in the final syllable of the stanza.

The poem's verbification of the noun "college" was, according to Hayden, inspired by a playful remark offered by Langston Hughes, who simultaneously called attention to Hayden's intellectual pedigree and subtly warned against making too much of it, saying, "Boy, you colleged!"⁴¹ The vernacular neologism attributed to Hughes suggests that an original subject has been acted upon by some exterior energy or force and definitively changed by it. In Hayden's poetic usage, the verb, "was colleged," condenses "the inexorable social processes" that inevitably strain the relation between the Black artist intellectual and the folk community.

Readers of the African American literary tradition recognize that this strain – and the internal storm – stirred up by the colleged condition of the Black intellectual was archetypally captured by Du Bois in "Of the Coming of John," the single chapter of fiction in *The Souls of Black Folk* (1903). Du Bois' protagonist leaves the Southern rural matrix, attends an imagined Black college and is transformed in "body and soul," only to find himself speaking the language of an epistemology that fundamentally alienates him from the Black folk who gave him life.[42]

By explicitly demonstrating that college education brought on "engagement with the *traditional* (Euro-American) categories of intellectual endeavor" that led to a troubling dissonance for the Black intellectual aspirant, at the beginning of the twentieth century Du Bois laid bare a tectonic question in African American literary art: Could the formally learned Black artist speak to or for the folk? In 1960s poems like "Electrical Storm," Robert Hayden offered up his version of the answer to this question by suggesting that, although he spoke from the folk experience, he could not easily align himself with the denizens of the Black majority that were not really intellectual brethren, immersed in the logics of secular humanism or the plenitude of Western literary culture. But Hayden – who would ask rhetorically: "how thrive but by the light / of paradox?"[43] – also refused complete devotion to materialist philosophies that might have inexorably distanced him from folk roots. In "Electrical Storm," Hayden remains ambivalent about the answer to the fundamental philosophical question at the heart of the poem: Is the journey through life determined by "heavenly design / or chance"? Theories of heavenly design, articulated by the poem's vernacular-speaking "neglected ones" are never fully jettisoned by the colleged artist. Instead, two seemingly antithetical epistemologies – one linked to Black folk life, the other to Western intellectualism – are allowed to collide and perpetually compete in the consciousness of the poet-speaker.

In Hayden's 1966 *Selected Poems*, "Electric Storm" appears as the second poem in the book. It is preceded only by "The Diver," a symbolist piece that contemplates the allure of suicide and the will to life (and thus *the* primary existential question – Why live?). The prominent positioning of the poem in the book, replicated in his *Words in the Mourning Time* (1972) and *Angle of Ascent* (1975), indicates that the cleaved relation between the artist-intellectual and his folk roots was essential to Hayden's self-perception and artistic project.

His most famous 1960s poem, "Those Winter Sundays," is built on the self-same thematic topography that is established by "Electric Storm." Hayden's poetic persona – the colleged speaker whose limpid, expertly calibrated voice guides the poem – recalls his time in the folk matrix, centering on his cleaved relation to a paternal figure whose love was not expressed in words, but whose "cracked hands that ached / from labor in the weekday weather made / banked fires blaze," vanquishing the cold of winter Sundays.[44]

The genius wedding of form and content in the quasi-sonnet is routinely recognized by anthologists and critics who attend to the poem's technical precision, such as the alliterative flourishes that bring to life both the "blueblack cold" of the winter morning, and the warming fire nurtured by the vigilant father. But while Hayden uses poetic device to eloquently register the quotidian, sacrificing heroism of the working-class patriarch, he is also committed to an articulation of distance between father and son. While the former creates warmth on winter Sundays, he is also responsible for the "chronic angers" of the household, which repelled the possibility of filial affection and appreciation when the narrator was a boy, "Speaking indifferently to him, / who had driven out the cold." Distance is also ambient in the expostulation of the mature speaker who, in the poem's final couplet, cries: "What did I know, what did I know / of love's austere and lonely offices?" The pathos of the poem is kindled by the fact that the recognition of parental love comes belatedly to Hayden's adult speaker: Experience has given him emotional tools to fully perceive his father's love, but the passing of time needed for perception has robbed him of the opportunity to fully connect to the now absent father.

Moreover, the significant gulf separating father and son is implicit in the astonishing mastery of poetic language by the speaking persona, recalling his formational years in the household of a father who – in sharp contrast to his artist-intellectual progeny – has no words for his love. While it is through manual labor that the folk father attains expressive capacity, it is in erudite literary work that the colleged speaker expresses himself. Certainly, "Those Winter Sundays" is a meditation on intergenerational friction and the warmth of masculine familial love, but it is equally a representation of the poet's cleaved relation to the formational folk world which he sincerely loved, yet eagerly "escaped" – as he put it in one personal letter.[45]

The Paradigm of Distance After the 1960s

Hayden's work in poems like "El-Hajj Malik El-Shabazz," "Electrical Storm," and "Those Winter Sundays" exemplifies a writerly, distanced, and introspective approach to Black life that contrasts significantly with the political aesthetic advanced by that cadre of Black poets who in the 1960s eschewed signs of intellectual and literary training as they developed speakerly, expressive forms rooted in vernacular orality, dramatic performance, and the appearance of full identification with the lower-class folk world of the Black majority. The delineation and explication of these contrastive modes of Black poetics is, in and of itself, important to textured appraisals of the literary 1960s; and careful noting of this bifurcation in African American poetic expression is thus essential to the genealogy of post-Civil Rights-era poetics.

Although anthologists and literary historians have often marginalized Hayden's contributions to the 1960s while focusing on the radical developments in the poetry associated with the BAM, Hayden's commitments to aesthetic distance and contemplation of his cleaved relation to the Black folk world have proven paradigmatic for a significant sector of poets working in the wake of the 1960s. As Charles Rowell argues in the introduction to *Angles of Ascent: A Norton Anthology of Contemporary African American Poetry* (2013), after the 1960s:

> the poets of the next generations, who have ascended to great heights on the North American literary scene, are not direct aesthetic and ideational descendants of the poets of the Black Arts Movement; they are more akin to Robert Hayden and the poets contemporary to the Movement who wrote outside the Black Aesthetic. (xl)

An attempt to account for the institutional, cultural, and social processes that led to the literary prominence of post-1960s poets who followed after Hayden, rather than the BAM, would require analysis that delved into: (1) the emergence of the university based MFA program as the primary producer of literary poets from the 1970s onward; (2) the 1970s coalescence of hip-hop and spoken word poetries as "aesthetic and ideational descendants" of the BAM; and (3) the widening of the experiential gap between the Black artist-intellectual class and the Black poor who bore the brunt of neoliberal socioeconomic policies in the post-civil rights/hyper-incarceration era. Suffice it to say, 1960s activism opened up predominantly white universities to greater numbers of Black students and a modest collection of Black poet-professors, who, in the context of MFA poetry workshops, practiced a mostly page-based, literary poetics that was the flipside of the street-inflected rhyming of hip-hop MCs who were – in many respects – the aesthetic scions of BAM poets who, according to Amiri Baraka, "created the word as living music raising it off the still, Apollonian, alabaster page."[46]

While it is the vernacular-saturated, performance-oriented, Dionysian aesthetic of the BAM that makes its way into hip-hop and spoken word, it is the imprint of Hayden's distancing methods and curatorial relation to Black vernacular that is felt in the field-shaping, academically rewarded literary poetry of the 1980s and 1990s produced by writerly poets like Rita Dove, Yusef Komunyakaa, and Elizabeth Alexander, and the founders of the Cave Canem Foundation, Toi Derricotte and Cornelius Eady.

As a primary production house of early twenty-first-century Black literary poetics, Cave Canem has built upon the work of successful poets of the 1980s and 1990s, who themselves built upon the 1960s work of Robert Hayden. To offer just one example, Komunyakaa – who is a Cave Canem Fellow and Honorary Director – published "My Father's Love Letters" in 1992. The poem is a thematic homage to "Those Winter Sundays," and it helps establish Komunyakaa as one of Hayden's most distinguished descendants. Komunyakaa's poem conjures no wistful sense of filial love as its speaker remembers his illiterate father. But, like Hayden's 1960s classic, the poem is alive with the same marveling distance between the articulate poet-speaker and the hard-working (but abusive) father figure, who – "With eyes closed & fists balled, / Laboring over a simple word" – dictates letters to his scribe-son. Here there is a vast gulf between the erudite poet-speaker and the unschooled father who comes to voice only in the vernacular rhythm-and-blues-like lyrics he would send to the mother of the boy-scribe: "Love, / Baby, Honey, Please."[47]

If the differing degrees of literacy distancing the poet-speaker and the hard-laboring father was an undercurrent in Hayden's civil rights-era poem, it is a primary feature of Komunyakaa's poem published in the neoliberal era. Like Hayden, Komunyakaa uses the poem and the figure of the laboring father, to consider not only his distance from a formational familial matrix, but also from a folk world populated by Black masses only minimally exposed to "the *traditional* (Euro-American) categories of intel-lectual endeavor" that shape the voice and the thinking of the mature poet. In some ways, Hayden's frequent poetic return to the distance between himself and all others, including those Black folk nearest to him – his artistic exploration of a "sense of alienation that nothing could alter" and his cleaved relation to the Black folk world – provided an instructive model for Black poets, like Komunyakaa, who forged rewarding careers in academia in the decades following the 1960s.

Until the era of campus integration, high-profile Black poets were – almost exclusively – faculty at historically Black colleges; but by the late 1980s, the most successful Black poets frequently found themselves in the uncharted professional-cum-social territory of predominantly white institutions of higher learning. In these new offices, Black poets were afforded economic stability and a degree of material comfort; but like an emergent class of Black university professors (and post-1960s Black profes-sionals generally), in their occupational offices, these poets were racially isolated – Black voices in ivory towers.

Concomitantly, tenured and tenure-track Black faculty, reaping the benefits of 1960s campus activism, also found themselves distanced from the experience of large swathes of working-class and poor Black folk who were most vulnerable to 1960s backlash policies, like the dismantling of the welfare state and the vast expansion of the penal state. While the experience of stark economic and social dispossession was reflected in the folk poetry of hip-hop, which grew ubiquitous in the 1980s, the formal poetry of post-1960s poet-professors was reflective of the growing distance between the upper and lower strata of the Black class structure.

In the same year that University of Indiana associate professor, Yusef Komunyakaa, published "My Father's Love Letters," Henry Louis Gates, Jr., penned a *Forbes* magazine editorial entitled "Two Nations ... Both Black." Writing from his tenured professorship at Harvard, and as the most visible member of that Black professorate that had expanded significantly in the decades following the 1960s, Gates called attention to "a rift within black America" – one that had widened along class lines that separated culturally and economically capitalized Blacks from the Black majority.[48] Gates declared that "we members of the black upper middle class, the heirs of the Talented Tenth ... are isolated from the black underclass."[49] Using the pejoratively coded language of the era, Gates gave shape to a feeling that some of his professor-peers may have articulated in different terms, but none could fully deny: a wide gulf had emerged between the life-experience of Black professionals and the Black folk who labored in post-industrial service sector jobs, or in shadow economies, and who bore the brunt of neoliberal socioeconomic policies.

As the poet-professors of the neoliberal/post-civil rights era gazed across the experiential gulf that distanced the ivory tower from the ebony ghettos, it was impossible for them to write in the manner of their 1960s predecessors who had attempted to meld themselves to "wild guys" of the Black lumpen. Although the poet-professors remained vulnerable to the ambient racism of late twentieth-century America, and while many may have subscribed to "linked fate" theories that bound together political interests at all levels of the Black class structure, the middle-class security provided by university employment and the epistemological and linguistic demands of academic life meant that poet-professors could not easily pass themselves off as vernacular practitioners whose art was organic to the Black majority.

Stephen Henderson, who was one of the leading interpreters of what he called the "New Black Poetry" that emerged in the 1960s, would in the early 1970s look back upon the history of African American poetics and declare:

"there are two traditions or levels of Black poetry – the folk and the formal – which must be seen as a totality, since they often intersect and overlap one another, and since the people who create them are one people."[50] But by the time Gates wrote of the "rift within black America," Henderson's logic was no longer as defensible as it may have once seemed.

In the wake of the 1960s, as the connections between Black professionals and the Black folk world further attenuated, it became increasingly difficult to meaningfully describe African Americans as "one people"; it also seemed hard to join the folk and the formal levels of Black poetry in a single "totality." The "high-culture" page-based poetry that flourished in the academy and the "low-culture" hip-hop poetry that thrived in the commercial marketplace seemed to emanate from very different Black worlds. While hip-hop drew from heterogeneous aesthetic traditions, its devotion to the vibrancy of Black vernacular language, its affiliation with the lower segments of the class structure, and its demand for oral performance rooted it in the 1960s innovations of Black poets who sought to bring on what Houston Baker once called a "generational shift."

With purveyors of the 1960s Black aesthetic in mind, Baker described this kind of shift as "an ideologically motivated movement overseen by young or newly emergent intellectuals dedicated to refuting the work of their intellectual predecessors and to establishing a new framework for intellectual inquiry."[51] In the 1960s, BAM poets certainly helped to inspire a generational shift that made possible the late twentieth-century efflorescence of Black "folk" poetry in the shape of hip-hop. But at the "formal" level of Black poetics that is most frequently studied and produced in academic settings, Hayden's 1960s contributions to American literary production figure most prominently.

And yet, in narratives of African American literary history, Hayden's advancement of writerly aesthetic models during the decade is often overshadowed by the radical shifts in aesthetic-politics that emerged among Black artist-intellectuals who were his younger peers. However, the most productive histories of African American poetry do not appear in zero-sum narratives that displace Hayden's potent 1960s work while documenting the development of the Black Arts Movement. It is rather in dialectical appraisals of the decade, cognizant of the tensions between its writerly and speakerly expressive modes, and attentive to both generational shifts and generational continuities, that Hayden appears as a major figure of the 1960s.

Notes

1. Mullen (2012), 79.
2. Ibid., 80.
3. Neal (2007), 79.
4. Henderson (1973), 32.
5. Neal (2007), 654.
6. Ibid., 654.
7. Henderson (1973), 33.
8. Llorens (1966), 62.
9. Neal (2007), 655.
10. Rambsy (2011), 53.
11. Malcolm X (1990), 59.
12. Randall and Burroughs (1969), 16.
13. Ibid., 15; my emphasis.
14. Bullough (1994), 461.
15. Locke (2014), 48.
16. Malcolm X (2013), 113.
17. Randall and Burroughs (1969), 21.
18. Ibid., 5.
19. Ibid., 32.
20. Ibid.
21. Ibid.
22. Du Bois (2002), 76, 80.
23. Brooks (1972), 85.
24. Baraka (2007 [1969]), 302.
25. Ongiri (2010), 119.
26. Hayden (2001b), 22.
27. Hayden (1940), 44.
28. Ibid., 54.
29. Smethurst (1999), 193.
30. Ibid., 194.
31. Hayden (1984), 22.
32. Smethurst (1999), 194.
33. Hayden (1984), 79.
34. Ibid., 20–21.
35. Ibid., 25.
36. Fetrow (1984), 5.
37. Hayden (1984), 22.
38. Harper (1996), 51.
39. Hayden (1966), 13.
40. Ibid.
41. Hayden (2001a), 38.
42. Du Bois (2002), 224.
43. Hayden (1975), 12.

44. Hayden (1966), 55.
45. Hayden (1977).
46. Baraka (1996), xiii.
47. Komunyakaa (1992), 43.
48. Gates (1992), 138.
49. Ibid., 135.
50. Henderson (2000), 102.
51. Baker (1985), 67.

References

Baker, H. A. 1985. *Blues, Ideology, and Afro-American Literature: A Vernacular Theory*. University of Chicago Press.
Baraka, A. (L. Jones). 1996. "Foreword." In *On a Mission: Selected Poems and a History of the Last Poets*, by A. Oyewole and U. Bin Hassan, xiii–xvii. New York: Henry Holt.
  2007 [1969]. "Black Art." In *Black Fire: An Anthology of Afro-American Writing*, ed. A. Baraka and L. Neal, 302–3. Baltimore, MD: Black Classic Press.
Brooks, G. 1972. *Report From Part One*. Detroit, MI: Broadside Press.
Bullough, E. 1994. "'Psychical Distance' as a Factor in Art and as an Aesthetic Principle." In *Art and Its Significance: An Anthology of Aesthetic Theory*, ed. S. D. Ross, 458–68. Albany: State University of New York Press.
Du Bois, W. E. B. 2002. *Du Bois on Education*, ed. E. Provenzo. Lanham, MD: Rowman & Littlefield.
  2014. *The Souls of Black Folk*. New York: Simon & Schuster.
Fetrow, F. M. 1984. *Robert Hayden*. Boston, MA: Twayne Publishers.
Gates, H. L., Jr. 1992, September. "Two Nations . . . Both Black." *Forbes* 150.6: 132–38.
Harper, P. B. 1996. *Are We Not Men? Masculine Anxiety and the Problem of African-American Identity*. Oxford University Press.
Hayden, R. 1940. *Heart-Shape in the Dust*. Detroit, MI: Falcon Press.
  1966. *Selected Poems*. New York: October House.
  1975. *Angle of Ascent: New and Selected Poems*. New York: Liveright.
  1977, October. "Letter to Dorothy Lee." In *Hayden Papers*. Washington, DC: Library of Congress.
  1984. *Collected Prose*, ed. F. Glaysher. Ann Arbor: University of Michigan Press.
  2001a. "A Conversation with A. Poulin, Jr." In *Robert Hayden: Essays on the Poetry*, ed. L. Goldstein and R. Chrisman, 30–40. Ann Arbor: University of Michigan Press.
  2001b. "An Interview with Dennis Gendron." In *Robert Hayden: Essays on the Poetry*, ed. L. Goldstein and R. Chrisman, 15–29. Ann Arbor: University of Michigan Press.
Henderson, S. 1973. *Understanding the New Black Poetry: Black Speech and Black Music as Poetic References*. New York: William Morrow.

2000. "Saturation: Progress Report on a Theory of Black Poetry." In *African American Literary Theory: A Reader*, ed. W. Napier, 102–12. New York University Press.

Komunyakaa, Y. 1992. "My Father's Love Letters." In *Magic City*, 43. Middletown, CT: Wesleyan University Press.

Llorens, D. 1966. "Writers Converge at Fisk University." *Negro Digest* 15.8: 54–68.

Locke, A. 2014. "Negro Youth Speaks." In *The New Negro*, ed. A. Locke, 47–53. New York: Touchstone.

Malcolm X. 1990. *Malcolm X Speaks: Selected Speeches and Statements*, ed. G. Breitman. New York: Grove Weidenfeld.

2013. *The Portable Malcolm X Reader*, ed. M. Marable and G. Felber. New York: Penguin.

Mullen, H. 2012. *The Cracks Between What We Are and What We Are Supposed to Be: Essays and Interviews*. Tuscaloosa: University of Alabama Press.

Neal, L. 2007. "And Shine Swam On." In *Black Fire: An Anthology of Afro-American Writing*, ed. A. Baraka and L. Neal, 302–3. Baltimore, MD: Black Classic Press.

Ongiri, A. A. 2010. *Spectacular Blackness: The Cultural Politics of the Black Power Movement and the Search for a Black Aesthetic*. Charlottesville: University of Virginia Press.

Rambsy, H., II. 2011. *The Black Arts Enterprise and the Production of African American Poetry*. Ann Arbor: University of Michigan Press.

Randall, D., and M. Burroughs, eds. 1969. *For Malcolm: Poems on the Life and the Death of Malcolm X*. Detroit, MI: Broadside Press.

Rowell, C., ed. 2013. *Angles of Ascent: A Norton Anthology of Contemporary African American Poetry*. New York: W. W. Norton & Co.

Smethurst, J. E. 1999. *The New Red Negro: The Literary Left and African American Poetry, 1930–1946*. Oxford University Press.

CHAPTER 3

Breathing
Sonia Sanchez's Call to Coalition Building

Patricia Herrera

People need to learn to lean into each other's breath, and realize that it's okay to breathe other's breath, this African breath or this Cuban breath. If people could learn to do that, it would be much more healthy and we would maintain this climate the way it needs to be maintained.
Sonia Sanchez, *Conversation with Sonia Sanchez*

The 1950s and 1960s, decades of prosperity and protest, profoundly impacted Black Americans.[1] These periods not only gave birth to the Civil Rights Movement and the Black Power Movement but also saw an expansion of Black identity as diasporic. Sanchez stands out as one of the most prominent feminist writers in these movements creating Afro-diasporic connections. Writing in various modalities, from feminist poetry to novels to plays, she advocates for racial equity and social justice; her body of work creates a transnational discourse that signals the ongoing relationship between African American and U.S. Latinx/Latin American communities. Whether she infuses her work with experiences gained in her visits to Mexico and Cuba, or acknowledges the influence of Latin American poets such as Nicolás Guillén, Federico García Lorca, and Pablo Neruda, or chooses to retain a Spanish-language last name from her first marriage to a Puerto Rican, Sanchez produces work that forges strong links between African American and Latinx communities. Her work, I argue, models a coalition building practice of breathing each other's breath – "this African breath or this Cuban breath." The act of breathing expands our understanding of the shared histories and lived experiences of Black Americans and Latinxs/Latin Americans.

The breath takes on larger ramifications in the context of 2020's global pandemic, the multiple murders of unarmed Black people, and the consequent global Black Lives Matter movement. Against the backdrop of the pandemic, we witnessed the brutal murder of George Floyd. His words

"I can't breathe" hang heavy in the air, haunting our contemporary moment, as the white police officer squeezes his breath out of him. His last words are a reminder of how racism and oppression suffocate Black, Indigenous, and people of color (BIPOC). It is with this urgency in mind that I turn to Sanchez's methodology of breath and breathing as a mode of coalition-building. The disproportionate cases of police brutalities experienced by Black people and the disparate social inequities are symptomatic of the entrenched systemic racism existing over many centuries. What can we learn from our Black artists and activists of the 1960s fighting in the trenches for social justice? Through a closer reading of Sanchez's work, readers can see and hear intercultural resonances and connections between African American and Latinx cultures. The breath and breathing practice, as Sanchez explains, helps us to "be much more healthy and . . . maintain this climate the way it needs to be maintained."[2] In making the many points of intersections visible, this essay aims to not only garner a greater understanding of the resonances among people of color across time and space, but also moves toward coalition-building as a methodology for today's time of crisis.

Drawing from Afro-diasporic as well as theater and performance studies, I turn to Sanchez's work, in particular *The Bronx Is Next*, to demonstrate how she breathes and leans into the breath of others to create an intimate collective understanding of how communities of color locally and globally fight for justice and equality. Her first play, *The Bronx Is Next* (1968), concurrently upholds the ideals of the Black Power Movement that called for self-determination, self-respect, and self-defense for Black Americans while also preparing fertile ground for building alliances across ages, races, and socioeconomic status. Even when she anchors Black nationalism, she draws affinities that derive from New World experiences of slavery, racism, and colonialism to build bridges among U.S. Latinx, Latin American, and African American communities. I examine how Sanchez, an African American artist and cultural producer, breathes into existence new coalitional possibilities by charging her work with historical and cultural resonances among communities of color.

As is true for Black revolutionary authors and artists of the 1960s, Sanchez's works recover Africa and expand Black American literary expression by signaling affiliation with Third World feminist perspectives. If the 1960s was marked by Black pride and outright protestation for racial justice, the 1970s sought a need for African Americans to connect with the world outside of America and to link their struggle to the liberations of all Black people as well as those resisting domination. Both the recovery of Africa and the perspective of the Third World provided civil rights activists with a broader understanding of history and social experience. Sanchez and other Black revolutionaries were radical in their communal approach toward unifying people in terms of their experiences of oppression and resistance to politicizing them.[3] Sanchez's travel to Mexico (1965), Jamaica (1973), and Cuba (1978) shifted and broadened her vision of Black heritage from a separatist to a collectivist point of view. As such, Sanchez falls in line with Brent Hayes Edwards' claim that the diaspora is a set of practices through which Black intellectuals pursue international alliances.[4]

While her work in the 1980s explicitly links African American, U.S. Latinx, and Latin American communities, her work in the late 1960s is not as overt. On many occasions, Sanchez has spoken openly about her interest in the eradication of racial and political oppression on an international level, and has incorporated the concerns and culture of the Latinx community in her work. This commitment is reflected in various poems in the 1980s. For instance, in "MIA's" in *Homegirls and Handgrenades* (1984) she references the "disappeared" villagers of El Salvador's repressive government. In so doing, she calls attention to the political oppression on an international level, as well as exposes the United States' complicit role in both supporting the civil war by providing aid to the El Salvadoran military and remaining silent in the face of human rights abuses in El Salvador.[5]

Impacted by her travels to Cuba, she also wrote the two-part poem "At the Gallery of La Casa de Las Américas Habana. Dec. 1984" in *Under a Soprano Sky* (1987), as part of the first Havana Biennial Art Exhibition. This poem serves as a response to the visual artwork of Canadian-Mexican Arnold Belkin and Chilean Roberto Matta. The first part of the poem, titled "Picture No. 1 / Arnold Belkin: *Attica*," was inspired by Belkin's painting as well as her visit to Attica Prison after the 1971 uprising, when prisoners demanded better living conditions and political rights. In the second part of the poem, "Picture No. 2 / Roberto Ma[t]ta: *Chile: Sin T[i]tulo*," Sanchez associates the painting with the cultural wasteland back home. As noted in the titles of the poems, Sanchez offers an international dimension to her writing by linking the struggles of African Americans to that of U.S. Latinxs and Latin Americans. These explicit points of intersection link the local and global intercultural pursuits of social justice.

"Breathe This African Breath or This Cuban Breath"

The practice of leaning into each other's breath is a profoundly intimate act that is as literal as it is metaphorical. To physically breathe in someone's breath, one would need to get a little closer to someone. During this current pandemic moment, getting a little close does not come easy. Naturally, to be near a stranger is not only awkward but is also not safe. And yet, that is precisely what Sanchez is inviting readers and audiences to do – to lean into the uncomfortable space of closeness and then sit in this discomfort with people from different walks of life; different racial, ethnic, and cultural backgrounds; different genders and sexual orientations; different ages, social classes, religious beliefs, and physical abilities or attributes.

Leaning into someone's breath demands a level of conscientious attentiveness. Not only do I need to be close to a person to breathe their breath, but I also need to carefully observe the rise and fall of their chest and listen deeply to their inhalation and exhalation. Being in close proximity to someone requires me to bring the gentle, caring, and generous side of myself, which can be difficult, especially with strangers. However, when we practice leaning into each other's breath we discover that the breath unites us. As Jacqueline Wood reminds us: "Contrary to many European perspectives, the African worldview values the individual only in relation to others, embracing the correlative 'I am because we are.'"[6] Breathing into someone's breath means shifting our worldview from "I" to "we," from the individual to the collective.

Sanchez's call to "lean into each other's breath, and realize that it's okay to breathe other's breath, breathe this African breath or this Cuban breath," not only proposes a different way of relating to each other but also expands on the concept of "Afro-Latinx."[7] This label of identification often refers to both Latinxs in the United States and Latin Americans who acknowledge their African roots. While U.S. Latinxs might use the term to affirm the history and legacy of the African diaspora, Black Latin American tend to identify themselves along regional or national lines, such as Afro-Caribbean, Afro-Cuban, or Afro-Dominican. However, as Petra R. Rivera-Rideau, Jennifer A. Jones, and Tianna S. Paschel demonstrate in the anthology *Afro-Latin@s in Movement: Critical Approaches to Blackness and Transnationalism in the Americas* (2016), the term Afro-Latinx necessitates a framework that takes into account the back-and-forth movement across national borders and racial divides that impact cultural production.

Sanchez's instruction to breathe the breath of individuals from Africa and Cuba, two distinct geographic locations that are culturally and historically connected, allows us to focus on the process of fertilizing the grounds for "cross-cultural interpenetrations" through literature, history, or culture.[8] Cuba, in particular, resonates with many Black Americans on many fronts. Many African Americans came to know Cuba through the history of slavery. Their enslaved descendants passed through the Caribbean during the middle passage and were auctioned in the islands or in Brazil.[9] In addition to its African heritage, African Americans relate to Cuba because of its anti-colonial struggle, support of the African liberation movements, and resistance to U.S. domination. Additionally, there existed a long working relationship with Cubans and African Americans – from abolitionists jointly forging organizations, to leftist and trade unions exchanging strategies, to musicians and baseball players sharing the same cultural venues.[10]

In many ways, Cuba, along with countries in Africa, were places where freedom seemed to be tangible. While the constitutional amendments granting Blacks citizenship and voting rights at the end of the Civil War brought about hope that Blacks could integrate into American society, the establishment of the Ku Klux Klan during the Reconstruction era instilled terror. By the mid-nineteenth century, the discourse around abolition, resistance, freedom, and integration weighed heavily in America. Black intellectuals and abolitionists such as Frederick Douglass, Sojourner Truth, Henry Highland Garnet, Martin Delany, and Alexander Crummell, among others, debated over whether emigrating outside of the United States; integrating into American society based on equality; or organizing a revolution to overthrow the system would be effective strategies for attaining freedom.[11]

Garnet, Delany, and Crummell advocated for Blacks' emigration outside of the United States, since they believed that Blacks would otherwise continue to struggle against bias and oppression and ultimately would never attain true independence. Truth and Douglass did not endorse emigration. Douglass insisted that Blacks should defend their humanity and should reap the benefits of that revolutionary spirit by staying, building, and integrating into American political society while maintaining racial pride and equality.[12] Similarly, Truth asserted that Blacks should not leave America.[13] For many Black female abolitionists, emigration simply replicated a colonial and capitalist project that emulated gender discrimination.[14]

These various approaches – from integration to emigration to revolution – framed many of the mobilization strategies in the United States and informed the ways African Americans viewed other multiracial nations. While Cuba was proposed as a place where all three visions were possible, it stood out because of its history of rebellions by the enslaved.[15] On June 15, 1825, in the sugar-producing area of Matanzas, for instance, a group of enslaved Africans organized large-scale plantation revolts that then spread to other plantations.[16] This uprising began a cycle of slave rebellions that would end with the Conspiración de la Escalera in 1844 and 1845. Spanish colonial officials found out that there was a conspiracy to promote revolts by enslaved people and they immediately responded by imprisoning, torturing, and executing thousands of Afro-Cubans, regardless of whether they were free or enslaved. The conspiracy was referred to as La Escalera (the ladder) because any person that was suspect was bound to an *escalera* for interrogation and whipped to instill state terror.[17]

Despite the U.S. blockade on Cuba, the latter's long history of anti-colonial organizing, mobilizing dissidents, leading effective Black insurgents, and fighting for emancipation – as evidenced by the Bay of Pigs Invasion and the Missile Crisis – became a significant part of African American consciousness. In bringing Africa and Cuba, two distinct geographies, together in the same breath, Sanchez uses her writing to create cross-racial and cross-ethnic affinity spaces linking African Americans to Latinx and Latin Americans.

Spatial Historical Resonances

Working within the ideologies of the Black Power Movement, Sanchez documents the growing spirit of Black self-determination and Black cultural unity in *The Bronx Is Next*. Though she never utilizes James Brown's lyrics from "Say it Loud, I'm Black and I'm Proud," the unofficial anthem of the Black Power Movement, this racial and cultural affirmation reverberates throughout the play. *The Bronx Is Next* was part of *The Drama Review*'s special issue on "Black Revolutionary Theatre and Theatre of Black Experience" (Summer 1968). It was also included in Ed Bullins' anthology, *New Plays from the Black Theater* (1968), which many scholars argue, became a manifesto for Black revolutionary theater and provided a sociocultural context for understanding Black theater history and aesthetics.[18] Revolutionary theater, as Amiri Baraka claims, "should force change, it should be changed . . . Revolutionary theater must EXPOSE! Show up the insides of these humans, look into black skulls. White men will cower before this theatre because it hates them."[19] Sanchez's work is most notable for simultaneously dramatizing Black pride, power, and nationalism while unapologetically exposing the negative impact of Black militant practices, especially in terms of the existing Black male chauvinism and sexism.

Influenced by the work of Chilean writer Pablo Neruda, Sanchez directly engages with Harlem to mirror back the socioeconomic hardship Black Americans face, to galvanize the Black community into action, and to inspire hope. She "shows [us] a picture of an alienated person and hostile person, but there are reasons for it, and lessons to learn, too."[20] In an interview with Joyce A. Joyce, Sanchez shares that *The Bronx is Next* was inspired by a newspaper article she read about a cop chasing a boy down 125th Street because he was simply running down the street.[21] He was presumed guilty because he was a Black boy in Harlem running away. Concerned with how Harlem was being decimated by urban neglect and the future of her community, Sanchez was interested in dramatically portraying the racial and economic disparities that oppressed the Harlem community – "how urban cities were killing Black folks, how death permeated our souls as it is in these ghettos, tenements, in these houses that people didn't care about."[22] Sanchez specifically sets the play in Harlem to acknowledge the contested social history of this space and place, which undoubtedly shaped and influenced the experiences and actions of Black residents in that neighborhood.

During the turbulent period of the Civil Rights Movement, Harlem faced a fast decaying housing stock with a high concentration of under-privileged residents, but it was enriched by the political action of Black nationalist groups, such as Malcolm X's Nation of Islam and the Black Panther Party (BPP). Faced with rising operating expenses, some landlords committed arson as a way of salvaging what they could from unprofitable buildings. Other landlords – knowing that the foreclosure process took over five years – abandoned the maintenance of their buildings but continued to collect rent from tenants who had no other options.

Interestingly, even when Sanchez sets the play in Harlem, the title shifts the focal setting to the Bronx. The South Bronx in particular became home for many Puerto Ricans. In fact, by the early 1960s, New York City had a larger Puerto Rican population than San Juan, Puerto Rico.[23] Characters in the play burned down Harlem as a way of protesting the lack of investment in housing, basic services, and social services. Sanchez proposes that in order to resurrect a community, like Harlem, it must be burned down. Now that Harlem has been burned down, Sanchez predicts that the Bronx will be next.[24]

Like Harlem, the Bronx, along with Brooklyn's Brownsville, Bushwick, and Bedford-Stuyvesant neighborhoods, as well as Manhattan's Harlem and Lower East Side, was not only a neglected neighborhood ridden by poverty but was burning down. When Sanchez references in the title that the Bronx is the next place to burn down, she links the devastating socio-political conditions of the Bronx and Harlem to the pursuit of justice by the African American and Latinx communities. Geographic emphasis of the Bronx rather than Harlem in the title demonstrates how she practices breathing into each other's breath, bringing people and their histories in closer proximity to each other.

Just as the title creates spatial resonances, her stage direction also brings the social justice efforts of the Young Lord Organization in conversation with the BPP. As she notes, "The scene is a block in Harlem – a block of tenement houses on either side of a long, narrow, dirty street of full garbage cans."[25] Again, while the location is Harlem, the world Sanchez creates on stage is representative of the living conditions faced by not only Blacks but many Latinxs in poverty-stricken neighborhoods.

Inspired by the BPP, the Young Lord Organization, a Puerto Rican revolutionary national group, was started in Chicago in 1968. A year later, a chapter opened in New York City, the same year *The Bronx Is Next* was produced. When the Young Lords began polling East Harlem residents as to the most pressing issues, they identified garbage as the biggest problem. The sanitation services were virtually nonexistent in that area and the neighborhood was overrun with piles of rotting garbage. Sanchez's stage directions visually turn our attention to the garbage problem, reminding us that one of the first initiatives that the Young Lords took part in was the Garbage Offensive, where they spent time sweeping the streets and bagging rubbish. Even with the Young Lords' direct action, sanitation service failed to improve. Frustrated, they built 5-foot (1.5 meter) tall barricades of garbage bags across Third Avenue and set them on fire, halting traffic and getting the attention of police, firefighters, and the media.

The media coverage raised national awareness of the inhuman living conditions in East Harlem. As a result, the sanitation service improved. The staging of garbage in *The Bronx Is Next* points to the urban neglect and ultimate abandonment by the city, and signals how this devaluing led organizations like the BPP and Young Lords to mobilize and care for their people, neighborhood, and community by providing breakfast and clothing programs as well as educational and health services. Ultimately, Sanchez sets the play in Harlem, but leans into the breath of the Bronx, scripting resonances between the two communities and modeling coalition-building strategies.

She further deepens the practice of breathing into someone else's breath by making the setting of the play timeless. Though the drama is deeply rooted in the rhetoric and ideology of the Black Power Movement and the Black Arts Movement of the 1960s, Sanchez explicitly states in the stage direction: "The time is now."[26] Similar to how Sanchez grounds the play in

Harlem while turning our attention to the Bronx, she establishes the time as the present while using conventional liberation rhetoric of the 1960s and 1970s, a colloquial language with the central purpose of agitation for the freedom of individuals and condemnation of white supremacy.[27] Regardless of the reader's present, the 1960s, or the twenty-first century, the past always lives in the present. This temporal intersection brings a level of urgency to the past in the present moment. Urgency, as Harry Elam reminds us, "conveys the idea that the frustrations of the disenfranchised have reached crisis proportions; untenable circumstances have pushed oppressed people to the boiling point, and they erupt."[28]

In *The Bronx Is Next*, readers witness how three revolutionary characters have reached the point where they are no longer willing to endure subjugation and instead create an immediate reform, burning down Harlem. Sanchez sets the play in the present because she understands the timelessness of systematic oppression and the long-haul battle of civil rights activists. Setting the play in the present thus strikes a chord with today's escalating war on Black and Brown bodies and the fight to end police brutality and disproportionate incarcerations of young people.

Dramatic Resonances: The Inversion of Power

Enraged by the inhumane conditions experienced by Harlem's tenants Charles, Roland, and Jimmy, the three revolutionary characters in *The Bronx Is Next*, organize a protest plan. They decide that the best way to address this social injustice and protect their community is to take their destiny into their own hands by forcing tenants into the streets and burning the tenement buildings down. While the idea of burning down Harlem is seemingly destructive, Sanchez wanted to ignite hope in a community in which hopelessness was the status quo. Burning down a place that is destroying the community and "organizing people to take them South where they had come from," Sanchez suggests, demands that the community rebuild and create spaces and places that nurture them.[29] What begins as a model of Black revolutionary activism results in an exposé of the internal generational differences, sexism, and political violence within the Black community. The two female characters, Old Sister (an elderly Black woman) and Black Bitch (a Black single-mother), as well as the White Cop, are at the core of exposing the contradictions and conflicts of the Black Power Movement.

Old Sister has packed too much for the exodus, and the organizers automatically see her as a burden to the movement and send her back to her apartment with promises that they will handle her belongings, but with all intentions to leave her behind to burn:

CHARLES: Look. Someone will help you get back to your apartment. You can stay there. You don't have to come tonight. You can come some other time when we have room for your stuff. OK?

OLD SISTER: Thank you, son. Here let me kiss you. Thank the lord there is young men like you who still care about the old people. What is your name son?

CHARLES: My name is Charles, sister. Now I have to get back to work. Hey Roland. Jimmy. Take this one back up to her apartment. Make her comfortable. She ain't coming tonight. She'll come another time.

ROLAND: Another time? Man, you flipping out? Why don't you realize . . .

CHARLES: I said, Roland, she'll come another time. Now help her up those fucking stairs. Oh yes. Jimmy, see too that she gets some hot tea. You dig? Ten o'clock is our time. There ain't no time for anyone. There ain't no time for nothing 'cept what we came to do. Understand? Now get your ass stepping.[30]

Sanchez reveals the contradictory actions of revolutionaries who claim to serve their community yet neglect their elders. Old Sister pleads that she cannot leave behind belongings that she traveled with from Birmingham forty years ago. Charles pretends to take into account her request, but plans on leaving her behind, ultimately to burn with the tenement houses. Old Sister is not only symbolic of an older generation, but she is also a reminder of the individuals who were part of the Great Migration (1910–70) from the South to escape the atrocities of Jim Crow and to search out economic opportunities in the industrial North. In pursuit of justice, the revolutionaries have lost sight of what matters – their history and people – especially as it concerns their past and their elders.

The play moves from one negative encounter to another. This time a hostile interaction with a white cop and a younger Black woman. As Larry, one of the revolutionaries, hurriedly tries to get tenants out of their apartments, he finds the White Cop leaving Black Bitch's place. At first Roland, Charles, and Larry think that he is a spy, but when they cross-examine him, they find out that Black Bitch is his mistress. The revolutionaries immediately perceive her as a traitor for having a relationship with a white man. Unaware of the exodus, the White Cop attempts to inquire about it only to reveal his disconcerting negative racial attitudes toward Black Americans living in poverty. "The hardest thing for me to understand," he explains, "was that all you black people would even live in these conditions. Well. You know. Everybody has had ghettos, but they built theirs up and there was respect there. There is none of that . . . But all this hopelessness. Poverty of the mind and spirit. Why? Things are so much better. All it takes is a little more effort by you people."³¹

Realizing White Cop's ignorance of the institution of racism and negative racial stereotypes about people living in poverty, the revolutionaries decide that perhaps switching roles with him would broaden his perspective. The White Cop assumes the role of the "black dude walking down a ghetto street," and Charles, Jimmy, and Roland would be "three white dudes – white cops on a Harlem street."³² The White Cop hesitates, but when Roland pleads that he has always wanted to be a white cop, he agrees to the role reversal.

Reminiscent of the newspaper article that inspired Sanchez to write *The Bronx Is Next*, Charles directs the White Cop, now playing the Black man, to run. As the White Cop, who now plays a Black dude, runs, Charles, Jimmy, and Roland, now playing the white cops, stop him and question why he is running. While the White Cop/Black dude insists that he is running because he feels like it, Charles, Jimmy, and Roland, as white cops, assume that he is running away because he has stolen something or is escaping from jail. To prove that he is innocent, the White Cop shows them that he does not have anything in his pockets. Jimmy immediately responds by drawing his gun out and alerting the White Cop to get his hands out of his pockets, and demands that he goes against the wall. As the scene unfolds, we learn about the power dynamics and abusive behavior of a dominant class, one with economic and social power, experienced by Blacks.

JIMMY: (Draws gun) Get your hands out of your pockets boy. Against the wall right now.
WHITE COP: But what have I done? I was just running. This is not legal you know. You have no right to do this . . .
ROLAND: You are perfectly correct. We have no right to do this. Why I even have no right to hit you, but I am. (Hits WHITE COP with gun)
WHITE COP: (Falls down. Gets up) Now wait a minute. That is going just a little too far and . . .
CHARLES: I said why were you running down that street boy?
WHITE COP: Look. Enough is enough. I'm ready to stop – I'm tired.
JIMMY: What's wrong nigger boy – can't you answer simple questions when you're asked them. Oh, I know what's wrong. You need me to help you remember. (Hits WHITE COP with gun)

WHITE COP: Have you gone crazy? Stop this. You stop it now, or there will be consequences.

ROLAND: What did you steal black boy – we can't find it on you, but we know you got it hidden someplace. (Hits him again)

WHITE COP: Oh my god. Stop it . . . this can't be happening to me. Look – I'm still me. It was only make believe.

CHARLES: Let's take him in. He won't cooperate. He won't answer the question. Maybe he needs more help than the three of us are giving him.

JIMMY: I don't know. Looks like he's trying to escape to me. Take out your guns. That nigger is trying to run. Look at him. Boy, don't run. Stop. I say if you don't stop, I'll have to shoot.

WHITE COP: Are you all mad? I'm not running. I'm on my knees. Stop it. This can't continue. Why . . .

ROLAND: You ain't shit boy. You black. You a nigger we caught running down the streets – running and stealing like all the niggers around him.[33]

The moment the now turned cops begin to be violent, the White Cop wants the role reversal to stop, but Charles, Jimmy, and Roland don't break out of the dramatic role playing. They don't want him to access his white privilege so easily: their point being that Black folks experience this police harassment and they do not have the luxury to say I am tired of being Black. They cannot break away from the social reality of racism. They must live in their skin. This role reversal inverts the conventional hierarchy of power and legitimates not only the actions of the Black revolutionaries but Black Power. The racial discrimination and harassment Black folks experience at the hands of police authorities in the 1960s strike a similar chord with America's current state of affairs with racial profiling and harassment.

Committed to disrupting racial stereotypes, Black cultural nationalist of the 1960s were very much concerned with controlling and dismantling "the machineries and regimes of representation,"[34] what Stuart Hall calls, "the politics of representation."[35] Sanchez, for instance, challenges mainstream representations of Blacks by foregrounding the sociopolitical circumstance of Black Americans and valorizing Black culture in the liberation struggles. While Sanchez's dramatic tactic of role inversion is specific to the Black community, it also resonates with the work of El Teatro Campesino, the farmworkers' theater. Luis Valdez, who was present at the Grape Pickers strike in Delano led by the United Farm Workers Organizing Committee, was interested in creating a troupe of farmworkers using theater to assist in the fight against discriminatory labor and immigration practices. Valdez implements the strategy of role reversal to raise consciousness about race, privilege, power, and the complexities of systematic oppression. Role reversal allows the audience to witness the impact of systemic racism on Blacks and

Latinxs, and offers a moment of escape from oppression, even if it is temporary.

First performed on the picket lines in Delano, California by El Teatro Campesino, *Las dos caras del patroncito* ("The Two Faces of the Little Boss"; 1965) is an *acto* that attempts to satirize the *patrón* (boss, in this case, landowners) as well as those who crossed the picket lines, known as *esquiroles*, scabs or undocumented Mexicans imported to break strikes. *Actos* were brief improvisational-agitational theatrical vignettes collectively created to expose the social inequities of the farm labor system. The Patroncito,[36] who feels the pressures of being a capitalist landowner, longs for the simple, carefree life of the Farmworker: "Sometimes I sit up in my office and think to myself: I wish I was a Mexican."[37] Curious about the Farmworker's life, he asks if they can switch roles. The two characters exchange props that signal their position of power, or lack thereof. The Patroncito gives the Farmworker his pig mask, cigar, and whip and the Farmworker takes the sun hat and shears. The previously oppressed worker disempowers the boss by subjecting him to the same oppressive language and abusive working conditions.

Unlike *The Bronx Is Next*, in *Las dos caras* all the characters would have been played by farmworkers. In staging the brown bodies of farmworkers, Valdez demonstrates cultural affirmation and commitment to resist race and class oppression. This in turn offers a realistic portrayal of the abuse perpetrated by the patron toward the farmworker, and opens up the possibility for the audience to conceive a future where individuals are no longer defined by limited labor and ethnic roles. By suggesting that the roles of oppressed and oppressor are interchangeable, audience and performers alike are encouraged to consider the potential power of social change achieved through collective farmworker participation in the strike.

The Bronx Is Next serves as a model of how Sanchez creates resonances whether in terms of space, time, or history to demonstrate how she practices "breathing into each other's breath." Sanchez links the experiences of Black Americans and Latinx/Latin Americans by evoking the shared history of racism and colonization in the role inversion scene. As the trauma of racism and sexism persists in the Americas, this communal approach from the 1960s and 1970s is now more than ever essential for communities to cope with and cleanse from racial trauma. The escalating mass incarceration of people of color and the unprecedented high percentage of young minority men at the hands of law enforcement today leaves no doubt that anti-Black racism persists. Our current moment of pandemics, from racism to COVID-19, has further emboldened the most abhorrent expressions of hatred, racism, misogyny, and xenophobia, inevitably dividing and alienating the inhabitants of the United States. While the toxic racial climate today unjustifiably divides and alienates, this essay shows how breathing into someone's breath, if only for a brief moment, makes palpable and possible the affinities, intimacies, intertextualities, and cross-cultural interpenetrations among Blacks, U.S. Latinxs, and Latin Americans.

Notes

1. Elam and Krasner (2001); Ward and Ward (1971).
2. Sesay (2007), 147.
3. Wood (2010).
4. Edwards (2003).
5. Joyce (2007).
6. Wood (2010), xiv.
7. Sesay (2007), 146.
8. Jackson (1998), Kutzinski (1985).
9. Smallwood (2008), Brock (1994).
10. Guridy (2010), Brock and Castaneda Fuertes (1998), Brock (1994).
11. Brock (1994).
12. Myers (2013).
13. Washington (2009).
14. Peterson (1998).
15. Finch (2015), Pérez (2014), Barcia (2012), Childs (2006).
16. Barcia (2012).
17. Finch (2015).
18. Wood (2010).
19. Baraka (1965), 4.
20. Leibowitz (2007), 12.
21. Joyce (2007).
22. Melhem (2015), 162.
23. Sánchez Korrol (1994).
24. Flood (2010) argues that the impact of building codes as well as repeated budget cuts and lack of investment in housing led to greater devastation when disastrous fires happened.
25. Sanchez (2010), 26.
26. Ibid., 25.
27. Wood (2010).
28. Elam and Krasner (2001), 23.
29. Joyce (2007), 199.
30. Sanchez (2010), 26.
31. Ibid., 28.
32. Ibid., 29.

33. Ibid., 30–31.
34. Elam and Krasner (2001), 29.
35. Hall (1995).
36. While the diminutive -*cito* in Spanish is often used as term of endearment, in this case Valdez uses Patroncito as a way of "demeaning a person of prominence, as it brings him down to human dimensions rather than elevating him to Olympian standards" (Huerta 1982, 20).
37. Valdez (1990), 23.

References

Baraka, A. (L. Jones). 1965, July. "The Revolutionary Theatre." *Liberator* 5: 4–6. nationalhumanitiescenter.org/pds/maai3/protest/text12/barakatheatre.pdf [accessed September 23, 2021].

Barcia, M. 2012. *The Great African Slave Revolt of 1825: Cuba and the Fight for Freedom in Mantanzas*. Baton Rouge: Louisiana State University Press.

"Black Playwrights Present New Plays." 1970, October 17. *New York Amsterdam News* (1962–93): 20.

Brock, L. 1994. "Back to the Future: African-Americans and Cuba in the Time(s) of Race." *Contributions in Black Studies* 12.1: 9–32.

Brock, L., and D. Castañeda Fuertes. 1998. *Between Race and Empire: African-Americans and Cubans before the Cuban Revolution*. Philadelphia, PA: Temple University Press.

Childs, M. D. 2006. *The 1812 Aponte Rebellion in Cuba and the Struggle against Atlantic Slavery*. Chapel Hill: University of North Carolina Press.

Edwards, B. H. 2003. *The Practice of Diaspora: Literature, Translation, and the Rise of Black Internationalism*. Cambridge, MA: Harvard University Press.

Elam, H. 2005. *Taking it to the Streets: The Social Protest Theater of Luis Valdez and Amiri Baraka*. Ann Arbor: University of Michigan Press.

Elam, H., and D. Krasner, eds. 2001. *African American Performance and Theater History: A Critical Reader*. Oxford University Press.

Finch, A. K. 2015. *Rethinking Slave Rebellion in Cuba: La Escalera and the Insurgencies of 1841–1844*. Chapel Hill: University of North Carolina Press.

Flood, J. 2014. *The Fires: How a Computer Formula, Big Ideas, and the Best of Intentions Burned Down New York City – and Determined the Future of Cities*. New York: Riverhead Books.

Guridy, F. A. 2010. *Forging Diaspora: Afro-Cubans and African Americans in a World of Empire and Jim Crow*. Chapel Hill, NC: University of North Carolina Press.

Hall, S. 1995. "New Ethnicities." In *The Post-Colonial Studies Reader*, ed. B. Aschroft, G. Griffiths, and H. Tiffin, 223–28. London: Routledge.

Haslip-Viera, G., and S. Baver, eds. 1996. *Latinos in New York: Communities in Transition*. University of Notre Dame Press.

Huerta, J. 1982. *Chicano Theater: Themes and Forms*. Ypsilanti, MI: Bilingual Press.

Jackson, R. 1998. *Black Writers and Latin America: Cross-Cultural Affinities*. Washington, DC: Howard University Press.

Joyce, J. A. 2007. "Interview with Sonia Sanchez: Poet, Playwright, Teacher, and Intellectual Activist." In *Conversations with Sonia Sanchez*, ed. J. A. Joyce, 177–206. Jackson: University Press of Mississippi.

Kutzinski, V. M. 1985. "The Logic of Wings: Gabriel Garcia Marquez and Afro-American Literature." *Latin American Literary Review* 13.25: 133–46.

Leibowitz, H. 2007. "Sonia Sanchez: An Interview." In *Conversations with Sonia Sanchez*, ed. J. A. Joyce, 6–16. Jackson: University Press of Mississippi.

Melhem, D. 2015. *Heroism in the New Black Poetry: Introductions and Interviews*. Lexington: University Press of Kentucky.

Myers, P. C. 2013. "Frederick Douglass on Revolution and Integration: A Problem in Moral Psychology." *American Political Thought* 2.1: 118–46.

Pérez, L. A., Jr. 2014. *Cuba: Between Reform and Revolution*. Oxford University Press.

Peterson, C. L. 1998. *"Doers of the Word": African-American Women Speakers and Writers in the North (1830–1881)*. New Brunswick, NJ: Rutgers University Press.

Rivera-Rideau, P. R., J. A. Jones, and T. Paschel, eds. 2016. *Afro-Latin@s in Movement: Critical Approaches to Blackness and Transnationalism in the Americas*. Palgrave Macmillan.

Ro, S. 1985. "'Desercrators' and 'Necromancers': Black American Writers and Critics in the Nineteen-Sixties and the Third World Perspective." *Callaloo* 25: 563–76.

Sanchez, S. 2010. *I'm Black When I'm Singing, I'm Blue When I Ain't and Other Plays*, ed. J. Wood. Durham, NC: Duke University Press.

   2015. *Homegirls and Handgrenades*. Buffalo, NY: White Pine Press.

Sánchez Korrol, V. E. 1994. *From Colonia to Community: The History of Puerto Ricans in New York City*. Berkeley: University of California Press.

Sesay, K. 2007. "Interview with Sonia Sanchez: Poet, Joy of Writing Poetry." In *Conversations with Sonia Sanchez*, ed. J. A. Joyce, 144–57. Jackson: University Press of Mississippi.

Smallwood, S. 2008. *Saltwater Slavery: A Middle Passage from Africa to American Diaspora*. Cambridge, MA: Harvard University Press.

Valdez, L. 1990. *Early Works: Actos, Bernabe, and Pensamiento Serpentino*. Houston, TX: Arte Público Press.

Ward, F., and V. G. Ward. 1971. "The Black Artist – His Role in the Struggle." *The Black Scholar* 2.5: 23–32.

Washington, M. 2009. *Sojourner Truth's America*. Champaign: University of Illinois Press.

Wood, J. 2010. "Introduction: The Power Plays of Sonia Sanchez." In S. Sanchez, *I'm Black When I'm Singing, I'm Blue When I Ain't and Other Plays*, ed. J. Wood. Durham, NC: Duke University Press.

CHAPTER 4

Reconsidering "the Revolution in Music"

Eric Porter

During the Black Arts Movement moment, the improvised Black experimental music called jazz signified possibilities for social, political, spiritual, and intellectual transformations differently than it had in earlier periods. Black and non-Black musicians were, after all, engaging in an ever-expanding project of artistic experimentation. Drawing inspiration from contemporary Black freedom and liberation struggles, musicians – and this included "straight ahead" players as well as members of "the avant-garde" – were also commenting frequently on social and political issues in lyrics and composition titles, speaking out about broader social issues in public, and actively seeking to improve the conditions under which they labored.

Black Arts Movement poets, novelists, playwrights, and visual artists also promoted the idea that there was a revolution in jazz that was intertwined with broader social revolutions. Some simply heard political purpose in the new music that they encountered on record or in clubs. But others gathered in living rooms, classrooms, and cultural institutions like Harlem's Black Arts Repertory Theater/School (BART/S) and thought together with musicians about how cultural workers should respond to the contemporary conjuncture and how, at that moment, expressive culture might inspire and even transform people intellectually, spiritually, and politically.

The question of how the so-called "jazz revolution" might reflect changing attitudes of and actions by Black people was a vexing one from the beginning. For some jazz critics, the very idea of radical Blackness, whether aesthetic or political, was unappealing. Others simply did not like the new music, despite their support for Black liberation. But the question could also be a challenge for those who embraced both. For one thing, many of "the people" the music was thought to emanate from and, ideally, inspire and transform, were not listening to it. Amiri Baraka's celebrated 1966 essay (when still writing as LeRoi Jones), "The Changing Same: R&B and New Black Music," for example, struggled to reconcile the importance of

90

the socially and spiritually redeeming aspects of avant-garde jazz with the fact that this style had relatively limited popularity with Black audiences. He hoped for a future "Unity Music," a synthesis of the New Black Music and rhythm and blues that would resolve the "artificial oppositions" that genre had imposed on Black music. For these expressions were, after all, "the same family looking at different things. Or looking at things different."[1]

A similar theme was taken up by Jayne Cortez in her 1969 poem "How Long Has Trane Been Gone." Recently deceased saxophonist John Coltrane might be, like Malcolm X, the "True image of Black Masculinity," but too few Black people knew his music – a phenomenon Cortez explained as a function both of the music industry's division of the music into separate genres *and* of a more general lack of historical and cultural awareness among the people themselves.[2] But, more fundamentally, while music might be political, it was not the same as politics. Theorizing the connection between the two was a conceptual as well as political challenge. As Baraka and others recognized and tried to come to terms with, musicians and their audiences were connecting at the levels of the body and the spirit as well as that of the conscious intellect; and that exchange was phenomenologically transformative in ways that were not reducible to singular, unidirectional processes of politicization.[3]

Scholars in jazz studies (e.g., Iain Anderson, 2007; Steven Isoardi, 2006; George Lewis, 2008; Ingrid Monson, 2007; Eric Porter, 2002; and Daniel Widener 2010) have, over the past couple of decades, wrestled with the question of jazz and politics during the Black Arts Movement era. They have generally been careful about positing too neat a connection between music and the social, making clear that we should avoid neat homologies among radical aesthetic expressions, political intent on the part of musicians, and broader ideological currents. Yet, they have also tried to be attentive to the varying ways experimental musicians (and others) actually were making politically themed music and engaging in political or community uplift activities.

Scholars have looked at the power of the critiques they have voiced, the successes of the political projects they have engaged in, and their musical achievements, while sometimes keeping in mind the limitations of their vision as well as the challenges they faced given critical hostility, economic precarity, and a shrinking audience. They have pointed out the androcentrism of this movement in terms of the demographics of participation, the gender politics within artist networks, and the discourse and visual economy around the music. And they have shown that while women tended to be quite marginalized on the national music scene and in liberal, left, and Black nationalist conversations about it, they played key roles developing the music and associated social and political projects locally.[4]

For some in the field, the work of the white-Jewish, Marxist jazz writer and historian Frank Kofsky has been an important reference point. Writing for *Jazz* magazine and other publications during the 1960s, and then in his 1970 book *Black Nationalism and the Revolution in Music* and subsequent volumes that revised and augmented its content and basic arguments,[5] Kofsky championed the jazz avant-garde; linked its emergence to the Black freedom struggle; took seriously the ideas of activist musician-theorists like Archie Shepp, Cecil Taylor, and Bill Dixon; and insisted on foregrounding the asymmetrical financial arrangements that shaped the careers of performers. By doing so, he and his work have for decades drawn scholars' attention to matters of jazz and politics and the political economy of jazz.

Yet Kofsky had his critics as well. He was a controversial figure in life, and he has remained so after his death in 1997, in no small part because of his withering critiques of jazz business people and fellow writers. He lambasted club owners, whom he called "cockroach capitalists," and took well-known jazz critics such as Leonard Feather and Martin Williams to task for what he saw as their implicit racism, complicity with capitalist exploitation, and banal writing. He referred to such liberal critics as "active ideologists," whose refusal to adequately describe the music's social context and the conditions under which its practitioners labored helped to make seem more benign an exploitative "colonial" relationship that extracted value from Black artistic labor for the benefit of white capitalists. In return, fellow jazz critics (in the 1960s and 70s and later) took him to task for what they considered a doctrinaire Marxism that distorted his analysis; intemperate, ad hominem attacks; and sometimes for being a reverse racist.[6]

But even jazz studies scholars who are more sympathetic to Kofsky's views often see his work as emblematic of the problems that arise when one imposes too much (or too narrow a) politics onto the music. As John Gennari puts it, as "incisive as Kofsky's analysis could be, often it sagged under the weight of a dogmatic and rigid ideological purity." One problem was that he could be very condescending toward musicians "who didn't pass a litmus test of black nationalist revolutionary zeal."[7] Another, as Ingrid Monson points out, is that Kofsky's assumptions about the homologous relationship between "revolutionary music" and "revolutionary politics" led to a "failure to recognize the cross-generational relationship of jazz as a whole to the culture of commitment that characterized the 1960s."[8] In other words, Kofsky has also been a negatively productive influence in the jazz studies present, serving as inspiration for scholarly efforts to treat the cultural and materialist politics of jazz in the 1960s and 1970s with more care and nuance.

Many of Kofsky's critics point specifically to his 1966 interview with John Coltrane, first published in *Jazz* in 1967 and then in *Black Nationalism*, as exemplifying his ideological blinders. There, the saxophonist spends a significant part of the interview patiently correcting the critic's assumptions about his artistic motivations and the political significance of the music. Responding, for example, to Kofsky's suggestion that "there's a relationship between some of Malcolm's ideas and the music," Coltrane says: "Well, I think that music, being an expression of the human heart, or of the human being itself, does express just what *is* happening. I feel it expresses the whole thing – the whole of human experience at the particular time that it is being expressed."[9]

Preceding Coltrane's interview in *Black Nationalism* is a less discussed one with his pianist, McCoy Tyner, in which Kofsky asks many of the same questions. Receiving almost no mention in the scholarly literature is that Kofsky describes the Tyner and Coltrane interviews as part of a group of "approximately two dozen" that he conducted with participants in the "revolution in music" during the summer of 1966. This lack of attention is not surprising. Kofsky did little with them in the book. He mentions them in the introductions to the Tyner and Coltrane interviews, and in the latter alludes to similar conversations with trumpeter Bill Dixon, bassist David Izenson, and keyboardist Sun Ra.[10] But in only three other instances in the book, all in the lengthy introduction, does he explicitly draw upon the interviews to support his arguments. He claims that the interviews show that "radical nationalist ideas" are common among many young Black musicians and some white musicians too (he mentions Izenson, trombonist Roswell Rudd, and saxophonist Frank Smith); that Malcolm X has been an inspirational figure for a younger generation of jazz musicians; and that musicians often express such political affinities in tentative, sometimes inchoate ways because of the dangers being outspoken politically can pose to one's career. But these references are brief and not substantiated with quoted material.[11]

About a decade ago, recordings of these interviews came to light as part of a collection of Kofsky's correspondence, photographs, and research materials donated by his widow, Bonnie Kofsky, to University of California Santa Cruz, where I work.[12] These interviews offer an occasion to revisit Kofsky's work (especially *Black Nationalism*) and legacy given the way that the one with Coltrane, at least, has been used as a primary vehicle for critiques of it. And, for purposes of this volume, and following the lead of Kofsky's original, albeit only partially realized, intent to theorize the revolution in music through them, they provide a chance to reconsider the complicated and vexing question of the relationship of experimental (or avant-garde) jazz and politics as both were going through profound transitions during the mid-1960s.

I begin by discussing how Kofsky appears to have originally wanted to use the interviews in *Black Nationalism* to extend the ideas he had developed through his criticism. Turning to their content, I discuss the rough consensus that emerged among musicians and Kofsky on certain issues – agreements that he actually might have used to support some of his arguments about jazz and politics – but I also examine the differences in thinking among musicians and Kofsky. An examination of such divergences, I suggest, helps us understand the multiplicity of the so-called jazz revolution, at the level of the individual player and as a composite expression, that exceeds any simple notions of politics or identity. It also helps us understand how the weight of political expectation vis-à-vis "the Black community" and "the revolution" was itself an aesthetically productive force, whether musicians were working with or against it.

* * *

Kofsky began developing his analysis of jazz, race, economics, and politics in the late 1950s and early 1960s as a graduate student in biophysics at UC Berkeley, where he helped found the Students for Racial Equality, an organization whose activities included fundraising for the Student Nonviolent Coordinating Committee (SNCC). Kofsky further honed his commitments after he left the Berkeley program and began doing graduate work in History. He obtained an MA from California State University Los Angeles in 1964 and subsequently enrolled in the PhD program at the University of Pittsburgh in 1965. Along the way he was influenced by Black musician-theorists such as Archie Shepp, Cecil Taylor, and Bill Dixon, as well as the ideas of LeRoi Jones (Amiri Baraka) and other early Black Arts Movement figures.[13]

Kofsky also drew from a Trotskyist analytical and political orientation. In tune with George Breitman's and the Socialist Workers Party's (which published his book) veneration of Malcolm X, support for militant Black nationalism more generally, and theorization of the latter as a potentially vanguard revolutionary movement, Kofsky saw practitioners of what Jones called the "new Black music" performing with revolutionary purpose and articulating the aspirations of urban African America. He tried to bring attention to the aesthetic and social pronouncements of politically vocal musicians, and he positioned himself as their ally, often decrying that some had suffered career repercussions for speaking out. Although cognizant of gendered exclusions in the jazz world, Kofsky, like most contemporaries in jazz critical circles, wrote primarily about male musicians. He often expressed his admiration for political and aesthetic expressions of Black masculinity, most notably when comparing Malcolm X and John Coltrane.[14]

In a January 1966 *Jazz* article, "The Avant-Garde Revolution: Origins and Directions," which eventually became chapter 4 of *Black Nationalism*, Kofsky wrote about the possibility of conducting interviews to verify some of his admittedly speculative conclusions about music and the Black revolution and African Americans' disavowal of U.S. cultural norms. Although he admitted to "treading over extremely treacherous ground" by making these connections, he thought with "ample time and patience and blessed with the kind of research endowment that the affluent foundations prefer to lavish on comparatively trivial and irrelevant problems, a definite answer favorable to my thesis would ultimately be forthcoming."[15] Several months later, Kofsky found support in the form of a grant from the not-so-affluent Louis M. Rabinowitz Foundation, which supported progressive and Jewish-related research and political work.

Kofsky's working thesis, he told the Foundation in his May 1966 grant application, was "that the same currents which find political expression in the ideology of Black Nationalism are also reflected in what has been called (by LeRoi Jones and others) the New Black Music or, alternatively, the music of the Jazz Revolution." As would eventually be the case, he envisioned a book largely made up of previously published, recently submitted, and in-progress essays. Subjects already covered in his writing included revolutionary music, radical Black nationalism, and the connections between them; jazz criticism, the jazz business, and their connections to state power and capitalism; the writings of Malcolm X and LeRoi Jones; and the music and influence of John Coltrane. But even though "the manuscript was largely finished," he still hoped to research and write a chapter titled "A Social Profile of the Jazz Revolutionary," for which he wanted to interview "20 to 25 of the leading musicians of the Jazz Revolution" about topics including "the relationship between jazz (especially the new jazz) and the Negro ghetto; the views of the musician on Black Nationalism, the war in Vietnam, socialism vs. capitalism, and related topics." Not only did he want to create a collective "profile" of the "revolutionary" cohort; he also "hope[d] to submit my thesis – that the

Black Nationalist radicalism of the ghetto pervades the new music – to empirical verification."[16] Thus the need for Rabinowitz funding.

Kofsky's proposal was successful, and a few months later, in addition to interviewing Coltrane, Dixon, Izenson, Rudd, Smith, and Sun Ra, Kofsky spoke with drummer Rashied Ali, multi-instrumentalist Marion Brown, bassist Ron Carter, trumpeter Don Cherry, saxophonist Joe Henderson, multi-instrumentalist Joseph Jarman, reed player Giuseppe Logan, trombonist Grachan Moncur III, trumpeter Charles Moore, saxophonist Pharoah Sanders, saxophonist Wayne Shorter, pianist Cecil Taylor, drummer Tony Williams, and, in a joint conversation, trumpeter Ric Colbeck and drummer Mark Levin. With the exception of the interviews with Moore, conducted on July 16 while Kofsky was in Michigan to give talks at the Friday Night Socialist Forum, and Jarman, whom Betty Schmae interviewed with Kofsky's questions in hand for WDET radio on August 1, all extant interviews were conducted by Kofsky in New York between August 8 and 19, 1966.[17]

The group was reasonably representative of a musical movement whose prominent figures were predominantly, but not entirely, African American, mostly between twenty and forty years old (the outlier was Sun Ra, who was fifty-two), and male. The fact that Kofsky included five white musicians and several Black musicians who were not commonly associated with the "jazz revolution" (Henderson, Carter, Shorter, and Williams) may indicate an attempt to cultivate a broader perspective on the movement. The absence of the profoundly influential Ornette Coleman and Archie Shepp, whose political and aesthetic analyses shaped Kofsky's, indicates that the composition of the group may have reflected who was in New York that August and willing to talk.

Although there is usually a significant degree of improvisational give-and-take between Kofsky and his subjects, all the interviews are based on a set of common questions evident in the Coltrane and Tyner transcripts.[18] Kofsky was likely compelled to use this approach because he thought it would help him support his "thesis" while helping him create a manageable archive for the new chapter on jazz revolutionaries. Indeed, Kofsky's questions are closely related to the primary political and theoretical assumptions guiding the analysis in *Black Nationalism* and the articles upon which it is based – i.e., that avant-garde jazz has developed hand-in-hand with the Black freedom movement, its Black nationalist trajectories in particular, and is otherwise connected to Black urban society.[19]

Kofsky usually starts off by asking musicians to comment on the usefulness of Jones' phrase "new Black music" to describe current directions in jazz. He typically adds follow-up questions regarding the political significance of recent musical trends; whether whites can play this music; whether it emerges from, is relevant to, or popular in "the ghetto"; or whether the interviewee's own music can be labeled "new Black music." As he does with Coltrane, Kofsky asks most musicians to comment on the significance of Malcolm X having spent time with jazz musicians. One typical follow-up question is whether any of Malcolm's ideas are expressed in the new music. Another is whether the interviewee would consider doing a musical tribute to Malcolm or another important figure. Often asked near this point in the conversation is whether musicians notice different responses to their music from primarily Black or primarily white audiences, and whether they have a preference for performing in front of either.

Kofsky typically then asks his subjects if they agree that jazz is opposed to social injustice and inequality and, if so, whether they would characterize it as opposed to the war in Vietnam. This question builds from a 1966 statement by Archie Shepp in *Down Beat*, quoted in the introduction to *Black Nationalism*:

> [Jazz] is antiwar; it is opposed to Viet Nam; it is for Cuba; it is for the liberation of all people. That is the nature of jazz. That's not far-fetched. Why is that so? Because jazz is a music itself born out of oppression, born out of the enslavement of my people. It is precisely that.[20]

Rounding out the discussion of the new music's sociopolitical function are questions regarding the extent to which musicians discuss such social and political issues among themselves and whether they have a duty to educate their audiences about their aesthetic and political goals.

Kofsky asks all his subjects about working conditions for jazz musicians and, assuming they are less than desirable, how they explain the situation. Follow-up questions address whether these conditions can be explained by a high representation of "Negroes" among jazz musicians, and whether Black and white jazz musicians are treated differently. Kofsky usually tries to get his subjects' opinions on recent efforts to address working conditions, such as Cecil Taylor's call for a musicians' boycott and the Jazz Composers Guild's efforts to organize musicians collectively. He also raises questions about how critics' (particularly white critics') social positionalities or ideological orientations factor into their lack of understanding of or outright hostility to recent musical trends.

Kofsky generally moves the conversation back to music, with emphasis on how recent stylistic developments might be connected to social

transformations. He asks about the growing importance of group improvisation and whether that might be linked to a broader collectivist spirit in
African American communities. He notes musicians' increasing interest in
Asian and African music and asks whether this interest is inspired by
anticolonial movements or "the non-Western or anti-Western stance of
the musicians themselves." He also asks most of his subjects about the
waning interest in Third Stream's fusion of jazz with Western classical
music, compared to its popularity in the late 1950s, suggesting in several
interviews that its decline represents a rejection of Eurocentrism as well as
the failure of integrationist politics in society.[21] Near the end of most
interviews, Kofsky asks his subjects to discuss the major influences on the
new music, provide basic biographical information (age, birthplace, education, etc.), and add anything they want to discuss that has not been
covered by the interview questions.

The musicians' responses to Kofsky's questions vary widely. A few of the
interviews are simply disasters. Kofsky is audibly flummoxed by Tony
Williams' curt, hostile responses in an interview that lasts only 8 minutes,
and by Sun Ra's enigmatic ramblings about the blackness of outer space
and Black earthlings' misbehaviors in a conversation that goes for almost
100 minutes. There is better rapport in most of the other recordings, which
average about 55 minutes in length, although these still range significantly
in terms of how well they prove Kofsky's suppositions or even how well
they demonstrate the ability of human beings to listen to one another
carefully and to respond in kind.

There is the most agreement among interviewees, and between their
assessments and Kofsky's, on issues regarding working conditions in the
jazz business. Although a handful express satisfaction with their lot, most
interviewees agree that conditions are "shitty," to quote both Colbeck and
Moore, given the low wages, infrequent gigs, and the difficulty of performing in cramped, noisy nightclubs. A few interviewees, perhaps out of fear of
repercussion from industry people, refuse to touch questions about the
racial politics of the industry. Most, however, agree that a long history of
racism in society, a concomitant denigration of jazz for decades, and racial
power differentials in the contemporary music business produce a situation
where all but a small number of commercially successful musicians are
exploited. Most, including the white players, are of the opinion that Black
musicians typically have it worse than whites and that experimental musicians struggle more than straight-ahead players.[22] Compounding the situation for experimentalists, many agree, is hostility from jazz critics. Some
concur with Kofsky's claim that assessments of Black experimental music

often have a racial and class bias, especially when such work has an identifiable political valence, while others see the hostility primarily stemming from critics' anachronistic aesthetic investments in bebop or other established styles.

Most believe the jazz business should be transformed, although there is little agreement on what is to be done. Few are optimistic that conditions will improve. Several see potential in protest, but more – including Dixon and Taylor, who had been directly involved in such activities – see activism in the jazz community being constrained by individual career aspirations and fear of repercussions.[23] Jarman emphasizes the self-help aspects of collective organizations, providing some specifics from personal experience in the fledging Association for the Advancement of Creative Musicians' efforts to support its members' original music by producing its own concerts. Moore argues that broader social transformation would be necessary before music industry conditions improve, suggesting that Kofsky might spend less time cataloguing the ideas of revolutionary musicians and more time promoting revolution itself.

In a few conversations, Kofsky makes clear his disappointment that his interviewees' colleagues did not offer more insightful analyses of the music business. Although Taylor disagrees with Kofsky's observations about the cluelessness of certain individuals, he ultimately agrees that only a "small percentage" of musicians are "solidly equipped to really think about" the conditions under which they labor. Yet Kofsky is still buoyed up by the level of politicization he hears in the interviews and by their reports of the depth of conversation about social, political, and philosophical issues among musicians. Although he describes some of his subjects as "apolitical," most are not, as they generally express opposition to the war in Vietnam, admiration for Malcolm X, and a desire to transform society. He points out these trends to Izenson: "Even though I knew, in front, that musicians were concerned with social and political questions, and even related their work to it, I wasn't prepared for the strength of the response that I've gotten and the unanimity."

But musicians' opinions are more divided – among themselves and, as a group, from Kofsky's – when the conversations turn to the relationship of music to politics. His subjects may be opposed to the Vietnam War, but none agree with Shepp's assessment that *the music* is opposed to the war or to suffering more generally. Several interviewees refuse to engage with the question, or claim there is simply no relationship. Another group sees jazz as potentially against war but only indirectly. Some make comments similar to Coltrane's about the music as an expression of "higher ideals," being intrinsically antithetical to "poverty" and "war." Others suggest that any antiwar sentiment in the music stems from it being an expression of the sum total of experiences and attitudes of the performers. If musicians have antiwar attitudes, it will come out in the music along with everything else they believe.

The interviewees see little or no political relevance in Malcolm X's friendships with jazz musicians and they are divided on the question of whether Malcolm's ideas are inflected in the new music. Ali and a few others see Malcolm and their generation of musicians linked by a commitment to "freedom," but the connection is usually less direct. Moore hears Malcolm in the new music but also Martin Luther King, Jr., and "anything Black that is happening." For Shorter, what is evident is "the change that [Malcolm] went through after he came back from Mecca." Brown sees Malcolm's character being expressed in the music, "the finer manhood" that is also evident in the efforts of musicians to improve minds and bodies by eschewing drugs and practicing yoga and meditation. And while some express interest in dedicating (or already have dedicated) a recording to Malcolm or other Black activists, the range of responses to the question – the Creator and Pope Paul (Shorter), JFK (Henderson), Dag Hammarskjöld (Rudd), Walt Disney and "his Donald Duck" (Moncur), Sonny Liston (Dixon) – reflecting both a breadth of political and social affinities and at least some degree of sarcasm, does not exactly support the argument that their aesthetic sensibilities are being primarily driven by Black nationalism.

This range of politics and ideological orientation is even more evident when Kofsky asks more generally about connections between the music and the contemporaneous Black freedom struggle. Taylor emphatically says "the music is always political." Brown, himself a theorist of Black culture and experimental music as well as an associate of Jones, imbues the music with contemporary political relevance: "The music is definitely a part of what's going on in the Black revolution in America, and in musical terms it's just a musical expression of the general attitudes."[24] Yet Brown also explains that any received political meaning is on some level dependent on the predisposition of the listener. Regardless of musicians' intent, some listeners will likely only hear a "kind of entertainment." Henderson and Moncur emphasize that some musicians indeed express an explicit political agenda in their music – Henderson points to Shepp, specifically – yet for others the connection is only incidental, a reflection of an "emotional standpoint," as Moncur put it, generated in a political context. Moncur reminds Kofsky that even the activist wing of avant-garde musicians is composed of people with a range of social and political commitments and orientations. Indeed, Sanders and Coltrane describe their music as a kind of spiritual activism that exceeds a specifically Black nationalist politics. As Coltrane put it: "I want to be a force for real good. In other words, I know that there are bad forces, forces put here that bring suffering to others and misery to the world, but I want to be a force which is truly for the good."[25] Sun Ra expresses an activist sensibility in his inimitable way, suggesting his music promotes the "precision and discipline" that Black people need more than "freedom" in the wake of the Watts insurrection.

The most widely shared response to the general question of the new music's relation to Black political movements is that while one's experience with that struggle and one's own political beliefs have an influence on the creative process, they are but a few of many factors that inspire an art form that is, ultimately, an expression of its creators' total being at the spiritual, intellectual, emotional, and social levels. As Carter puts it: "Any small thing or any event no matter how minute it may seem always affects how you play, whether you're conscious and aware of it or not." Similar comments are voiced by Ali, Cherry, Henderson, and Moncur. Moreover, Carter, along with Cherry, Jarman, and Shorter, states that any attempt to restrict the music to political expression, to lessen the commitment of making music for the sake of the music itself, whether through the intent of the musician or the prescriptive interpretation of audience or critic, potentially diminishes its quality. Dixon, anticipating publication of his interview, later added a postscript to his copy of the recording. He said he edited out comments he saw as no longer relevant and added information about his own creative output, particularly his collaborations with dancer and choreographer Judith Dunn, as a means of making the interview less beholden to Kofsky's politics and more focused on his own somewhat differently political interests.

Concerns over critical and ideological reductiveness also arise when discussion turns to the term "new Black music." Brown embraces it, asserting that he and other Black innovators were creating something "new" as they built upon a foundation of African American musical practice. Most of the others, however, do not like it, rejecting it outright or calling into question aspects of the formulation. Henderson and Jarman assume it is a term imposed by white critics that reflects their hostility to recent musical trends. Moore and Ali have no problems with "Black music," but think the designation "new" obscures the extent to which contemporary music is built upon a longer jazz history. White interviewees, on the other hand, while cognizant of the centrality of Black contributions to the art form, are concerned that widespread adoption of the term might marginalize them as practitioners of a racially defined genre. Rudd suggests "new world music" as an alternative. Some of those (Black and white) most dismissive of the term think it runs contrary to the universalist ethos driving recent developments in the music, whether conceived of in terms of reaching a broad (multiracial, international) audience or in terms of the music's multicultural roots. As Jarman puts it:

> No. It has nothing to do with the music I play, but it has everything to do with the music I play. . . . That has to do with the whole cultural development of America. And it is Black music, white music, table music, cigarette music – it's just music. It has nothing to do with those pronouns, nouns, and all that.

Cherry and Henderson think "new Black music" might be relevant to the work of some of the politically vocal or active musicians, but would not use it to describe their own music. Taylor worries that the term has a kind of flattening effect when brought to bear on the very different musical projects of those – e.g., Marion Brown, Archie Shepp, Sun Ra – theoretically defined by it.

Comments about audiences call into question Kofsky's formulation of how the music expresses a specifically Black urban political aspiration. Although a few interviewees argue that Black audiences express their appreciation for the music more enthusiastically than others, more point out that support for the new music by Black audiences and the Black press is less than desirable, and that their livelihoods depend significantly on a white audience. The consensus is no preference for Black, white, or mixed audiences. What is important is having an audience. Kofsky ultimately sees some solidaristic potential in mixed audiences. This sentiment is evident as well in the exchanges about the potential for white musicians to play the "new Black music." Although the white interviewees note some difficulties in being accepted by certain Black colleagues or audiences, both they and African American interviewees see possibility in interracial musical collaboration, so long as white practitioners remain confident in their own self-expression while self-aware of their relative privilege and cognizant of the centrality of Black innovation in the genre.

Musicians diverge significantly from Kofsky's analytical assumptions about the growing influence of "Asian" and "African" musical elements or the declining significance of "European" ones. Some claim to be unaware of such trends. Those who confirm them usually either see them as part of a much longer interest in "non-Western" music in the jazz community, or as a recent trend that has less to do with politics than cultural affinity or the need to find new elements (scales, rhythms, and so on) upon which to base improvisations. Only a few see anticolonial or internationalist perspectives behind the trend, and then only with Kofsky's prompting.[26] Musicians are similarly split on whether "group improvisation" is a growing trend or whether it is simply a fundamental part of the music going back to its early development in New Orleans. Only Brown makes Kofsky's desired point about collective improvisation being an expression of "the whole idea of togetherness [that] is sweeping black communities and sweeping America." There is no consensus that Third Stream is a failed experiment, and absolutely no support for the idea that its lack of popularity signifies the limitations of integration as a political project.

Kofsky did not follow through with plans to write the "Social Profile of the Jazz Revolutionary" chapter, or otherwise draw substantially from the full set of interviews in *Black Nationalism*. This was the case for the version published in 1970, as revised into his eponymous 1973 University of Pittsburgh dissertation with the subtitle "Social Change and Stylistic Development in the Art of John Coltrane and Others, 1954–1967," and as expanded into his 1998 book *John Coltrane and the Jazz Revolution of the 1960s* (Pathfinder).[27] Nor did Kofsky realize plans, per his application to the Rabinowitz Foundation, to complete an "in-progress" chapter on "The Social Significance of Collective Improvisation in the Jazz Revolution," or to compose another chapter from excerpts from a panel discussion on "Jazz and Revolutionary Black Nationalism" as serialized in *Jazz*.[28] Instead, he gave greater emphasis to Coltrane by adding chapters on his influence on the "rock revolution" and on Elvin Jones' drumming, as well as the Coltrane and Tyner interviews.[29]

One wonders why Kofsky did not draw more significantly from the interviews in *Black Nationalism* and beyond. His critics might argue that he ditched them because they did not affirm his already established conclusions. Yet, this does not seem right. Clearly, some elements of his thesis – connecting the failures of Third Stream and integration, for example – could not be supported by the interviews. Nor would his subjects' comments have given him much useful information for the in-progress chapter on collective improvisation. Still, Kofsky made clear on tape that he found validation in the interviews. He easily could have adhered to and effectively strengthened some of his existing arguments about the politics of jazz and especially about exploitation in the jazz industry by quoting selectively from them. And while the group as a whole would not have produced the "profile" he was looking for, he could have created a satisfying one by drawing substantially from interviews with Ali, Brown, Dixon, and Taylor. Moreover, he was satisfied enough after he completed the interviews to seek (and eventually receive) a small amount of additional funding from the Rabinowitz Foundation for transcribing them after initial estimates for funds required fell short.[30]

It seems more likely that Kofsky would simply have found it too difficult, if not impossible, because of ideological orientation *and* the sheer conceptual difficulty of the task, to reconcile the wide range of opinion voiced in the interviews into something like "A Social Profile of the Jazz Revolutionary." The fact that he did not draw even minimally from like-minded musicians to substantiate his conclusions also suggests the possibility that Kofsky may have simply run out of time, money, and energy – even with the additional Rabinowitz Foundation funds – to transcribe the interviews and integrate them into the study. Friends describe the period of 1967 to 1969 as a difficult one for Kofsky. He was making little headway on a planned dissertation on U.S. foreign relations and having a hard time supporting himself on adjunct teaching and writing jobs. He also went through a period of depression after the 1967 death of John Coltrane, whom he considered a hero.[31]

These factors combined may have made it difficult to produce anything, save the book introduction, beyond what he had already written for the project, and encouraged him – perhaps also at the behest of colleagues, editors, and his publisher – to make the volume more of a homage to the saxophonist. After all, his own thinking about jazz – rooted in his Trotskyist politics but also, importantly, influenced by Shepp and other publicly outspoken musicians – was congruent enough with information in some of the interviews to provide "empirical verification" for much that he had already written. And, he already had significant sources to work with in the form of published commentary by Shepp, Dixon, and Taylor.[32] When Kofsky explains in his book's introduction that musicians' some-times inchoate, tentative commentary or refusal to speak to interviewers at all is often the result of the dangers that speaking out might pose to their careers, he voices simultaneously a real concern for musicians' professional standing *and* a theoretical justification for using a vanguardist interpret-ation to focus on the ideas of already outspoken, activist musicians.[33]

But what happens if we listen more carefully to the broader range of perspectives voiced in the 1966 interviews than time, inclination, or cir-cumstance enabled Kofsky to do himself? We can accomplish this best not simply by lining up with Kofsky's critics, but also by following some of the leads he set forth in his writing and in the 1966 interviews. After all, he did recognize the problems with reductionist cultural analysis, and in the 1966 *Jazz* article reproduced in *Black Nationalism*, he left the door open for a different assessment:

> I am *not* contending, first of all, that every avant-gardist has affiliated himself with this musical persuasion out of the direct desire to undermine and overthrow the *status quo*, or because he hates whites, or because he is choking with the suppressed rage of the downtrodden. Such a mechanical formulation would really be untenable, . . . (On the other hand, certain of the avant-garde fraternity, notably Archie Shepp but others as well, have left no doubt that to them the aesthetic revolution is closely linked with the social-political one.) Beyond that, some of the avant-gardists (though a minute fraction, my guess would be) may be true apoliticals: they are involved in the movement out of considerations that are solely aesthetic, and are by and large impervious to the influence of social currents external to the narrow sphere of art.[34]

Moreover, while Kofsky sometimes comes across as brusque, opinionated, and tone-deaf in the interviews, at other moments he is generous and sensitive, clearly listening to his subjects carefully and, at least temporarily, reconsidering some of his statements when interviewees disagree with them. He finds himself, for example, agreeing with Taylor's assessment that the music was multidimensional and not easily categorized by the term "new Black music." And he tells Dixon that in cases where he and musicians disagree about matters related to the music, the musician is, by definition, correct. Moreover, even as some musicians disagree with him, one gets the sense that they often find him engaging and appreciate the sincerity of his beliefs.[35]

Even the Coltrane interview suggests the value of more careful listening. More apparent on the recording than in the transcript is a rapport between the two men. Kofsky comes across as a respectful interlocutor. The exchange about Malcolm X does not seem as forced as it appears on the page, with both men seeming to take seriously this question of how music can best be connected to the current sociopolitical context.[36] When, in an interview several years later, Alice Coltrane gently pushes back on Kofsky's attempts to find political meaning in her husband's work, he acknowledges the range of perspectives and positionalities within the avant-garde movement and how that complicates the project of ascribing political meaning to it:

> Someone like Marion or Archie will say that it's very definitely connected with politics and they'll talk about working with SNCC and so forth, and so

on. And then other people will say it's not connected at all. And they'll think
about it a little and say, "well maybe here it is and here it is," but overall
that's not the major reason. No, I don't think it is the reason. People go into
music to play music, they don't go into music to be politicians. But, again,
it's very hard to escape being influenced by the overall situation in which
you find yourself. I mean John couldn't ignore those four girls.

With such perspectives in mind, then, how might musicians' ideas
voiced in response to Kofsky's questions about the "jazz revolution" enable
us to theorize that "revolution" differently? Or, perhaps another way to put
it is, what might we best learn from musicians who, confronted with the
responsibility of being jazz revolutionaries, thought about both the possibilities and limits of connecting music to a political present? The remainder of this essay attempts to answer these questions, albeit with the caveat
that the interviews were shaped by the form of Kofsky's questions, the
choices (along lines of race, generation, gender, aesthetic orientation, and
so on) he made about whom to interview, and that, with the exception of
the conversation with John Coltrane, he seldom posed questions to his
subjects about their own music and goals as artists.

* * *

The interviews confirm some of what we already know from comments
these and other musicians active in 1966 have had to say elsewhere about
the music and its social context. They remind us, first and foremost, that
we cannot assume a neat, homologous relationship among avant-garde
jazz, the radical intent of its practitioners, and the aspirations of inhabitants
of "the ghetto." What LeRoi Jones called "the new Black music" was
a multifaceted musical movement, created by a group of people with
diverse aesthetic, social, and political orientations, and such diversity
must be taken into account when attempting to characterize the musical
movement and its practitioners.

Some musicians were active politically, whether consistently and inter-
mittently, in the broader Black freedom struggle, in community organizing
and education, or in efforts to improve the conditions under which they
labored. Others were politically conscious in the moment – especially
around labor issues – but not politically active in any commonly understood sense. And some, as Kofsky pointed out, were relatively apolitical.
Even the politically conscious exhibited a wide range of opinion on how
their music may or may not have been shaped by the political moment.
Some did see their music as an extension of their own political beliefs or
commitments to cultural nationalist uplift projects. A few viewed it as

a reflection of the collective aspirations of a broader Black community. Yet others saw the music as connected only insofar as the political context shaped one's "emotional standpoint," or they viewed one's political commitments as significant but not determinative, as only one among many factors inspiring the music. Still others saw their music functioning at a spiritual or therapeutic level, in ways that were relevant to the political moment but not necessarily restricted to the realm of Black politics. And this range of political orientations does not correlate neatly to style of performance or generation. There were politically committed and politically apathetic musicians playing experimental music, straight-ahead music, and other styles.

Moreover, as Brown pointed out, any political meaning in a performance was in part dependent on audience reception, and Black listeners exhibited a wide range, from enthusiastic embrace to disdain to obliviousness. In other words, the music was revolutionary because some people – Blacks, whites, and others – heard it as revolutionary, talked about it as such, and sometimes wrote about it in those terms. But any attempt to see experimental music as an unmediated reflection of, or generative force for, the production of a collective militancy, spiritual quest, or other orientation in urban Black America was deeply fraught. While some musicians developed their aesthetic sensibilities in "the ghetto" or saw their music as articulating the feelings, aspirations, or condition of people living in Black urban communities, and while there was a dedicated Black audience for this music, there was widespread recognition of, and no shortage of anxiety about, the fact that the Black audience was relatively small and that the so-called "jazz revolution" was significantly dependent on a white audience for its survival.

Yet, even though we acknowledge that politically active musicians' work is not fully representative of members of the contemporaneous jazz community or even the contemporaneous avant-garde, most scholars working on such questions still focus on those musicians who put themselves out there, whether through politically themed music, activism, statements in interviews, or writings. The Kofsky interviews, however, suggest a few directions scholarship might take in the future to theorize somewhat differently the relationship of Black experimental music and politics at this moment by paying attention to less obviously intentional, public expressions.

First, the interviewees encourage us to spend more time thinking about how certain musical expressions may be seen as products of politically generated creative inspiration, even if they cannot be reduced to that.

Moncur's statement about the political context shaping the "emotional standpoint" from which one approaches the music suggests the need to better come to terms with internal processes of interpretation and translation when thinking about how the political context may become manifest in music. Various musicians' assertions that political events are only a few among many factors, at the spiritual, intellectual, emotional, and social levels, whether consciously processed or not, that affect one's musical decisions on a given day, encourage deeper consideration of the generative ground of the vague, inchoate political orientations of individuals, and to do so in ways that do not necessary assume a primary mode of political attachment but remain open to exploring the multiplicity of affinities and influences. Such approaches suggest avenues for productively analyzing experimental music in its political context in the absence of evidence of programmatic intent, and while avoiding the analytically flawed practice of projecting such intent onto musicians, or the equally flawed (and often racist and sexist) assumption that experimental music was a kind of unconscious reflection of the contemporaneous political gestalt.[37]

Musicians' comments in these interviews also suggest the possibility of moving away from analyses rooted in assumptions about the coherence of social and cultural formations, even if the orientation is to focus on how experimental music is the product of extensions, collisions, or fusions of these formations. We often see the jazz avant-garde or Black experimental music more generally as expressions of an expansive Black subjectivity with cosmopolitan orientation that is formed at the productive interface of discrete cultural formations, be they racial (Black/white), geographical (North American/European/Third World), or aesthetic and temporal (modernism/postmodernism). Yet such analyses potentially reduce meaning of these expressions to their relationships with the cultural formations they are thought to engage, even if antagonistically so.

The interviewees' comments suggest the possibility of finding meaning and functionality of music in the "actual exercise" of its "capacities" rather than in our assumptions about the nature of its constitutive wholes, to draw upon the language of assemblage theorist Manuel DeLanda.[38] In other words, when analyzing a piece of Black experimental music, the acoustics of the recording studio, one player's atheism, another's recent conversion to Islam, a simmering debate over back wages, three straight days of thunderstorms – may be as relevant to the sound and its meaning in its political context as a long history of the sonic affirmation of Black life and spirit and the fact that two of the six players are members of a community organization providing free music instruction in urban schools. This does not mean that the work is not relevant or meaningful in its political or cultural context, but that it is relevant in multiple ways and through the complicated processes by which its practitioners live the conjuncture as artists, thinkers, workers, lovers, siblings, parents, and so on.

Finally, the interviewees' comments suggest consideration of the *weight* of "the jazz revolution" as community bound discursive formation and how it served as both a positively and negatively productive force for creativity. Again, scholars have examined with great complexity the ways musicians during the 1960s rose to the challenge of "speak[ing] to the spiritual and cultural needs of black people," to quote Larry Neal.[39] But what about the ways they sought to resist that challenge – not necessarily because of apathy but because of the limits that political necessity might put on creativity? This was not simply an iteration of the old "art-for-art's-sake versus propaganda" dilemma, but rather a challenge that was particular to the politics of the movement and the meanings various observers were trying to place on the music.

For Cecil Taylor, the responsibility to the ideal of Black community and the act of drawing inspiration from it are difficult negotiations. When one is "essentially living really within the aesthetic curve of the art," the experimentalist must

> separate himself and yet understand that he is also a part of what he's separating himself from. Where it's different ... where it's special is that he supposedly is dealing with absolutes and trying to resolve those absolutes into workable theories. He knows since society doesn't ask anyone, doesn't encourage anyone to evolve themselves into mystical creations, he obviously lives outside by virtue of his choice from the masses.

The avant-garde, in other words, is Black *and* alienated from Blackness in a certain sense, yet that tension is also a resource for perseverance.

And, as noted, several politicized musicians simply worry that making the music responsive to the contemporary political movement would limit the range of creative inspiration that went into it. Some think political commitment would fix the music too firmly in time, either by erasing the creative foundations upon which it is built – thus several interviewees' objections to the "new" in "new Black music" – or by making it dated after the fact. And Joseph Jarman's rejection of "new Black music," his insistence that "pronouns, nouns, and all that" are completely inadequate for describing the full range of the music, calls attention to the power of labels such as "Black" or "revolutionary" to restrict the experience of playing or listening to experimental music. Evident in a number of responses that trouble a political definition of the music – whether through generic label or prescriptive definition of its function – is not so much a dissembling rejection of politics, but an effort to protect the spiritual, emotional, intellectual, and creative joy in music from being lost within a political discourse. As Grachan Moncur states: "I don't think that word is as big and as meaningful and as intricate as the music. I think there would be a lot left out of the real meaning of this music to label it just plain a revolution, revolutionary music."

Notes

1. Jones (1967), 210–11.
2. Cortez (1996), 1958.
3. Mathes (2015).
4. See, for example, Lewis' (2008) discussion of women in the Chicago and New York branches of the Association for the Advancement of Creative Musicians (AACM), and Isoardi's (2006) discussion of women in the Union of God's Musicians and Artists Ascension (UGMAA) in Los Angeles.
5. Kofsky (1998a) and (1998b).
6. Such analysis can be found throughout Kofsky (1970) and in his *Jazz* magazine essays that provided the foundation for the book. For an excellent discussion of Kofsky's work, see Gennari (2006), especially 252–53, 258–59, 262–64. For a posthumous critique from an old adversary, see Chris Albertson's 2010 blog post: http://stomp-off.blogspot.com.es/2010/07/i-dont-know-how-many-of-you-remember.html [accessed August 30, 2016].
7. Gennari (2006), 262–63.
8. Monson (2007), 201.
9. Kofsky (1970), 225. For discussions of this interview that are critical of Kofsky, see, e.g., Gennari (2006), 263; Nisenson (1995), 178–81; and Porter (2002), 367n.11.
10. Kofsky (1970), 6, 207, 221–22, 232.
11. Ibid., 53, 62–64.
12. At present most interviews can only be accessed by listening to the recordings at UCSC's Special Collections. The exceptions are those with Coltrane and Tyner and one with Rudd that was published as Kofsky (1967).
13. Joan Bailey, "Frank Kofsky: Chronological Summary, 1957–1974," personal communication in the author's possession.
14. Kofsky (1970), 65–66, 223–24. Asked about the lack of women in *Black Nationalism* in a 1970 interview for KPFA radio, Kofsky makes clear his understanding of the jazz world as "male dominated, male chauvinist" in terms of critical discourse, the instruments women are expected to play, and

social relations among musicians. He brings up such matters again in the 1971 interview with Alice Coltrane.

15. Kofsky (1966), 16.

16. Frank Kofsky to Victor Rabinowitz, May 25, 1966, with "Prospective Table of Contents for *Black Nationalism and the Revolution in Jazz.*" Box 30, Folder: Correspondence: Acceptances: Ko-Ku, Rabinowitz Records. The Foundation informed Kofsky on June 16 that he received a US$600 grant to pay for travel, lodging, and transcriptions. See Carole Remes to Frank Kofsky, June 16, 1966, Box 26, Folder: Correspondence: 1966 (II), Rabinowitz Records. Kofsky reiterated this plan in his interview with Cherry as well as in a brief biographical sketch preceding the published version of his interview with Rudd (Kosfky 1967, 36).

17. Kofsky may have interviewed other musicians in August 1966 and subsequently lost or taped over the recordings. This possibility is suggested by the absence of the Tyner interview in the Kofsky archive, and the more recent addition of the Dixon interview to it. The latter was given to UC Santa Cruz by Dixon's estate executor, Sharon Vogel, several years after the original gift. Although it is not dated, comments Kofsky makes in the Coltrane interview suggest the Dixon interview happened during the two-week period in August.

18. Kofsky tells Coltrane: "I had a lot of questions here that were related just to you. Many of those questions about music I don't ask of the other musicians; but I've always had a very special interest in your work, so I took this opportunity, since I don't know when I'll ever have a chance to get you down on tape again" (Kofsky 1970, 241). It is a bittersweet statement given the saxophonist's death from liver cancer less than a year later.

19. Kofsky sometimes explains to his subjects that the form of his questions reflects his desire to show the world that they are thinking clearly and intelligently about their craft and its connection to the social. See interviews with Ali, Henderson, Izenson, Moore, Smith, Sun Ra, and Taylor.

20. Kofsky (1970), 64.

21. For similar arguments, see ibid., especially 136–38.

22. Jarman complicates this assessment a bit by suggesting that all practitioners of "contemporary" music are facing difficulties. Colbeck, while cognizant of white privilege, says whites playing the new music or laboring in integrated bands face similar conditions to Black musicians.

23. See also the interviews with Ali, Izenson, Moncur, Rudd, Shorter, and Smith.

24. See Brown (1973) and (1984) for examples of his writings. For a discussion of them, see Porter (2002), 246–54, and Mathes (2015), 49–54.

25. Kofsky (1970), 241.

26. Coltrane was one of these. See ibid., 230.

27. Kofsky (1973) and (1998b). The primary difference between *Black Nationalism* and the dissertation is the addition in the latter of chapter 6, a lengthy treatment of the jazz business consisting of new writing. The 1998 volume is a substantially revised and expanded version of *Black Nationalism*, with some of the analysis of the music business shifted into the companion volume, *Black*

Music, White Business (Kofsky 1998a). Kofsky draws on later interviews with musicians and producers in these subsequent works, but does not expand his use of the 1966 conversations.

28. Frank Kofsky to Victor Rabinowitz, May 25, 1966. The panel discussion was serialized in *Jazz* over fourteen issues between April 1966 and July 1967. Participants included Kofsky, Shepp, Jones, pianist Steve Kuhn, critic Nat Hentoff, jazz impresario George Wein, art historian Robert Farris Thompson, and Father Norman J. O'Connor, who served as moderator.

29. The Elvin Jones piece was published in *Jazz* in 1967. The piece on Coltrane's influence on rock was commissioned by *Rolling Stone* but never published. He also decided to foreground the politics of jazz criticism, leading with two chapters on the subject rather than with a planned pair of chapters on the "jazz revolution" itself.

30. See Frank Kofsky to Carol Remes, August 23, 1966; Carol Remes to Frank Kofsky, August 31, 1966; Frank Kofsky to Carol Remes, September 1, 1966, Box 30, Folder: Correspondence: Acceptances: Ko-Ku; Carol Remes to Frank Kofsky, October 6, 1966, Box 26, Folder: Correspondence: 1966 (II), Rabinowitz Records.

31. Joan Bailey, personal communications to author, July 27, 2012, and August 2, 2012; Tom McCormick to Joan Bailey, undated; Bailey, Chronological Summary – all in author's possession.

32. Kofsky opens *Black Nationalism* by quoting from Shepp's 1965 *Down Beat* essay, "An Artist Speaks Bluntly," in which he describes Black musicians as "a reflection of the Negro people"; notes their liberatory, vanguardist function; and champions the central, innovative role Black people have played in the development of jazz (Shepp 1965). Later in the introduction, after quoting Shepp on Vietnam, Kofsky says that "all of the writing" in *Black Nationalism* is "informed" by this "point of view" (Kofsky 1970, 64). He makes clear his interpretation of Shepp's vanguardist role in his interview with Smith: "And it isn't that we're just talking to Archie [Shepp], we're really talking about a whole milieu and it just happens that Archie is the spearhead of that movement."

33. Kofsky (1970), 62–63. Friends of Kofsky's have suggested to me that he did not use the interviews with less established figures than Coltrane and Tyner because he did not want to damage their careers by bringing attention to their controversial statements. On the other hand, he easily could have concealed the identities of vulnerable informants by drawing selectively from their interviews or quoting them anonymously.

34. Kofsky (1966), 16. This passage is reproduced in Kofsky (1970), 131–32, with minor revisions.

35. Colbeck told him flat out that he had been well-received in the community, even though he was a white man, because of the potential power he wielded as a critic *and* because of his sincerity.

36. Kofsky heard this himself in their exchange, even though he recognized that Coltrane did not agree with much of his analysis. See comments in the 1970 radio interview.

37. A moment where Kofsky himself gestures toward this approach is when he thinks through the question of influence regarding Coltrane's effect on Albert Ayler: "The artist's individuality is never the only root out of which his art grows. Every artist lives at a certain time, in a certain place; absorbs certain social and intellectual conventions, some implicit, some explicit; undergoes certain formative experiences, artistic and otherwise, and so on. All of these things, to a greater or lesser degree are the 'influences' that shape the man's art" (Kofsky 1970, 173). Kofsky cites Trotsky (1960, 59–60) to get at this multiplicity, while avoiding the class determinism of the original's formulation.
38. DeLanda (2006), 9–11. DeLanda presents assemblage theory as an alternative to social theories that presuppose "the component parts [of a social formation] are constituted by the very relations they have to other parts of the whole." Assemblage theory instead emphasizes "relations of exteriority," out of which "the properties of a whole cannot be reduced to those of its parts [because] they are the result not of an aggregation of the components' own properties but of the actual exercise of their capacities."
39. Neal (1968), 29.

References

Archival Collections

Frank Kofsky Audio and Photography Collection of the Jazz and Rock Movement (A Gift of Bonnie Kofsky), UC Santa Cruz, McHenry Library, Special Collections.

Interviews in the Kofsky Collection

Rashied Ali, New York City, August 16, 1966.
Marion Brown, New York City, August 9, 1966.
Ron Carter, New York City, August 8, 1966.
Don Cherry, New York City, August 9, 1966.
Ric Colbeck and Mark Levin, New York City, August 19, 1966.
Alice Coltrane, Berkeley, California, April 23–24, 1971.
John Coltrane, Deer Park Station, Long Island, New York, August 18, 1966.
Bill Dixon, undated – probably New York City, August 1966.
Joe Henderson, New York City, August 13, 1966.
David Izenson, New York City, August 15, 1966.
Joseph Jarman (interviewed by Betty Schmae), Detroit, Michigan, August 1, 1966.
Frank Kofsky (interviewed by KPFA radio), 1970.
Giuseppi Logan, New York City, August 14, 1966.
Grachan Moncur III, New York City, August 19, 1966.

Charles Moore, Detroit, Michigan, July 16, 1966.
Roswell Rudd, New York City, August 11, 1966.
Pharoah Sanders New York City, August 19, 1966.
Wayne Shorter New York City, August 8, 1966.
Frank Smith, New York City, August 13, 1966.
Sun Ra, New York City, August 9, 1966.
Cecil Taylor, New York City, August 14, 1966.
Tony Williams, New York City, August 8, 1966.

Other Recordings in the Kofsky Collection

Frank Kofsky, lecture: "Jazz and the New Black Nationalism," Sacramento City
    College, 1964.
Frank Kofsky, lecture: "Jazz, the Cold War, and the Establishment," Friday
    Night Socialist Forum, Detroit, Michigan, July 1966.

Victor Rabinowitz Papers, Series V: Records of the Louis M. Rabinowitz
Foundation, 1954–1991, The Tamiment Library and Robert F. Wagner
Labor Archives, New York University.

Books and Articles

Anderson, I. 2007. *This Is Our Music: Free Jazz, the Sixties, and American Culture.*
    Philadelphia: University of Pennsylvania Press.
Brown, M. 1973. *Afternoon of a Georgia Faun: Views and Reviews.* Nia Music.
    1984. *Recollections: Essays, Drawings, Miscellanea.* Frankfurt: Juergen A. Schmitt.
Cortez, J. 1996. "How Long Has Trane Been Gone." In *The Norton Anthology of
    African American Literature*, ed. H. L. Gates, Jr., and N. Y. McKay, 1957–59.
    New York: W. W. Norton & Co.
DeLanda, M. 2006. *A New Philosophy of Society: Assemblage Theory and Social
    Complexity.* London: Continuum.
Gayle, A., Jr. 1971. *The Black Aesthetic.* New York: Doubleday.
Gennari, J. 2006. *Blowin' Hot and Cool: Jazz and Its Critics.* University of Chicago
    Press.
Isoardi, S. 2006. *The Dark Tree: Jazz and the Community Arts in Los Angeles.*
    Berkeley: University of California Press.
Jones, L. 1967. *Black Music.* New York: William Morrow.
Kofsky, F. 1966, January. "The Avant-Garde Revolution: Origins and Directions."
    Jazz: 14–19.
    1967. "A New World Music? An Interview with Roswell Rudd." *American
    Dialog* 4.1 (Spring): 33–36.

1970. *Black Nationalism and the Revolution in Music.* New York: Pathfinder Press.

1973. "Black Nationalism and the Revolution in Music: Social Change and Stylistic Development in the Art of John Coltrane and Others, 1954–1967." PhD dissertation, University of Pittsburgh.

1998a. *Black Music, White Business: Illuminating the History and Political Economy of Jazz.* New York: Pathfinder Press.

1998b. *John Coltrane and the Jazz Revolution of the 1960s.* New York: Pathfinder Press.

Lewis, G. E. 2008. *A Power Stronger than Itself: The AACM and American Experimental Music.* University of Chicago Press.

Mathes, C. 2015. *Imagine the Sound: Experimental African American Literature after Civil Rights.* Minneapolis: University of Minnesota Press.

Monson, I. 2007. *Freedom Sounds: Civil Rights Call Out to Jazz and Africa.* Oxford University Press.

Neal, L. 1968. "The Black Arts Movement." *The Drama Review* 12.4 (Summer): 28–39.

Nisenson, E. 1995. *Ascension: John Coltrane and His Quest.* New York: Da Capo Press.

Porter, E. 2002. *What Is This Thing Called Jazz? African American Musicians as Artists, Critics, and Activists.* Berkeley: University of California Press.

Shepp, A. 1965, December 16. "An Artist Speaks Bluntly." *Down Beat*: 11, 42.

Trotsky, L. 1960. *Literature and Revolution.* Ann Arbor: University of Michigan Press.

Widener, D. 2010. *Black Arts West: Culture and Struggle in Postwar Los Angeles.* Durham, NC: Duke University Press.

II

Culture and Politics

CHAPTER 5

The Rights of Black Love

Dagmawi Woubshet

No other American writer embodies the 1960s more so than James Baldwin. Not only did the decade cement his reputation as a rare artist, it saw also his rise as one of America's preeminent public intellectuals. Taking Baldwin's own literary timeline, we might say "the Sixties" commenced for him in 1957, the year he left France and returned to the United States to report on the early days of the civil rights struggle in the South; and concluded, we might add, in 1972 with the publication of *No Name in the Street*, his elegiac meditation on the Civil Rights Movement and the revolution that America and the world underwent in a such a short span of time. And yet Baldwin would continue to return to the 1960s in his late works, using the advantage of hindsight to reexamine the significance of the era in its extended wake. As Raoul Peck's documentary film *I Am Not Your Negro* (2017) has recently brought to light, in 1979 Baldwin had begun to sketch *Remember This House*, a book he never completed but intended to be a personal recollection of his friends, the assassinated civil rights leaders Medgar Evers, Malcolm X, and Martin Luther King, Jr. And he appeared in the 1982 film *I Heard It Through the Grapevine*, a documentary in which he retraces his initial journey to the South, reflecting on that journey from a new historical horizon – the 1980s. In fact, at the very beginning of *I Heard It Through the Grapevine*, articulating the film's multiple timeframes, says Baldwin:

> It was 1957 when I left Paris for Little Rock. 1957. This is 1980. And how many years is that? Nearly a quarter of a century. What has happened to all those people, children I knew then? What happened to the country? What does it mean for the world? What does it mean for me?[1]

Since Baldwin sought to make meaning of the 1960s in real time as well as in retrospect, I find it instructive, even necessary, to take an expansive view of his ever-changing outlook on the era, one that looks beyond the confines of historical periodization based on decades (1960–69) or the strict timetable of the Civil Rights Movement (1954–68). This shift in perspective is particularly important in understanding a writer like James Baldwin, so closely linked with the 1960s/Civil Rights Movement that that association has come to define and, too often, delimit his work. Because what still remain under examined are the many books and essays he wrote from the mid-1970s until his death at the end of 1987. One of my aims, then, is to read *The Fire Next Time*, a 1960s classic, alongside "To Crush a Serpent" (1987), one of Baldwin's last essays and an exemplary piece of the author's late style. In "To Crush a Serpent," Baldwin returns to a formative experience he'd written at length about in *The Fire Next Time* – his years as a teenage evangelist preacher – but this time he recasts that experience as a *sexual* coming-of-age story. As a queer sequel to the iconic Civil Rights-era text that now includes the flesh and its reservoir of desires and fears, "To Crush a Serpent" significantly revises the definitive account of Baldwin's ministry in *The Fire Next Time*. I will focus on their intertextual relationship later in this chapter, and elaborate why Baldwin waits until the end of his career to emplot his own sexuality. But first I want to read *The Fire Next Time* on its own terms, paying careful heed to Baldwin's theory of love. To expound on love is also to expound on the most abiding theme and moral principle of Baldwin's work, and so my other aim is to examine the uses of love in the early 1960s in *The Fire Next Time* and to see how love fares in another era in "To Crush a Serpent."

Love and Liberation

The Fire Next Time is arguably Baldwin's finest collection of essays, a lucid example of his ability to weave together aesthetics, politics, and ethics into one exquisite tapestry. Although it appeared in book form in 1963, its two missives were originally published the year before – the shorter piece, "A Letter to My Nephew," in *The Progressive*, and the longer, near 40,000-word "Letter from a Region in My Mind" in *The New Yorker*. Both exemplify Baldwin's signature essay form, which employs the author's personal story as text for collective self-reflection. And here the epistolary form gives him ample room to shift points of view, sometimes in an instant, from the personal to the national to the global; from critical analysis of race, religion, and nation to existential meditations on why human beings need these categories in the first place. Because the measure of the letter is not as prescribed as the essay's is to weigh a specific subject matter, Baldwin can leap across a range of subjects while still sustaining the book's overall coherence. The epistolary form complements *Fire* in another way, too, since the set of feelings that often infuse Baldwin's essays – e.g., intimacy, vulnerability, righteous discontent, and yearning – become all the more acute for the reader willing to be hailed as the epistles' direct addressee. Moreover, form and feeling cohere in *Fire* because the book's organizing principle is love; and the letter, perhaps next to lyric, is the literary genre in which love finds its everyday expression.

Love is mentioned in over a dozen important passages in *Fire*, but it is only in the last few pages that Baldwin presents us with a definition. He writes:

> Love takes off the masks that we fear we cannot live without and know we cannot live within. I use the word "love" here not merely in the personal sense but as a state of being, or a state of grace – not in the infantile American sense of being made happy but in the tough and universal sense of quest and daring and growth.[2]

This highly intricate and suggestive definition resists easy summing up; still, at the very least, we can glean from it that love is both an act and a condition. As an act, it has the power of revelation. Not divine or supernatural disclosure about human life coming from above, but human insight rooted in our worldly existence and experience, which holds the power to confront our deepest fears, as well as the power to extricate our private and public lives from the state of quagmire those fears trap us in. As a state of being, love stands opposed to a state of fear. Love is a state of grace, Baldwin adds, not in the Christian sense of a condition free of sin, nor in the American ideal of the pursuit of happiness, but rather as a constant universal striving that rests on human inquiry, courage, and maturity.

In many ways, this definition is a distillation or abstraction of the other key claims on love that precede it, which posit love as a countervailing force against white power, on the one hand, and Christianity, on the other. *Fire* offers Baldwin's most trenchant critique of white power, revealing how white supremacy is contingent on Black subjugation, and how that asymmetry totally warps America, its people, institutions, and moral character. But as one example, consider how with characteristic economy Baldwin describes this racial asymmetry in the New York of his youth:

> It was absolutely clear that the police would whip you and take you in as long as they could get away with it, and that everyone else – housewives, taxi-drivers, elevator boys, dishwashers, bartenders, lawyers, judges, doctors, and grocers – would never, by the operation of any generous human feeling, cease to use you as an outlet for his frustrations and hostilities. Neither

civilized reason nor Christian love would cause any of those people to treat you as they presumably wanted to be treated.[3]

The law is not the sole instrument of white power; that power, as Baldwin enumerates, also rests in the hands of fellow Americans across gender, age, social rank, and profession, whose very whiteness is the law that licenses them to harm and humiliate Black people with impunity and with disregard to the political, civic, and religious virtues the nation ostensibly cherishes.

To compound its power, moreover, whiteness relies on a structure of feeling that disavows the harm done in its name, a feeling that Baldwin brilliantly terms *innocence*. Perhaps Baldwin's most original insight in theorizing race is to identify innocence as a constituent feature of white power: "it is not permissible that the authors of devastation should also be innocent. It is the innocence which constitutes the crime."[4] To author devastation entails a certain kind of force, and, as Baldwin delineates here, it takes yet another kind to willfully ignore and deny its consequences. As a structure of feeling, innocence masks and voids America's violent racial past and present record, enabling white Americans not only to shirk responsibility, but to reify an idea of themselves and of America based on the republic's noble ideals rather than its ignoble history. No substantive racial progress, and no fundamental transformation of the self and the nation, could be achieved so long as innocence remained the organizing feeling of American whiteness. It traps white Americans in a false reality; it is the mask they must take off in order to reckon with themselves and their country. This is where love comes in, vis-à-vis whiteness, as a countervailing force, as Baldwin argues, in fact the only remaining force powerful enough to free whiteness from its arrested state of fear, violence, and innocence: "if love will not swing wide the gates, no other power will or can."[5]

In reading *Fire*, critics jump to the book's penultimate sentence to represent Baldwin's vision of love:

> If we – and now I mean the relatively conscious whites and the relatively conscious blacks, who must, like lovers, insist on, or create, the consciousness of the others – do not falter in our duty now, we may be able, handful that we are, to end the racial nightmare, and achieve our country, and change the history of the world.[6]

A vision of a vanguard of Americans made flesh in the simile of interracial lovers was certainly evocative and provocative in 1963, when *de jure* segregation and anti-miscegenation still reigned. But taking this image out of its textual context – without heeding closely the argument that Baldwin builds up to culminate in these final words – obscures the initial set of demands he places on this handful lot to reach a new level of consciousness they could then use to achieve America. And the demands to each group, white and Black, are qualitatively different. Early on in *Fire*, Baldwin writes:

> White people in this country will have quite enough to do in learning how to accept and love themselves and each other, and when they have achieved this – which will not be tomorrow and may very well be never – the Negro problem will no longer exist, for it will no longer be needed.[7]

The function of love in this loaded statement is echoed in the definition cited earlier, but additionally it resounds Baldwin's pointed claim of what love can do specifically for white people. He intertwines race and love here via a sentence that is both chiastic and conditional: it inverts the conventional paradigm that equates Black people and the race problem and instead figures white people as the problem of race; and, it articulates the conditions under which this problem could be resolved. That is, if white people loved and accepted themselves and each other – that is, confronted and rid themselves of an identity based solely on supremacist power and innocence – then there wouldn't be a need for a racial "other" against whom to measure and define self-worth.

Love functions differently for the disenfranchised, however. The passages where Baldwin speaks of love in relation to Black people emphasize love as an instrument of both intramural survival and interracial transformation. In the letter to his nephew, notice Baldwin's propositions of familial and intraracial love:

> Well, you were born, here you came, something like fourteen years ago; and though your father and mother and grandmother, looking about the streets through which they were carrying you, staring at the walls into which they brought you, had every reason to be heavyhearted, yet they were not. For here you were, Big James, named for me – you were a big baby, I was not – here you were: to be loved. To be loved, baby, hard, at once, and forever, to strengthen you against the loveless world. Remember that: I know how black it looks today, for you. It looked bad that day, too, yes, we were trembling. We have not stopped trembling yet, but if we had not loved each other none of us would have survived. And now you must survive because we love you, and for the sake of your children and your children's children.[8]

In the first instance, love is a birthright: "For here you were, Big James, named for me – you were a big baby, I was not – here you were: to be loved," writes Baldwin, creating with a colon a philosophical proposition that to be loved is the very purpose and prerogative of human existence, a natural right possessed by everyone. And in this instance, this birthright, if we follow Baldwin's brilliant sentence, is embodied by *both* Jameses. The interlacing of the two names and the repetition of "here you were" create an overlay we are meant to notice and ask about. Does the *you* refer to Big James or to his namesake or to both?, we wonder, passing as we do through the same construction "here you were" twice. Baldwin himself haunts the sentence with his own possibility, conceiving himself and his nephew within a larger proposition on *being*. Existence is a matter of space and time – "here" = location, "were" = time – Baldwin reminds us, and also a matter of love – "to be" = love. In this passage, furthermore, he tells his nephew that love also fortifies, especially a people stripped of the rights of full humanity and citizenship, becoming a vehicle for surviving a death-dealing world, for ensuring futurity.

Black love is also key to realizing interracial America. Addressing his nephew in the first example, and a Black collective in the second, he writes:

> The details and symbols of your life have been deliberately constructed to make you believe what white people say about you. Please try to remember that what they believe, as well as what they do and cause you to endure, does not testify to your inferiority but to their inhumanity and fear. Please try to be clear, dear James, through the storm which rages about your youthful head today, about the reality which lies behind the words *acceptance* and *integration*. There is no reason for you to try to become like white people and there is no basis whatever for their impertinent assumption that *they* must accept *you*. The really terrible thing, old buddy, is that *you* must accept *them*. And I mean that very seriously. You must accept them and accept them with love. For these innocent people have no other hope.[9]
>
> And if the word integration means anything, this is what it means: that we, with love, shall force our brothers to see themselves as they are, to cease fleeing from reality and begin to change it.[10]

In both instances, Baldwin positions Black love to be essential for integration. The same rhetorical move we see above with the phrase "the Negro problem" applies here, whereby Baldwin attacks and inverts the racial assumptions of American keywords – like integration, which in 1963 widely meant the acceptance of Black people by white people, institutions, and standards. He overturns this assumption with an italicized chiasmus, and repurposes the word "*integration*" to signify Black acceptance of white people and, by extension, the transformation of American institutions and

standards on Black terms. Writing on the eve of the end of legal segregation, then, this is what Baldwin demands of Black people: not only to
accept whites, but to do it *with love*, the prepositional construction in both
examples indicating Black love as a vital instrument for white liberation
and interracial/national renewal.

In *Fire*, Baldwin is concerned with demystifying and debunking power,
wherever that power resides: "The unprecedented price demanded – and
at this embattled hour of the world's history – is the transcendence of the
realities of color, of nations, and of altars."[11] And, indeed, his searing
critique of white power is matched by his fierce confrontation with
Christianity. It is in "Down at the Cross" that Baldwin offers a moving
account of his days in the Church: what led him there in the first place,
what propelled him to become an adolescent preacher, and, eventually,
what brought him down from the pulpit and forced him out of the temple.
I will rehearse this story later, but for now it is worth recalling why Baldwin
gives up God and with what power he replaces Him. Baldwin rejects
Christianity, on the one hand, because of its collusion with white supremacy, a collusion that has left the American Church morally bankrupt. On
the other hand, as a teen preacher, Baldwin had witnessed how the Church
functioned, like other American institutions, also for personal gain rather
than the collective good, for instilling fear and safety rather than fellowship
and daring; he had seen firsthand the disconnect between a preacher's
public sermon and his private conduct, including his own – all of which
reasons led him to question his Christian faith and ultimately to abandon
the Church.

When describing his personal experience in the Church, as well as the
general principles of Christianity in America, Baldwin's tone is acerbic,
even indignant. He characterizes his early calling not as a vocation but
a career and a gimmick ("it was my career in the church that turned out,
precisely, to be my gimmick"); the Church not as a holy institution but
a dishonest scheme ("I found myself in the church racket"); and his role
not as a minster of religion but an actor or magician ("Being in the pulpit
was like being in the theatre; I was behind the scenes and knew how the
illusion was worked").[12] Moreover, of the principles of both Black and
white churches, he writes:

> I was also able to see that the principles governing the rites and customs of
> the churches in which I grew up did not differ from the principles governing
> the rites and customs of other churches, white. The principles were
> Blindness, Loneliness, and Terror, the first principle necessarily and actively
> cultivated in order to deny the two others. I would love to believe that the

principles were Faith, Hope, and Charity, but this is clearly not so for most Christians, or for what we call the Christian world.[13]

And, as his ultimate statement on religion, he closes out the first section of "Down at the Cross," which focuses on his ministry, with these emphatic words:

> It is not too much to say that whoever wishes to become a truly moral human being (and let us not ask whether or not this is possible; I think we must *believe* that it is possible) must first divorce himself from all the prohibitions, crimes, and hypocrisies of the Christian church. If the concept of God has any validity or any use, it can only be to make us larger, freer, and more loving. If God cannot do this, then it is time we got rid of Him.[14]

Baldwin's rejection of Christianity, at root, is not unlike his rejection of white power. In both cases, he is challenging doctrines that he reasons limit human freedom and possibility, and thwart love's intrinsic values and virtues; why in the absence of his Christian faith, the authority that he summons – for its ethical and political resources, for its edifying power – is love.

To be sure, while Baldwin gives up Christian foundationalism, he never abandons the cultural and spiritual raw materials of the Church. How fitting that the essay in which he rejects God and Christianity is titled "Down at the Cross," and the book itself, *The Fire Next Time* – both references obviously drawn from the Bible. It would be inconceivable to imagine the corpus of James Baldwin emptied out of the language, music, and pathos of the Black Church; if that were to happen, we wouldn't have his first novel, *Go Tell It on the Mountain*, nor his last, *Just Above My Head*, nor his plays, *The Amen Corner* and *Blues for Mister Charlie*, to name but a handful of texts. But using the resources of the Black Church and the parables and metaphors of Christianity for artistic purposes, or to forge a secular worldview, is not the same as keeping Christian faith; his writings do not bear out the latter, whereas they cannot exist without the former. Surely, one of Baldwin's achievements as an artist is to blur – even, erase – the division between the sacred and the profane. Conventions tell us that the sacred is tethered to the Divine, and the profane to the worldly. Sacred words, rites, and spaces – say, holy, prayer, and place of worship – are bound up with a higher, spiritual power we show total reverence and devotion; whereas the profane is outside the purview of religion and deals with human affairs that are earthbound, temporal, and often of the flesh. But in Baldwin's hands this sacred/profane binary comes undone, as he rewrites religious idiom to describe worldly experiences that range from inner, sexual turmoil to external, social, and political crisis.

I have been reading love textually so far, paying close attention to how Baldwin defines and delineates it in *Fire*, and how he fashions rhetoric to work out the relationship among love, race, and religion. I would be remiss, however, not to point out the ideological and political implications of Baldwin's enterprise. American civilization is founded on the assumption that, because we were deemed subhuman, Black people were incapable of love. American slavery buttressed, and was buttressed by, an Enlightenment discourse that inscribed an intrinsic and fixed difference between white and Black people; reasoned that the latter were an inferior class who lacked the physical form and the mental and emotional faculties that distinguished the human from the animal. A paragon of his age, Thomas Jefferson wrote in *Notes on the State of Virginia* that in body (color, figure, hair), mind (the ability to reason, compose, narrate), and emotion (the ability to grieve and to love), Black people were deficient, subordinate, and substandard to whites. Notice, for instance, how Jefferson uses love as one of the criteria for measuring the difference between the races:

> But never yet could I find that a black had uttered a thought above the level of plain narration; never seen even an elementary trait of painting or sculpture. In music they are more generally gifted than the whites with accurate ears for tune and time, and they have been found capable of imagining a small catch. Whether they will be equal to the composition of a more extensive run of melody, or of complicated harmony, is yet to be proved. Misery is often the parent of the most affecting touches in poetry. Among the blacks is misery enough, God knows, but no poetry. Love is the peculiar oestrum of the poet. Their love is ardent, but it kindles the senses only, not the imagination. Religion indeed has produced a Phyllis Whately [sic]; but it could not produce a poet. The compositions published under her name are below the dignity of criticism.[15]

Wheatley, he misspells her name, apparently fails as a poet because of her under-developed sense of love. Black love, according to Jefferson, is capable of arousing *only* the senses (meaning the body) and not the imagination (meaning the mind), since the mind is a faculty that only humans possess, whereas the senses are common among all animals. And it is not the religious content of her verse that disqualifies Wheatley's work from meriting the "dignity" of the secular arts, but her inchoate love made so because of her race. Since she is Black, in other words, Wheatley lacks the requisite feelings to be a proper poet, indeed, to produce art, which is the prerogative of a human being who loves and not "a black" who cannot.

It turns out that love is among the categories that Jefferson uses to rationalize Black people's ostensible ontological difference and inferiority. He adds, "love seems with them to be more an eager desire, than a tender delicate mixture of sentiment and sensation," employing again the (Black) body/(white) mind schism that underwrites the Enlightenment.[16] In fact, here, Jefferson suggests with the graded quantifier "more" that by comparison Black love is not love per se, but simply the expression of physical (read: sexual) desire, devoid of love's other features like tenderness, exquisiteness, and sentience. It is within this warped world, that rendered Black love a contradiction in terms and relied on love as a category to reify white supremacy, that Black love assumes a radical ideological power. Since in constituting the United States and modernity's master discourse, emotional faculty was also a category manipulated for measuring and establishing racial difference, we have to interrogate not just the grand claims about Black physical and mental difference, but also about Black people's feelings.

Baldwin understood this very well, and part of the achievement of *The Fire Next Time* is its overturning of a paradigm of race built on the belief that Black people were inherently unequipped to exercise love's full prerogatives. This is why chiasmus becomes the key rhetorical *and* political device in *Fire*, enabling Baldwin to overturn America's racial equations in the same way Frederick Douglass uses the trope to topple the discourse of racial hierarchy in his own time. As Henry Louis Gates, Jr. reminds us:

> since chiasmus always entails a form of reversal, its potentially political uses are as great as its aesthetic uses, particularly if one is a fugitive slave implicitly making the case for his common humanity with his white reader through the text that reader is holding in her or his hands. Here, rhetoric is called upon to reverse the world's order, the order in which the associations between "slave" and "Black" and "white" and "free" appear to have been willed, fixed, and natural.[17]

And what such reversal ultimately reveals is how "these associations [were] wrong all along, that there was nothing natural or fixed about them after all; that they were constructed, arbitrary, and in fact, evil perversions of the natural order of things in which all men and women are meant to have equal rights."[18] Baldwin may not be writing during the era of chattel slavery; still, he is writing at a time when Black people remained *legally* disenfranchised; Black people may not have been enslaved in 1963, but still they remained in the grip of slavery's afterlife – a point he intimates at the outset of *Fire* by retitling the first essay, "My Dungeon Shook: A Letter to

My Nephew on the Hundred Anniversary of Emancipation." (Later, in 1979, he called the Civil Rights Movement "the latest slave rebellion."[19]) And, of course, Baldwin is writing amid a mass movement determined to overturn American apartheid, and as a skilled writer deliberate is his use of chiasmus not simply for aesthetic ends, but ideological and political ones as well. Surely, *Fire* stages a successful coup against (white) American grammar – including its definition of integration and of love – which, in itself, is a political act.

Black love is political, a fact that the Civil Rights Movement definitively established. Lest we forget, the awesome mass movement that Martin Luther King, Jr., led, and the nonviolent resistance that he championed and deployed to extraordinary effect, was anchored in love. Constitutive of nonviolent militant action is *agape* love, a point that King articulated in countless religious sermons, political speeches, philosophical essays, and, indeed, in practice. Distinct from *eros* (sexual love or desire) and *philia* (friendship or affection), *agape* is selfless love, and in Christian theology it is embodied in Christ and the love covenant between God and human-kind. In a speech he delivered in 1957, "The Power of Nonviolence," King put it this way:

> *Agape* is understanding, creative, redemptive good will for all men. Biblical theologians would say it is the love of God working in the minds of men. It is an overflowing love which seeks nothing in return. And when you come to love on this level you begin to love men not because they are likable, not because they do things that attract us, but because God loves them and here we love the person who does the evil deed while hating the deed that the person does. It is the type of love that stands at the center of the movement that we are trying to carry on in the Southland – *agape*.[20]

There is a binding kinship between King's and Baldwin's philosophies in that both endow love with transformative, redemptive power – in fact, as *the* power that could alter the course of America's history and moral character; and both recognize the capacity of Black people to unleash love in a way that could counter the forces of white supremacy and regenerate the nation. And yet there is a fundamental difference. King's idea of love rests on a religious, transcendental epistemology (i.e., the existence of God and of God's love), while Baldwin's, however inviolable, is rooted in human existence and experience. This is where the preacher and ex-preacher part ways: King's love is authorized by God, whereas Baldwin's is licensed by the best in us, fellow, flawed human beings. Still, religious or secular, however distinct their worldview, both championed love as the lever that could lift the country out of its racial and moral quagmire, as well as the firm ground upon which a new America could be built.

Baldwin was keenly aware that his use of an emotional/spiritual category like love to intervene in the political public sphere might raise objections. It was one thing for a religious leader like King to invoke love as part of the social gospel, yet another for a secular, literary artist and public intellectual to do the same, especially at a time when other leading intellectuals were theorizing love's uselessness in arbitrating matters of public politics. Take, for example, Hannah Arendt's *The Human Condition*, a book published in 1958 and contemporaneous with *Fire*. While Arendt recognizes love's power in the context of the private life, she invalidates its public uses. Of love's signal (private) power, she writes, incisively:

> For Love, although it is one of the rarest occurrences in human lives, indeed possesses an unequaled power of self-revelation and unequaled clarity of vision for the disclosure of *who*, precisely because it is unconcerned to the point of total unworldliness with *what* the loved person may be, with his qualities and shortcomings no less than with his achievements, failings, and transgressions.[21]

But love's "unequaled power of self-revelation and unequaled clarity of vision" applies only in the private realm and is snuffed out when taken out in public: "love, in distinction from friendship, is killed, or rather extinguished, the moment it is displayed in public . . . Because of its inherent worldlessness, love can only become false and perverted when it is used for political purposes such as the change or salvation of the world."[22] She adds: "Love, by its very nature, is unworldly, and it is for this reason rather than its rarity that it is not only apolitical but antipolitical, perhaps the most powerful of all antipolitical forces."[23] The private/public distinction Arendt holds is dissolved in Baldwin's theory of love (recall his definition, "I use the word 'love' here not merely in the personal sense"), laying claim to love's public properties. And, needless to say, Arendt's thesis that love is "perhaps the most powerful of all antipolitical forces" is belied by the American Civil Rights Movement, which proved that *with love* Black people could wage a mighty political battle and gain (even if it is partial) victory.

One cannot fully understand power like white supremacy without its emotional drive, its innocence, for example, which Baldwin considered to be a powerful, inimical structure of feeling to be distinguished from other instruments of power. In any political system, there is always collusion between formal politics and sentiment, between political institutions and the feelings that guide and govern them. So, when Baldwin speaks of political matters in ostensibly non-political terms, it is to expose how the political and the emotional/spiritual are deeply entangled. As Baldwin put it: "It can be objected that I am speaking of political freedom in spiritual terms, but the political institutions of any nation are always menaced and are ultimately controlled by the spiritual state of the nation."[24]

And since the architects of this nation chose love as one of the categories with which to design white supremacy, then, it is wise to consider love's deleterious public applications in the founding of this republic, as well as love's insurrectionary role during the Civil Rights Movement. In the extraordinary poem "Middle Passage," Robert Hayden says the American experience begins with a "voyage whose chartings are unlove."[25] Perhaps *The Fire Next Time* was Baldwin's attempt to change course, even embark on a new journey whose chartings this time could be love.

Love Is Where You Find It

Leap with me to 1987, to the publication of "To Crush a Serpent," the year that Baldwin died. Originally published in *Playboy* magazine in January 1987 and anthologized in *The Cross of Redemption: Uncollected Writings* in 2010, this short essay is a gem, illustrative of Baldwin's late style – a distinguishing feature of which is the unflinching characterization of the author's sexuality.[26] Thematically, a signal difference between Baldwin's novels and his essays is that while the question of queer sexuality is central to the former enterprise, it is negligible to the latter. Only two early book reviews, "The Preservation of Innocence" (1949) and "The Male Prison" (1951), make it a focus; and, when he broaches his own sexuality in *No Name in the Street* (1972) it is in very fraught passages, including a distressing reply to Eldridge Cleaver's homophobic attack against him. It is only in the late essays "Freaks and the American Ideal of Manhood" (1985) and "To Crush a Serpent" (1987) that Baldwin uses his signature genre to explore his sexual coming of age, revealing the close imbrication of sexuality, race, and religion in American life.

Why does Baldwin wait until the end of his career to emplot his sexuality in the essay form? Not a negligible fact for a writer who redefined the personal essay. Why revise a steadfast position, one that he maintained in many interviews, that his sexuality was a private matter not a public subject? For instance, when asked about it in 1970 in Sedat Pakay's lyrical short film, *James Baldwin: From Another Place*, he responds (visibly annoyed):

> I don't really know how to answer that question. In the first place, I don't exactly resent it, but I don't feel it's somebody's business whatever goes on in anybody's bedroom. But in my own case I can see that it's a very big issue for a lot of people. I don't know, I have a certain Puritan thing about two things – a certain kind of privacy, which is everybody's right, certainly mine, a certain kind of pride.[27]

How do we explain then this deliberate self-breach of privacy and pride in the late essays? Does it matter that Baldwin had withdrawn from the kind of intense public life he led in the 1960s, and was no longer beholden to the role of the race man which was thrust upon him, and which he embraced, during the Civil Rights era? What about the rise of Black women authors and the renaissance of Black gay art in the 1980s, and the overall cultural ferment of that decade to think together questions of race, gender, and sexuality – did those events have any bearing on Baldwin's late works? Since a defining feature of the Baldwin essay is the way it leverages the author's personal experiences as text for collective reflection, this pivotal shift toward sexuality in the late essays is noteworthy and merits close consideration.

With these questions in mind, I want to read "To Crush a Serpent" as a late sequel to the second epistle of *The Fire Next Time*, "Down at the Cross." Both essays relay the story of Baldwin's adolescent years in the ministry, a kinship reflected in their opening lines. "Down at the Cross" begins:

> I underwent, during the summer that I became fourteen, a prolonged religious crisis. I use the word "religious" in the common, and arbitrary, sense, meaning that I then discovered God, His saints and angels, and His blazing Hell. And since I had been born in a Christian nation, I accepted this Deity as the only one. I supposed Him to exist only within the walls of a church – in fact, of *our* church – and I also supposed that God and safety were synonymous. The word "safety" brings us to the real meaning of the word "religious" as we use it. Therefore, to state it in another, more accurate way, I became, during my fourteenth year, for the first time in my life, afraid – afraid of the evil within me and afraid of the evil without.[28]

And in "To Crush a Serpent":

> I was a young evangelist, preaching in Harlem and other black communities for about three years: "young" means adolescent. I was fourteen when I entered the pulpit and seventeen when I left. Those were very crucial

years, full of wonder, and one of the things I most wondered about was the fellowship of Christians in the United States of America.[29]

These initial words set the narrative slant for both essays, as explorations of the collision of adolescence and faith in the author's life, and, we anticipate, the collusion of race and religion in American Christianity. But while "Down at the Cross" goes on to cast this collision and collusion as a religious and racial coming-of-age story, "To Crush a Serpent" recasts it also as one of sexual awakening, focusing on the feelings of an adolescent boy coming to physical and sexual maturity at the same time he was a minister of the faith. We might say, "Down at the Cross" reckons with the young Baldwin's fear of the "evil without," but says very little about the "evil within" that was also the source of his adolescent fear; that is, the internal turmoil that fed "his prolonged religious crisis" is barely discussed in *Fire*, whereas it is fully fleshed out in "To Crush a Serpent."

Early on in "To Crush a Serpent," Baldwin frames the essay with a key (re)definition of adolescence:

> Adolescence, as white people in this country appear to be beginning to remember – in somewhat vindictive ways – is not the most tranquil passage in anybody's life. It is a virgin time, *the* virgin time, the beginning of the confirmation of oneself as *other*. Until adolescence, one is a boy or a girl. But adolescence means that one is becoming *male* or *female*, a far more devastating and impenetrable prospect.
>
> Until adolescence, one's body is simply there, like one's shadow or the weather. With adolescence, this body becomes a malevolently unpredictable enemy, and it also becomes, for the first time, appallingly *visible*. Everybody sees it. *You* see it, though you have never taken any real notice of it before. You begin to hear it. And it begins to sprout odors, like airy invisible mushrooms. But this is not the worst. Other people also see it and hear it and smell it. You can scarcely guess what they see and hear and smell – can guess it dimly, only from the way they appear to respond to you.[30]

There is such a compression of language and ideas in this prose. Baldwin's definition begins with a space-clearing gesture, negating an American grammar of adolescence tethered to white innocence. Severed from its racial meaning, adolescence is then redefined in positive form as "*the* virgin time," which Baldwin characterizes as a time of both innocence and profound rupture: a rupture that is cognitive ("the confirmation of oneself as *other*"); social ("becoming *male* or *female*"); and physical ("this body becomes a malevolently unpredictable enemy"). Notice Baldwin's use of the word "virgin" as an adjective to modify time that is in radical flux, not as a noun to mark a static state of being; a choice word also in the context of defining adolescence because unlike its proxies (innocence, purity, naïveté) its sphere of activity is the flesh. Notice, too, the economy with which he captures the cognitive, social, and physical dissonance of adolescence. To begin to see oneself as "other" is a rupture from how one had previously introjected the external world; also, a reflection of one's conscription into a world fastidious about enforcing social categories. The word "other" is double-edged, of course, descriptive and prescriptive: as a descriptive category it may indicate individual difference, a way of distinguishing oneself from another; but as a prescriptive category, "other" is an instrument of power, a way of reifying a hierarchy of social difference (for instance, within a discourse of race, we say "other" to stipulate nonwhite). Moreover, the shift from boy to male and girl to female indexes not merely physical change, but the hardening of prescribed gender roles, as Baldwin stresses, "a far more devastating and impenetrable prospect." Then, there is the body itself, also witnessing a metamorphosis, becoming (to itself and to others) visible, audible, redolent, physically and sexually woke. Baldwin is right: Going through these extraordinary changes "is not the most tranquil passage in anybody's life."

Having to reconcile one's inner sexual awakening with the rigid expectations of the outside world is hard enough for any adolescent, let alone a teen preacher. After outlining the general parameters of adolescence, Baldwin fills in the details of how the onset of these changes fueled his evangelism. He writes:

> It is not the best moment to be standing in the pulpit. Though, having said that, I must – to be honest – add that my ministry almost certainly helped me through my adolescence by giving me something larger than myself to be frightened about. And it preserved, as it were, an innocence that, in retrospect, protected me.
>
> For, though I had been formed by sufficiently dire circumstance and moved in a severely circumscribed world, I was also just another curious, raunchy kid. I was able to see, later, watching other kids like the kid I had been, that this combination of innocence and eagerness can be a powerful aphrodisiac to adults and is perhaps the key to the young minister's force.
>
> Or, more probably, only one of many keys. Certainly the depth of his belief is a mighty force; and when I was in the pulpit, I believed. The personal anguish counts for something, too: it was the personal anguish that made me believe that I believed. People do not know on what this anguish feeds, but they sense the anguish and they respond to it.[31]

What's striking about Baldwin's characterization of his ministry in "To Crush a Serpent" is the revelation of how desire mediated his personal faith as well as his relationship with his congregation. On the one hand, his ministry helped to ease the terrors of adolescence, since there were otherworldly terrors to preoccupy the young believer and preacher. "When I was in the pulpit, I believed," says Baldwin, a belief deeply shaped by a hermeneutics of biblical literalism Pentecostalism espouses. We can suppose for Baldwin the evangelist that Hell's eternal fire was not a metaphor but a literal, inextinguishable blaze that awaited the wicked, unrepentant soul; and, the awe and reverence with which he held God was equally matched by the fear of His wrath. Imagine: the vision of the Apocalypse can strike terror in even the adult skeptic and non-believer, to say nothing of the young who cling to faith blindly; the end times as near and proximate, a doctrine so prized in evangelical Christianity, is a real and terrifying prospect, and for the adolescent evangelist preacher we might imagine he felt it was easier to mortify the flesh to gain salvation than be concupiscent and face damnation.

We glean from these passages that as a believer the combination of adolescent and religious innocence informed Baldwin's blind faith, while, on the other hand, as a preacher the "combination of innocence and eagerness" imbued the rapport with his flock. After all, says Baldwin, however sanctified, he was "just another curious, raunchy kid," and it was this confluence of sexual chastity and keen carnal appetite that the young possess, and that adults covet in the young ("a powerful aphrodisiac," Baldwin calls it), which helped to charge his ministry.

During his adolescent years, Baldwin tells us:

> I was in love with my friend, as boys indeed can be at that age, but hadn't the faintest notion of what to do about it – not even in my imagination, which may suggest that the imagination is kicked off by memory. Or perhaps I simply refused to allow my imagination to wander, as it were, below the belt.
>
> Judging from my experience, I think that all of the kids in the church were like that, which is certainly why a couple of us went mad. Others simply backslid – went "back into the world." One relentless and realistic matron, a widow, determined to keep her eighteen-year-old athlete in the flock, in the pulpit, and in his right mind, took him South and found him a bride and brought the son and the girl – who scarcely knew each other – back home. The entire operation could not have taken more than a week.
>
> We went to see the groom one morning, and as we left, my friend yelled, "Don't do anything we wouldn't do!"
>
> The groom responded, with a lewd grin, "You all better not be doing what I'm doing!"
>
> Which suggests that we endured out repression with a certain good humor, at least for a time.[32]

Spelling out the source of his anguish further, Baldwin explains the signal role that desire and sexuality played in initiating his vocation as a preacher and in bringing it to a close:

> My sexuality was on hold, for both women and men had tried to "mess" with me in the summer of my fourteenth year and had frightened me so badly that I found the Lord. The salvation I was preaching to others was fueled by the hope of my own.
>
> I left the pulpit upon the realization that *my* salvation could not be achieved that way.
>
> But it is worth stating this proposition in somewhat harsher terms.
>
> An unmanageable distress had driven me to the altar, and once there, I was – at least for a while – cleansed. But at the same time, nothing had been obliterated: I was still a boy in trouble with himself and the streets around him. Salvation did not make time stand still or arrest the changes occurring in my body and my mind. Salvation did not change the fact that I was an eager sexual potential, in flight from the inevitable touch. And I knew that I was in flight, though I could not, then – *to save my soul* – have told you from what I was fleeing.[33]

These are remarkable paragraphs, for they make clear – for the first time in Baldwin's writing – that what compelled him to devote his life to God was a deep sense of fear that accompanied his sexual coming of age: a fear prompted by the experience of being a sexual target as well as the recognition of oneself as a sexual subject; and also a fear compounded by a Christian belief warning the high price to be paid for the sins of the flesh. Baldwin sought refuge from this fear in his ministry and, however temporary, found relief there; and the salvation he sought and preached were intimately connected to this collision between faith and desire. For a time, his sins were cleansed, but his fears remained, and it is the recognition of this contradiction – that matters of the flesh cannot be resolved in evangelical terms – that prompts Baldwin to leave the pulpit.

It is important to recall here the particular reason Baldwin gives in "Down at the Cross" for leaving the Church. He writes in 1963: "I date it – the slow crumbling of my faith, the pulverization of my fortress – from the time, about a year after I had begun to preach, when I began to read again. I justified this desire by the fact that I was still in school, and I began, fatally, with Dostoyevsky."[34] And in "To Crush a Serpent," in 1987:

> So, in time, a heavy weight fell on my heart. I did not want to become a liar. I did not want my love to become manipulation. I did not want my fear of my own desires to transform itself into power – into power, precisely, over those who feared and were therefore at the mercy of their own desires . . . In

my experience, the minister and his flock mirror each other. It demands a very rare, intrepid, and genuinely free and loving shepherd to challenge the habits and fears and assumptions of his flock and help them enter the freedom that enables us to move to higher ground. I was not that shepherd. And rather than betray the ministry, I left it.[35]

Reading is our gateway to the largeness and complexity of the world, and I am sure it helped to ungate the young Baldwin's narrow worldview. That said, as "To Crush a Serpent" belies, his apostasy entailed more than reading Dostoyevsky; it required a personal confrontation with the fear of his own desires, a fear he did not want to exploit in the service of his teaching nor in serving his congregation. While "Down at the Cross" repeatedly stresses fear as a governing force behind Baldwin's short-lived ministry – for example, "That was the most frightening time of my life, and quite the most dishonest, and the resulting hysteria lent great passion to my sermons – for a while" – it does not explain what fueled this fear, much less why Baldwin deems the years of his ministry "the most dishonest."[36]

I asked earlier: Why does Baldwin wait until the end of his career to emplot his sexuality in the essay form? In answering this question, I want to take heed of first the historical context in which this late essay appeared, and how that context alters the terms of the Baldwin essay. Reagan's America saw the rise of the religious right as a powerful arm of politics and public policy in the 1980s. The Moral Majority reigned, for instance, by making homosexuality and the gay rights movement a principal issue and target. As the Reverend Jerry Falwell, the founder of the Moral Majority, put it in 1981: "I refuse to stop speaking out against the sin of homosexuality ... I believe that the mass of homosexual revolution is always a symptom of a nation coming under the judgment of God."[37] And, a few years later, as thousands of his fellow citizens (many of whom were fellow Christians) suffered and perished from AIDS, then widely considered "a gay disease," he said: "AIDS is not just God's punishment for homosexuals; it is God's punishment for the society that tolerates homosexuals."[38] A cadre of religious-political moralizers like Falwell and Pat Robertson amplified such hateful sentiments, and the rhetoric of political demonology that they employed would have devastating consequences, not only in ginning up support for anti-gay laws and public policies, but also in compounding the AIDS crisis into a mass catastrophe. The public demonization of queer people and queer resistance to that demonization in the 1980s during the early era of AIDS hence put the question of sexuality center stage in American cultural and political life unlike at any other prior time.[39]

"To Crush a Serpent" comes out of this new historical and discursive context. And like the best Baldwin essays, which use the author's personal story to reflect on a pressing moral and political crisis, it characterizes the author's private life alongside a public debate around sexual identity that raged in the 1980s. Indeed, the essay recollects the collision of faith and desire during Baldwin's adolescence in as much as it confronts the homophobia and moral bankruptcy of "the present-day gang that calls itself the Moral Majority or its tongue-speaking relatives, such as follow the Right Reverend Robertson."[40] As in "Down at the Cross," Baldwin's critique of religion in the 1980s has a depth of perception afforded perhaps only to an ex-minister. But while "Down at the Cross" only reveals the entanglement of race and religion in both the author's and American life, "To Crush a Serpent" also threads in sexuality, giving the Baldwin essay a new analytic scope and critical texture. Since the essay is the medium in which Baldwin assumed the role of the public intellectual, it is not surprising that he focuses on sexuality in his 1980s essays at a time when sexual identity became a matter of fierce public debate and, indeed, a matter of life and death. In other words, I read his late turn toward sexuality in his late essays in part as a matter of the time, as the result of a new discursive, cultural, and political context that emerged in the 1980s, one in which Baldwin the public intellectual is called upon to reflect on not just racial but also sexual identity.

Personal context matters, too. Although he remained an indispensable public intellectual, in the 1980s Baldwin was no longer the race man of the Civil Rights Movement, and no more beholden to the heteronormative trappings of that role. As Dwight McBride rightly observes, as a spokesman of the race during the 1960s, Baldwin would employ a heteronormative rhetoric that effaced his sexuality. As one example: in 1968 on the Dick Cavett show, speaking to white liberal America, Baldwin says: "You want me to make an act of faith risking myself, my wife, my woman, my sister, my children on some idealism which you assure me exists in America which I have never seen?"[41] McBride argues that in words like these:

> when Baldwin affects the position of race man, part of the performance includes the masking of his specificity, his sexuality, his difference. And in race discourse, when all difference is concealed, what emerges is the heterosexual Black man "risking [himself], [his] wife, [his] woman and [his] children." The image of the Black man as protector, progenitor, and defender of the race is what Baldwin assumes here. The truth of this rhetorical transformation is that in order to be a representative race man, one must be heterosexual and male.[42]

And, moreover, as Henry Louis Gates, Jr., Douglas Field, and others have persuasively argued, by the late 1960s Baldwin's sexuality had become the focus of Black nationalist vitriol and a liability to his public role as a race man. As Gates puts it: "A new generation, so it seemed, was determined to define itself by everything Baldwin was *not*. By the late 1960s, Baldwin-bashing was almost a rite of initiation."[43]

One notorious example of such bashing is Eldridge Cleaver's *Soul on Ice*, which uses (hetero)sexuality as the criterion with which to dispossess Baldwin, and by extension "the black homosexual," of the authority of collective representation vested in the race man. Cleaver claims that Baldwin is unfit to represent the race because there is in his work "the most grueling, agonizing, total hatred of the blacks, particularly of himself, and the most shameful, fanatical, fawning, sycophantic love of the whites that one can find in the writings of any black American writer of note in our time."[44] And, according to Cleaver, this hatred of self and of a larger Black collective, and the fawning love of white people, is rooted in Baldwin's homosexuality:

> The case of James Baldwin aside for a moment, it seems that many Negro homosexuals, acquiescing in this racial death-wish, are outraged and frustrated because in their sickness they are unable to have a baby by a white man. [...]
>
> The black homosexual, when his twist has a racial nexus, is an extreme embodiment of this contradiction. The white man has deprived him of his masculinity, castrated him in the center of his burning skull, and when he submits to this change and takes the white man for his lover as well as Big Daddy, he focuses on "whiteness" all the love in his pent up soul and turns the razor edge of hatred against "blackness" – upon himself, what he is, and all those who look like him, remind him of himself. He may even hate the darkness of the night.
>
> The racial death-wish is manifested as the driving force in James Baldwin. His hatred for blacks, even as he pleads what he conceives as their cause, makes him the apotheosis of the dilemma in the ethos of the black bourgeoisie who have completely rejected their African heritage, consider the loss irrevocable, and refuse to look again in that direction.[45]

In Cleaver's opinion, "the black homosexual" is a contradiction in terms, since Blackness is a sign of hetero-masculinity and homosexuality one of emasculation; that is, to be a Black homosexual is to cancel out the very properties constitutive of Blackness, to "completely reject" one's Africanity, which Cleaver configures as *essentially* heteronormative. Therefore, such an essentially compromised figure as Baldwin as a Black homosexual – full of Black self-loathing, in total submission to white power, and driven by a "racial death-wish" – does not have the faculty nor the credibility to represent himself, let alone a Black collective yearning and working for self-determination and empowerment.

What I find surprising, and distressing, is not Cleaver's tirade and its essentialist and heteronormative assumptions, but Baldwin's response to it in *No Name in the Street*, which excuses Cleaver's words and moreover adopts a heterosexist idiom to debase other sexual minorities. Writes Baldwin:

> I was very much impressed with Eldridge, too – it's impossible not to be impressed by him – but I felt a certain constraint between us. I felt that he didn't like me – or not exactly that: that he considered me a rather doubtful quantity. I am used to this, though I can't claim to like it. I knew he'd written about me in *Soul On Ice*, but I hadn't yet read it. Naturally, when I did read it, I didn't like what he had to say about me at all. But, eventually – especially as I admired the book, and felt him to be valuable and rare – I thought I could see why he felt impelled to issue what was, in fact, a warning: he was being a zealous watchman on the city wall, and I do not say that with a sneer. He seemed to feel that I was a dangerously odd, badly twisted, and fragile reed, of too much use to the Establishment to be trusted by blacks. I felt that he used my public reputation against me both naively and unjustly, and I also felt that I was confused in his mind with the unutterable debasement of the male – with all those faggots, punks, and sissies, the sight and sound of whom, in prison, must have made him vomit more than once.[46]

As Field argues:

> [Baldwin's] justification of Cleaver's homophobia not only exonerates Cleaver, but complicity borrows from his former critic's vocabulary . . . By employing a rhetoric (faggots, punks, and sissies) that even the Black Panther Party had by then officially prohibited, Baldwin not only distinguishes his sexual preference from [an ostensibly] more deviant and degenerate behavior, but comes dangerously close to mimicking Cleaver's own homophobic diatribe.[47]

Indeed, I cannot think of another sentence in Baldwin's vast corpus, like the last one in the above passage, where he "others" in such a deliberately unethical way: where he explicitly renders others abject in order to bolster his own normative self-image. One of Baldwin's kernel truths about human affairs is that what one says about another reveals the addresser more so than it does the addressee – why he insisted, for instance, that white people's characterization of Black Americans hardly described the latter but reflected the former's self-projections. As he put it memorably in the 1963 documentary, *Take This Hammer*:

> Anyone who's tried to live knows this: That what you say about anyone else reveals you. What I think of you as being is dictated by my own necessities, my own psychology, my own fears and desires. I'm not describing you when I talk about you, I'm describing me. Now, here in this country, we've got something called a nigger. We have invented the nigger. I didn't invent him. White people invented him. I've always known, I had to know by the time I was seventeen years old, what you were describing was not me, and what you were afraid of was not me. It has to be something else, something you were afraid of you invested me with.[48]

By this measure, *all those faggots, punks, and sissies* whom Baldwin debases are but a projection of the author's anxieties about his own sexuality and gender embodiment: they are *his* inventions, a group he invests with abject meaning. For a dialectical writer like Baldwin, to other others – for any personal gain – is a betrayal of the self; and, in this instance, it is also a betrayal of the core principle of love that he had articulated in *Fire* (that "love takes off the masks we fear we cannot live without and know we cannot live within") and of his principle for leaving the pulpit ("I did not want my fear of my own desires to transform itself into power – into power, precisely, over those who feared and were therefore at the mercy of their own desires"). Wisdom I have learned from Baldwin – and indeed, what has allowed me to think of myself as a self-avowed faggot, punk, and sissy – is that the image of the "other" is a reflection of the self I must embrace, not estrange.

In his essays, Baldwin's reticence (and sudden outburst of invective in *No Name*) about sexuality was a result of both external and internal pressures. It cannot be an easy thing for everybody – from the FBI to *Time* magazine, from John F. Kennedy to Eldridge Cleaver – to make your sexuality a point of ridicule and use it to cast a pall of animus over your brilliant existence. I read Baldwin's reticence, then, as a reflection of a constricted and inimical public sphere and discourse that not only saw race and sexuality in mutually exclusive terms, but moreover used the author's queer sexuality to tarnish his public reputation and to make him feel ashamed. I also read his reticence as a reflection of his own limited sense of sexuality as a private matter and of an uncritical allegiance to Black manhood; and, furthermore, as a silent acquiescence to the widespread homophobia leveled against him. These external and internal pressures vis-à-vis sexuality, which informed his essays of the 1960s, would give way by the 1980s, however; and Baldwin's earlier view of sexuality as a mere private matter (as "whatever goes on in anybody's bedroom") would significantly change later to show how sexuality plays a pivotal role in defining a sense of the self, and how sexuality and race inform our lives not as discrete experiences but as mutually reinforcing ones.

To be sure, as he was of the nation's racial categories, Baldwin was deeply suspicious of the extant categorization of sexuality into "homosexual," "gay," or "queer" to sum up the range of human desire and sexual identity.[49] Nonetheless, there is a striking shift in Baldwin's late essays, a deliberate use of sexuality as a key analytic and heuristic. As he says emphatically in 1985 in "Freaks and the American Ideal of Manhood": "The idea of one's sexuality can only with great violence be divorced or distanced from the idea of the self."[50]

Baldwin closes out "To Crush a Serpent" with this observation of 1980s America: "what we are watching with Falwells and Robertsons is an attempt to exorcise ourselves. This demands, indeed, a simple-mindedness quite beyond the possibilities of the human being. Complexity is our only safety and love is the only key to our maturity. And love is where you find it."[51] The love we find in Baldwin's late essay embraces the flesh as a source of knowledge and possibility, not as a source of fear or a sin to be exorcised or a figure to be effaced. The unmasked love that Baldwin defines in *Fire* comes into sharper relief in late life, as Baldwin confronts the "fear within" that informed his private anguish and public ministry, and summons his philosophy of love to reject the religious right's "attack on the sexual possibility." And while "To Crush a Serpent" intervenes in a crucial debate of the 1980s, it also amends the past, casting a retrospective eye that now imbues Baldwin's iconic 1960s text with a new queer possibility as well as a new realization of love – a realization, a depth of perception, which comes perhaps only with age. Not only is love the key to maturity; love is the maturity where we find what is key.

Notes

1. Fontaine and Hartley (1982).
2. Baldwin (1993 [1963]), 95.
3. Ibid., 21.
4. Ibid., 5–6.
5. Ibid., 30.

6. Ibid., 105.
7. Ibid., 22.
8. Ibid., 6–7.
9. Ibid., 8.
10. Ibid., 9–10.
11. Ibid., 81–82.
12. Ibid., 24, 29, and 37, respectively.
13. Ibid., 31.
14. Ibid., 47.
15. Jefferson (1997), 99–100.
16. Ibid., 98.
17. Gates (2016), 27.
18. Ibid., 28.
19. In a lecture recalling the Civil Rights Movement, Baldwin (1979) says: "I am a witness to and a survivor of the latest slave rebellion." A recording of the lecture is available online: www.c-span.org/video/?170651-1/james-baldwin-speech [accessed October 9, 2021].
20. King (1991), 13.
21. Arendt (1958), 242.
22. Ibid., 52.
23. Ibid., 242.
24. Baldwin (1993), 89.
25. Hayden (1985), 51.
26. Baldwin (2010), 158–65.
27. Pakay (1973).
28. Baldwin (1993), 15–16.
29. Baldwin (2010), 158.
30. Ibid., 159.
31. Ibid., 159–60.
32. Ibid., 163.
33. Ibid., 160.
34. Baldwin (1993), 34.
35. Baldwin (2010), 160.
36. Baldwin (1993), 32.
37. Quoted in Smillie (2008), s95.
38. Quoted in McElvaine (2008), 35.
39. On the role AIDS played in reshaping the discourse around sexuality in American culture, see Woubshet (2015).
40. Baldwin (2010), 161.
41. The Dick Cavett Show was aired on June 13, 1968.
42. McBride (2005), 46.
43. Gates (1998), 12.
44. Cleaver (1968), 124.
45. Ibid., 127–29.
46. Baldwin (1985b), 539–40.

47. Field (2004), 469.
48. Moore (1963).
49. For an incisive interview, in which Baldwin challenges these terms, see Baldwin (1989), 173–85.
50. Baldwin (1985a), 678.
51. Baldwin (2010), 165.

References

Arendt, H. 1958. *The Human Condition.* University of Chicago Press.

Baldwin, J. 1979, January 15. Lecture delivered at the University of California, Berkeley. www.c-span.org/video/?170651-1/james-baldwin-speech

1985a. "Freaks and the American Ideal of Manhood," reprinted as "Here Be Dragons." In *The Price of the Ticket: Collected Nonfiction, 1948–1985,* 677–90. New York: St. Martin's Press.

1985b. *No Name in the Street.* In *The Price of the Ticket: Collected Nonfiction, 1948–1985,* 539–40. New York: St. Martin's Press.

1989. "'Go the Way Your Blood Beats': An Interview with James Baldwin (1984)." In *James Baldwin: The Legacy,* ed. Q. Troupe, 173–85. New York: Touchstone.

1993 [1963]. *The Fire Next Time.* New York: Vintage.

2010. "To Crush a Serpent." In *The Cross of Redemption: Uncollected Writings,* ed. R. Kenan, 158–65. New York: Pantheon Books

Cleaver, E. 1968. *Soul on Ice.* New York: Delta.

Field, D. 2004. "Looking for Jimmy Baldwin: Sex, Privacy, and Black Nationalist Fervor." *Callaloo* 27.2 (Spring): 457–80.

Fontaine, D., and P. Hartley, dirs. 1982. *I Heard It Through the Grapevine.* Living Archives Inc.

Gates, H. L., Jr. 1998. *Thirteen Ways of Looking at a Black Man.* New York: Vintage.

2016. "Frederick Douglass's Camera Obscura." *Aperture* 223: 27–29.

Hayden, R. 1985. "Middle Passage." In *Robert Hayden: Collected Poems,* 51. New York: Liveright Publishing Corporation.

Jefferson, T. 1997. "The Difference Is Fixed in Nature." In *Race and the Enlightenment: A Reader,* ed. E. Chukwudi Eze, 99–100. Malden, MA: Blackwell.

King, M. L., Jr. 1991. "The Power of Nonviolence (1958)." In *A Testament of Hope: The Essential Writings and Speeches of Martin Luther King, Jr,* ed. J. M. Washington, 12–15. San Francisco: Harper.

McBride, D. 2005. *Why I Hate Abercrombie & Fitch: Essays on Race and Sexuality.* New York University Press.

McElvaine, R. S. 2008. *Grand Theft Jesus: The Hijacking of Religion in America.* New York: Three Rivers Press.

Moore, R. O., dir. 1963. *Take This Hammer.* KQED TV.

Pakay, S., dir. 1973. *James Baldwin: From Another Place*. Hudson Film Works.

Peck, R., dir. 2017. *I Am Not Your Negro*. Magnolia Pictures.

Smillie, D. 2008. *Falwell Inc.: Inside a Religious, Political, Educational, and Business Empire*. New York: St. Martin's Press.

Woubshet, D. 2015. *The Calendar of Loss: Race, Sexuality, and Mourning in the Early Era of AIDS*. Baltimore, MD: Johns Hopkins University Press.

CHAPTER 6

Albert Murray Beyond Plight and Blight

Paul C. Taylor

It is fitting that Albert Murray's landmark text, *The Omni-Americans*, appeared in 1970. The essays in that volume aim, in their way, to finish off one of the animating ideas of the 1960s as surely as the calendar brought the decade to a close. That decade stands out as a moment, as a period of time worthy of commemoration and exploration for a great many reasons, but chief among these is the rise of a distinctive approach to the politics of Black aesthetics and culture. Figures like Stokely Carmichael, Gwendolyn Brooks, James Baldwin, and Amiri Baraka insisted on linking the political and the cultural dimensions of Black life in the USA and beyond. They imagined the content and the politics of the Black Aesthetic in different ways, to be sure, but all insisted on treating the linkage between politics and culture as an essential way of responding to the persistent threat of Black oppression, self-doubt, and immiseration. Murray spends most of *The Omni-Americans* refusing and even ridiculing this approach to Black culture work. In the passage that informs the title of this chapter, he complains that an attempt at this sort of cultural politics during the interwar years had produced particularly untoward results. At that time, he points out: "Blackness as a cultural identity was all but replaced by blackness as an economic and political identity – or condition, plight, and blight."[1]

Murray was prepared to blame a great many culprits for what he regarded as an unfortunate effacement of culture by social condition. Social scientists routinely suffer his scorn, along with the gullible artists and journalists and others who in his view fell for the "social science fictions" that the likes of Kenneth Clark produced. But he's even more troubled by the writers, artists, and critics who accept these fictions, because in doing so they abdicate the special duties that accrue to the custodians of aesthetic experience. As Murray sees it, writers like Baldwin should know better than to hide the richness, vitality, and heroism of Black culture beneath the gloom of dire sociological analyses. Even worse, they should know better than to fetishize the Blackness of Black art and culture so completely as to obscure its broader human significance, its intimate connections to the wider American culture, and its debts to the life-affirming, order-imposing work of human experience as such.

In response to the naïve mix of particularism and pessimism that Murray found at the heart of the "plight and blight" school of the Black Aesthetic, *The Omni-Americans* offered a life-affirming concrete universalism rooted in the blues as a mode of phenomenology. Murray's modified Black aesthetic established a fully American Blackness as an instance and emblem of universal human experience, and animated his work for the rest of his career. By the 1980s, Murray's relationships with influential figures like Henry Louis Gates, Jr., and Wynton Marsalis led to the promulgation and enshrinement of his blues phenomenology in various elite cultural institutions. This public affirmation of an integrationist Black aesthetic, enacted in part through a tendentious reading and consequent refusal of Black particularism and pessimism, was a fitting reflection of the containment, exhaustion, and co-optation of 1960s liberationism in the 1970s and 1980s.

While this essay approaches Murray's work as a matter of refusal and rejection, it is impossible to think productively about his work without understanding the positive claims that animate it or the contexts that framed these claims. The next three sections will offer a short summary of these contexts and claims. The first will provide a brief sketch of Murray's life, the second will (swiftly) discuss the intellectual commitments he shared with his most important interlocutor, Ralph Ellison, and the third will explain what Murray did with these shared commitments to produce his own distinctive philosophical apparatus. The final section will then explore one consequence of what may be the clearest difference between Murray and Ellison: Murray's willingness to cultivate followers like Gates and Marsalis, pivotal culture workers in the post-Civil Rights shift in U.S. racial politics.

Murray's Intellectual Journey

Albert Murray created himself as a thinker and culture worker in a series of stages, and did so while drawing from an evolving store of resources and influences. During his early years, from 1916 to 1947, he developed an almost axiomatic sense of race pride, though he declined to think of it in those terms, and a presumptive commitment to an expressivist cultural pluralism. From 1947 to 1969, he refined his ideas through continued formal study and voracious informal study, with the latter including sustained conversations with figures like James Baldwin, Romare Bearden, and Ralph Ellison. In 1970, his mature thinking began to lift him to national prominence, as he began to publish his best-known books. And in 1987 his influence began to manifest itself in earnest in elite U.S. cultural institutions like Lincoln Center.

Murray was born in 1916 in Nokomis, Alabama. He received his secondary education at the segregated Mobile County Training School (MCTS) and his tertiary education at Tuskegee Institute, the celebrated historically Black college founded by Booker T. Washington. These schools inspired, nurtured, and informed his lifelong commitment to liberal and humanistic inquiry and learning, not least by cultivating the interest in art and literature that would eventually form the core of his intellectual life, and by introducing him to the philosophy of John Dewey, to which this discussion will return. They also enabled him to assume both the reality of Black excellence and community and the relationship between these phenomena and broader human strivings. These assumptions grounded Murray's intellectual journey while also making him forever skeptical of campaigns to raise Black self-esteem – because he couldn't imagine any need for them – or to separate Black achievement from broader human experience.

He speaks to this strand in his development in a telling passage from *South to a Very Old Place*, where he explains the approach adopted by his favorite teacher at Tuskegee (Morteza Drexel Sprague), as well as by the dominant figure at MCTS (Benjamin F. Baker). Sprague, he says:

> expected you to proceed in terms of the highest standards of formal scholarship among other things not because he wanted you to become a carbon copy of any white man who ever lived, not excepting Shakespeare or even Leonardo da Vinci. But because to him you were the very special vehicle through which contemporary man, and not just contemporary black man either, would inherit the experience and insights of all recorded or decipherable time. Because to him (as to everybody else on that all-black faculty) your political commitment to specific social causes of your own people went without saying.[2]

Murray graduated from Tuskegee with a degree in English in 1939. After spending a term as the principal of a junior high school in Georgia and another at the University of Michigan taking graduate courses in education, he returned to Tuskegee to teach English. In 1943 he joined the Army Air Corps (soon to become the Air Force), and completed his active service "at the Tuskegee Army Air Field where the 'Tuskegee Airmen' were being trained."[3]

Murray met Ellison during his active service, during a trip to New York City in 1942. But the "ongoing literary dialogue" with Ellison that would so profoundly shape the work of both men began in earnest in 1947.[4] The second phase of Murray's journey began in this year, not only because of the relationship with Ellison but also because Murray began working toward his MA in English at NYU. He later reported that it was while composing his thesis on T. S. Eliot and Ernest Hemingway that he first developed the insight that would become central to his later work: that the problematic that animated the blues also informed the more profound achievements in canonical Anglophone literature:[5]

> My master's thesis was a comparative study of *The Wasteland* and *The Sun Also Rises* . . . [W]hat I realized was that Hemingway's approach was much more profound than T. S. Eliot's . . . Hemingway's confrontation was more like the blues. Life is a low-down dirty shame that shouldn't happen to anyone – futility. All is futile. I appropriated that in my interpretation of the blues. You come back to this, and it's not nihilism, and it's not despair, and it's not hedonism. It's a sober recognition that you have so many bars, and the more you can make them swing, the better. Then when you're gone, it doesn't matter.[6]

After earning his degree in 1948 on the G.I. Bill, Murray traveled across Europe and North Africa, with much of this travel coming after he returned to active duty in the military in 1951. He met Baldwin in Paris, where he also began a long friendship and collaboration with the great painter Romare Bearden. He gave a series of unpublished lectures on jazz in Morocco, and published his first short story and nonfiction during this time. But perhaps his most impactful writing unfolded behind the scenes. During this time, he continued to work on the drafts that would eventually become the books of his mature period, and he continued his correspondence with Ellison, which both men used to affirm and advance their thinking. Murray retired from the Air Force in 1962 and moved to New York City, where he began to work in journalism and media as a writer, reviewer, and researcher.[7]

The third period in Murray's intellectual journey began with the publication of *The Omni-Americans* in 1970 and continued through his collaboration with Count Basie on the great bandleader's autobiography. During this time he published his most influential and best-known books, each in a different idiom. After the social-critical essays of *The Omni-Americans* came *South to a Very Old Place* (1971), an oddly dialogic travelogue and memoir that one commentator describes as "a kind of anti-travel book, in which observable facts [about the southern USA after segregation] are constantly eclipsed by the author's memories and associations";[8] *The*

Hero and the Blues (1973), an ambitious series of lectures laying out his core theoretical commitments; *Train Whistle Guitar* (1974), a novel; and *Stomping the Blues* (1976), "an idiosyncratic study in the history, aesthetics, rituals, and anthropology of jazz" that has since won a wide following among jazz critics.[9] His reputation and influence grew, earning him a number of awards, honorary degrees, visiting posts to teach and lecture, and institutional appointments. His circle of friends and interlocutors, which was always wide and diverse, grew to include figures like Robert Penn Warren, Stanley Crouch, Gary Giddins, Henry Louis Gates, Jr., and Wynton Marsalis.

   Good Morning Blues: The Autobiography of Count Basie as Told to Albert Murray appeared in 1986, and marks the transition to the last stage of Murray's career. At this point, Murray's status as a celebrated national figure was secure, as evidenced by the national media coverage for the Basie project book party, by a tribute at the Modern Language Association convention in the same year, and Murray's appearance in an episode of the PBS documentary, *The Story of English*. This lofty profile enabled him to pivot comfortably into the role of cultural influencer, as prominent figures like musician-composer Wynton Marsalis and writer Stanley Crouch eagerly presented themselves as Murray's students and as conduits for his ideas. In 1987, Murray joined Crouch, Marsalis, and others in launching the program that would eventually become Jazz at Lincoln Center (JALC). Marsalis became artistic director of the program, while Murray served actively on the board of directors from 1996 to 2005.[10] JALC would ride Marsalis' popularity to become perhaps the most influential – and controversial – arbiter of jazz excellence as the twentieth century drew to a close.

   Murray remained active during this last period almost until the end, though his lasting influence traces to the ideas he articulated most clearly in the third period writings, and that informed his tutelage of Marsalis, Crouch, and others. He was elected to the American Academy of Arts and Letters in 1997, appeared in Ken Burns' *Jazz* documentary series in 2001, continued to receive accolades and awards, and kept writing. His last piece of original writing, as opposed to collections of previously unreleased material, appeared in 2005 (when his last novel, *The Magic Keys*, appeared). He died in New York City in 2013.

An Aside and a Setting Aside: The Ellison Problem

Murray's rise to prominence since 1970 has crucially involved a slow journey out of the shadow of his better-known friend and interlocutor,

Ralph Ellison. By the time Murray's mature work began to appear, Ellison had firmly established himself in the U.S. literary pantheon. Ellison's first novel, *Invisible Man*, won the National Book Award in 1953 and cemented its author's reputation as one of the country's most incisive commentators on race, culture, and democratic politics. Ellison's much earlier arrival on the literary and cultural scene encouraged many early commentators to think of their relationship as that of mentor to pupil, or icon to epigone. But the documentary record – as revealed, for example, in the recently published volume of their collected correspondence, *Trading Twelves* – suggests a different picture. As Gates puts it:

> It was a great mistake to regard Murray simply as Ellison's sidekick, the way many people did, but he was without question the most fervent and articulate champion of Ellison's art. The two were, in a sense, part of a single project: few figures on the scene shared as many presuppositions and preoccupations as they did.[11]

The burden of this essay will be to clarify what Murray did with the presuppositions and preoccupations that he shared with Ellison. Their ideas are so closely aligned that there is considerable value in marking quite precisely just where they diverge from each other, preferably by comparing their different ways of proceeding from similar starting points: but limitations of space prevent that from being the work of this piece. The aim here will be to offer a generalized picture of the philosophical dimensions of the project as Murray developed it. The existence and easy availability of a vast literature on Ellison, especially the precincts of it that follow Ross Posnock in reading Ellison against the American pragmatist tradition, should be sufficient compensation for setting Ellison's work aside here.

Murray's Theory and Its Apparatus; or, "Cosmos Murray"

Murray's intellectual ambitions were lofty, as evidenced by his willingness to refer to the constellation of intellectual commitments he developed as "Cosmos Murray."[12] The "cosmic" dimension of this project derived from its reliance on quite general philosophical principles that committed him to definite accounts of the workings of culture as such, experience as such, and much more, all in the same fully general spirit. But the real purchase of this project derived from the way it turned these general principles into a theory of society and culture that aimed specifically to illuminate the promise and perils of U.S. social arrangements and cultural practices.

Radical Empiricism, Social Science Fiction, Folklore, and Fakelore

The first philosophical commitment at the core of Cosmos Murray is an abiding radical empiricism. Put very crudely, though as carefully as the space allotted to this essay allows, to endorse this view is to insist that human experience is richer than the more common and narrower empiricisms typically allow. Attending properly to this greater richness means accepting that scientific generalizations – or, better, any judgments that aspire to the condition of knowledge – have at least two important limitations.

First, epistemic judgments can't capture everything that makes experience matter for us. Dewey's way of making this point often involved the reminder that knowing is one way to experience something, but not the only or always the best way. This was most saliently for him a way of insisting on the value and validity of aesthetic experience, *pace* the dismissiveness with which Western philosophers (he argued) sometimes subordinated art and the aesthetic to science, knowing, and the (narrowly) empirical.

The second limitation of epistemic judgments is that they tend to have trouble accommodating dynamism, both in the world and in human attempts to engage the world productively. This is in part a point about the continual human quest for epistemic progress, and about the need to prepare for the possibility that ongoing inquiry will reveal the inadequacy of today's best ideas about how things are. But the deeper point is that epistemic judgments are context-specific and therefore reductive, which means that they necessarily, by design, for the sake of expediency, exclude considerations that might in other contexts prove essential.

The radical empiricist tendencies in the Ellison-Murray project come through most clearly in complaints about reductive generalizations and in appeals to the necessity of art in managing the complexity of experience. Murray's complaints in this spirit often pertain to the limits of what he calls "social science fiction." He is careful to make clear that his target is not social science as such: the problem is that "most social science survey findings are not scientific enough," beholden as they are to *a priori* myths and images of Black life that obscure the evidence that responsible inquirers would gather and analyze. Still, the problem is widespread enough that "[t]he bias of *The Omni-Americans* is distinctly proliterary." His explanation for this bias clearly draws on the radical empiricist commitment discussed above: "the counter-formulations posed in [the book] ... are submitted as antidotes against the pernicious effects of a technological enthusiasm inadequately counter-balanced by a literary sense of the ambiguities and absurdities inherent in all human experience."[13]

The Omni-Americans, in particular, is shot through with these complaints. A subsection of one chapter, entitled "White Norms for Black Deviation," focuses on the social scientists themselves, including the two figures who emerged from the 1960s as perhaps the most obvious targets, in the eyes of many, for this sort of complaint: Daniel Patrick Moynihan and Kenneth Clark. Another chapter, entitled "A Clutch of Social Science Fiction Fiction," takes William Styron and two lesser-known novelists to task for managing to "mistake the illusions of social science for actuality." Richard Wright receives the same treatment later in the book, but perhaps the worst offender in Murray's eyes is James Baldwin. "[W]hat Baldwin writes about," Murray claims, "is not really life in Harlem. He writes about the ... material *plight* of Harlem."[14]

For Murray, Baldwin's problem has to do with a failure of literary craft, specifically in relation to the writer's obligation to experience. Baldwin's fiction, Murray explains:

> reflects very little of the rich, complex, and ambivalent sensibility of the novelist, very little indeed, no more than does the polemical essay *The Fire Next Time*. What it actually reflects ... is the author's involvement with oversimplified library and laboratory theories and conjectures about the negative effects of racial oppression.[15]

Murray goes on to point out many of the features of Harlem life, of Harlem *Negro* life, that Baldwin speeds by. Then he pithily sums up the meaning of these oversights. Baldwin, he says, "writes as if he had never heard the comedians at the Apollo Theatre. Life in Harlem is the very stuff of romance and fiction, even as was life in Chaucer's England."[16]

The most obvious problem with social science fiction is that it gets the world of human experience wrong, especially in relation to Black people. But this is a reflection of at least two deeper problems that Murray is keen to point out. In addition to producing specific errors about particular ways of experiencing the world, these "fictions" belong to structures of meaning and practice that systematically promote error and severely constrain the possibilities for experience as such.

Murray often discusses the mechanisms for routinely producing ignorance in terms of "the folklore of white supremacy" and "the fakelore of black pathology." These are his names for what scholars now call "epistemologies of ignorance," or the epistemic and discursive mechanisms that systematically distort or block knowledge of U.S. racial matters (and much else). In discussing racial folklore and "fakelore," Murray was most interested in structures that promote "the systematic oversimplification of black tribulations," and that allow the population that benefits from white supremacy to "create the impression that it deserves to be where it is."[17] These are in effect two sides of the same coin, as the ideologies that establish the normativity of whiteness also create the conditions for marking Blackness as deviant.

As one might expect based on Murray's complaints about Baldwin and Wright, *The Omni-Americans* reserves special scorn for Black people who peddle "fakelore" in the name of Black liberation or advancement. On Murray's reading of Kenneth Clark's *Dark Ghetto*, for example, Clark "insists that slavery and oppression have reduced Negroes to such a tangle of pathology that all black American behavior is in effect only a pathetic manifestation of black cowardice, self-hatred, escapism, and self-destructiveness." For Clark, as for Baldwin, "Harlem is ... an urban pit writhing with derelicts" who are ill prepared for the demands of white civilization.[18]

Heroic Experimentalism and the Acceptance Frame

If the first layer beneath the problem of social science fiction is the epistemology of ignorance that sustains it, then the second is the phenomenology of despair that frames it. Producing errors of fact is bad enough; producing them routinely, even systematically, is even worse. But misrepresenting experience *itself*, reducing it to something that, for some people at least, simply *cannot* involve beauty, joy, or heroism, is a rather different, and in some sense deeper, problem. In this spirit, Murray complains about the "wailing wall polemicists" who read the African American tradition in much the way shortsighted observers view Jewish life. After reporting Baldwin's claim that "a tradition expresses, after all, nothing more than the long and painful experience of a people," and that "[w]hen we speak of the Jewish tradition we are speaking of centuries of exile and persecution,"[19] Murray explains:

> A tradition involves *much more* than the long and painful experiences of a people. The modern Jewish tradition, which someone has referred to as an instantly erectible wailing wall, may well represent centuries of exile and persecution, but it also represents much more. As did the ancient Greek and Roman traditions. As do the modern French and English traditions.[20]

Murray continues his assault on Clark in the same spirit. After reporting Gunnar Myrdal's description of *Dark Ghetto* as a book animated by the determination to reveal "the ugly facts of life in the Negro ghetto," Murray complains that this approach "implies that *ugly* facts are more important and more useful than *plain* or even *beautiful* facts, not to mention *comprehensive* facts."[21]

This existential argument from the need for "beautiful facts" points to a vital level of significance in Murray's focus on the blues. The blues impulse, variously encoded in "Negro" practices of folk, popular, and fine art in various media, attests to the human capacity for imposing order on chaos and for doing so in aesthetically and existentially rich ways – that is, with style. To focus just on "ugly facts," in the manner of Baldwin, Wright, or Clark, is to ignore the rich capacity for creativity and heroic invention that "Negro" American culture epitomizes.

For Murray, the blues idiom's determination to embrace the beauty *and* the ugliness of experience embodies "an attitude toward the nature of human experience ... that is both elemental and comprehensive."[22] We might think of this attitude as a kind of heroic experimentalism, which holds that all human projects are flawed and at risk of disaster; but insists that this fact, rather than being cause for despair, simply sets the conditions for the exercise of heroic agency and the virtuous work of self-cultivation. This is the second philosophical principle underwriting Cosmos Murray.

Murray draws out this claim about the existential and phenomenological depth of the blues in a couple of key directions. Sometimes he leans toward the naturalist phenomenology of Deweyan pragmatism, which clearly hovers in the background of this passage from "The Blues as Statement" in *Stomping the Blues*:

> [The blues] is a statement about confronting the complexities inherent in the human situation and about improvising or experimenting or riffing or otherwise playing with ... such possibilities as are also inherent in the obstacles, the disjunctures, and the jeopardy. It is also a statement about perseverance and about resilience and thus also about the maintenance of equilibrium despite precarious circumstances and about achieving elegance in the very process of coping with the rudiments of subsistence.[23]

At other times, though, he draws on resources from literary and rhetorical theory, as when he borrows the opposition between an "acceptance frame" and a "rejection frame" from Kenneth Burke:

> Burke is discussing ... a disposition to accept the universe with all its problems or to protest against it, and in the category of Acceptance he ...

includes tragedy, comedy, humor, and the ode. What is accepted, of course, is not the status quo ... [but] the all too obvious fact that human existence is almost always a matter of endeavor and hence also a matter of heroic action. In the category of Rejection ... Burke places the plaint or elegy, satire, burlesque (plus such related forms as polemic and caricature) .... [W]hat is rejected by such statements of lamentation, protestation, and exaggeration is the very existence of the circumstances that make heroic endeavor necessary.[24]

Murray fleshes out the links between epic heroism and the blues in a variety of places, most obviously in *The Hero and the Blues*. But this passage from *Stomping the Blues* makes the point clearly and concisely:

There are those who regard blues music as a statement of rejection because to them it represents the very opposite of heroism. To many it represents only the anguished outcry of the victim, displaying his or her wounds and saying that it is all a lowdown dirty shame ... Blues music, however, is neither negative nor sentimental. It counterstates the torch singer's sob story ... What the customary blues-idiom dance movement reflects is a disposition to encounter obstacle after obstacle as a matter of course ... Indeed the improvisation on the break, which is required of blues-idiom musicians and dancers alike, is precisely what epic heroism is based on.[25]

Concrete Universalism and the Omni-American

Murray appeals to the blues in part to support his "counterstatement" to the phenomenology of despair that he finds in Baldwin, Clark, and many others. But he also makes this appeal in order to advance the claims in history, sociology, politics, and philosophical anthropology that underwrite both his partnership with Ellison and his argument in *The Omni-Americans*. Black culture, he wants to say, just is American culture; blues-derived or blues-resonant practices are at the heart of both; and this dynamic exchange of cultural practices just is how experience and culture work, and how these things have manifested themselves in the American context.

This insistence on the Americanness of Black culture points to the third philosophical principle behind Cosmos Murray, and points beyond it to the theory of society and culture that the principles jointly underwrite. This principle involves a kind of concrete universalism, and unfolds on three levels. One level has to do with the metaphysics of culture; a second has to do with the broad sociohistorical fact of racialization in modern cultures; and a third has to do with the narrower dynamics of racialization and identity formation in the specific context of U.S. national culture.

At the level of metaphysics, concrete universalism involves a commitment to the dependence of human universals on human particularity. The idea here is that while talk about human universals – truth, right, beauty, and the like – is commonplace and unobjectionable as far as it goes, there is a sense in which it doesn't go very far. This is because the only way to instantiate or encounter these universals is through the efforts of specific human individuals and the practices of concrete human cultures. All human cultures have music, for example, but the experience of music depends on the abstract capacity for musicking becoming manifest in particular sociocultural settings, through concrete and specific conventions for handling phenomena like rhythm, melody, and harmony. This way of thinking – perhaps most famously and infuriatingly worked out by Hegel, though in ways that made Dewey and Marx possible – reconciles the otherwise conflicting impulse to venerate humanity as such, while also celebrating particular parochial instantiations of the human – like the people Murray most often preferred to call "Negroes."

Bringing concrete universalism a trifle closer to the ground leads to a second level of significance that is specific to racialized contexts. Here, too, conflicting impulses are in play. On the one hand, in deference to the universal dimension of human strivings, one wants to say with Alain Locke that "cultures have no color": that the superficial markers of racial identity do not necessarily or neatly map onto the ability or right to participate in cultural practices. On the other hand, though, as a matter of contingent but concrete historical fact, modern cultures come into being and evolve under conditions that make racial markers meaningful, and that encourage members of certain racialized populations to make common cause and find community with each other.

Attending to the way racial dynamics play out in the setting that most concerns Murray leads to the third level of significance in his concrete universalism. He insisted that universal human strivings manifested themselves not in broadly racial practices, but in the historically specific practices of concrete societies shaped not just by racial dominance but also by narratives of national identity. He was most interested in the way this happened in U.S. society in particular, a society that for reasons internal to the accidents of its history produced cultural and political forms that rewarded sustained scrutiny.

The commitment to thinking the racial, the national, and the universal all at once is what led Murray to begin the mature phase of his work with his book *The Omni-Americans*. The book's core conceit, as announced in its title, signifies on the convention of signaling ethnoracial difference with hyphenated gestures at Americanness – Irish-American, African-American, and so on. But it subverts the convention by preempting the hyphen with a gesture at the universal, even as it insists on the national context – on the American character – of this preemption.

There is of course much else to grapple with in the book, and in the complex of ideas it announced to the world. There is, first of all, the fact that it uses "American" to mean something that the Spanish language names more effectively than English does: an *estadounidense*, or "United-States-er." And there is the additional fact that the rich combination of Indigenous, European, and African cultures that the book locates at the core of the Omni-American's identity turns out to be a matter largely of turning Africans into "Negroes" – "American blacks" – and creating the conditions for both complicating and reinforcing a Black-white binary. But the key consideration here is the way the book declares from the very beginning, in its title, the concrete universalist commitment to yoking the human, the racial, and the national together in a single conception of culture and identity.

This synthesis animates Murray's work in a variety of places. Consider, for example, this passage from a lecture late in his career, explaining to a group of college students the way he approached his work:

> I'm trying to deal with . . . the blues statement as a representative American anecdote: one little . . . image that encapsulates a whole lifestyle. On one level you're talking about American culture, American identity, American objectives; but you're always talking about human life . . . So, universality: something which is . . . valid for everybody . . . So, the writer tries to create images which . . . enable us to realize what we are doing here on this planet, to face chaos, to face nothingness, and whatnot. And my main metaphor comes out of the blues.[26]

This passage shows Murray toggling back and forth between a national frame, a universal perspective, and a racialized practice. The blues is all at once an American inheritance, a "Negro" creation, and an "adequate image" of universal human condition.

"Negro" Culturalism and/or Dialectical Integrationism

Murray's insistence on the blues as an adequate image of both American life and human experience is the centerpiece of his distinctive theory of society and culture. He combines heroic experimentalism, radical

empiricism, and concrete universalism into a contingent "Negro" culturalism. This view in turn entails a kind of dialectical integrationism that
may be the clearest takeaway from an encounter with Cosmos Murray.

"Negro culturalism" is an ugly name for what's left of cultural nationalism when a liberal but historicist individualism gets done with it. It denotes
a proud but always provisional insistence on American identity "in black,"
though Murray would often resist describing it in this way. For him, what
most of us now think of as African American culture is just one of the forms
that the existential adventure of human culture-making has taken under
specific conditions.

The particularity of the American cultural setting turns out to be vital
for this "Negro culturalism," and warrants a redescription of it, seen from
the other side, as it were, as a kind of *dialectical integrationism*. If "Negro
culturalism" is cultural nationalism "lite," then dialectical integrationism
is cultural pluralism on steroids. For Murray, "Negroes" and America are
mutually constitutive, and irremediably so. This interracial entwining is
not just a thesis of philosophical anthropology and the philosophy of
culture; it is also a political reality and commitment. He insisted that
Blacks had always been an essential part of American society and that
U.S. political culture simply needed to catch up to, or stop repressing, this
fact. As he saw it, failing to recognize this meant failing to see the intimate
connections between the sensibilities behind jazz and blues and the pro-
spects for American democracy and human heroism.

As before, the title of Murray's first book signals his commitment to
dialectical integrationism with admirable clarity and efficiency. But the
commitment shines through just as clearly, and more eloquently, in what
might be his most famous assertion. The claim in question appears at the
end of a passage guardedly endorsing the political impulses of Black
nationalists, while resisting their "ill-digested . . . ideologies of blackness,
blackmanship, and blackman spokesmanship":

> White Anglo-Saxon Protestants do in fact dominate the power mechanisms
> of the United States. Nevertheless, no American whose involvement with
> the question of identity goes beyond the sterile category of race can afford to
> overlook another fact that is no less essential . . . Identity is best defined in
> terms of culture, and the culture of the nation over which the white Anglo-
> Saxon power elite exercises such exclusive . . . control is not all-white by any
> measurement ever devised. *American* culture, even in its most rigidly segre-
> gated precincts, is patently and irrevocably composite. It is, regardless of all
> the hysterical protestations of those who would have it otherwise, incontest-
> ably mulatto.[27]

Institutionalizing the Cosmos

The preceding sections show, if they have done their jobs, that it is possible to explain Murray's core ideas by reference almost entirely to his major writings from the 1970s. It is, however, impossible to explain his cultural influence fully without turning to the institutional work of his later period. Murray passed his "blues theory" and the rest of "Cosmos Murray" down not just through his writings but also, in ways Ellison was loathe to do, through a vast personal network and array of institutions. As a member of this network explains: "Murray was at the center of something perhaps resembling an ancient Greek university, and its curriculum often circulated through talk. Among the ranks of alumni are numerous writers, musicians, and academics of renown."[28]

Of Murray's many students, two stand out as powerful vectors for the promulgation and development of his ideas. Henry Louis Gates, Jr., and Wynton Marsalis have testified openly to Murray's influence on them, and they have worked, in different ways and to different degrees, to promote those ideas in elite cultural spaces. Along the way, they have also clearly revealed tensions between those ideas, or their most straightforward application, and some of the core cultural achievements of the 1960s.

Henry Louis Gates, Jr.: Learning How to Be Black

Henry Louis Gates, Jr., is, by any measure, a towering figure in U.S. elite culture, especially as that culture intersects with Black and African American life. He holds an endowed chair at Harvard, spent fifteen years running what is now the department of African and African American Studies, and has led (what is now called) the Hutchins Center for African and African American Research since 1991. He was in the first class of MacArthur "genius" grantees; he serves on the boards of powerful organizations like the Aspen Institute; and he has parlayed his credibility in elite cultural institutions into a remarkable public presence. He has won Emmy Awards for his television documentaries; he has appeared on *Time* magazine's list of the 100 most influential Americans; and he once routinely wrote for high-profile publications like *The New York Times* and *The New Yorker*.

Gates has on occasion publicly insisted that Murray is central not just to his own work but to the wider work of understanding American and

African American life. Consider this passage from an article he wrote on
Murray for *The New Yorker*:

> When *The Omni-Americans* came out in 1970, I was in college, majoring in
> history but pursuing extracurricular studies in how to be black. Those were
> the days when the Black Power movement was the mode and rage de
> rigueur ... Such was the milieu in which Murray published *The Omni-
> Americans*, and you couldn't imagine a more foolhardy act. This was a book
> in which the very language of the black nationalists was subjected to a strip
> search ... The contrarian held his own ... by writing a book that was so
> pissed off, jaw-jutting, and unapologetic that it demanded to be taken
> seriously ... [I]n Murray the bullies of blackness had met their most
> formidable opponent. And a great many blacks – who, suborned by "soli-
> darity," had trained themselves to suppress any heretical thoughts – found
> Murray's book oddly thrilling ... You'd read it greedily, though you just
> might want to switch dust jackets with *The Wretched of the Earth* before
> wandering around with it in public.[29]

He goes on to add, "my first two books can be read as footnotes to *The
Omni-Americans*."[30]

This passage shows Gates using Murray – either in the moment, as
a young scholar, or retrospectively, as an established figure constructing
a usable past – to narrate a journey to contemporary influence that skirts
the radical activism of the later 1960s. The Black Power Movement was
exciting, the story goes, but ultimately unsatisfying. Murray redeemed the
"heretical thoughts" of "a great many blacks," a company that Gates'
conspiratorial shift to the second person ("*you'd* read it greedily") expands
to include not just the author but also the sympathetic reader. Thus
reinforced, the heretic could refuse the "subornations" of Blackness-
obsessed "bullies" and the seductions of a mode of "solidarity" that was,
in retrospect, sufficiently odious to require the distancing work of scare
quotes.

More to the point: Gates uses Murray to chart a path to contemporary
influence *in relation to the study of Black folks* that deflates 1960s-style
appeals to politics and authenticity. Murray helps Gates articulate a kind
of Black authenticity that is neither aggressively political nor narrowly
solidaristic. Whatever its intellectual merits, this was a useful posture when
Gates took the reins at Harvard. To put it crudely: a Murrayite vision for
Black studies could only be an asset in the quest for mainstream credibility
during an era of Clintonian centrism in relation to racial politics. Under
Gates' leadership, Harvard threw its full institutional weight behind
a liberal multiculturalist vision for Black studies, a vision that was at

times actively deployed against the dominant models that emerged from the late 1960s campus upheavals: an Afrocentric cultural nationalism in the mold of Molefi Asante, and a praxis-oriented radical egalitarianism in the mold of Manning Marable.

Houston Baker offers a precise account of this deflation of 1960s-style Blackness – what he calls a "swerve" – in a laudatory but critical essay celebrating the twenty-fifth anniversary of Gates' germinal text, *The Signifying Monkey*. Gates, he says, "wanted a praxis and politics of integration that opposed and refuted the work of the Black Arts and Black Power movements as he conceived them."[31] He found resources for this work in Murray, and assembled them into one of the more influential Black studies operations in the contemporary academy.

Marsalis, Classicism, and the Jazz Canon

Just over a decade after his *New Yorker* encomium, Gates presented Murray with an award from his Harvard research center. He drew the presentation to a close with these words:

> [Murray] has presided over black cultural life for several decades. He spurred Ralph Ellison's thinking for decades (and sparred with him as well), and sharpened the "narrative" of Romare Bearden's gorgeous art. Today, Stanley Crouch and Wynton Marsalis still labor under his dictates, and I do, too.[32]

Gates went on to report that "Wynton Marsalis, who is joyfully present today, is more than a protégé of Al's – he is a disciple."[33]

With these words Gates clearly marked a second major vector of concrete impact for Murray's ideas. Just as Gates' liberal reimagining of Black studies shaped opportunity structures, scholarly work, and public discourse around inquiry into Black life, Marsalis' jazz conservatism shaped opportunity structures, critical work, and public tastes around Black expressive culture. By their own testimony, both Gates and Marsalis did this work under Murray's "dictates."

Marsalis was able to exert this cultural influence because of his centrality to a crucial moment in the histories of jazz and American culture. Here's how one writer described it in 2003:

> For twenty years the fates of Marsalis and jazz music have appeared inextricably intertwined ... Extraordinarily gifted and fluent in both jazz and classical music, not to mention young, handsome, black, impassioned, and articulate, especially on the importance of jazz history and jazz masters, Marsalis was ideally equipped to lead a cultural-aesthetic movement suited

to the time, a renaissance that raised public esteem for and the popular appeal of jazz through a return to the music's traditional values: jazz for the Reagan revolution. In 1990 *Time* magazine put him on the cover and announced the dawn of "The New Jazz Age."[34]

There is insufficient space here to explore the defining commitments of this "cultural-aesthetic movement," or to track the details of this view through Marsalis' own written and oral pronouncements. Luckily, a great deal of commentary already does this work.[35] The aim here is to read his influence as itself a function of Murray's influence on him, and to see in his cultural impact the same elision and refusal of the 1960s that we find in Murray. For that purpose, it will suffice to report Marsalis' own account of his relationship to Murray, to track Murray's involvement in his core projects, and to gesture at certain common reactions to their interventions.

Marsalis has often testified openly to Murray's impact on him, as in the interview that produced this remark:

> Albert Murray gave me an education that no amount of money could buy . . . He'd suggest books for me to read, and I'd read them, then call him, maybe at 10:30, 11 o'clock at night. "You up?" I'd ask. "Yeah, man, I'm up," he'd say. "Come on over." I'd go over, we'd sit down, I'd pull out my notepad, and he'd start talking . . . He always has something to tell me that I need to know . . . I don't do anything serious unless I get his perspective on it.[36]

Having received this education, Marsalis went on to work with Murray on two extraordinarily influential projects: Jazz at Lincoln Center and Ken Burns' *Jazz* documentary. These ventures gave Marsalis – and the Murrayite ideas he championed – the kind of reach that most jazz musicians could only dream of.

In the early 1990s, the esteemed Lincoln Center for the Performing Arts in New York City added to its already illustrious constellation of enterprises an organization devoted entirely to jazz composition, education, and performance. In 1996, after years of preparation, Jazz at Lincoln Center joined the New York Philharmonic, the Metropolitan Opera, and the New York City Ballet as a "full constituent" of the Lincoln Center complex. This remarkable affirmation of jazz's status as "America's classical music" grew directly out of the efforts of Marsalis, who as of this writing still serves as JALC's managing and artistic director. For his part, Marsalis is clear about the true source of the intellectual framework for the organization:

> When I started with Lincoln Center, there wasn't really anything to be on board with. It was just three concerts I was asked to do in the summer. But

> Al [Murray] developed the intellectual foundation of what was to become
> Jazz at Lincoln Center . . . That foundation came from him.[37]

Murray was in fact one of the co-founders of the classic jazz concert series
that eventually became JALC, a series that he described in one interview as
"essentially based on *Stomping The Blues*," and he went on to serve as
a member of the JALC board of directors for many years.[38]

JALC grew in importance and complexity after its formal establishment,
but this process was not without controversy or difficulty. Some of the
problems related to complaints about the racial and gender politics of its
hiring practices. But more salient for current purposes are the concerns
related to the impact of JALC's cultural conservatism on the viability of
jazz as a living art form.

Murray and Marsalis put an explicitly monumentalist vision of the jazz
tradition at the center of the JALC enterprise. Paul Devlin, another of
Murray's self-confessed disciples, describes this vision as a self-conscious
"movement toward jazz repertory" that produced "jazz conservation
orchestras," like the Marsalis-led JALC ensemble.[39] The aim of this movement was to resist a specious presentism that, as Murray saw it, conflated
excellence in jazz with novelty. Consumers of European concert music, he
noted, venerate Bach, and "are not going to criticize anyone if they play
Bach instead of Aaron Copland, just because Copland is more recent
than Bach."[40] Similarly, students of jazz should focus on the timeless
achievements in the tradition, instead of discounting excellence because
fashions have changed. Once the focus shifts from novelty to excellence,
Ellington and Armstrong have to receive their due, especially in light of
presentist efforts to sideline them.

This emphasis on canonization and conservation also clearly shaped
director Ken Burns' 2001 *Jazz* documentary. Burns' film told the story not
just of jazz in America, but also of jazz *as* America, in a manner deeply
beholden to the "integrationist idealism" that Ellison and Murray marked
out many years before.[41] This was no accident, of course. Marsalis was
a senior creative consultant on the film as well as a frequent on-screen
presence. And there was a Murrayite contingent among the film's small
army of senior advisors and interviewees, including critic Gary Giddins,
writer-critic Stanley Crouch (who introduced Marsalis to Murray), and
Murray himself.

In order to gauge the impact of Burns' film and, by extension, of the
ideas that animated it, it is important to be clear about what Ken Burns was
at the time. By the time of the film's initial release, he was a towering figure

in U.S. media culture. His renderings of the American Civil War and of baseball were so popular that one could plausibly claim, with historian Stephen Ambrose, that "More Americans get their history from Ken Burns than from any other source."[42] Burns' popularity was the result not just of his filmmaking skill but also of his team's marketing savvy. His films were cultural happenings, complemented by campaigns to sell companion books, video and audio recordings, and much more.

Burns put his cultural influence and the marketing machinery that supported it fully in service of the *Jazz* project. This led to an "unprecedented and all-pervasive campaign" with General Motors, Starbucks, the National Basketball Association, Sony Music, and Universal Music Group as partners.[43] The picture of the jazz tradition that it painted was vigorously pushed to millions of viewers and consumers, among them a great many students who received free educational materials based on the film.

As it happens, the picture that Burns' culture-production machinery promoted was closely aligned with Murray's views. Burns himself made this clear in his comments about the film. In an interview before the documentary was released, he declared: "we want to convince someone in Dubuque that jazz is the Rosetta Stone of American culture."[44] He went on, in unmistakably Ellisonian-Murrayite terms:

> JAZZ is this wonderful portrait of not only the 20th century, but of our redemptive future possibilities. In JAZZ, we see the ultimate of the democratic idea. Different races, different styles, different souls, all negotiating their agendas together. When jazz works, it's a kind of model . . . of what democracy is about.[45]

Jazz was precisely the sort of cultural happening that Burns' track record suggested it would be, in part because it was as controversial as it was meticulously constructed. The primary source of controversy related directly to the Murrayite inheritance of Marsalis-style jazz conservatism. Many critics and musicians complained that *Jazz* subordinated a living and dynamic art form, practiced by living people with new ideas, to an obsession with Great Men like Ellington. One commentator sums up this worry by pointing out that in Burn's film:

> several of jazz's most garrulous spokespersons held forth for more than nineteen hours, brandishing a vocabulary full of such juicy words as "heroic," "erotic," "majestic," and – the film's mother of all jazz words – "genius." And yet the film couldn't carry the jazz story past the 1960s, which meant virtually excising nearly a third of the music's century-long

history and strongly implied that jazz is now entombed in a condition of permanent epilogue. One critic of the film has likened it to a "funeral celebration," while another has characterized the curatorial, neoclassical aesthetic of the film's main talking head – the trumpeter and Lincoln Center jazz program artistic director Wynton Marsalis – as a form of "musical necrophilia."[46]

This general worry about "musical necrophilia" has quite specific, and dire, consequences for denizens of the contemporary jazz artworld. The call to celebrate the jazz world's mighty dead was a gift to the music industry's margins: the enterprises we once called "record companies" could market and re-sell already recorded work without committing themselves to supporting living artists. Contemporary performers ended up splitting the audience with each other *and* with Thelonious Monk, Miles Davis, and Duke Ellington. The former proprietor of the great jazz club Sweet Basil, lamented the impact of this shift while reflecting on the worsening conditions that led him to sell the club: "They've been saying jazz is America's classical music, and it deserves respect. Well, now it's America's classical music. Thanks a lot. What do we do now?"[47]

This picture of Marsalis as a musical "necrophiliac" whose vices have led to jazz's declining fortunes appears here not as a claim this essay means to endorse, but as data. Whatever the ultimate probity of the charge, its initial plausibility provides evidence that Murray's refusal of core elements of the 1960s finds an echo in the uses to which Gates and Marsalis put his ideas. One might contest the reading that Baker gives of Gates, or the reading that many jazz critics gave of Burns' film and of the JALC repertory impulse. But the targets of these accusations gave their critics enough material to make a *prima facie* case. Those materials at least appear to reveal the worldview that Baker found in Gates' work. According to this view, in the 1960s people got confused about how to be Black, and about what was really central to jazz music. The remedy for this was to construct alternative traditions, to read Black identity through Murray and Ellison instead of Baraka and Brooks, and to read jazz history through Ellington and Armstrong instead of through those figures *and* Ornette Coleman and Eliane Elias. This re-recovery of the past supports a different model of authenticity in relation to Black cultures, one grounded not in a radical critique of American racism or a celebration of post-Civil Rights assertiveness, but in a reinvention of integrationism, a reclamation of America not just for Blacks but also *as* Black, and of Blacks as American, and of Black culture as the key to a multicultural mosaic that the "bullies of blackness" ignore at their peril.

Conclusion

The aims of this piece are, all things considered, fairly modest. The aims have not been to evaluate Albert Murray's views, or the views he encouraged people like Gates and Marsalis to adopt, for truth or falsity, risk or promise. Nor have they been to weigh the costs and benefits of his cultural impact on the United States or any proper subset of the U.S. population. The aims have been to tease out the core philosophical commitments that define his work, to dwell briefly on the way these commitments worked through his followers and found their way into influential cultural institutions and objects, and to consider how all this constitutes a "swerve" against, or around, the 1960s.

These objectives aside, the argument probably still feels somewhat judgmental. If so, this is in part a function of the attempt to locate Murray's work and impact relative to the ferment of the 1960s. Murray's most important written work self-consciously aspires to interrogate the forces in Black cultural politics that define the 1960s for a great many people. But the half century that has passed since that moment gives contemporary commentators a different relationship to those forces, and makes it possible for the forces to appear more central and less irruptive to Black intellectual and cultural traditions than they must have seemed to Murray. As a result, simply indicating his role in theorizing and underwriting the refusal of (among other things) post-Civil Rights Black nationalism will involve indicating his distance from the kind of social-theoretic common sense that now supports a cottage industry devoted to exploring the Black Power Movement, the Black Panther Party, and other developments that he regarded mostly with scorn.

If the hint of judgment that runs through this piece derives in part from the intellectual distance that contemporary students of Black life have to travel in order to inhabit Murray's "cosmos," it also derives in part from the difficulty of dispassionately discussing – borrowing again from Gates – this most "pissed-off" and "jaw-jutting" of writers. To engage with Murray is to engage a pugnacious barbershop ethos, an ethos that, at least until the final phase of his career, led him to make outrageous claims that one lets pass only with difficulty. Some of these claims seem calculated mainly to provoke, as when he says to an interviewer that since Thomas Jefferson's genius was bound up with slaveholding, "I want to wake him up and give him ten more slaves."[48] Other claims appear more sincerely held but simply seem shortsighted, like his insistence that Toni Morrison's literary reputation far outstrips the value of her work.[49]

Expanding on most of these evaluative gestures and traces would require exceeding the scope of this essay. The merits of Murray's complaints about "wailing wall polemicism" and "social science fiction" are matters to take up from the perspective of social science, social criticism, and social theory. Similarly, the plausibility of his objections to Morrison and Baldwin as writers, like the probity of the theoretical resources that he relentlessly champions, are matters to take up with literary critics and cultural theorists. But it would not be amiss to close with a few thoughts on how to understand one of the less satisfying pieces of expressly philosophical argument in his work.

One throughline for many of Murray's diatribes is his insistence on "the acceptance frame." As noted above, one of his key concerns about people like Baldwin is their focus on the negative dimensions of Black life. Baldwin's Harlem writhes with derelicts, he complains, while the real Harlem also laughs with the Apollo's comedians. This negativity misrepresents the complexity of experience, which is a mistake of phenomenological analysis; but it also invites one to approach the world as an inherently gloomy or dire place, which is a mistake of existential orientation. Remember, one moral of the blues tradition is that ugly facts have no more validity or weight, and are no more comprehensive, than beautiful facts. So why, Murray asks, focus on the one and not the other? Comprehensiveness demands that both receive their due.

But what does it mean to give negativity its due, and to give it only its due and nothing more? How does one know when one succeeds at this? One way to approach the question is broadly empirical or vaguely utilitarian, and involves making sure that representations of Black life depict the same ratio of good to bad, of pleasure to pain, that one finds in the world. This is a deeply unsatisfying way to go, not least because hedonic measurement and comparison are notoriously knotty undertakings. Another way to approach the question, though, is to ask what people *need to believe*, or *what stance they need to adopt*, in order to manage whatever negativity they happen to encounter. This approach is not empirical but broadly psychological, volitional, and therapeutic, and appears to run precisely counter to Murray's refusal of arguments about Black self-esteem. Blacks are not psychologically broken or self-hating, he was always eager to say, usually before reporting some conversation, memory, or encounter that was meant to prove the depth of Black strength and self-confidence. But if that's right, then why engage in a relentless boosterism about Black heroism, dignity, and elegance, a campaign so all-encompassing that it crowds out the more sober reflections of Baldwin and Morrison?

Murray sometimes writes as if his emphasis on beautiful facts is simply a personal predilection, as if he just happens to be built so that beauty resonates with him and ugliness doesn't. Generalizing from here, and crediting the concrete universalist sensibility that he displays elsewhere, one might say that he sees the universe as capacious enough to contain both beauty and ugliness, and generous enough to divert its energies into distinct channels for focusing on one or the other. His job as a vehicle for the elaboration and refinement of human experience – one of his favorite ways to think about art – was to insist on the positive, knowing that the negative would take care of itself, using other vehicles. His barbershop impulse toward provocation led him to shower disdain on the vehicles for negativity, and his American naturalist impulse toward phenomenological comprehensiveness bred in him a heightened sensitivity to the prospect of the negative taking more than its due. But the overall aim might have been to achieve, across the community of inquirers and agents that we call humanity, the condition that Cornel West calls the tragicomic sense.[50]

Neither pessimistic nor optimistic, always aware of life's precariousness but never so hardened by it as to forget the prospect for enjoyment and beauty, tragicomic thinkers accept the unavoidable burden of cultivating resources for resisting despair and dread. They do this not grudgingly but in the joyful, improvisational spirit that Murray, at his best, championed. Murray at his best is not the thinker who indulges lazy broadsides against "the victim mentality" or "welfare sociology." He is someone who sounds like this:

> Jazz is . . . central to American culture, because it is there, like all art forms, to condition us to do what we're supposed to do. Like an epic. An epic conditions you for heroic action. You are born to fight the dragon, You are born to turn back the enemy . . . So you don't say, "It's unfair that I have to fight the dragon." That's life. Even if you're a Southerner and it's the Grand Dragon. It's life . . . [W]e're supposed to live as if the dragon exists in order to make heroes, just as plagues exist, and great medical disasters exist, to make great doctors . . . When you get that view of life, you see, then you are conditioned to heroic action.[51]

Whether jazz and the blues can bear all this weight is a question for another time. One hears in the background at moments like this the charge that Ellison levied against Baraka: this kind of thinking could give the blues the blues. For now, though, it is clear that the attempt to assign Black expressive practices this burden was central to a cultural project that helped complicate the reception and understanding of the legacy of the Black 1960s.

Notes

1. Murray (2016c), 148.
2. Murray (1971), 132.
3. Murray (2000b), Kindle locations 214–16.
4. Murray (2000a), Kindle location 261.
5. Noble (2010), 130–37.
6. Ibid., 135.
7. Murray (2016a), 915–41.
8. Marcus (2013).
9. Murray (2016a), 930.
10. For a fuller account of Murray's role in the JALC see, generally, Devlin (2016), Kindle locations 598–648.
11. Gates (2010a), 17.
12. "Cosmos Murray" is a name for, as one commentator puts it, "the vast swirl of . . . interests and influences . . . that define Murray's worldview." Devlin (2016), Kindle location 433.
13. Murray (2016c), 10.
14. Ibid., 144, 129.
15. Ibid., 128.
16. Ibid., 129.
17. Ibid., 12, 32, 37.
18. Ibid., 39, 40.
19. Baldwin (2012), 36.
20. Murray (2016c), 126.
21. Ibid., 41.
22. Gates (2010a), 26–27, citing Albert Murray, *Stomping the Blues* (New York: Random House, Inc., 1982), 250–51.
23. Murray (2016b), 509.
24. Ibid., 509–10.
25. Ibid., 512.
26. Murray and Devlin (2016), Kindle locations 2295–303.
27. Murray (2016c), 24.
28. Devlin (2016), Kindle locations 426–30.
29. Gates (2010a), 17–19.
30. Ibid., 36.
31. Baker (2015), 835.
32. Gates (2010b), 203.
33. Ibid., 202.
34. Hajdu (2003).
35. See, for example, Sanchirico (2015) and Gray (2005).
36. Maguire (2010), 200.
37. Ibid., 201.
38. Murray and Devlin (2016), Kindle locations 2275–76, 2374.
39. Devlin (2016), Kindle locations 605, 616.

40. Ibid., Kindle locations 639–40, citing Maita (2001).
41. Sundquist (2005).
42. Stephen Ambrose, quoted in Blumenthal (2000), para. 2.
43. Blumenthal (2000), paras. 36–42.
44. Ibid., para. 11.
45. Interview with Ken Burns, cited in Sanchirico (2015), 300.
46. Gennari (2006), 1, 2, 4; quoting Watrous (2002), 204 ("funeral procession") and Nicholson (2002), 126 ("necrophilia").
47. Hajdu (2003), para. 65.
48. Gates (2010a), 20.
49. Ibid., 21.
50. See, for example, West (1996).
51. Neff (2016), Kindle locations 2435–556, 2468–87.

References

Baker, H. A. 2015. "The Urge to Adorn: Generational Wit and the Birth of The Signifying Monkey." *Early American Literature* 50.3: 831–42.
Baldwin, J. 2012. *Notes of a Native Son*. Boston, MA: Beacon Press.
Blumenthal, B. 2000, December 1. "Ken Burns' Jazz." *Jazztimes*. https://jazztimes.com/features/ken-burns-jazz/ [accessed September 23, 2021].
Burns, K., dir. 2001. *Jazz: A Film by Ken Burns* [Film]. Public Broadcasting Service.
Devlin, P. 2016. "Albert Murray: Making Words Swing, on and off the Page." In *Murray Talks Music: Albert Murray on Jazz and Blues*, ed. P. Devlin, xvii–xlvi; Kindle locations 598–648. Minneapolis: University of Minnesota Press.
Gates, H. L. 2010a. "King of Cats (1996)." In *Albert Murray and the Aesthetic Imagination of a Nation*, ed. B. Baker, 15–36. Tuscaloosa: University of Alabama Press.
2010b. "Albert Murray's Du Bois Medal Citation (2007)." In *Albert Murray and the Aesthetic Imagination of a Nation*, ed. B. Baker, 202–3. Tuscaloosa: University of Alabama Press.
Gennari, J. 2006. *Blowin' Hot and Cool: Jazz and Its Critics*. University of Chicago Press.
Gray, H. 2005. *Cultural Moves: African Americans and the Politics of Representation*. Berkeley: University of California Press.
Hajdu, D. 2003, March. "Wynton's Blues." *The Atlantic*. www.theatlantic.com/magazine/archive/2003/03/wyntons-blues/302684/ [accessed September 23, 2021].
Maguire, R. S. 2010. "Wynton Marsalis on Albert Murray (2001)." In *Albert Murray and the Aesthetic Imagination of a Nation*, ed. B. Baker, 199–201. Tuscaloosa: University of Alabama Press.
Maita, J. 2001, August 29. "The Ralph Ellison Project: Albert Murray, Author of Trading Twelves: The Selected Letters of Ralph Ellison and Albert Murray."

Jerry Jazz Musician. http://jerryjazzmusician.com/2001/08/the-ralph-ellison-project-albert-murray-author-of-trading-twelves-the-selected-letters-of-ralph-ellison-and-albert-murray/ [accessed September 23, 2021].

Marcus, J. 2013, May/June. "Home Truths." *Columbia Journalism Review*. http://archives.cjr.org/second_read/home_truths.php [accessed September 23, 2021].

Murray, A. 1971. *South to a Very Old Place*. New York: McGraw-Hill.

———. 2000a. "Introduction to Part I." In *Trading Twelves: Selected Letters of Ralph Ellison and Albert Murray*, ed. A. Murray and J. Callahan, Kindle location, 261. New York: Vintage-Random House.

———. 2000b. "Preface." In *Trading Twelves: Selected Letters of Ralph Ellison and Albert Murray*, ed. A. Murray and J. Callahan, Kindle locations, 214–16. New York: Vintage-Random House.

———. 2016a. "Chronology." In *Albert Murray: Collected Essays & Memoirs*, ed. H. L. Gates and P. Devlin, 915–41. New York: Library of America.

———. 2016b. "Stomping the Blues." In *Albert Murray: Collected Essays & Memoirs*, ed. H. L. Gates and P. Devlin, 411–514. New York: Library of America.

———. 2016c. "The Omni-Americans." In: *Albert Murray Collected Essays & Memoirs*, ed. H. L. Gates and P. Devlin, 1–189. New York: Library of America.

Murray, A., and P. Devlin. 2016. "'Hear that Train Whistle Harmonica!' Talk at St. John's University." In *Murray Talks Music: Albert Murray on Jazz and Blues*, ed. P. Devlin, 96–104; Kindle locations 2295–303. Minneapolis: University of Minnesota Press.

Neff, R. 2016. "'A Real Conservative? I'm Not One. I'm an Avant-Garde Person.' Interview [with Albert Murray]." In *Murray Talks Music: Albert Murray on Jazz and Blues,* ed. P. Devlin, 105–13; Kindle locations, 2435–556, 2468–487. Minneapolis: University of Minnesota Press.

Nicholson, S. 2002. "Low-Budget Careers: The Business of Jazz." In *The Future of Jazz*, ed. Y. Taylor, 109–28. Chicago, IL: A Cappella Books.

Noble, D. 2010. "A Conversation with Albert Murray (1996)." In *Albert Murray and the Aesthetic Imagination of a Nation*, ed. B. Baker, 130–37. Tuscaloosa: University of Alabama Press.

Sanchirico, A. 2015. "The Culturally Conservative View of Jazz in America: A Historical and Critical Analysis." *Jazz Perspectives* 9.3: 289–311.

Sundquist, E. J. 2005. "Dry Bones." In *The Cambridge Companion to Ralph Ellison*, ed. R. Posnock, 217–30. Cambridge University Press.

Watrous, P. 2002. "The Ghost in the Machine: Jazz Institutions, Infrastructures, and Media." In *The Future of Jazz*, ed. Y. Taylor, 189–206. Chicago, IL: A Cappella Books.

West, C. 1996. "Black Strivings in a Twilight Civilization." In *The Future of the Race*, ed. C. West and H. L. Gates, 53–112. New York: Alfred A. Knopf.

CHAPTER 7

Espionage and Paths of Black Radicalism

GerShun Avilez

If we realize how indispensable is responsible militant organization to our struggle, we create it as we managed to create underground railroads, protest groups, self-help societies and the churches that have always been our refuge, our source of hope and our source of action.

Martin Luther King, Jr.[1]

As the historiography of the Civil Rights Movement and the Black Power Movement attests, there were rich and complex developments in African American political thought during the 1960s, which impacted every component of social life.[2] This essay seeks to determine how art refashions and advances the shifts that come to define the Black radicalism of this period. Sam Greenlee's novel *The Spook Who Sat by the Door* (1969/1973) reveals key changes in African American literary history and political theorizing about revolution, and also captures major concerns of the historical moment.[3] The novel is an artistic translation of the intellectual and social terrain of the Black Power Movement. It chronicles how the activism of this period modified the sociopolitical discourse around Black identity. *Spook* presents the case for new strategies to achieve the sought-after revolution that would improve the social position of African American citizens.

Greenlee uses the conceit of espionage to articulate new modes of Black radicalism. Espionage involves intelligence gathering, the creation of informed and empowered networks capable of social and political action, and equipping oneself for self-protection alongside the protection of others. Accordingly, Greenlee uses the narrative frame of espionage as a metaphor for the development and dissemination of techniques for liberation, strategic community-building, and, importantly, the cultivation of Black radical personhood.[4]

The novel is a narrative guide to engineering social rebellion and infiltrating institutions. The basic plot of the novel involves a Korean

173

War veteran, Daniel Freeman, who wants to mobilize African Americans and start a revolution to overthrow the U.S. government in hopes of unseating white supremacy. The character decides that the best way to undermine the U.S. state and foment insurgency is to gain access to the Central Intelligence Agency (CIA), the hub of national security and confidential strategic policy. Greenlee bases the novel on his own experiences working for the U.S. Information Agency, a Cold War-era public diplomacy organization, in the 1950s and 1960s.[5] In the novel, Freeman is the first African American to be hired as an operative. Becoming a veritable double agent, Freeman joins the CIA to learn methods to create his own revolutionary army and wage war on the United States. He takes what he learns in the CIA and transforms a street gang in Chicago into a sophisticated paramilitary operation that becomes the beginning of a national network of highly trained and armed revolutionaries. To be successful, Freeman has to keep his radical plans a secret, requiring him to have a public identity as a mild-mannered social worker even though he secretly plans a radical insurgency.

Making manifest W. E. B. Du Bois' concept of double consciousness, Freeman has to navigate two different worlds; in fact, the double agent motif is a purposeful extension and restructuring of double consciousness.[6] The systematic plan to overthrow the government made Greenlee's manuscript controversial, and he was unable to find a publisher in the United States for several years – it was rejected by dozens of mainstream publishers before being published in the United Kingdom.[7] In this provocative text, Greenlee uses the protagonist to imagine innovative strategies for revolution by questioning the two prevailing ways of thinking about Black advancement in the social world during the 1960s: (1) integrating into the body politic through legislation, or (2) separating from it through Black institution-building.

Rather than falling into the trap of choosing either an ostensibly integrationist (i.e., Civil Rights) strategy or a separatist (i.e., Black Power) strategy, the protagonist of the novel, Dan Freeman, links the two together, rejecting the kind of binaristic logic that dominated some of the Black political thought at the time. Working both inside the system and outside of it, he integrates in order to separate, offering a somewhat counterintuitive path to revolutionary action. I argue that the novel employs *and* challenges recognizable Civil Rights and Black Power discourses of social change to destabilize institutionalized racism and socioeconomic discrimination, and to begin to imagine untested paths to resistance. In the process, Greenlee's novel gestures toward revisions in how thinkers and activists were conceptualizing social change as well as the parameters of Black identity.

In the first section of this essay, I consider how Greenlee uses espionage to reconfigure familiar political ideals and modes of leadership. The second section explores how the imagined integration of the CIA becomes a device for critiquing employment discrimination and the state's half-hearted deployment of affirmative action. The final section shows how spy training and spycraft offer Greenlee opportunities to rethink the connections among gender, sexuality, and revolution, while additionally illustrating how heterosexual masculinity dominates the space of the revolutionary. Through the frame of espionage, Greenlee reimagines Black identity and activism.

The Search for New Forms

In a May 1969 issue of the *Negro Digest*, contributor Rukudzo Murapa insists that what the political situation in the United States requires is an "attitudinal revolution" among Black citizens.[8] Murapa's point is that there is not only a need for redefining the political state and social policies; rather, there is also a need for rethinking the meaning of Blackness, the social situation of African Americans, and the most effective methods for creating change. The revolution is not simply about social struggles, rallies, and marches; it is also about "revolutionizing the mind" or adopting new mindsets in regard to social matters.[9]

This understanding of a radical change in attitude is the defining component of Greenlee's presentation of revolution in his novel. A reorientation of thinking will enable social change. Murapa's essay appears just one month before Greenlee publishes a short section of his novel in the African American owned and operated magazine *Negro Digest*.[10] This excerpt of the novel is the only portion of the work to appear in print in the United States until the entire novel is finally published four years later. Greenlee found support from this arm of the Black press, whereas major publishing houses in the United States routinely rejected the manuscript. Murapa provides a framework for understanding how Greenlee's novel presents a different perspective on the path to revolution. The novel is about the logistics of an actual revolution, but it is also a call for an attitudinal revolution in that it is asking African Americans to reassess accepted ideas about collaboration, activism, and leadership. Espionage functions as the medium for this attitudinal revolution.

In one of the few extended reviews to appear when the novel was published in 1969, literary critic Charles D. Peavy characterizes the book as being about the "changing attitudes" about the possibility revolution.[11] The review appears in the second issue of the newly created *Journal of Black Studies*, so once again it is a periodical dedicated to Black experience and media that is the initial publication vehicle for Greenlee's work.[12] Peavy sees the novel as a prime example of the "Black revolutionary novel," which, he argues, has its origin in Sutton Griggs' 1899 *Imperium in Imperio*, a novel that has at the heart of its plot a secret Black society that plans to revolt against the United States and create a Black nation out of the state of Texas. Peavy states that the question of political revolution had been basically absent from twentieth-century African American fiction until the Black Power era, and that novels such as Greenlee's not only capture the zeitgeist of the late 1960s, but they also materialize a genre that had remained underutilized for decades. Works such as Greenlee's, then, recall Griggs' novel, but put the question of revolution into different historical and political registers and imagine change. In that sense the narratives of revolution are both backward- and forward-looking. Peavy's assessment suggests that the 1960s become a historical moment in which revolution (again) represents a point of genuine consideration. More than anything else, Peavy emphasizes that Greenlee's narrative catalogs a movement toward confrontation, as well as a reappraisal of the most effective methods with which to address African American civic dilemmas.

Both Murapa and Peavy reference the idea of a shift in attitudes at their historical moment, and this notion reflects the general tenor of Black Power reasoning. Activists and writers during the 1960s situate the rhetoric of Black Power as an improvement on and replacement for Civil Rights strategies, as Malcolm X's 1964 speech, "The Ballot or the Bullet," shows in its spurning of a "turning-the-other-cheek" strategy, which is often connected to Civil Rights nonviolent protest.[13] The idea that emerges is that Civil Rights methods have become exhausted or are not capable of addressing fully the social and economic dilemmas that continue to stymie the Black community. Some felt that Civil Rights calls for integration and legislative change had made no net results. In a speech given on October 29, 1966, after being released from jail in Greenwood, Mississippi, Stokely Carmichael asserts: "We been saying freedom for six years and we ain't got nuthin'. What we gonna start saying now is Black Power!"[14] Many people began to believe that a new set of approaches was needed, as were different ways of expressing social dissatisfaction.

Confrontational politics and promises of violent retaliation began to replace the rhetoric of nonviolence. Protesters were more likely to be armed with guns than Bibles. Demands for revolution replaced calls for reform. These shifts reflect the movement from traditional Civil Rights activism to Black Power activism. Black Power ideologies, as they get articulated by political groups such as the Black Panthers or adapted by artistic collectives such as the Black Arts Movement, result from the desire for new tactics that move away from more familiar Civil Rights strategies.

However, what was to keep Black Power adherents from being vulnerable to critiques comparable to those leveled at Civil Rights activists? Although Black Power sets itself up as the more attractive alternative, what happens if it does not immediately solve social problems? One finds that Black Power ideologies faced the challenge of keeping themselves from becoming exhausted in the way many claimed Civil Rights methods had become. In other words, how would Black Power keep from being displaced? These questions point to areas of concern that plague Black Power almost from its inception. These considerations are the cause of much of the anxiety and disagreement among different Black Power adherents. As scholars such as William Van Deburg, Peniel Joseph, Jeffrey Ogbar, and James Smethurst show, activists did not always agree about the most effective ways to proceed.[15]

Greenlee's novel is written during the peak of the Black Power Movement and appears in the United States as the movement begins to wane. Part of what the novel addresses is the anxiety about how to ensure a long lifespan for Black Power ideologies: how to keep them from dying out. During the 1960s, many writers expressed concerns about the possibilities of desired revolution (political and personal) and question Black Power rhetoric, as texts such as LeRoi Jones' play *The Slave* (1964), John A. Williams' novel *The Man Who Cried I Am* (1967), James Baldwin's novel *Tell Me How Long the Train's Been Gone* (1968), Alice Walker's poetry collection *Once* (1968), Sonia Sanchez's poem "blk rhetoric" (1969), and Toni Morrison's novel *The Bluest Eye* (1970) all make clear. Throughout the period there is circulating doubt about revolutionary sentiment even in texts that recognize the value of such sentiment.

Offering an unexpected perspective, Greenlee suggests that the best way to vitalize Black Power and safeguard its future is to commingle it with older strategies, making it new and keeping its versatility through adaptation. He indicates that Civil Rights and Black Power ways of thinking must be made to cooperate instead of being seen as diametrically opposed. He even goes further in offering ideas that build on, yet also move away from either of these ideologies. It is from this perspective that one begins to recognize the attitudinal shift for which Murapa calls within Greenlee's fiction. His narrative asks the reader to think differently about past strategies and the possible trajectories for present ones.

As a whole, *Spook* is an extended meditation on the methods that constitute Black Power activism. Inasmuch as Greenlee's book is a "handbook on urban guerilla warfare,"[16] *Spook* can also be read specifically as a narrative exploration of Kwame Ture and Charles V. Hamilton's highly influential treatise, *Black Power: The Politics of Liberation* (1967). This important text offers a theorization of the increasingly popular conception of "Black Power" as well as a systematic analysis of racial relations in the United States alongside a framework for translating a new consciousness about Black identity into a politics of action. It is a key text of political thought during the 1960s. In many ways, the novel builds on the thinking that emerges in *Black Power*.

Key issues from Ture and Hamilton's social analysis shape the development of Greenlee's plot: the middle class is presented as a key element of institutionalized racism; urban spaces are the sites of focus for revolutionary organizing; there is an emphasis on Blacks defining themselves; and there is a premium on communal identification and community-building. Because these basic elements of radical political thinking provide the foundation for Freeman's experiences and philosophy, one can think of the novel as primarily a fictional mirroring of the political treatise published two years earlier.

Perhaps the most important way that the novel picks up the argumentation of the critical volume and expresses a Black Power ethos is in its apparent criticism of integration. Integration, as Ture and Hamilton understand it, has to do with the loss of Black culture and the destruction of Black communities. They describe integration as "a subterfuge for the maintenance of white supremacy" and as a device that attempts to force "black people to give up their identity, deny their heritage."[17] They go on to say that integrationist strategies (i.e., "the large scale transfer of black students to white neighborhoods") are ultimately unfeasible and mostly concern the idea that "the closer you get to whiteness, the better you are."[18] From the perspective of Ture and Hamilton, integration functions as a threat to Black culture and represents a state-sponsored policy riddled with problems.

Similarly, Greenlee's novel casts aspersions on assimilation into white culture, especially in its presentation of the Black middle class. Freeman insists that he "had no more love for the black middle class than they had for him," because their "definition of integration is to have their kids the only niggers in a white private school; their wives with a well-paying job in an otherwise all-white firm and balling white chicks looking for some African kicks."[19] Freeman is not interested in interracial connections or advancing through white-dominated business networks; he is more interested in undermining white supremacy and creating Black autonomous spaces. Freeman is consistently critical of Black characters who seek to emulate whites and gain a middle-class status that alienates them from the majority of Black people.

That being said, Greenlee situates integration as a tactic that can be successfully manipulated to protect and cultivate Blackness as opposed to diminishing it. The novel is an exploration of the ideas in *Black Power*, but it also moves in other directions. There is a redeployment of the notion of integration itself that ultimately repurposes it for the task of Black liberation rather than for the sustaining of the stability of white communities and values. Having a Korean War veteran join the CIA symbolizes (re) uniting with a major arm of the state as well as an emblem of U.S. white power – the CIA is 100 percent white when the narrative opens. Freeman is a character who appears to be working within the system. To some extent, he is a model figure of one strain of Civil Rights philosophy. Integration here is a viable means for setting the stage for revolution. Greenlee refuses an "either-or" way of thinking about Civil Rights and Black Power ideologies. The result is that Freeman and his colleagues become unrecognizable – even invisible – in their actions because they do not rely on typical or expected strategies for street gangs or other insurgent groups.[20] In this way, the novel challenges and advances how we think about the best political strategies for radicals.

Part of the value of Greenlee's book is that it not only insists on re-evaluating the relationship between Civil Rights and Black Power methods; it also begins to formulate ways of thinking that depart from both paradigms. *Spook* questions the investment in a leadership model of social activism. It asks: what is the proper role for a leader of the movement and what are the best strategies for a successful revolution? Civil Rights activism and the Black radical movement in general in the twentieth century have often been memorialized through references to specific charismatic – often male – leaders: Marcus Garvey, A. Philip Randolph, Ella Baker, Martin Luther King, Jr., Fannie Lou Hamer, Malcolm X, Huey Newton, Angela Davis. We often tell stories and write history through the actions of individuals. It is not just that leaders such as these are instrumental; to some extent, there is also a cultural belief that charismatic leaders are elemental to effecting real change, as Erica Edwards demonstrates.[21] From this perspective social change is dependent upon a leader, and without that leader, change will be obstructed, if not impossible.

Throughout *Spook*, Greenlee offers a recurring rejection of a charismatic leader paradigm for social change. To be more specific, he employs this paradigm to undo the hold that it has on the radical imagination. Dan Freeman is a charismatic leader: he is persuasive, powerful, and effective in terms of achieving results, and he gets what he wants for nearly the entire narrative. That being said, Greenlee consistently rejects that model as being one that is detrimental to achieving revolution. Freeman refuses a way of thinking that would position only him or someone exactly like him as a revolutionary lynchpin:

> Look, goddamnit, there ain't no head niggers in this outfit! The whole scene is designed to have the man below move up at least three steps whenever necessary. If I go, Do-Daddy takes over and right down the line. Every nigger revolt in the history of America has ended when they wasted the head nigger. That won't happen to us.[22]

Freeman's strategy is not about recruiting revolutionary fighters trained to follow him. Rather, he wants to help every person to understand that he is capable of changing the social world and occupying the space of the "leader." Later in the novel, Freeman insists that no one is "indispensable," meaning that specific leaders are not necessary or vital to a plan of action. He forsakes the idea of an indispensable leader, and this narrative move abandons ostensibly the investment in a cult of personality.

The novel critiques what political theorist Cedric Robinson would later call the "myth of leadership."[23] Robinson understands political leadership as a social construct for expediency. His overall goal is to "dismiss political leadership as the manifestation of authority, that is as the instrument through which an authority which manages the integration of a community is maintained."[24] Robinson pushes against the framework of leader-as-authority that dominates political movements as well as state politics. He ponders, what ways of thinking, or terms of order, are apparent when the leader paradigm is not seen as a constant and inevitable way of organizing? How might one formulate leaderlessness and still make decisions and produce results? Robinson offers two alternatives to the leader-as-authority paradigm that plagues and arrests the social imaginary:

> near-leaderlessness in a group can be achieved functionally by the *succession* of leader-guides, a succession which "exaggerates" the capacities of nearly all

the members of the community by ensuring to each actual mobility (in contrast to potential mobility) with several delimited periods of eminence [. . .] Leadership or dominance, followership or submission are only some forms that dependence may assume, but as such, they should not be taken as the nature of the thing. [. . .]

The second alternative may be considered either as the logical consequence and thus the goal of the first or as a process and end in and of itself. It is to be characterized as true leaderlessness. True leaderlessness as a consequence of "transitional" leaderlessness would follow from the accumulated development of each group member.[25]

That which Robinson describes as "near" leaderlessness resonates with Freeman's strategy of preparing everyone to be a leader. Again, he insists that there would be no "head nigga" and that no one would be indispensable because all would share the knowledge base that creates the privileged place of the leader. The fact that every man was trained to move three steps up conveys the idea of a succession of leader-guides; moreover, the extensive training itself, the development of each group member that Robinson envisions, can be the first step toward "true" leaderlessness.

In *Spook*, Greenlee charts out a conceptual terrain that Robinson would develop about a decade later in his political history. The novel signals a movement away from leader-focused conceptions of activism that would be realized later in Black political theory. Freeman's revolution seeks to be a leaderless one, which pushes against common conceptions of how social movements are organized. In part, the novel questions a popular way of thinking about the Civil Rights Movement: singular, charismatic leaders are essential to political change – an idea that often prevails in the general political domain. Freeman's repudiation of the indispensable leader framework signals a shift in the public conceptions of leadership and the dynamics within groups and organizations. The emphasis is on collective action and, importantly, collective empowerment and institution-building as opposed to singular, charismatic leadership.

Tokenism and Tropes of Redress

The immediate historical context for *Spook* includes the ongoing discussion of employment discrimination faced by African Americans. Though incredibly specific, the challenges that the Black characters have in getting a job at the CIA is reflective of much larger patterns in the social world. To put it simply, during the 1960s, employers refused to hire African Americans across the nation. Historian Terry H. Anderson explains:

> Nationally, black men held only about 1 percent of all white-collar positions; they usually only could get labor and service jobs. [. . .] Most unions also refused to train black apprentices. The National Urban League revealed that African Americans were almost completely excluded from printing and plumber unions. [. . .] For the African American in 1960, then, the result was a vicious circle. Job discrimination reduced employment opportunity, resulted in low income, and that in turn limited availability of education and training programs, keeping skills low and reducing employment opportunities and income.[26]

This inability to obtain employment was challenging for Black men and even more complicated for Black women, who often had far fewer opportunities to access white-collar positions and union memberships. The employment stasis that this "vicious circle" of discrimination created dominated Civil Rights discourse and the political terrain throughout the decade. This situation led to increased conversation on the part of Black activist groups such as the Congress of Racial Equality (CORE) about "compensatory hiring," which would be aimed at addressing decades of discrimination.[27] In addition, politicians and federal officials also took it upon themselves to tackle this problem through public policy. The federal intervention into the problem of employment discrimination in the 1960s resulted in the emergence of affirmative action and a new discourse of racism and employment practices that would impact cultural production.

The language of "affirmative action" first appears in an official document when President John F. Kennedy issued Executive Order 10925 in March 1961. This order sought to undermine employment discrimination by declaring that the federal government would seek to ensure that employers would take

> affirmative action to ensure that applicants are employed, and that employees are treated during employment, without regard to their race, creed, color, or national origin. Such action shall include, but not be limited to, the following: employment, upgrading, demotion or transfer; recruitment or recruitment advertising; layoff or termination; rates of pay or other forms of compensation; and selection for training, including apprenticeship.[28]

The mandate was later supplanted by Kennedy's Executive Order 11114 of June 1963, which extended the reach of the policy from jobs created by contracts to all entities that received federal funds. It explicitly proclaimed the use of affirmative action to eliminate discrimination and to create employment opportunities. This order would later be effectively absorbed into Title VII of the Civil Rights Act of 1964.[29] These documents represent landmark pieces of policy in U.S. history.

On paper, affirmative action seems to address the problem of employment discrimination; however, for many there was little to no change in terms of hiring practices or the government's intervention into those practices. More importantly, far too often a few African Americans were hired to make it appear as if there was a change in the preferential treatment given to white applicants.[30] In this way, affirmative action quickly became linked to *tokenism*, or minimal and merely symbolic representation in the workplace, in the minds of many Black activists and thinkers. It is here, through the concept of tokenism, that Greenlee enters the emergent conversation surrounding affirmative action during the 1960s. In *Spook*, Greenlee offers a narrative critique of affirmative action as practice rather than as a policy, while using the ideas behind it to investigate Black identity.

The novel opens with the question of integrating the CIA to address the history of preferential treatment of whites in its selection process for field agents. Unfortunately, this integration results in mistreatment of the applicants and the most debasing form of tokenism. From the start, integrating the CIA is meant to be a wedge issue to stir up votes for a senatorial race. It is a technique for gathering Black electoral support: "This question of the Negro vote could be serious. I never thought I'd ever be in trouble with those people. We have to come up with something which will remind them I'm the best friend they have in Washington, and soon."[31] After discussing a new Civil Rights bill, a fact-finding tour of African countries, and a speech critiquing apartheid at the University of Cape Town, the senator's advisory committee decides to focus on the CIA's "discriminatory hiring policy."[32] Although the senator and his advisors resolve to undermine employment prejudice, from the start of the novel African Americans are situated as pawns in a larger struggle for state power and white social control. The idea that integration becomes a priority because it supports white desires demonstrates how the novel resonates with Derrick Bell's notion of interest convergence theory, which proposes that white people will support racial justice only when it benefits themselves.[33]

The recruitment process that Greenlee details showcases the presumption that Blacks are always already unqualified, as well as the system-wide refusal to undo discrimination in a real way. Following the senator's campaign against the CIA's employment practices, hundreds of African Americans are considered but only twenty-three men are finalists for employment. They arrive together at the CIA training barracks excited about what this prospect represents for their own lives and for the social realm in general. These men believe that each will get a job with the CIA because they have made it through the screening, but they are disappointed to learn that their arrival is simply the next phase of a series of elimination tests. There are not *jobs*; there might be one job, and the hope on the part of the administration is that none of the men will make it through the assessments. They want to be able to say that they tried, but that no Black men proved to be of the right caliber for employment with the CIA:

> When this group is finished, I want you to begin screening another. Don't bother to select Negroes who are obviously not competent; they have already demonstrated their inability to close the cultural gap and no one is in the position seriously to challenge our insistence not to lower standards for anyone. It will cost us a bit to flunk out six or eight a year, but we needn't worry about harassment on this race thing again in the future if we do. It's a sound investment.[34]

There is an overriding supposition or expectation of Black failure and incompetence. The general does not believe that any Black candidate will be qualified, and he effectively details a hiring strategy that preempts it because his strategy is based on that belief. Integration here is little more than a performative act. Going through the steps of showing concern or investment gets confused with actualizing change. This moment in the text illustrates how and why affirmative action policies can, and sometimes do, fail. Racial inequality was thought of as social and scientific fact, as opposed to the result of the privileging of one group historically.

That being said, Greenlee's plot pivots around the fact that one candidate does get through: Daniel Freeman. He manages to stay under the radar, and he performs well. The officers in charge are unable to eliminate him, so they give him a job as the "top secret reproduction section chief" – he makes copies of confidential files in the basement of the CIA.[35] After months of tests and surpassing every other candidate and every possible expectation, Freeman gets a job working at a copy machine in the basement of a building instead of as a field agent. Occasionally, he is asked to lead tour groups. In Freeman's mind, his "job was to be black and conspicuous as the integrated Negro of the Central Intelligence Agency of the United States of America. As long as he was there, one of an officer corps of thousands, no one could accuse the CIA of not being integrated."[36] Ultimately, integrating appears in terms of the most rudimentary tokenism. Integration means adding literally one. Having one employee in the CIA who is not white manifests integration and seemingly addresses the employment problem substantially. Greenlee exposes and criticizes the idea that hiring one employee (or even a handful) can effectively address decades of employment discrimination. In fact, from his perspective, it represents a purposeful misunderstanding of diversity as well as an ignoring of the history and dynamics that structure the working world specifically and the public world more generally.

The idea of Freeman's conspicuousness is crucial to the text overall, because there is an ongoing tension between conspicuousness and inconspicuousness that subtends the narrative. Being a token means being both visible and invisible, both present and effectively absent through a refused presence. The title of the novel emblematizes this idea on several levels. The word "spook," from the first part of the title, is a way of referring to a spy as well as a derogatory way of referring to Black people. There is a play on words here: Freeman is a spook who is a spook. His Blackness makes him legible, yet spies are supposed to be unseen. The remainder of the title moves beyond this pun. The metaphor of sitting by the door implies the idea of being seen and not heard and being seen but not acting. This sitting by the door represents the logic of the visual example. In other words, the title frames the narrative with the notion of conspicuous, immobilized racial presence – but one that is also gathering information. Greenlee's title indicates a concern with image-making and public perception. This is the realm of tokenism: a focus on public perception as opposed to a concern with actual structural change.

As the title demonstrates, conspicuousness is paired with motifs of invisibility. Freeman might be conspicuous, but he is also concealed. As a spy, he purposefully tries not to be seen to achieve his goals. This strategic invisibility becomes the basis on which the novel consolidates some of the major motifs of African American racial performance and identity: invisibility, masking, jiving, and the trickster. These four tropes recur throughout the novel. In the context of Black cultural history, invisibility describes the lack of a social presence and the denial of civic membership. Greenlee regularly frames Freeman through invisibility: "I somehow forgot that [Freeman] existed. He has a way of fading into the background. You can't remember his face, or what he looks like, or what he has said"; "Freeman moved through Washington like an invisible man."[37] Masking refers to historical acts of shielding or concealing one's true self or feelings for survival: "Freeman the Tom became Freeman the hipster" depending on the situation, to protect himself and achieve his goals.[38] Later on, Freeman thinks: "the cover had to be complete, no holes anywhere. It had to be that way and now he was ready. Or was he? Had his mask become him?"[39] Jiving is the cultural practice of joking with and manipulating another person; it often involves games of one-upmanship. In the text, Freeman is part of an advisory board in Chicago that studies local gang culture. Although the board members believe Freeman is getting them unfettered access to the gang so that it can ultimately be destabilized, he uses their resources to transform a street gang into revolutionaries.[40]

Finally, the trickster is a mythic figure that clandestinely disobeys rules in order to upend tradition and defy figures of authority; the trickster relies upon language play and double meanings to outwit others. Freeman taught the Cobras to use "the linguistics of deception; subterfuge, to strike when least expected and then fade into the background."[41] As one can readily see, these four concepts are interrelated; they often appear together, and all have been crucial elements of African American cultural expression. Significant texts such as Paul Laurence Dunbar's poem "We Wear the Mask" (1896), Zora Neale Hurston's book of folklore, *Mules and Men* (1935), Langston Hughes's Jesse B. Simple stories (1950–61), Ralph Ellison's novel *Invisible Man* (1952), and Cecil Brown's novel *The Life and Loves of Mr Jiveass Nigger* (1969), all reflect the artistic engagement of one or more of these folkloric tropes. Greenlee's active use of these four motifs registers his consciousness of the contours of African American literary history and indicates his attempt to situate his work in that lineage. Collectively, the four tropes all refer to ways of negotiating racial dynamics in the social world, and Greenlee turns to them to illuminate the multiple techniques Freeman uses to infiltrate the CIA and set the stage for a social revolution.[42]

Part of what these strategies point to is a consideration of the most effective means for revolutionary action. The covert is situated as being as important as the overt in terms of revolution. This idea about the value of the covert that is advocated here pushes against common conceptions of Black Power politics as necessarily being more confrontational than Civil Rights strategies. In effect, the simultaneous employment of invisibility, masking, jiving, and the trickster enhances and helps to make possible Greenlee's technique of linking together Black Power and Civil Rights plans of action. They become devices for expressing radical ways of thinking about Black political action. I situate these strategies as creative renderings of notions of compensation that responded to histories of discrimination. As affirmative action policies indicate, compensation has to do with addressing an ongoing history of suppression and discrimination. These four figures are representational methodologies by which African American literary artists have sought to push against and undermine such suppression over time. These literary devices provide ways of reading that recast the seemingly powerless as agential, and trouble power hierarchies instead of reinforcing them. Most often, they take stereotypes and turn them on their heads: an Uncle Tom is feigning subservience; an oblivious, weak-willed individual actually has a plan for insurrection; and so on. Policymakers sought to determine ways to address inequity within the economic sphere; creative writers sought to recuperate the Black character from acts of erasure and constraint within the social imaginary and to challenge the power and meaning of stereotypes.

In the context of this novel concerned with employment discrimination, I read invisibility, masking, jiving, and the trickster as figures of redress because they confront historic and ongoing discrimination and inequity as they emerge in the cultural imagination. In this sense, they reject and move beyond tokenism, which does little to attend to such issues. In fact, one could go so far as to say that tokenism perpetuates disparity and imbalances of power. Through the four figures that Greenlee uses as a collective unit, even tokenism can become the basis for outwitting the powerful and establishing a community of activists. In other words, these devices provide a lens through which one can use tokenism as the foundation for revolutionary action. This reorientation of tokenism through rhetorical figures of redress lays the conceptual terrain of Greenlee's narrative of espionage and rebellion.

Gender Politics and Black Revolutionary Thought

In her 1970 essay, "On the Issue of Roles," Toni Cade Bambara insists that revolution "begins with the self, in the self."[43] Recalling and extending Murapa's ideas about attitudinal revolution, Bambara makes the point that any revolutionary sentiment must begin with a reimagining of individual identity, particularly in regard to conceptions of gender. The rhetoric of revolution driving the movement is not only about revamping the social world. This idea that radical political thought has implications for gender identity and the means for expressing it forms an important component of Greenlee's narrative of espionage. There is a questioning of gender identity and sexual expression that emerges prominently in the inciting of revolt. Greenlee inquires, how might revolutionary thought impact gender expression? The reader finds that in the novel, gender becomes a site for both progressivism and stereotyping. Greenlee uses Freeman's plan for insurrection to shape his presentation of gender and sexual identity.

However, the reformulation of gender ideologies is unevenly radical in its representations of masculinity and femininity.

An important device for articulating masculinity in *Spook* is martial arts. Learning judo is an integral part of Freeman's training as a spy. The goal of judo is to use one's competitor's strength to your own advantage: "a judo match is a contest of skill, not strength. A judo master seeks to minimize the amount of strength he needs to apply [. . .] The goal of movement is to weaken your opponent's position, getting him off balance and taking away his edge."[44] Greenlee is interested in the image of hand-to-hand combat for the narrative about rebellion, but he also seeks to tap into the symbolic value of judo. The instructor of the CIA class is a Korean named Soo, but the supervisor of the instruction is a white man from North Carolina named Calhoun, who takes it as his personal objective to frighten the Black male applicants into leaving or to "break their necks." That being said, he "broke no necks, but he did break one man's leg and dislocated another's shoulder."[45] Calhoun's motivation toward violence illustrates how the recruiters for the CIA were actively attempting to disqualify the Black applicants so that there would be none left to integrate the intelligence agency. He seeks to prove white male superiority over Black men even in an Asian sport. In fact, he tells Freeman directly: "This is a team for men, not misplaced cottonpickers."[46] In the hopes of ridding the program of the high-performing Freeman, Calhoun challenges him to a match, telling him that if he did not resign immediately, he would "whip" him until he walked out, crawled out, or was carried out and resigned. Freeman is able to best Calhoun relatively easily during the match because the latter immediately moves in for the attack and assumes his larger frame and size will result in a quick win. However, judo is less about mastering an attack or simply overwhelming an opponent with strength, and more about evading attack and using a person's strength or force against them.[47] Calhoun, in his race-based anger and fear, is more concerned with overpowering than with demonstrating the skills he has mastered to be a black belt. Judo is a form that emphasizes adeptness and skill that can allow a smaller or weaker individual to outwit and topple to the ground a stronger or larger opponent. This understanding is part of the reason it is an attractive device for Greenlee. Judo is a perfect metaphor for a minority group overcoming a majority population. The minority will never be able to compare in size, but it can cleverly use the majority group's resources to topple the intimidating adversary. This idea lies at the base of the plot; in this sense, the match with Calhoun stands as a metonym for the narrative: a minority using an apparatus of the United States (CIA culture) to overthrow the state.

In addition to indicating the possibility of a minority outmaneuvering a majority, judo is important to the logic of this novel about revolution because of its emphasis on self-defense. Judo – and martial arts in general – consists of a set of techniques for protecting oneself from attack. It is not about fighting or aggression, but rather about personal safety, restraint, self-possession, and self-awareness. These ideas resonate deeply with the Black Panther Party's ideology. Upon its creation, the party originally called itself the Black Panther Party *for Self-Defense*. Such intraracial protection is often remembered in terms of the bearing of arms and the performing of patrolled watches to lessen police brutality in Black communities.

However, the Black Panther-created Oakland Community Learning Center offered a variety of educational and recreational programs including martial arts classes.[48] Accordingly, self-defense did not only mean claiming access to the Second Amendment and policing the police; it also meant equipping community members with a skill set to safeguard themselves. There is a genuine investment in the philosophy of self-defense among Black radicals of this period, which leads some, such as the Panthers, to Eastern martial arts like judo, a physical and mental pedagogy, as opposed to a more aggressive sport such as boxing.

This emphasis on self-defense, though, cannot obscure the fact that judo (and self-defense in general) gets expressed through a limited gender frame. Greenlee uses martial arts primarily to convey masculine empowerment. The image of two men fighting becomes the symbol for the revolutionary action that the novel tracks; in fact, the novel ends with a scene of two Black men (Freeman and Dawson) in fatal conflict. Revolutionary action is a masculine endeavor from the beginning to the end of *Spook*. After successfully joining the CIA and learning all he can from the inside for five years, Freeman decides to quit and go work for a nonprofit foundation back in Chicago. Being a harmless social worker becomes his new cover. In effect, he continues to work as a spy. He organizes a local gang, the Cobras Athletic and Social Club, into a paramilitary group while he is working for the nonprofit.

Although Freeman had been a leader of the group as a teenager, the current Cobras members are reluctant to trust him because he is now considered to be an outsider and not nearly as radical and anti-establishment as they are, given his occupation. However, he reassures them: "You really want to fuck with whitey, I'll show you how!"[49] His full-time work becomes instructing them on how to become revolutionary soldiers. His training includes learning how to steal weapons from the government, how to rob a bank successfully (which they do), how to use triangulation to figure out range when working as a sniper, as well as training in physical combat and judo. Throughout the different levels of preparation, Freeman emphasizes discipline and not anger to these young men. At one point, he does admit that women can and should be useful in their plans for revolution,[50] but Freeman's army is a male army, and his revolution has all the trappings of androcentrism. This kind of thinking recalls some of the critiques of the Black Panther Party early on made by women members of the Party, as well as recognizable critiques of social activism during the 1960s.[51] Whether Greenlee was merely replicating the dynamics that emerged in real-life radical groups or was expressing his own inclination toward male-centered activism, the novel chiefly imagines revolution through the young, able-bodied, and heterosexual male body.

What about revolutionary women and sexual minorities within this landscape of rebellious activism? Although one particular body dominates the expression of revolutionary action in the novel, it is not the only one that is reimagined. There are only two women characters of any significance, neither of whom gets much narrative space: Freeman's occasional girlfriend, Joy, and a nameless sex worker, who appears in the story under the appellation of the "Dahomey queen" and has an ongoing relationship with Freeman. Joy principally serves as a device to critique the Black middle class; she aspires to financial stability – if not excess, has no concern for struggling Black communities, and wants Freeman to prioritize this desire if they are to be together.

However, the Dahomey queen character stands as a complicated exploration of sexual dynamics in the context of Freeman's subversive actions. Although she does sell sex to men, she uses the language of homosexuality to characterize herself.[52] She repeatedly remarks that men "would never be her scene."[53] She confidently asserts her non-normative sexual identity and refuses heterosexuality except as a means for her financial stability or occasional pleasure. Her character represents a refusal of patriarchy while at the same time she claims a right to desire men if she so chooses. Through the character, Green gestures toward a radical Black womanhood that does not have to make a complete concession to heterosexual patriarchy.

Throughout the novel, Greenlee presents homosexuality as a given, a social fact, and not as a moral dilemma or as in need of censure. Freeman has no problem socializing with gay men; he can make them "feel at ease and turn down their propositions without bruising their ego."[54] At the beginning of the novel, a couple of the recruits to the CIA are dismissed from consideration because they are gay. Freeman acknowledges that their sexuality makes them vulnerable, but he is not critical of their sexual preferences. This understanding differs from critical stances that some Black male writers such as Amiri Baraka and Eldridge Cleaver ostensibly take on homosexuality, especially male homosexuality, during this period.[55] Same-sex desire is a recurring element of *Spook*; one finds that Greenlee's narrative of insurrection cannot be told without reference to homosexual desire.[56] My point is not that the text is absolutely progressive in terms of its rendering of homosexuality. Rather, the narrative reflects increasing attention to the place of sexuality within political rhetoric.

The Dahomey woman character forms an important part of Freeman's information network and helps to establish the narrative's uneven investment in undermining conventional ideas about Black gender identity. In her own way, she is also a secret agent providing the protagonist with important information. She alerts Freeman to the plans of the general, who seeks to stop the revolutionary action, because she is the general's escort.[57] In fact, Elizabeth Reich describes her as "a prostitute who becomes an Africanist queen-spy for the revolution," enhancing the overall motif of espionage.[58] The challenging aspect of her power and access is that she manifests them through her sexuality and through heterosexual sex acts. Following this logic, women can gain information and social power through intercourse, unlike the Cobras who train their bodies as well as their minds, with no recourse to sexual pleasure. The Cobras' spycraft consists of being a sniper or performing surveillance; her spycraft is solely sexual. She consistently claims an agency and independence for herself, but it appears in a stereotypical and sexist manner: this Black women's value derives from the fact that she is a sex worker.[59] Moreover, even though the Dahomey queen character insists that men are not her scene, Freeman is. She never rejects her self-professed homosexuality, but she does concede that Freeman is the only man who would ever lead her to question it.[60] Accordingly, through their relationship, Freeman appears as exceptional, the superlative Black man, who *possibly* has the power to reorient queer desire.

Although the novel resists recapitulating the notion of the charismatic, exemplary leader in terms of the description of Freeman's paramilitary organization, there is a kind of heterosexual male sexual charisma that emerges through the relationship with the Dahomey spy character. This is important for two reasons. First, it reminds the reader that Black Power politics steadily explores the fraught terrain of gender and sexuality in the context of social change. There was a recognized link made between political action and sexual action. Second, Freeman's ability to charm the Dahomey spy in a way that no other man ever could demonstrates how Greenlee's novel simultaneously takes up and bypasses Bambara's call for revolutionary selfhood. The novel indicates that you do not have to be the biggest or the strongest to be successful. It also suggests that defense sometimes matters more than offense (militancy). There is an attempt to offer a variety of tactics and understandings about struggle. Nevertheless, this alternative theory of radical empowerment never fully rises above masculine empowerment. The novel espouses revolution and seeks to refashion political rhetoric as well as Black gender identity, but it also reflects an investment in old-fashioned and even reactionary ways of thinking. It proffers new models for activism and for imagining Black masculinity, while at times upholding clichéd and problematic conceptions of Black femininity. The Black female spy as a figure registers the protagonist's masculine appeal. However, I maintain that this spy is also an emblem of an emerging discourse around the politics of homosexuality within Black literary culture, which would become an important site for radicalizing Black identity during the 1970s and 1980s, as the works of Barbara Smith, Audre Lorde, and Joseph Beam (among others) illustrate.[61]

Conclusion

To conclude, I turn to a figure who might be seen as an unexpected addition to an examination of Black Power politics: Martin Luther King, Jr. In his final book, published the year before he died, *Where Do We Go From Here?*, King argues:

> We need organizations that are permeated with mutual trust, incorruptibility and *militancy*. Without this spirit we may have numbers but they will add up to zero. We need organizations that are responsible, efficient and alert. We lack experience because ours is a history of disorganization. But we will prevail because our need for progress is stronger than the ignorance forced upon us. If we realize how indispensable is responsible *militant* organization to our struggle, we create it as we managed to create underground railroads, protest groups, self-help societies and the churches that have always been our refuge, our source of hope and our source of action.[62]

Throughout this book, King attempts to answer the question that he uses to frame this volume. He emphasizes militancy, an idea that may not generally be connected to his avowed philosophy of nonviolence. This important book is one that might not be assumed to be a contribution to the discourses around militant radicalism of the 1960s. In reality, much of

King's book uncovers the connection between his own thinking and that of other Black radicals. As the above passage illustrates, King essentially formulates a synthesis of Civil Rights logic and Black Power ideologies. He is interested in institution-building and pointing out the disappointment with the implementation of Civil Rights legislation.[63] King negotiates the complex terrain of Black political thought. He is a Civil Rights icon who is actively negotiating Black Power principles. He is doing in his analysis what Greenlee hopes to achieve in his fiction: merging different paradigms. His work, like Greenlee's, gestures toward a new avenue for conveying and inciting Black activism.

Spook makes a demand for and imagines alternative possibilities for activism, leadership, and identity. Notwithstanding this idea, the text is consistently both forward- and backward-looking in terms of its rendering of these elements – just as it is in relation to the form of the revolutionary novel. In Greenlee's analysis, the boundaries between the old and the new become blurred, sometimes beneficially and sometimes detrimentally. This characteristic means that Greenlee's novel sits on the precipice of the innovative, though complete newness is not fully realized within the pages of the novel because of the dependence on older forms and ideas. The novel represents a world in flux.

This understanding of Greenlee's novel as existing between the old and the new in terms of political rhetoric and racial representations indicates how *The Spook Who Sat by the Door* is ultimately a novel about Black liminality. This term denotes being on the threshold of change or being on the verge of transition. Greenlee's decision to use the spy as an organizing lens supports the notion of the liminal state of Blackness. Freeman asserts: "The nigger was the only natural agent in the United States, the only person whose life might depend from childhood, on becoming what whites demanded, yet somehow remaining what he was as an individual human being."[64] In the context of the novel, liminality connotes a necessary way of existing in the social world that African Americans inhabit. Black positionality is spy positionality, given the former's social circumstances, and the spy is a liminal figure. Therefore, because of sociohistorical realities, Black identity can best be expressed through metaphors of liminality. In fact, Greenlee's title encapsulates this understanding. The act of sitting by the door describes a state of liminality: being in-between, on the threshold, and so on. Therefore, the novel situates Blackness at a moment of transition and in-between dominant ways of thinking.

Given this idea, the narrative functions as an archive of the shifting terrain of Black Power, specifically how activists and cultural producers diligently adapt and transform the militant philosophy of revolution to move it forward and achieve desired change. Greenlee's spy novel shows the twenty-first-century reader how Black Power is an open-ended process of searching for meaning rather than a singular static philosophy.

Notes

1. King (1968), 161.
2. For historical accounts of the period, see Brown (1994), Seale (1970), Davis (1974), Malcolm X (1992), King (1964), Joseph (2006), Ransby (2003), and Countryman (2006).
3. Greenlee had difficulty getting his novel published in the United States. The novel was first published in the United Kingdom in 1969. It was not published in full in the United States until 1973. A film version of the novel also appeared in 1973.
4. Much of the scholarship on Greenlee's text is on the 1973 film adaptation of the novel that considers it in the context of the Blaxploitation film genre. I focus on the novel and its relationship to issues of Civil Rights during the 1960s.
5. See Schudel (2014).
6. See Du Bois (2007 [1903]).
7. Greenlee talks about the challenges he faced getting the book published, and claims that the FBI attempted to suppress the film version, in the 2011 documentary *Infiltrating Hollywood: The Rise and Fall of the Spook Who Sat by the Door*, directed by Christine Acham and Clifford Ward (Acham and Ward 2011).
8. Murapa (1969), 9.
9. I discuss how the concept of "revolutionizing the mind" is a dominant paradigm in 1960s-era Black political thought in Avilez (2016).
10. The selection appears under the title "The D.C. Blues" (Greenlee 1969, 86–92).
11. Peavy (1970), 223. The review discusses three novels in particular: J. Denis Jackson's *The Black Commandos* (1967), John A. Williams' *Sons of Darkness, Sons of Light* (1969), and Greenlee's novel.
12. Peavey expanded the review and published it the following year in the academic journal *Studies in the Novel* (Peavey 1971).
13. Malcolm X (1990).
14. Carmichael (2003), 507.
15. See Van Deburg (1992), Joseph (2006), Ogbar (2005), Smethurst (2005).
16. Acham (2005).
17. Ture and Hamilton (1992 [1967]), 54, 55.
18. Ibid., 157.
19. Greenlee (1969b), 12, 56.
20. Ibid., 204.

21. For a consideration of Black leadership and notions of charisma in twentieth-century African American culture, see Edwards (2012).
22. Greenlee (1969b), 107.
23. Robinson (2016).
24. Ibid., 67.
25. Ibid., 67–68.
26. Anderson (2004), 55–56.
27. Ibid., 76.
28. See Executive Order 10925 (March 6, 1961). www.presidency.ucsb.edu/docu ments/executive-order-10925-establishing-the-presidents-committee-equal-empl oyment-opportunity [accessed September 22, 2021].
29. www.ourdocuments.gov/doc.php?flash=false&doc=97&page=transcript [accessed September 22, 2021].
30. See Anderson (2004).
31. Greenlee (1969b), 4.
32. Ibid., 6. Actually, it is the mayor's wife who suggests this possibility to the committee. They are unable to come up with the idea on their own.
33. Bell (2004).
34. Greenlee (1969b), 20.
35. Ibid., 40.
36. Ibid., 47.
37. Ibid., 28, 60.
38. Ibid., 48.
39. Ibid., 75.
40. Ibid., 89–93, 103–4.
41. Ibid., 135.
42. These tropes connect the novel to important works of African American literary and cultural history. See, for example, Zafar (1997) and Gates (1988).
43. Bambara (1970), 133.
44. Yoffie and Kwak (2001), 9–11.
45. Greenlee (1969b), 23.
46. Ibid.
47. See Reay (1985) and Pedro (2001).
48. Jones (1998), 191.
49. Greenlaw (1969b), 88.
50. Ibid., 96.
51. See critiques of masculinism in Black political organizations in Collier-Thomas and Franklin (2001) and Brown (1994).
52. Greenlaw (1969b), 36.
53. Ibid., 39, 61.
54. Ibid., 82.
55. See Baraka (2001 [1964]), and Cleaver (1991 [1968]), 205–20.
56. I discuss the employment of homosexuality in relation to revolutionary thought in Avilez (2016).
57. Greenlaw (1969b), 235.

58. Reich (2012), 335.
59. Patricia Hill Collins' discussion of "controlling images" provides a language with which to discuss the presentation of Black women through sexual means (Collins 1991).
60. Greenlee (1969b), 36.
61. See Smith (1983) and (1998); Lorde (1992) and (1984); and Beam (1986).
62. See King (1968), 160–61 (emphasis added).
63. Ibid., 34.
64. Greenlaw (1969b), 109–10.

References

Acham, C. 2005. "Subverting the System: The Politics and Production of *The Spook Who Sat by the Door.*" *Screening Noir* 1.1: 113–36.

Anderson, T. 2004. *The Pursuit of Fairness: A History of Affirmative Action.* Oxford University Press.

Avilez, G. 2016. *Radical Aesthetics and Modern Black Nationalism.* Champaign: University of Illinois Press.

Bambara, T. C. 2005 [1970]. "On the Issue of Roles." In *The Black Woman: An Anthology*, ed. T. C. Bambara, 123–36. New York: Washington Square Press.

Baraka, A. (L. Jones). 2001 [1964]. *Dutchman and the Slave.* New York: Perennial.

Beam, J., ed. 1986. *In the Life: A Black Gay Anthology.* New York: Alyson Publications.

Bell, D. 2004. *Silent Covenants: Brown v. Board of Education and the Unfulfilled Hopes for Racial Reform.* Oxford University Press.

Brown, C. 1991 [1969]. *The Life and Loves of Mr. Jiveass Nigger.* New York: Ecco Press.

Brown, E. 1994. *A Taste of Power: A Black Woman's Story.* New York: Anchor Books.

Carmichael, S. 2003. *Ready for Revolution: The Life and Struggles of Stokely Carmichael [Kwame Ture].* New York: Scribner.

Cleaver, E. 1991 [1968]. *Soul on Ice.* New York: Delta.

Collier-Thomas, B., and V. P. Franklin, eds. 2001. *Sisters in the Struggle: African American Women in the Civil Rights–Black Power Movement.* New York University Press.

Collins, P. H. 1991. *Black Feminist Thought: Knowledge, Consciousness, and the Politics of Empowerment.* New York and London: Routledge.

Countryman, M. J. 2006. *Up South: Civil Rights and Black Power in Philadelphia.* Philadelphia: University of Pennsylvania Press.

Davis, A. 1974. *An Autobiography.* New York: Random House.

Deslippe, D. 2012. *Protesting Affirmative Action: The Struggle over Equality after the Civil Rights Revolution.* Baltimore, MD: Johns Hopkins University Press.

Du Bois, W. E. B. 2007 [1903]. *The Souls of Black Folk.* Oxford University Press.

Dunbar, P. L. 1993. "We Wear the Mask." In *The Collected Poetry of Paul Laurence Dunbar*, ed. J. M. Braxton, 71. Charlottesville: University of Virginia Press.

Edwards, E. 2012. *Charisma and the Fictions of Black Leadership*. Minneapolis: University of Minnesota Press.

Ellison, R. 2002 [1952]. *Invisible Man*. New York: Random House.

Executive Order 10925. 1961, March 6. www.presidency.ucsb.edu/documents/ex ecutive-order-10925-establishing-the-presidents-committee-equal-employ ment-opportunity [accessed September 22, 2021].

Executive Order 11114. 1963, June 22. www.presidency.ucsb.edu/documents/execu tive-order-11114-extending-the-authority-the-presidents-committee-equal-e mployment [accessed September 22, 2021].

Gates, H. L., Jr. 1988. *The Signifying Monkey: A Theory of Afro-American Literary Criticism*. New York: Oxford University Press.

Greenlee, S. 1969a, June. "The D.C. Blues." *Negro Digest* 18.8: 86–92.

1969b. *The Spook Who Sat by the Door*. Chicago, IL: Lushena Press.

Jones, C. E., ed. 1998. *The Black Panther Party [Reconsidered]*. Baltimore, MD: Black Classics Press.

Joseph, P. E. 2006. *Waiting 'Til the Midnight Hour: A Narrative History of Black Power in America*. New York: Henry Holt.

King, M. L., Jr. 1964. *Why We Can't Wait*. New York: Harper & Row.

1968. *Where Do We Go from Here: Chaos or Community?* Boston, MA: Beacon Press.

Lorde, A. 1984. *Sister Outsider: Essays and Speeches*. Trumansburg, NY: Crossing Press.

1992. *Zami: A New Spelling of My Name*. Freedom, CA: Crossing Press.

Malcolm X. 1990. *Malcolm X Speaks: Selected Speeches and Statements*, ed. G. Breitman. New York: Grove Weidenfeld.

1992 [1965]. *Autobiography of Malcolm X*. New York: Ballantine.

Murapa, R. 1969. "The Real Revolution: Race Pride and Black Political Thought." *Negro Digest* 18.7: 6–10.

Ogbar, J. 2005. *Black Power: Radical Politics and African American Identity*. Baltimore, MD: Johns Hopkins University Press.

Peavy, C. D. 1970. "Four Black Revolutionary Novels, 1899–1970." *Journal of Black Studies* 1.2: 219–23.

1971. "The Black Revolutionary Novel: 1899–1969." *Studies in the Novel* 3.2: 180–89.

Pedro, J. 2001. *Judo: Techniques and Tactics*. Champaign, IL: Human Kinetics Publishers.

Ransby, B. 2003. *Ella Baker and the Black Freedom Movement*. Chapel Hill: University of North Carolina Press.

Reay, T. 1985. *Judo: Skills and Techniques*. Marlborough: Crowood Press.

Reich, E. 2012. "A New Kind of Black Soldier: Performing Revolution in the Spook Who Sat by the Door." *African American Review* 45.3: 325–39.

Robinson, C. J. 2016 [1990]. *The Terms of Order: Political Science and the Myth of Leadership*. Chapel Hill: University of North Carolina Press.

Schudel, M. 2014, May 14. "Obituary: Sam Greenlee." *Washington Post*.

Seale, B. 1970. *Seize the Time: The Story of the Black Panther Party and Huey P. Newton.* New York: Random House.

Sheppard, S. N. 2013. "Persistently Displaced: Situated Knowledges and Interrelated Histories in The Spook Who Sat by the Door." *Cinema Journal* 52.2: 71–92.

Smethurst, J. 2005. *The Black Arts Movement: Literary Nationalism in the 1960s and 1970s.* Chapel Hill: University of North Carolina Press.

Smith, B., ed. 1983. *Home Girls: A Black Feminist Anthology.* New York: Kitchen Table Press.

    1998. *The Truth that Never Hurts: Writings on Race, Gender, and Freedom.* New Brunswick, NJ: Rutgers University Press.

Ture, K., and C. Hamilton. 1992 [1967]. *Black Power: The Politics of Liberation.* New York: Vintage.

Van Deburg, W. 1992. *New Day in Babylon: The Black Power Movement and American Culture, 1965–1975.* University of Chicago Press.

Yoffie, D., and M. Kwak. 2001. *Judo Strategy.* Boston, MA: HBS Press.

Zafar, R. 1997. *We Wear the Mask: African Americans Write American Literature.* New York: Columbia University Press.

CHAPTER 8

The Necessary Violence of Frantz Fanon and Malcolm X in Global Black Revolution

Kelly M. Nims

The World the Slaves Made

"We assert that in those areas where the government is either unable or unwilling to protect the lives and property of our people, that our people are within our rights to protect themselves by whatever means necessary."
I repeat, because to me this is the most important thing you need to know.
I already know it.

Malcolm X, reading from the Charter for the Organization of Afro-American Unity ("By Any Means Necessary," 1964)

Forged out of slave labor, imperialism, genocide, and the failed promises of revolution for those outside of white national manhood, violence is the bedrock of the United States.[1] This goes without saying. Enslaved people built the United States, as Eugene Genovese's masterpiece lays bare, under unspeakable oppression and violence.[2] Enslaved people also resisted. Their descendants resist. This essay is in engagement with the iteration of this resistance in 1960s America, specifically the relationship between violence and rebellion: in times of resistance, what happens to the violence that is required for slavery and world-making, the ongoing violence that props up the white power structure that undergirds the nation? How is this violence rechanneled and appropriated during revolt? Historically, with empathy and hope as their structuring affects, mainstream U.S. social movements aimed at redressing ongoing violent exploitation and degradation have championed peaceful protest and persuasion, the sympathetic fellow feeling of putting oneself in the shoes of the oppressed always already coupled with the Christian mandate of turning the other cheek.[3] This is to say that the violence that structures the social is absorbed in new forms by the body of the oppressed, in what is often described as "nonviolent" protest or civil disobedience. The masochistic choice to take on the violence of the oppressor while loving that oppressor ("love thy enemy" and the like) does not place one ideologically or physically outside of violence as the qualifier "nonviolent" suggests.

The irony of a nation formed out of the violence of revolution that in turn criminalizes its colonialized desiring the same liberty is not lost on Malcolm X, an excellent student of American history: it was at his "white school" that "the white man made the mistake of letting [him] read his history books."[4] Patrick Henry's "Liberty or Death" is an early lesson for Malcolm in the dialectical relationship between freedom and violence: "These thirteen little scrawny states, tired of taxation without representation, tired of being exploited and oppressed and degraded, told that big British Empire, 'Liberty or death.' And here you have twenty-two million Afro-Americans, Black people today, catching more hell than Patrick Henry ever saw."[5] In a rhetorical strategy that is cross-racial and transhistorical, Malcolm appropriates (white) American history as a shared narrative of rebellion which it is his right to emulate. Henry's cry becomes a maxim for Black resistance in the 1960s. If thirteen "scrawny states" can effect revolution, certainly twenty-two million Afro-Americans who have suffered in ways unimaginable to Henry can. Rather than be "castrated" by white institutions structured to deny Blacks power and a Civil Rights Movement that advocates nonviolent protest, in comparing their numbers to the thirteen colonies, Malcolm X challenges Blacks, through a shaming logic, to respond appropriately: violently resisting by any means necessary, just like the nation's founders.[6] For Malcolm, the redress to castration is outwardly directed violence.

Yet in times of revolt, given the accepted narrative of American history, the violence of nation-building and empire is usually reabsorbed in forms of masochistic resistance, from mainstream nineteenth-century abolitionism to a Civil Rights Movement for whom Dr. Martin Luther King, Jr., continues to serve as the defining metonymy. Contra civil disobedience, flows of outwardly directed violent resistance erupt, breaking with the mainline of reform and protest movements centered on empathetic persuasion and its attendant inwardly directed violence: David Walker, John Brown, Nat Turner, slaves like Celia Newsom who kills her master/rapist in an act of self-defense.[7] These violent acts are flashpoints, shut down and often framed as footnotes or solitary moments within larger historical narratives that privilege civil disobedience. However, a strain of U.S. Black resistance in the 1960s becomes what Alain Badiou in *Being and Event* describes as an event proper, that which happens when the excluded flash up, suddenly, violently, drastically. The outwardly directed violence of such revolt ruptures the normative and clears the ground to produce what James Baldwin refers to as the void that the revolutionary must embrace, the space in which to reimagine the social.[8] What Badiou theorizes as the startling "inconsistent multiplicity" of the oppressed, that multiplicity unrealized by the oppressor, makes the event possible – in this case, the unexpected multiplicity of outwardly directed violence erupting as an organizing force in the face of the dominance of nonviolent protest and white supremacy. Given the historical record, with civil disobedience as the expected model of resistance in the United States, outwardly directed violent protest becomes unforeseen, inconsistent with how the oppressed have rebelled.

Yet in the 1960s, outwardly directed violence was officially on the table, organized and structured, part of a decolonial, transnational philosophy of Black resistance. Black violence against white supremacy became a viable strategy, one that openly competed with nonviolent protest. The event of "by any means necessary" moves from the margin to the center, grounded specifically in the theory and praxis of Malcolm X, whose own inconsistent multiplicity in vision can be traced to his time abroad as he moves from calls against the "white devil" to white institutions, from religion to the economy. This movement from margin to center is global in force, inspired by revolutionaries in Latin America and Africa, most directly by Frantz Fanon's *The Wretched of the Earth*, what we might read as the doctrine that undergirds the event of the 1960s in America through Malcolm X and the Black Panthers, both of whom share an affinity with Fanon's call for the violent dismantling of colonialization as the only way for the oppressed to claim their humanity and freedom.

If we then frame the Civil Rights Movement as a deterritorialized, Black revolutionary event, we reveal the complexities and contradictions inherent in Black resistance that complicate the narrative we have created retroactively about the 1960s. Engaging with the rich complexities of revolution, this essay troubles the accepted narrative of Black resistance in 1960s America, specifically the uses of violence and the ways it stretches the movement across space and time. I consider the violence of Black protest in the 1960s in more expansive terms, beyond the turn-the-other-cheek violence of what often is described as nonviolent protest. Engaging with Malcolm X's *Autobiography* (1965) and selected speeches, read through the influence of Fanon's *The Wretched of the Earth* (1961), this essay reads the two as representative of a global Black model of revolution predicated on outwardly directed violence.

Alongside, against, and often rendered peripheral to the tradition of civil disobedience in America, radicals from Malcolm X to the Black Panther

Party reject nonviolent resistance in favor of an outwardly, rather than an inwardly, directed violence aimed at white supremacy and a political model that limit social justice to merely a "seat at the table," circumscribing Black potentiality. This essay's counter-narrative challenges the geography, temporality, and structure of Black revolution in the 1960s, decentering the United States, acknowledging the influence of French intellectualism, and reaching back to acts of resistance of earlier generations, ultimately complicating the linear narrative of nation-bound, peaceful protest that has come to define civil rights.

The violence out of which the oppressed are formed is the quilting point for transitions in Black resistance. White responses to peaceful protest were often extremely violent. There is no place where this is better exemplified than in the assassination of King in 1968. Frustrated with civil disobedience and Elijah Muhammad, conversant with the ideologies of revolutionaries like Fanon and Jomo Kenyatta and Kwame Nkrumah in Africa, Malcolm X advocates what he describes as an act of self-defense against the ongoing physical and psychic brutality of racism.[9] Malcolm X reads police brutality against peaceful protesters as a plantation scene, alive and well, post-emancipation, perpetuated by both oppressed and oppressor, with Black men passively witnessing white men beat Black women.[10] Given his logic, nonviolent resistance parallels the plantation hierarchy, with the Black body absorbing the white violence that maintains white power – instead, Malcolm X calls for less religion, "less singing and more swinging."[11] Inspired by the African struggle, Malcolm X argues that outwardly directed violence embodies a sadistic, generative power manifest in a self-love and pleasure in Blackness unfettered from assimilation into a white power structure that is dependent on the demonization of Blackness.

Malcolm's philosophy represents the idea that violence can be what is necessary to bring an end to oppression, a position that echoes Fanon's claim that "The naked truth of decolonization evokes for us the searing bullets and bloodstained knives which emanate from it."[12] In his "Message to the Grassroots" (1963), Malcolm X unites his Black audience through a "common enemy . . . the oppressor, the exploiter, the discriminator."[13] Tellingly, Fanon demonstrates a similar belief that the racial hierarchy of the colonial world will necessarily result in a "great showdown" between these two fundamentally opposed groups, an "inevitable emergence of the armed struggle against colonialism."[14] Thus, in both the African and the African American context, there is simultaneous acceptance of the necessity of violence in the quest for true revolution. Free from the politics of reform, the pleasure and empowerment that grow out of outwardly directed violence allow for the making of self and world outside of white supremacist institutions. This sadism adds an affective density to the narrative that we tell about Black resistance in the 1960s, placing Fanon and Malcolm X in a perhaps unlikely context that takes into account the ways in which resistance is shaped by desire and pleasure.

Although the Black struggle for civil rights in the United States and decolonialization in Algeria are contextually different, Malcolm X theorizes Black oppression in the United States through the lens of colonialism, arguing for the powerful affinity between the two movements:

> America is just as much a colonial power as England ever was. America is just as much a colonial power as France ever was. In fact, America is more so a colonial power than they because she's a hypocritical colonial power behind it. What do you call second class citizenship? Why, that's colonization. Second class citizenship is nothing but twentieth-century slavery.[15]

In keeping with the global, decolonial framework that Malcolm X arrives at, speaking to the Ghanaian Parliament in 1964, he describes the United States as "the master of imperialism without whose support, France, South Africa, Britain, and Portugal could not exist," and called upon all Africans to support Blacks in the United States, proclaiming: "The struggle for civil rights in the United States should be switched to a struggle for human rights to enable Africans to raise the matter at the United Nations."[16]

After his travels, then, Malcolm X transitions from an American-centered revolution that saw whites as "blue-eyed devils," to a Black diasporic revolution with its sights set on dismantling white power structures. Inspired by the Afro-commitment in other countries to American Civil Rights, as well as the interracial Muslim communities that he encountered, Malcolm X comes to make a case for both a pan-African and pan-racial revolution, where religion is left "in the closet," one that rechannels the violence of racism toward the white institutions, largely economic, that prop it up.[17] Coming to understand the necessity of globality, Malcolm X challenges Black Americans living abroad to join their brothers and sisters in their own decolonial revolutions.[18] In sum, the transitions in revolutionary vision that I trace permeate the 1960s. The Black Panther Party, for example, is conversant with previous generations like Fanon, and expands the coordinates of its resistance from protecting Black neighborhoods in the United States to supporting revolutions abroad and protesting the war in Vietnam. The Panthers provide a timely example given our current historical moment: police brutality at home, multiple wars abroad, xenophobic violence. Perhaps a reconsideration of

(Black) revolution beyond national boundaries and the dominance of empathy and peaceful protest is necessary.

Necessary Violence, Necessary Sadism

Since self preservation is the first law of nature, we assert the Afro American's right to self defense.

Everything in the universe does something when you start playing with his life, except the American Negro. He lays down and says, "Beat me, daddy."
Malcolm X, "By Any Means Necessary," 1964

As the above quotations attest, revolution and violence are entangled. The 1960s become a case in point for the oppressed's relationship to violence during rebellion. Malcolm X clearly reads nonviolent protest as positioning the Black person in a subservient position in relation to the master whom he begs for a beating. The pleading, the sexualized language of the address to "daddy" coupled with the masculine pronoun gendering the Black subject (doubling the humiliation given conventional gender norms) underscore the masochism that animates civil disobedience as well as the sadism that informs the master's position as the agent administering the violence. Countering this eroticized tableau of humiliation, outwardly directed violence empowers the colonized to move from the position of object to subject in the spectrum of power. The oppressed person is now in the position formerly occupied by the master. The sadistic violence that makes such a positionality possible allows for self-preservation for Malcolm X. Following Fanon, the outwardly directed violence permits the colonized to define her humanity after the annihilation of the master, and outside of the racist institutions that condition her existence. For both Malcolm X and Fanon, sadism is generative, producing subjects on their own terms. Masochistic passivity humiliates and keeps one an object to be used and abused for the master's enjoyment.

There is little doubt that in the history of slavery and colonization, violence and the power needed to ensure its domination is paramount in the creation of the European diaspora. Furthermore, violence is reflective of fear that later shaped subsequent attitudes toward the Other within the colonial/slave system. The fear was not only in the flight from the Old World to the New, but also in the hope of a limitless future, made more appealing by what was left behind. As Toni Morrison illuminates in *Playing in the Dark*:

> With luck and endurance one could discover freedom; find a way to make God's law manifest; . . . the habit of genuflection would be replaced by the

thrill of command. Power – control over one's destiny – would replace the powerlessness felt before the gates of class, caste, and cunning persecution. One could move from discipline and punishment to disciplining and punishing; from social ostracism to social rank.[19]

It was this kind of power – the power to turn a fearful impulse into law and – that was in turn appropriated into tradition. There is nowhere this tradition is better exemplified than in the system that was designed to reflect the interests of the ruler's oppression. Since "The economic substructure is also a superstructure," Fanon insists that a Marxist approach must be applied and stretched, for "the serf is in essence different from the knight, but a reference to divine right is necessary to legitimize this statutory difference. In the colonies, the foreigner coming from another country imposed his rule by means of guns and machines."[20] Can this "divine right" be reappropriated by the colonized in revolution?

Walter Benjamin's meditation on violence is useful in defining the violence of Black resistance in the 1960s in the United States. In his foundational "Critique of Violence," Benjamin argues that the state is deeply dependent upon circumscribing violence within the scope of the law, thus enabling the state to preserve the law; violence outside of the law always threatens the state "by its mere existence."[21] The outwardly directed violence of Black resistance may be closest to what Benjamin terms divine violence: neither the "law-preserving" violence of the state, nor the "law-building" violence outside of the state that erects counter-institutions that may be coopted and brought back under the state's purview.[22] Rather, divine violence erupts outside of the law and its organizing institutions. It protects what is sacred about humanity, allowing those stripped of their humanity and rendered bare life (humans rendered objects and property under slavery) by the violence of the law to define their humanity on their own terms. While not the violence of any god or God, divine violence is of a higher order beyond, not subservient to, the state.

Slavoj Zizek (2008) reads divine violence as manifesting itself after millions have suffered for a prolonged period of time, their suffering having accrued in the superstructure. Here perhaps Zizek is echoing Malcolm X, who further theorizes the danger and potentiality of sustained oppression, degradation, and accrued rage:

> Because Negroes have listened to the trickery and the lies and the false promises of the white man now for too long, and they're fed up ... And all

of this has built up frustrations in the black community that makes the black community throughout America today more explosive than all of the atomic bombs the Russians can ever invent. Whenever you got a racial powder keg sitting in your lap, you're in more trouble than if you had an atomic powder keg sitting in your lap. When a racial powder keg goes off, it doesn't care who it knocks out the way. Understand this, it's dangerous.[23]

What happens in the aftermath of the explosion? If we are to read the racial powder keg as divine violence's tear in the social fabric, it is important to note that according to Benjamin, divine violence is not the violence of organized revolutionary struggle (law-making violence); successful revolutions lead to the building of counter-institutions with their own laws (Cuba, the Soviet Union, Algeria). My claim, however, is that Black resistance in United States in the 1960s remains within the realm of divine violence because it never had the organizing power of the Civil Rights Movement and did not have the power of sustainability. Rather, in America, unlike Fanon's involvement with the Algerian revolution, it manifests itself in moments of unsustained violent resistance, with its leaders ultimately assassinated or incarcerated. This does not make its model of resistance any less real or potent. With Paul Klee's *Angelus Novus* painting as a touchstone, Benjamin reads the angel of history as "see[ing] one single catastrophe which keeps piling wreckage and hurls it in front of his feet"; the call to violence, unlike the "turn-the-other-cheek" mandate of nonviolent protest, counters the systemic violence building at the angel's feet.[24] To consider Benjamin's angel in perhaps less poetic or mythical terms: what I am calling the divine violence of Black resistance à la Malcolm X has no desire for assimilation into dominant institutions via reform, because it is of a higher, perhaps yet to be imagined order, whose contours can be glimpsed in the representation of the angel of history.

For Fanon, outwardly directed violence becomes law-making in the Algerian revolution. But in his writings, Fanon is most concerned with examining the colonial world through the lens of law-preserving violence: the world of the native/settler, colonized/colonizer, poor/rich, Black/white is divided into compartments, it is "a world cut in two . . . the frontiers are shown by police stations. . . . it is the policeman and the soldier who are the official, instituted go-betweens, the spokesmen of the [settler/colonizer/ rich/white] and his rule of oppression."[25] The rule of law is expanded into every facet of life, as the labor and educational system must respect the established order and "serve to create around the exploited person an atmosphere of submission . . . which lightens the task of policing considerably."[26] Residential areas reflect the rules of oppression as they adhere to "the rules of pure Aristotelian logic, they both follow the principle of reciprocal exclusivity."[27] Fanon highlights that the settler/colonizer/rich/white residential area is one that is illuminated and strongly built, one that is neat and spacious, while the native/colonized/poor/Black area is a "reservation, peopled by men of evil repute."[28] It is a place devoid of light and spaciousness, one that is starved and hungry for all things that the settler/colonizer/rich/whites have.

Fanon also analyzes the question of legitimacy in nationhood. Legitimacy has not been in question for the West since the Enlightenment, yet for colonized individuals who are offshoots of political parties that mobilize people, "the demand for national culture and the affirmation of the existence of such a culture represent a special battlefield."[29] In systems of oppression, cultural domination or obliteration is made possible by the legal regulations of the dominant group, in which "every effort is made to . . . [convince the oppressed person] to admit the inferiority of his culture and the confused and imperfect character of his own biological structure, [which in turn] leads to the systematic enslaving of men and women."[30] This itself is a violent act, one that leads Malcolm X to identify the white man as the enemy of Black people, as the slave master who "destroyed everything of [one's] past. Today [one] do[es] not know [his] true language . . . [he] know[s] nothing about [his] true culture."[31]

European culture had to exercise systematic discipline in order to manage and produce the Other in every way imaginable.[32] The relationship between Europe and Africa has always been defined by power, domination, and varying degrees of hegemony. Racial categories were created out of this relationship. A powerful theorization of the disciplinarity of colonization is Edward Said's third type of orientalism, wherein he describes Europe as a corporate institution that administers control over the Orient – making statements about it, authorizing views of it, teaching it, describing it, having authority over it.[33] The Orient and Africa in this sense are perceived as exotic, intellectually retarded, emotionally sensual, culturally passive, and politically penetrable. In studies on Black/white relationships, discussions circulating around sociopolitical and economic experiences were dominated by the two major binaries: settler and native or Black and white. This is linked to European dominance and control, as there has always been an accepted system of theory and practice created for filtering knowledge about Africa to the West.

In his *Autobiography*, Malcolm X outlines his experience as a Black man in America and the subsequent violence he endured personally, psychologically, and communally. His book chronicles a movement from

the naïve and benevolent schoolboy whom white guidance was bestowed
upon, to his involvement with crime, to his discovery of the physical and,
even more importantly, psychological domination of Black people in
America. His journey embodies the religious imagery of from darkness to
light, echoing the words of the Honorable Elijah Muhammad that the white
man is the devil incarnate himself, and as a result, he posits that "Western
society is deteriorating . . . and God is going to judge it and destroy it . . . so
let us, the black people, separate ourselves from this white man slave master,
who despises us so much."[34] Separation is key for Malcolm X, as he sees this
as a willful act of power, which is chosen, rather than segregation, which is
a regulated act of control over the life and liberty of the powerless.

   Malcolm views Christianity in the same vein – as a tool of control –
proscribing the masochism of a Christ-centered "turn-the-other-cheek"
model as the only form of resistance, and asserting that "the greatest
miracle Christianity has achieved is that the black man in white
Christian hands has not grown violent. It is a miracle that 22 million
black people have not risen up against their oppressors."[35] While most of
the *Autobiography* is rooted in mobilizing Black people psychologically and
economically (following in the steps of Marcus Garvey) in America against
their white oppressors with a handful of repeated themes, perhaps at the
intention of the author, Alex Haley, whose rendering of Malcolm
X Manning Marable (2011) calls "fictive"; there are early indications of
what would become his later understanding that violence was the only
remedy for dismantling the system of oppression. Frustrated with the
personal digressions of Elijah Muhammad, Malcolm X, like Fanon,
became less invested in the politics of Black/white relationships based on
identity, and firmly committed to a global Black consciousness aimed at
destroying the system of oppression for people of color worldwide after his
1964 *hajj*. Using Malcolm's diary from his travels to Africa and the Middle
East, Marable's research affirms Michael Eric Dyson's claim that

> These are new facts being unveiled, showing just how serious and sustained
> was Malcolm's interest in the global dimension of the domestic civil rights
> struggle . . . They really do suggest he was a subversive figure, trying to
> undermine the best interests of the U.S. government in the name of a larger
> pan-African cause.[36]

For Malcolm X, the outwardly directed violence of "by any means
necessary" becomes the unifying element in a global Black revolution. In
March 1964, after time in Africa and taking a pilgrimage to Mecca, where
he "spent many weeks . . . trying to broaden [his] own scope and get[ting]

more of an open mind," Malcolm X, although still Muslim, left the Nation of Islam and somewhat revised his separatist position.[37] However, he continues to advocate strongly for resistance predicated upon violence. It is in the speech that he gives after this time abroad that, with a nod to Jean-Paul Sartre, Malcolm proclaims:

> We assert that in those areas where the government is either unable or unwilling to protect the lives and property of our people, that our people are within our rights to protect themselves by whatever means necessary . . . If they don't want you and me to get violent, then stop the racists from being violent. Don't teach us nonviolence while those crackers are violent. Those days are over.[38]

Malcolm's travels push him past identity in some ways: he now sees white supremacist institutions, not necessarily all white people (only the violent "crackers") as the enemy; he urges Blacks worldwide to organize outside of religion, for what joins them in struggle is being Black, not being Christian or Muslim; he focuses more squarely on economic redistribution. In his post-Mecca speech, Malcolm identifies as an American when asserting the Black subject's constitutional right to bear arms in self-defense. In the same speech, he then takes on a global Black nationalist identity, arguing:

> There are more Africans in Harlem than exist in any city on the African continent. Because that's what you and I are, Africans. You catch any white man off guard in here right now, you catch him off guard and ask him what he is, he doesn't say he's an American. He either tells you he's Irish, or he's Italian, or he's German . . . And even though he was born here, he'll tell you he's Italian. Well, if he's Italian, you and I are African even though we were born here.[39]

Herein lies the rub of Malcolm's theorization of identity, which moves from fixed Black separatist to more fluid, global Black: he demands equal rights as the American citizen that he is, entitled to the same right to revolt against injustice as the nation's founders ("liberty or death"). He also demands the same privilege that the German or Italian has in identifying with what she sees as her culture and/or homeland beyond the bounds of the United States. In "The Ballot or the Bullet," (1964) another post-Mecca speech, he claims: "I'm no politician. I'm not even a student of politics. I'm not a Republican, nor a Democrat, nor an American – and got sense enough to know it."[40] He disavows his Americanness, along with the impoverished democracy of the two-party system, both of which he reads as segregationist: "If you black you were born in jail, in the North as well as the South. Stop talking about the South. As long as you south of the

Canadian border, you South . . . you can see that a Dixiecrat is nothing but a Democrat – in disguise." The Dixiecrat sells Black Americans the con of equality, deferred, of course, to an ever-receding post-election moment, which they never deliver on. Much like nonviolent resistance, politics is yet another con where Blacks get fleeced, serving as the perfect mark.

Malcolm's self-asserted right to take on and off both an American and African identity come together in his founding of the Organization of Afro-American Unity (OAAU) after his *hajj*, inspired by the Organization of African Unity's effective decolonial coalition-building, despite national differences:

> Our African brothers have gained their independence faster than you and I here in America have. They've also gained recognition and respect as human beings much faster than you and I . . . One of the first things that the independent African nations did was to form an organization called the Organization of African Unity. This organization consists of all independent African states who have reached the agreement to submerge all differences and combine their efforts toward eliminating from the continent of Africa colonialism and all vestiges of oppression and exploitation being suffered by African people.[41]

Malcolm's insistence on claiming both an American and African identity provides the name for this global organization, emphasizing the unity of African Americans and of Africans and Americans. Given his logic, liberation can only happen when it refuses to limit itself to the national or to the global, which it sees as a false choice. It is the guerrilla warfare of decolonization abroad that Malcolm urges fellow Black Americans to take up in the face of ongoing violence and what he sees as the failures of civil disobedience. In the OAAU, Fanon symbolically merges with Malcolm across the Atlantic. We cannot then view Black resistance in 1960s America as circumscribed by national boundaries.

Despite the necessary fluidity of identity that Malcolm arrives at in 1964, violence remains key to his doctrine; "by any means necessary" is the central tenet of the OAAU's charter. It is through violence that he can stand with his Black brothers and sisters regardless of whether they are Christian, Muslim, those faithful to civil disobedience, or "Uncle Toms" (Malcolm's description):

> We won't organize any black man to be a Democrat or a Republican because both of them have sold us out . . . Both parties are racist, and the Democratic Party is more racist than the Republican Party . . . One thing that we are going to do, we're going to dispatch a wire, a telegram that is, in the name of the Organization of Afro-American Unity to Martin Luther King in

St. Augustine, Florida, and to Jim Forman in Mississippi, worded in essence to tell them that if the federal government doesn't come to their aid, call on us. And we will take the responsibility of slipping some brothers into that area who know what to do by any means necessary.[42]

Without compromising his philosophy of outwardly directed violence, Malcolm X asserts that it is through violence that he can find common ground and form a coalition with Civil Rights leaders like Dr. King. Here, violence overrides difference. By using violence to defend his brothers and sisters, by remitting justice against the oppressor, violence might become world-building among the disparate collectives of Black resistance, across religion, doctrine, or nation. Although Malcolm shifts his focus from the "blue-eyed devil" to white institutions, he continues to see Blackness as the connective tissue that joins the oppressed across time and space. This is a "by us, for us" model. While Malcolm invites Black leaders with different ideologies to join him at the OAAU, while he extends an offer of violent retribution when the government fails them, he refuses to persuade non-Blacks to be allies: "instead of you and me running around here seeking allies in our struggle for freedom in the Irish neighborhood or the Jewish neighborhood or the Italian neighborhood, we need to seek some allies among people who look something like we do."[43] Blackness and violence remain the organizing forces – Malcolm X compromises on neither.

The affinities that Malcolm shares with Fanon are evident in the latter's revolutionary writings, which offer a more sustained and developed philosophy of colonialism and violent resistance than Malcolm's speeches or biography, and again, perhaps, the difference between unsustained divine violence and law-making violence. French-educated, Martinique-born psychologist Fanon's involvement in the Algerian resistance movement against France led him to the following conclusion: colonialism is created and perpetuated by violence and can only be destroyed by violence; thus, violence serves an important psychological purpose – it frees the colonized and gives them humanity. Fanon comes to this conclusion after analyzing his own identity in *Black Skin, White Masks*. First published in 1952, *Black Skin* examined colonial racism. which assumed that the colonized were inferior to the colonizers and imposed its own culture and values over the colonized while according them an inferior status.

Colonial racism had psychological affects on the colonized, as cultural assimilation denied the colonized an independent sense of identity and Western popular culture promoted the association of whiteness with purity and Blackness with evil, leaving them to internalize this negative view and aspire to be white. This is an impossible bind. Fanon argues that Blackness is an identity forced upon those who are considered Black, and that this social uniform functions to set apart, alienate, and ultimately destroy the Black man as he is forever subjected to images and ideas about himself.

In *The Wretched of the Earth*, his final work before his untimely death in 1961, Fanon sets out to establish a plan, a manifesto of sorts, to disrupt the feelings of inferiority, the loss of identity, and the lack of humanity experienced by people of color under oppression. Violence serves a cathartic function, one that enables liberation through self and world-making outside of the strictures of colonialism. Fanon outlines his belief that the same violence used to rule, must be the same violence that the natives must claim for themselves. It is a decision devoid of rationality. Turning Hegel on his head, Fanon writes: "I hope I have shown that here the master differs basically from the master described by Hegel. For Hegel, there is reciprocity; here the master laughs at the consciousness of the slave. What he wants from the slave is not recognition but work."[44] In Hegel's philosophy, the master and slave share a dependent relationship, one that operates by a recognition and reconciliation of the other. In his view, this is a relationship of mutual dependency rather than one of dominance and subordination – one in which power is shared by master and slave alike (the master is defined by the slave and the master needs the slave to legitimize his superiority). Yet for Fanon:

> decolonization is the meeting of two forces, opposed to each other by their very nature ... their first was marked by violence and their existence together – that is to say the exploitation of the native by the settler – was carried on by dint of a great array of bayonets and cannons. For it is the settler who has brought the native into existence and who perpetuates his existence.[45]

Only the oppressed can bring about true liberation as the native intellectual/liberal/middle class have allegiances to the ruling class from which they benefit, and as such, they would recreate the unequal system already in place (thus no social change): "National consciousness is the true node of revolutionary change and is always a violent phenomenon ... the proof of its success lies in the whole social structure being changed from the bottom up."[46] Furthermore, Fanon sees decolonization via violence as a moment of real liberation because it transforms the oppressed from objects to subjects.

Fanon tarries with the erotic in relation to racism, in that the violence that he advocates is conditioned by pleasure and empowerment – that is it say, it has a sadistic element. The sadism that informs violent resistance is part of what Sharon P. Holland (2012) defines as the erotic life of racism. Given the history of slavery and colonization, Holland challenges us to grapple with the ways in which racism shapes our intimacies and desires, engaging with the rich, complex, and often overlooked commingling of desire, racism, pleasure, and freedom (or, in academic speak, intersections of race, sex, and gender). I see my analysis here as part of a larger project of drawing attention to the routinely unacknowledged eroticism of racism and resistance, the ways in which sadistic pleasure makes possible a cathartic release and a severing of the oppressed from the oppressor. The psychological and physical pleasure of violent release returns control over mind and body to the newly liberated subject.

Robert Reid-Pharr (2001) also makes a case for the erotic life of racism in his reading of the overlooked homoeroticism informing Frederick Douglass' fight with the slave breaker Covey. Like Fanon, Reid-Pharr reads violence and domination in the master/slave dynamic. More overtly than Fanon, however, Reid-Pharr names the eroticism that informs this dynamic, specifically in relation to Douglass' battle with Covey, arguing that although Douglass asserts his own identity as man after defeating Covey, an identity that Douglass claims is free from any entanglement with the master (as do readings of Douglass' narrative), there is no escaping the homoerotic residue of the fight with the master. Reid-Pharr insists that we confront the "erotics of slavery."[47] Subscribing to an eroticized Hegelian dialectic, neither master nor slave emerge clean from their entanglement when it comes to identity formation. Despite his claim to the contrary, Douglass' newfound identity is partly conditioned by his (homoerotic) entanglement with Covey.

Like Reid-Pharr, but unlike Douglass, Fanon acknowledges the potentiality for self and world that this violent entanglement with the master makes possible. Placing Fanon and Malcolm X in conversation with contemporary critics like Reid-Pharr and Holland, enables us to more fully discern the erotic dimensions of violent Black resistance in the 1960s, not allowing this historical moment to be relegated to an antiseptic narrative (in the tradition of Douglass) that disavows the desire to dominate the colonizer and its attendant difficult affects.

Sadism is probably the most difficult key term in the counter-narrative about the 1960s that I am attempting to articulate. An unapologetic call to violence is challenging enough, given the stronghold that the narrative of nonviolent protest and loving one's enemy has on the United States imaginary, the ways in which empathy frames our story about Civil Rights and the 1960s for palatable consumption, textbook ready.

Naming the sadism that is a part of "by any means necessary" may be a radical act in and of itself as far as conventional historical narratives go. That pleasure and empowerment are part of this violence complicates the possible nobility or righteousness that one might be tempted to assign to violent protest in an effort to redeem it for certain audiences. I want to consider, as part of the story that we tell about Blackness and the 1960s, the sadistic pleasure, however difficult, that is part and parcel of the outwardly directed violence at the oppressor. As Fanon argues, racism colonizes one's interiority with an always already degraded Blackness that is thrust upon the oppressed, becoming one's skin, one's inner life, a cruel and deeply invasive disciplinarity that often registers symptomatically as mental illness. Fanon's involvement with the Algerian resistance led him to the conclusion that violence serves an important psychological purpose. It is the opacity of the inner life of racism that grabs me: how might the sadistic pleasure born of resistance allow for the colonized to gain control over their interiority? How might the pleasure in dominating one's oppressor rather than turning the other cheek short-circuit the mental degradation of white supremacy? How might this generative sadism allow for the colonized to claim and fashion her humanity rather than having it bestowed upon her by white allies (for Fanon, the white middle class), beyond state-sanctioned Blackness or a liberal definition of what it means to be human? To better understand the importance of the sadism that is a powerful affective component of the call for violence, it is necessary to set it against the sympathetic fellow feeling and masochistic resistance that dominate the landscape of protest in America.

Perhaps Harriet Beecher Stowe's *Uncle Tom's Cabin* (1852) is the urtext of civil disobedience in the U.S.: at worst, patronizing, sexist, racist, and imperialist; at best, a mess of good intentions. For James Baldwin, the novel's sentimental politics betrayed a "secret and violent inhumanity, the mask of cruelty" of the empathetic white abolitionist.[48] *Uncle Tom's Cabin* was the most socially and politically influential text in the United States in the nineteenth century, with its heartfelt pleas for empathy for the enslaved person, especially the enslaved mother, despite Stowe's post-liberation colonialization project (Liberia), racist caricatures, and refusal of any Black resistance that was not of the turn-the-other-cheek variety. That sentimental sympathy – putting oneself in the shoes of the oppressed, feeling their pain, and hence experiencing "right feeling" – will motivate one to act (nonviolently, expect for the violence taken up by the body of the one resisting), is the structuring logic of Stowe's vision and the hallmark of nonviolent protest. Taking a definitive stance against protest literature centered on sentimental sympathy, Baldwin goes as far as challenging Black writers like Richard Wright to disentangle themselves from the parameters of resistance articulated in *Uncle Tom's Cabin*. Specifically, he identifies in Wright's response to Stowe not enough distance from the racial politics of *Uncle Tom's Cabin*. Wright, according to Baldwin, remains caught in a tragic conflict where his heroes remain victims of the racist legacy his society inherited from the antebellum past. The persistence of this conflict is symptomatic of a fear of the dissolution of the bonds and institutions that make up modern society. Society, Baldwin reminds us, "is held together by our need; we bind it together with legend, myth, coercion, fearing that without it we will be hurled into the void, within which, like the earth before the Word was spoken, the foundations of society are hidden."[49] Baldwin calls for a break with the historic cycle that reproduces the categories, bonds, and institutions that regulate Black lives.

The cycle that Baldwin argues against, with its undercurrents of Christianity, of masochistic resistance, of "right feeling," of loving the oppressor, has come to define Civil Rights in the 1960s. Christianity and nonviolent resistance are conterminous. For Malcolm, the invention of Christian civil disobedience in America is yet another con, resulting in the tragic self-disciplinarity of the obedient Black. The logic of nonviolence projects justice and freedom into the afterlife, trapping both within a temporality of deferral. This is the politics of futurity, a politics that never has to deliver on its promise yet demands a Christ-like, or, within U.S. parlance, Tom-like, self-sacrifice. This is not to overlook the sporadic violent insurrections in the history of the nation, yet, for Malcolm X, there has never been a sustained ideology of violent resistance to rival the call for civil disobedience rooted in Christianity and the promise of future redemption.

The *event* of the 1960s presents a rare opportunity in U.S. history to engage with an unapologetic doctrine of violent resistance, one that exceeds national boundaries. Civil disobedience continues to have a stronghold on how we imagine resistance, and a history that we can trace back to the abolitionism of Stowe, whose world-making vision is aggressively shaped by race – in short, to revolutionize the United States by abolishing slavery but ship the newly liberated subject to Liberia – revealing a fear of post-emancipation miscegenation that threatens the generational transmission of racial sameness, white privilege, and wealth. Stowe's logic manifests itself in new iterations as it continues to structure and shape liberal models of reform in the United States. Against the mandate of nonviolence, the power and pleasure in redirecting the violence of the master, of self-sacrifice, outward, and the power and pleasure in articulating a philosophy of such resistance, cannot be swept under the proverbial rug in the name of civility and the uneasiness of grappling with the sadism that may animate this violence.

Following Fanon, I am arguing that violence, when directed outward, is animated by empowerment and pleasure, or, put another way, it is animated by sadism; that it is world and self-making: world-making in that it seeks not assimilation into and reform of dominant institutions, but rather a dismantling of such institutions, a clearing of the ground so that the social and economic may be reimagined (Baldwin's "void"). It is self-making in that it destroys the agent of power whom one's humanity or lack thereof is dependent on, and offers the colonized the only opportunity to define their humanity outside of whiteness and outside of the Blackness that Fanon claims is imposed on them. *The Wretched of the Earth* asserts that defining the colonized's humanity depends on violently taking back what was taken, rather than persuading, through empathy, the middle class, the (neo)liberal, to extend their definition of humanity to the oppressed. In short, Fanon calls for nothing less than the complete destruction of the colonial *world*, for a scorched-earth global-ity – a call from across the Atlantic that Malcolm X heeds. For Malcolm, the masochistic pleasure of "singing" while being harassed and beaten down by the police needs to be replaced by the bodily and psychological pleasure of "swinging"; of gaining control over one's body and mind by taking power away from the master in an act of outwardly directed violence.[50]

I chose to use the term sadistic to engage with the violence that Fanon and Malcolm X prescribe because I think that it most uncompromisingly embodies the empowerment and pleasure of world- and self-making in the face of assimilation that both advocate. It also provides a necessary contrast to the masochism that civil disobedience is often dependent on, rendering that challenging masochism more visible. In *The Wretched of the Earth*, Fanon evokes Sartre's mandate of shaming and intimidating European readers with his decolonial message, infusing his manifesto with a sadistic logic, or, at the very least, an acknowledgment of the sadism that is produced by outwardly directed violent resistance. Via Sartre, Fanon attaches the effects of sadism – shame, intimidation – to revolutionary action. As a psychologist, his attention to affect and interiority is not surprising. Diagnosing the inner life of racism, that oppression produces mental illness, Fanon in turn is concerned with the psychological potential of sadistic violence, reading violence as a cathartic, necessary form of destruction that may undo the damage of white disciplinary structures on the psyche of the oppressed.

The Wretched of the Earth's engagement with Sartre on violence and humiliation enables us to better see the sadistic component to Fanon's call to violence; Malcolm X's most famous words, "by any means necessary," are a translation of a phrase used by Sartre in his play *Dirty Hands* (1948). The Panthers were also influenced by French thinkers, especially Jean Genet. Within this Afro-French intellectual tradition, I want to argue that it is the Marquis de Sade's articulation of the affective density and potential to annihilate of what will come to be classified as sadism that best demonstrates Fanon's theorization of violent resistance. As Gilles Deleuze asserts in *Coldness and Cruelty* (1967), his analysis of de Sade and Leopold von Sacher-Masoch, the sadist is not interested in persuasion, but rather in demonstration: "The libertine may put on an act of trying to convince and persuade . . . But the intention to convince is merely apparent, for nothing is in fact more alien to the sadist than the wish to convince, to persuade, in short to educate."[51] The sadist will ask for what she wants but will not beg or persuade or try to override differences in an effort to get her audience to relate to her experience of suffering. How could an audience of middle-class whites, for example, identify with Black oppression? Malcolm X refuses to go into Italian or Jewish neighborhoods to persuade their residents to advocate on behalf of Blacks; rather, his concern is with people who look like him.[52] The persuasion and "love-thy-enemy" logic that civil disobedience is predicated upon is checked by sadistic resistance that does not wish to persuade but rather to annihilate.

Fanon's argument for violence and existence beyond identity, beyond the Blackness that is thrust upon individuals who are characterized as such by the oppressor, operates within the logic of de Sade. According to Deleuze, the Sadean subject seeks to transcend her identity/world and reach a space of pure power beyond good and evil, what Deleuze calls "primary nature."[53] Through a repetition of violence, the sadist's chief aim is to transcend the world of experience and reach primary nature, free from the constraints of secondary nature, that is, of dominant institutions and identities. Although they may make for strange bedfellows, my claim is that the generative violence that Fanon and Malcolm X advocate is in keeping with a Sadean model: in order to reimagine oneself and the world, outwardly directed violence is a prerequisite of dismantling colonialism (secondary nature). Blackness is never given a chance to construct an idea of itself, but is subjected to degraded images of Blackness. Outside of racial discourse, the terms Black and white have no function – a person only becomes Black by society as race is an effect of slavery and colonialization. Therefore, a society predicated upon white supremacy must be rebuilt in order for the playing field to be leveled, in order for the colonized to take their humanity, and not have to plead with or persuade the colonized to grant it to them.

The language of humiliation and castration is common in Malcolm X's speeches; shaming fellow Blacks, Black men in particular, into violent resistance against white supremacy seems to be one of his preferred rhetorical strategies. In turn, he mocks as castrated those who engage in nonviolent protest, or those who sit-in rather than stand up against the police.[54] The masochistic element of civil disobedience then robs one of power; following this logic, outwardly directed violence, that which is not dependent on white power recognizing the oppressed as fellow humans, gives power to the oppressed:

> It's not so good to refer to what you're going to do as a sit-in. That right there castrates you. Right there it brings you down. What – think of the image of someone sitting. An old woman can sit. An old man can sit. A chump can sit, a coward can sit, anything can sit. Well, you and I been sitting long enough and it's time for us today to start doing some standing and some fighting to back that up.[55]

Albeit the language is ageist, sexist, and able-bodyist, all of which have been well documented, what I want to focus on in the above challenge is its eroticization of power relations: one is either a masochist or sadist, castrated or virile, an active or passive agent of power, an object penetrated by violence or one who metes out violence. That Malcolm X chooses to eroticize resistance, to describe nonviolence as castrating, unmasculine, renders it of the body, part of pleasure and desire, intimate, that which deeply informs one's psyche and sense of self. In short, to evoke Holland's (2012) language, Malcolm's description demonstrates how resistance, whether nonviolent or not, is part of the erotic life of racism. He sexualizes resistance in all its forms. This is honest of him in that he draws attention to the ways in which the body registers resistance and its effects on our relationship to our bodies and to the bodies of others. When we deify Civil Rights leaders and cast them as Christ-like figures, we eclipse their bodies in the process. We may also evade the body and sensation when engaging with outwardly directed violence, not wanting to come to terms with the sadistic pleasure it may afford in our effort to read such violent militancy as righteous. For Malcolm X and Fanon, though, freedom demands violence, the sadistic pleasure of killing the master, as the only way to become a full subject with agency, in control of one's humanity. In short, the only way to be a man (given their perhaps limited worldview along gender lines). Their language does not allow us to overlook the body. In order not to be castrated, one must castrate white supremacy. This is necessary. This is empowering. This is pleasurable in the face of centuries of horrific oppression and degradation that remain foundational to America.

#BlackLivesMatter; or, "The Audacity of Hope"

> *So this is a con game, and this is what they've been doing with you and me all of these years . . . Whenever the Negroes keep the Democrats in power they're keeping the Dixiecrats in power. This is true! A vote for a Democrat is nothing but a vote for a Dixiecrat. I know you don't like me saying that. I'm not the kind of person who comes here to say what you like. I'm going to tell you the truth whether you like it or not.*
> Malcolm X, "The Ballot or the Bullet," 1964

The 1960s was a period of social change for people of color both domestically and internationally. In the United States, it was a period of protest and the passing of the Civil Rights Act in 1964; in Africa, it was the transfer of former European colonies back to their African majority. Yet it was also a period of violence, as Alice Walker highlights: "It was a decade marked by death. Violent and inevitable. Funerals became engraved on the brain, intensifying the ephemeral nature of life."[56]

Malcolm X and Frantz Fanon rechanneled the violence and offered the possibility of a new model – a new way of living for the oppressed – and this was taken up with temerity by the Black Panthers. The Panthers situated themselves in Fanon's and Malcolm X's framework, as Eldridge Cleaver saw Fanon's *Wretched of the Earth*, as "the Bible of the black revolutionary movement," tear down the status quo.[57] Stokely Carmichael pushed for the same revolutionary power, stating:

> we are oppressed as a group because we are black, not because we are lazy or apathetic, not because we're stupid or we stink, not because we eat watermelon or have good rhythm. We are oppressed because we are black. In order to escape that oppression we must wield the group power we have, not the individual power that this country sets as the criterion under which a man may come into it.[58]

The Panthers clearly posed a threat to the "security" of the United States – the security of keeping the oppressed in their place – and there were measures to ensure the party's demise. Not only were members under surveillance, but they were also killed and jailed, essentially targeted by the FBI. This policing and incarceration of Black men is historically rooted, but reached a particular significance in the 1960s as the Panthers took to armed resistance.

White power's response to uncompromising, organized Black militancy was a twenty-first-century incarnation of Jim Crow, which is Michelle Alexander's contention in *The New Jim Crow: Mass Incarceration in the Age of Colorblindness* (2010). Alexander describes the mass incarceration of Black men in America as the aftermath of the Civil Rights Movement, arguing that the prison system functions as a mechanism of racial control, as

> in the current system, but not because of what is commonly understood as old-fashioned, hostile bigotry. This system of control depends far more on *racial indifference* (defined as a lack of compassion and caring about race and racial groups) than racial hostility – a feature it actually shares with its predecessors.[59]

This indifference as control is echoed by Morrison, who insists that

> statements to the contrary, insisting on the meaninglessness of race to the American identity, are themselves full of meaning. The world does not become raceless or will not become unracialized by assertion. The act of enforcing racelessness . . . is itself a racist act. Pouring rhetorical acid on the fingers of a black hand may indeed destroy the prints, but not the hand. Besides, what happens in that violent, self-serving act of erasure to the hands, the fingers, the fingerprints of the one who does the pouring? Do they remain acid-free?[60]

Morrison suggests they do not.

Although Alexander and Morrison highlight the act of indifference to race and the promotion of a raceless society in their work, America, under its first Black president, suggests a more overt and brazen racial hostility at play – one that reaches back to pre-Civil Rights America. Eric Garner, Michael Brown, Sandra Bland, Freddie Gray, Walter Scott, and Philando Castile (and others) have all died at the hands of an oppressive force. Yet this time it is different. In the age of social and digital media, we are presented with actual visual and audible evidence of the dehumanization of people of color on a regular basis. Rather than addressing the issue of racism and oppression through reactionary and daily violence, the shooting to death of Trayvon Martin in 2012 and the acquittal of George Zimmerman the following year sparked the revival of a movement of civil disobedience. The Black Lives Matter movement (BLM) is the centerpiece of "allowable" responses to oppressive violence. Black Lives

Matter was organized as "an ideological and political intervention in a world where Black lives are systematically and intentionally targeted for demise." Like Malcolm X and Fanon, BLM "see [them]selves as part of the global Black family . . . and are unapologetically Black in their positioning. In affirming that Black Lives Matter, they need not qualify their position. To love and desire freedom and justice for themselves is a necessary prerequisite for wanting the same for others."[61]

Yet unlike Malcolm X and Fanon, they do not see violence as a necessary response. This is perhaps because the movement in steeped in the myth of a post-racial America following the campaign of "the audacity of hope" that carried Barack Obama to the presidency. Obama appealed to what has always been America's greatest obstacle to bring about real change to the lives of the oppressed – the hope of a better tomorrow. Like the Christian ideology used by the oppressors in the past, hope relies on the oppressed turning the other cheek and desiring to be recognized as human. Empathy, as Obama reminds us, is being able

> to see the world through the eyes of those who are different from us – the child who's hungry, the steelworker who's been laid off, the family who lost the entire life they built together when the storm came to town. When you think like this . . . it becomes harder not to act, harder not to help.[62]

In response, Paul Bloom argues that Adam Smith observed that having empathy is difficult, and our lack thereof may be as old as man himself: "though our brother is upon the rack, as long as we ourselves are at our ease, our senses will never inform us of what he suffers."[63] Following Smith, revolution cannot come from what Stowe terms "right feeling." Empathy may trap the subject in a weepy cycle, feeling bad but not wanting to dismantle the racist institutions that would require her to give up privilege and power. As Fanon argues, only the oppressed can fight for their revolution, since they do not serve the interests of the white middle class.

Malcolm X and Fanon, in their brief lives (Malcolm died at thirty-nine and Fanon at thirty-six), produced rhetoric for legitimate, justified global change for both the oppressor and the oppressed. While we do not know what either would have achieved or if their positions would have evolved over time, we do know that they each were certain of what they saw as the long con of the oppressor, namely, hope, empathy, and nonviolence, ultimately forms of self-regulation that keep the oppressed from violently dismantling the disciplinary institutions that organize and maintain white power. It is a con that capitalism and white power are dependent upon; this is why the house always wins.

Notes

1. Nelson (1998) defines national manhood as an ideal of white masculinity that came to structure social, economic, and political power and belonging after the Revolutionary War, a condition for representative and civic identity. The organization of the fantasy of white, male fraternity shaped the nation from its beginnings.
2. Genovese (1976).
3. On the dominance of hope and empathy is relation to protest and social change in the United States, specifically their iteration and popularity during the Obama years, see Paul Bloom (2013). Against a model of social justice centered on sameness and shared humanity as its defining logic, Bloom argues for keeping the radical alterity of the Other in place rather than overriding important differences in an attempt to empathize with the Other's suffering. The act of putting oneself in the Other's shoes is predicated upon colonizing the Other's experience as one's own. Bloom asserts that "our best hope for the future is not to get people to think of all humanity as family – that's impossible. It lies, instead, in an appreciation of the fact that, even if we don't empathize with distant strangers, their lives have the same value as the lives of those we love." Alain Badiou (2013a) makes a similar case for revolutionary coalition-building not dependent upon empathy or fellow feeling – one does not have to necessarily like or identify with the trauma of those for whom she is advocating. One need not do violence to another's alterity to fight for justice. We may do well to read Fanon's writings and their influence on Malcolm X and the Black Panthers as the first texts critical of the stronghold of civil disobedience and empathy in the West. Considered in this vein, thinkers like Badiou and Bloom become a part of a perhaps unexpected genealogy originating with Fanon and Malcolm X. Neither are traditionally linked to global Black militancy in the 1960s, but reading Badiou and Bloom within this context allows for a richer engagement with their work. Given Bloom's argument against empathy and hope, it is not President Obama who is the heir of Fanon and Malcolm X.
4. Malcolm X (1964a).
5. Ibid.
6. Ibid.
7. For a sustained analysis of Celia's case, see Hartman (1997).
8. Baldwin (1994).
9. Malcolm X (1992b), 246.
10. Malcolm X (1964a).
11. Ibid.
12. Fanon (1963), 28.
13. Malcolm X (1963).
14. Fanon (1963), 17.
15. Malcolm X (1964a).
16. Malcolm X (1964b).

17. Malcolm X (1964a) and (1992b).
18. Malcolm X (1992b).
19. Morrison (1992), 35.
20. Fanon (1963), 40.
21. Benjamin (1998), 281.
22. Ibid., 283.
23. Malcolm X (1964a).
24. Benjamin (1969), 249.
25. Fanon (1963), 38.
26. Ibid.
27. Ibid., 39.
28. Ibid.
29. Ibid., 209.
30. Ibid., 236.
31. Malcolm X (1992a), 291.
32. Here meant to be used as wide-range multiple cultures on the continent that had a significant influence on intellectual, religious, and scientific philosophies globally.
33. Said (1978).
34. Malcolm X (1992a), 282, 292.
35. Ibid., 282.
36. Dyson, quoted in Rohter (2011).
37. Malcolm X (1992b).
38. Ibid.
39. Ibid.
40. Malcolm X (1964a).
41. Malcolm X (1992b), 50.
42. Ibid., 49.
43. Ibid., 291.
44. Fanon (1963), 220.
45. Ibid., 36.
46. Ibid., 35.
47. Reid-Pharr (2001), 139.
48. Baldwin (1998), 21. Although Baldwin disagrees with Malcolm X's call to violence, making a case for the power in nonviolent resistance, and arguing in his 1963 debate with Malcolm that "maintaining calm in the face of vitriol demands a tremendous amount of power," and that one should not confuse power with equality, nevertheless his rejection of sentimental sympathy and protest literature like *Uncle Tom's Cabin* in "Everybody's Protest Novel" (Baldwin 1994) puts him in line with Malcolm's criticism of the same.
49. Baldwin (1998), 21.
50. Malcolm X (1964a).
51. Deleuze (1991), 18.
52. Malcolm X (1992b).
53. Deleuze (1991), 27.

54. Malcolm X (1964a).
55. Ibid.
56. Walker (2003), 21.
57. See http://libguides.gwu.edu/c.php?g=258982&p=1728991 [accessed September 23, 2021].
58. Carmichael (1966).
59. Alexander (2010), 198.
60. Morrison (1992), 46.
61. See www.blmla.org/guiding-principles [accessed September 20, 2021].
62. Obama (2006).
63. Quoted in Bloom (2013).

References

Alexander, M. 2010. *The New Jim Crow: Mass Incarceration in the Age of Colorblindness*. New York: The New Press.
Badiou, A. 2013a. *Being and Event*, trans. O. Feltham. London and New York: Bloomsbury Academic.
　　2013b. *Ethics: An Essay on the Understanding of Evil*, trans. P. Hallward. London and New York: Verso.
Baldwin, J. 1963. "Debate with Malcolm X." www.youtube.com/watch?v=sVNV b7sKwoU [accessed September 20, 2021].
　　1994. "Everybody's Protest Novel." In *Within the Circle: An Anthology of African American Literary Criticism from the Harlem Renaissance to the Present*, ed. A. Mitchell, 149–55. Durham, NC: Duke University Press.
　　1998. *James Baldwin: Collected Essays*. New York: Library of America.
Benjamin, W. 1969. "Theses on Philosophy of History." In *Illuminations: Essays and Reflections*, ed. H. Arendt, trans. H. Zohn, 253–64. New York: Schocken.
　　1998. "Critique of Violence." In *Reflections: Essays, Aphorisms, Autobiographical Writings*, trans. E. F. N. Jephcott. New York: Schocken.
Bloom, P. 2013, May 13. "The Baby in the Well: The Case Against Empathy." *The New Yorker*. www.newyorker.com/magazine/2013/05/20/the-baby-in-the-well [accessed September 23, 2021].
Carmichael, S. 1966, October 29. "Black *Power* [Speech]." Berkeley, CA. https://voicesofdemocracy.umd.edu/carmichael-black-power-speech-text/ [accessed August 26, 2021].
Deleuze, G. 1991. *Coldness and Cruelty*, trans. J. McNeil. New York: Zone Books.
Fanon, F. 1963. *The Wretched of the Earth*, trans. C. Farrington. New York: Grove Press.
　　1967. *Black Skin, White Masks*, trans. C. L. Markmann. New York: Grove Press.
Genovese, E. 1976. *Roll, Jordan, Roll: The World the Slaves Made*. New York: Vintage.
Hartman, S. 1997. *Scenes of Subjection: Terror, Slavery, and Self-Making in Nineteenth-Century America*. New York: Oxford University Press.

Holland, S. P. 2012. *The Erotic Life of Racism*. Durham, NC: Duke University Press.

Lacy, L. A. 1968. "African Responses to Malcolm X." In *Black Fire: An Anthology of Afro-American Writing*, ed. L. Jones and L. Neal, 19–38. New York: William Morrow.

Malcolm X. 1963. "Message to the Grassroots." www.blackpast.org/african-american-history/speeches-african-american-history/1963-malcolm-x-mes sage-grassroots/ [accessed September 20, 2021].

  1964a, April 12. "The Ballot or the Bullet." King Solomon Baptist Church, Detroit, Michigan. http://americanradioworks.publicradio.org/features/bla ckspeech/mx.html [accessed September 23, 2021].

  1964b, May 13. "Malcolm X at University of Ghana." http://malcolmxfiles.blogspot .com/2013/07/university-of-ghana-may-13,1964_1.html [accessed September 23, 2021].

  1992a. *The Autobiography of Malcolm X: As Told to Alex Haley*. New York: Ballantine Books.

  1992b. "By Any Means Necessary [1964]." In *By Any Means Necessary: Speeches, Interviews, and a Letter by Malcolm X*, 35–67. New York: Pathfinder Press.

Marable, M. 2011. *Malcolm X: A Life of Reinvention*. New York: Penguin.

Morrison, T. 1992. *Playing in the Dark: Whiteness and the Literary Imagination*. New York: Vintage.

Mudimbe, V. Y. 1988. *The Invention of Africa: Gnosis, Philosophy, and the Order of Knowledge*. Bloomington: Indiana University Press.

Nelson, D. 1998. *National Manhood: Capitalist Citizenship and the Imagined Fraternity of White Men*. Durham, NC: Duke University Press.

Obama, B. 2006, August 11. "Commencement and Katrina & Gulf Recovery Address." Xavier University, New Orleans. http://obamaspeeches.com/087-Xavier-University-Commencement-Address-Obama-Speech.htm [accessed September 23, 2021].

Reid-Pharr, R. 2001. *Black Gay Man: Essays*. New York University Press.

Rohter, L. 2011, April 1. "On Eve of Redefining Malcolm X, Biographer Dies." *New York Times*.

Said, E. 1978. *Orientalism*. New York: Vintage.

Sartre, J. 1989. *No Exit and Three Other Plays*, trans. S. Gilbert. New York: Vintage.

Smith, A. 2010 [1759]. *The Theory of Moral Sentiments*. New York: Penguin.

Walker, A. 2003. *Meridian*. New York: Harcourt.

Zizek, S. 2008. *Violence: Six Sideways Reflections*. New York: Picador.

III

Beyond the Canon

CHAPTER 9

Meanwhile, Back on the Home Front

Phillip Brian Harper

Among the myriad other occurrences that took place within African American literary culture during the 1960s, Vincent O. Carter's manuscript for the novel "The Primary Colors" was from 1963 through 1968 rejected by no fewer than eleven U.S. publishing houses, supposedly because "it was not what most publishers were looking for from an African-American writer."[1] This, in any case, was the conclusion reached by the author and editor Herbert Lottman, an acquaintance and supporter of Carter's who in the fall 1970 issue of the journal *Cultural Affairs* characterized Carter as a Black writer who, in "not seem[ing] to protest enough," failed to "stay within the accepted bounds of 'Negro fiction,'" and so was "a difficult person [for publishers] to place."[2] This assessment, for which Lottman provided no substantive evidence, was recapitulated in 1973 when Lottman's essay was reprinted as the preface to Carter's nonfiction volume, *The Bern Book*, and it has since then circulated as objective fact, unquestioningly disseminated by the publisher who eventually did issue Carter's novel in 2003, under the title *Such Sweet Thunder*, and by the whole cadre of that novel's reviewers, who have taken at face value what originated as pure speculation on Lottman's part.[3]

All these writers' pronouncements on what publishers of the period "were looking for in the way of 'Negro literature'" have a kind of performative effect, in that they bolster readers' conceptions of the 1960s as a decade in which African American cultural life was defined exclusively by public protest and political activism, and insofar as our access to the era is increasingly mediated by such discursive characterizations of it, we become increasingly incapable of developing an alternative understanding. Thus it can be difficult to counter such apparently self-evident propositions as the one by Lottman, whereby Carter's writing "so defied current conventions [during] the angry 1960s ... that it couldn't be published," the culture affording no space for "a black American who seemingly wasn't on the firing line";[4] and it becomes all the harder when the novel's eventual publisher reiterates the claim that press editors of the period "just weren't going for" Black authors who "w[ere]n't political," and when reviewers unequivocally assert that Carter's novel "didn't fit the mold of black literature in the 1960s," during which decade "American publishers expected books by black authors to be teeming with rage and discontent."[5]

One could, of course, cite contrary examples – 1960s-era fictions by such disparate African American writers as James Baldwin, Henry Dumas, Ernest J. Gaines, William Melvin Kelley, James Alan McPherson, Paule Marshall, Ishmael Reed, Margaret Walker, and John A. Williams that, even when they are racial-politically engaged, do not necessarily register as rageful protest. It is arguably more effective, however, to note that the only publisher's response to Carter's manuscript that Lottman actually cites does not at all fault the work for being insufficiently "political"; rather, it only regrets that the press cannot undertake the extensive editorial effort that Carter's evidently unwieldy manuscript would require, while at the same time lauding the novel for presenting "wonderful observation, real perception and feeling and some very graphic writing."[6] This praise might make us wonder what, exactly, was observed, perceived, and graphically rendered in Carter's manuscript pages; and it seems that our curiosity in this regard can be fairly well satisfied through a review of the posthumously issued *Such Sweet Thunder*, inasmuch as the publisher of that volume attests that his staff "copyedited the manuscript with the lightest possible hand and published it in its entirety."[7]

What, then, does *Such Sweet Thunder* offer? An autobiographical *Bildungsroman* set in 1930s Kansas City, Missouri, the novel follows protagonist Amerigo Jones from the age of five to the eve of his graduation from high school, tracking his stream of consciousness via an impressionistic third-person narration that gives the work overall a heavily modernist cast. Of course, both that impressionism and the book's retrospective orientation might be said to confirm the novel's detachment from its originary historical context, since the one precludes the social realism through which African American literature is conventionally understood to register political critique, while the other redirects whatever critique the novel *might* achieve toward a moment thirty years prior to the manuscript's completion in the early 1960s.[8] Just as the book's reviewers all tacitly accept that publishers during the 1960s wanted nothing but overtly political work from Black writers, however, so too do they all agree that in *Such Sweet Thunder* "Carter depicts, painstakingly, a mainly Black, urban community that is close-knit, organic and striving for uplift," as one of them put it in May 2003.[9] Whatever problems the concept poses (and they are considerable), *Black community* obtained as much in the 1960s as it did during the 1930s, and as *Such Sweet Thunder* itself implies is inevitably the case, that community was forged as much in the context of what we might call collective domesticity as in the properly political public sphere. Indeed, Carter's novel offers up three primary mechanisms for the establishment and maintenance of African American community that, precisely because they are by no means unfamiliar, certainly have to have been deployed throughout the entire period during which Carter was seeking a publisher: social dance and musical enjoyment; communal food preparation and consumption; and storytelling. If we trace some of the ways these mechanisms were implemented in that 1960s historical context, as I do in the remainder of this essay, we can arrive at a fuller understanding of what constituted African American life during the period than if we focus on political activity alone, with the likely result that we will also arrive at an expanded conception of African American literary culture during this pivotal decade.

* * *

While the most insistent invocations of dance in *Such Sweet Thunder* occur during the latter fifth of the novel, where they pertain to the relatively staid – because carefully chaperoned – entertainments that characterize Amerigo's junior-high- and high-school years, more relevant for our purposes are the earlier and somewhat more sporadic references to the dancing engaged in by Amerigo's parents, Rutherford and Viola, and other adult characters, as these provide a window onto the vernacular pursuits that are our primary concern. To be sure, these activities do not always end felicitously: one eagerly anticipated night on the town concludes with Rutherford striking Viola in a jealous rage and demanding: "Who was that niggah … ? That you had to dance with four times! Makin' a ass out a me in front a *ever* body! I'm sick a this crap! You hear me? *Sick of it!*"[10] And yet, generally speaking, Rutherford is proud of his wife's prowess and stamina on the dance floor, at one point bragging to his son:

> She breathes, Amerigo! Takes one breath to my three. I ain' kiddin'. That's why she's so strong! You know what she kin do? We kin go out an' dance down to the bricks! An' I mean d-a-n-c-e, an' her drinkin' right along with me. An' after a while I git tired an' sleepy, but she don' n-e-v-e-r git tired! … An' then after ballin' an' partyin' till two or three o'clock in the mornin' she kin git up at the crack a seven an' go to work, an' really work, I mean! … An' if it's somethin' goin' on the next night, she kin do it a-l-l o-v-e-r *agin!* B-o-y, your momma kin go!"[11]

This assessment is repeated later by Viola's friend, Allie Mae, who, when she comes to the Joneses' house so that Viola can style her hair, tells Amerigo: "We usta go to the dance, Amerigo, an'-an' Rutherford, he'd be wore out. But your momma, she'd be just as fresh as a daisy. Hey-hey!" During this same exchange, Viola herself acknowledges her ability to execute even ballet steps, "like them white gals do in the movies":

> I could go to the show ..., see 'um doin' it – once! honey – an' then come home – an' do it down to the bricks! ... I could do the splits standin' up against the wall. ... Just as good as on the floor. An' I mean layin' my head against my thigh!

When Allie Mae observes, "Rutherford made you stop, didn' 'e?" Viola replies: "Yeah, girl. He said it kept me too thin. I guess it did, at that. But it didn't make no bit a difference to me, 'cause I loved dancin' better 'n eatin'."[12] While Viola here attests her enjoyment in the sheer physicality of bodily movement, the novel elsewhere makes clear the importance of music and dance to the ongoing consolidation of neighborly community, as when the five-year-old Amerigo and his parents install themselves on the front porch of their apartment for a crawdad feast one late summer afternoon, surrounded by neighbors and acquaintances who are similarly enjoying the evening air and taking in the sonic atmosphere:

> a gentle swell of talk and laughter interspersed with music – from a radio, a Victrola, from someone singing or playing a guitar or playing a harmonica; accented by the sound of babies crying, a glass shattering against a floor, of automobiles whizzing up and down the boulevard, up and down the avenue.[13]

Into this scene enters "a baggy little man with a huge steel guitar slung over his shoulder," accompanied by "a little white mongrel dog"; and when this "Mr. Geetar man" obliges the gathered group with a song or two in exchange for spare coin, the party is uniformly surprised to see the lively response from "Miss Myrt ..., a large yellow gourd-shaped woman with dark eyes, a full head of almost black hair, and a small mouth full of fine teeth," who seems perennially ensconced in a perch at her upstairs window:

> "Look at Miss Myrt!" cried Viola. "She *lives* in that window! I don' care when it is, winter, summer, mornin', noon, or night, she's always there!" ...
> Aooooooow! The dog howled, and Mr. Geetar man continued to wang out his tune....
> Miss Myrt started popping her fingers....

... Miss Myrt, dressed in a yellow cotton housedress and Sam Brown shoes with elastic bands in the instep, ran swiftly down the steps and skipped on the toes of her tiny feet into the center of the alley.

"Aw-aw!" and "Will you look at that!" arose from the astonished crowd, who rushed up to the porch banisters and filtered into the alley.

"So grace-ful!" cried Viola, rising to her feet. "Why, her li'l head, an' tiny hands – they must be li'ller'n mine! Her legs are big but her ankles are as trim as a deer's. She come down those steps like a – a – an' she's almost *sixty* if she's a *day!*" ...

A roar rose from the alley.

"Looka that, Babe!" cried Rutherford. *"Unh!"*

"The *Charleston!*" cried Viola.

Miss Myrt bounced smoothly, effortlessly, gracefully to the rhythms of the Charleston, an exhilarated smile illuminating her face and firing her eyes, her tapering arms outstretched, her tiny fingers snapping like popping currents of fire wrung from her arms.

"An' on 'er *toes*, too!" cried Rutherford. The guitar man settled down to playing in earnest now, resting his guitar in the bend of his hip, with the weight of his right foot poised upon his toe, shoulders bent, fingers flying free, stringing the trills that flowed through Miss Myrt's body. The tempo increased. The onlookers began to clap their hands and shout words of encouragement to the old lady. The clapping, the solid beat, grew louder, so loud that it almost drowned out the music.

"Whew!" cried Miss Myrt.

"Don' stop now, honey!" cried Miss Nettie, baring her rotting teeth with a smile. "I knowed you could do it all the time!"

"Show these young cake eaters what it's all about!" shouted Mr. Harrison, throwing down a quarter that resounded upon the cobblestone with a tinkle.

The sweat rolled down Miss Myrt's face, and gradually the coolness of the September evening chilled her body. She slowed down to a halt. The guitar man threw up his hat. "Give the lady a hand!" he shouted, and the alley rang with thunderous applause, which, seconds later, dispersed like windblown rain in all directions, amid joyous commentary upon her extraordinary performance.[14]

If Rutherford's and Viola's exclamations here – "Looka that, Babe!" "The *Charleston!*" – register the pair's astonishment at the nearly sixty-year-old Miss Myrt's spryness, they also imply surprise at the spontaneous recrudescence of a dance whose heyday in the Black vernacular context had long since passed by the moment in which the scene is evidently set.[15] But of course, dances *do* reemerge, and by the time Carter completed his manuscript in 1963, key elements of the Charleston had resurfaced in the form of the "mashed potatoes" – a dance move made famous through James Brown's live performances and popularized by a number of rhythm-and-blues songs released by Brown and other artists from 1960 through 1962.[16]

The mashed potatoes itself, moreover, was one of a number of staple dances at block parties held throughout the long postwar period in African American neighborhoods across the country, to say nothing of more formal gatherings in venues fairly removed from the street.[17] Of course, to the extent that racial Blackness itself is understood as a necessarily vernacular phenomenon, these more rarified exercises have been highly susceptible to criticism for their supposed inauthenticity. Consider, for instance, this scathing passage from Nathan Hare's comprehensively scathing 1965 book, *The Black Anglo-Saxons*, which takes merciless aim at an African American bourgeoisie that it conceives as thoroughly alienated from its cultural roots and pathetically assimilated to white social norms:

> At exclusive gatherings of top society folk, you can now sit back and watch some 20 couples lined up on a patio, busily executing the Wobble and the Watusi. They are unaware that a good many such dance crazes were imported from the Southern backwoods, as well as Miami and Baltimore. Whereas it once was a mark of status to be "the smoothest dance couple on the floor," this acclaim now goes to the "best twisters" at Virginia Beach, or some other integrated locale. Local "professionals" acquire community fame for their unique versions of the Twist, which they perfect to demonstrate how much they are in the "modern swing of things." But since they are generally latecomers to the Twist, having learned it first from the whites, their styles are a burlesque of the pioneer Negro twisters.[18]

At the narrative center of this excerpt (from a putatively "sociological" study that Hare himself acknowledges is based on nothing more than informal "observation"[19]) is a process of cultural mediation that is understood to invalidate entirely any claim to proper Blackness that might be asserted by an African American social elite: Black patrons of rural jook joints in the post–Reconstruction South codified the West African-derived dance moves that in the early 1960s would be popularized throughout the United States as the Twist and the Watusi;[20] that very popularization – consisting as it did in the widespread adoption of the moves among middle- to upper-class whites – at once necessitated and signaled the extirpation of the dances' originary Black-vernacular import; a deracinated genteel Black bourgeoisie then "learned" the dances "from the whites," presumably through their promulgation in the mass media, and began to reenact them in what inevitably registered as a grotesque travesty of "real" Black musical entertainments. This, obviously, is one view of the matter. Alternatively, though, we could simply say that there are many different ways of being Black, and that these are simultaneously forged and deployed wherever two or more of African descent are gathered in social interaction. If any such mechanism might strike some observers as problematic – because, say, it is insufficiently rooted in Black-vernacular tradition – this fact is arguably moot so long as the participants themselves are effectively bound together in Blackness, however little they may be thinking about that effect.

Indeed, such unconsciousness is to a large extent part of the point, as it comports with the quotidian character of the community-building activities under consideration here, which typify the plot of *Such Sweet Thunder*. After all, if the novel impresses some readers as insufficiently Black to have achieved publication during the 1960s, this is because the events it depicts tend not to be framed in a specifically racialized way, either by the narrator or by the characters themselves. This is not to say that the narrative features no racial-political commentary at all: on the contrary, when, for instance, Rutherford pridefully boasts to Viola that his boss at the hotel where he is employed as an undercompensated maintenance man has praised his "fine work" and publicly extolled him as "a man you can depend on" after Rutherford has fixed the building's dysfunctional elevator, Viola responds sharply: "But he didn't pay you, did he? We can't eat praise! If you was a white man you'd have a hotel of your own! Instead a slavin' for somebody else – an' for nothin'!"[21] For that matter, she also acknowledges the racial hegemony that obtains within U.S. mass culture in her offhand reference to "them white gals … in the movies" in the passage quoted above. Still, such considerations are wholly unarticulated in the scene centered on Miss Myrt's impromptu performance, which suggests that they are far from the minds of the participants themselves. This seems reasonable enough, inasmuch as those participants really are only listening to music, which need not entail any conscious reflection on the vicissitudes of African American existence; and yet such existence is constituted and furthered in precisely such collective experiences as are depicted in this passage from Carter's novel – and as were undergone by innumerable Black people throughout the United States during the 1960s, across myriad and complex differences of class and political consciousness.

* * *

As is glancingly noted above, the spontaneous musical diversion in which Carter's characters participate ensues as the Joneses are indulging in a meal of crawfish that has been prepared and surreptitiously slipped to the family at no charge by Mrs. Derby, wife of the fisherman who harvests, cleans, boils, and then sells the crustaceans up and down the streets of the neighborhood:

> A soft knock on the screen door.
> "Yeah?" [Rutherford] said, turning around in his chair.
> "Ain' nobody but me," said Mrs. Derby, smiling broadly, thrusting a large steaming plate through the door, piled high with bright coral crawdads, with little round potatoes and onions that had been cooked in the juice. Here and there appeared small black peppers and red-hots and bay leaves and pods of garlic, the savory odors of which spiraled upward in coils of steam.
> "Unh – unh!" Rutherford exclaimed. "Looka that, Babe!"
> "You really laid it on us this time, Mrs. Derby. How much are they?"
> "Aw – take 'um for nothin'!" she said in a low cautious tone, making sure that Mr. Derby could not hear.
> "Aw, thanks a lot!" said Viola in a tickled whisper.
> "Yeah, that's sure nice a you," Rutherford added.
> "Just send 'Mer'go with the plate when you git through," waving her hand in such a way as to indicate what she really meant: when *he's* gone, meaning, her husband.[22]

Plentiful in the waterbodies of Missouri even today, the so-called "craw-dad" figured prominently in the Depression-era food culture of the Black Kansas City in which *Such Sweet Thunder* is set.[23] The numerous place references in the text suggest that the Joneses live in the northwest corner of what during the early twentieth century was "the largest area of African American housing and businesses" in the city, home to the legendary 18th and Vine jazz district that thrived during the 1920s and 1930s, thanks to an abundance of venues where, as Stanley Crouch puts it, "pork was served, liquor was drunk, and the bands played blues all night in the keys of B, D, and E."[24] Culinary historian Andrea Broomfield attests that "numerous club owners kept the music going by tying it directly to food. They put out kitties to collect musicians' tips, and they offered them cheap chili, coffee cans brimming with hot and spicy crawdads, and newspapers holding mounds of barbecue. Thus it is," she continues, "that when someone says 'Kansas City,' it often calls to mind jazz and barbecue, both tied to African American artistic and culinary culture, both deeply rooted in the South[, and both] often associated with celebration and optimism."[25] The above-cited scene with Mrs. Derby implies just this sense of celebration in relation to crawdads, and the suggestion seems to be borne out by the response among the neighbor folk to Mr. Derby's street-side sales cry:

> "Craw-pappy! R-e-d – hot!" A singing cry resounded from the top of the alley.

Mr. Derby! thought Amerigo. In his big white cook's hat and his white jacket with the white buttons and his apron – all white; with a tray with big, big crawdads on a little wagon. Coming down the alley. Hot dog! ...

"*Craw-pappy! R-e-d – h-o-t!*" Mr. Derby was coming closer....

"CRAW-PAPPY! R-E-D H-O-T!" ...

"GIT CHO RED-HOT CRAWDADS – CRRAW-PAPPY – R-E-D HOT!"

"Over here, Mister Derby!" cried a voice.

"I'll have a mess of 'um, too!" yelled another voice....

"CRAW-PAPPY!"

"Mister Derby! Aw – Mister Derby!"

"R-E-D – HOT!"[26]

Lest we succumb to a false and romanticized understanding of African American food culture, however, Broomfield herself reminds us that "at the foundation" of what might appear to be sheer culinary festival is "hunger – unrelenting physical hunger."[27] That hunger, moreover, was by no means limited to Blacks in the historical contexts in which we understand African American cuisine to have emerged. Indeed, if we recognize poverty to have been a principal factor in the development of the Black Southern cooking that would come to be known as "soul food," then we would do well to note that poverty itself was endemic across the South in the years following the Civil War, with the result that, as chef and food historian Adrian Miller has put it: "poverty food became the norm for almost everyone in the region regardless of class and race"[28] – belying what Miller claims was *always* only the "illusion," even during the heyday of antebellum slavery, that in the South, "blacks and whites ate differently."[29]

Needless to say, the thoroughgoing poverty that Miller rightly insists typified the South during Reconstruction was also a defining characteristic of the Depression-era context in which Carter's novel is set, and inasmuch as the Joneses' neighborhood itself is not exclusively Black, it stands to reason that Amerigo's gastronomic awareness should encompass not only his own mother's cooking (Amerigo and his parents have just finished a supper of fried buffalo fish and potatoes before repairing to their front porch in the scene under discussion) and the delicacies proffered by the Derbys, but also the foods prepared by the Irish American McMahons, who live next door. That family is evidently readying its own meal at the same time as the Joneses are eating their fish and potatoes and as the Derbys, who live above, are boiling crawdads;

the scent of the latter enables Amerigo to envision them in his mind's eye even as the smells of the other foods compete for his attention:

> The sharp pungent aroma of boiling crawdads filtered into the kitchen. ... They were hot and red with red and black peppers, Irish potatoes, and sweet white onions. The smell of crawdads mixed with the smell of buffalo fish and fried potatoes, and sausages and Boston baked beans from next door.[30]

This seemingly inconsequential scene substantiates Miller's point regarding the miscegenetic genealogy of African American foodways (to say nothing of African America as such), even as *Such Sweet Thunder*'s southern-plains setting comports with his observation that Civil Rights- and Black Power-era soul food discourses falsely equated vernacular African American cooking per se with the rather more narrowly delineated culinary traditions of the Black Belt. Instrumental in this regard, according to Miller, was the position paper on "The Basis of Black Power" issued by the Atlanta Project of the Student Nonviolent Coordinating Committee (SNCC) in the spring of 1966, which effectively posited the experiences of rural Black Mississippians as representative for all African Americans even as it trenchantly noted Black people's *non*-representativeness vis-à-vis "America" itself:

> Miss America coming from Mississippi has a chance to represent all of America, but a black person from either Mississippi or New York will never represent America. So that white people coming into the movement cannot relate to the black experience, cannot relate to the word "black," cannot relate to the "nitty gritty," cannot relate to the experience that brought such a word into being, cannot relate to chitterlings, hog's head cheese, pig feet, hamhocks, and cannot relate to slavery, because these things are not a part of their experience.[31]

Mistakenly attributing this statement to the "[Stokely] Carmichael-led SNCC," Miller notes that its list of quintessentially Black dietary items "focused on the most hard-core poverty foods of the area where Carmichael organized – Black Belt Mississippi." It correspondingly "glossed over the rich and varied culinary traditions within the black community. The Chesapeake Bay, the Lowcountry, and the Lower Mississippi Valley cooking styles were all subverted to Black Belt cooking."[32] Meanwhile, according to Miller, that cooking itself was simultaneously cast as an unassimilably Black cultural phenomenon, as contrasted with the cuisines of other U.S. minority ethnic groups:

> The conscious effort to create, politicize, and racialize soul food runs against the typical immigrant food story. After all, that was the point. ... [W]e can

tell when immigrants, or at least their food, have been accepted by the majority culture – their food is no longer viewed as "ethnic." Bagels, hamburgers, hot dogs, and pizza, all once strongly identified as ethnic foods, are now fundamental components of the American menu. Where soul food diverged from other immigrant cuisines was in its explicit rejection of the white mainstream. Soul food's authenticity now lay in its outsider status.[33]

By the same token, that "outsider status" rendered the cuisine a touchstone of racial identification among U.S. Blacks, the Atlanta Project statement having "transformed the marketable, happy-go-lucky term 'soul food' into edible Black Power": "Soul food was now a rallying cry for black solidarity. A cuisine 400 years in the making, melding African, European, and Native American influences, was now wholly black-owned. No matter where one lived, any black person could bond with another over this particular type of food."[34]

While Miller's ambivalence about it is palpable, this development arguably exemplifies the means by which *all* racial consciousness is established, inasmuch as such consciousness entails a group's laying exclusive claim to one set of cultural practices or another, regardless of whether the validity of the claim is borne out by the historical record. To the extent that this process approximates the consolidation of *individual* consciousness chronicled in *Bildungsromane* like *Such Sweet Thunder* (whereby all manner of promiscuously social experience is assimilated specifically to the psychic identity of the protagonist), Amerigo's own coming into being *as* Amerigo – including his delectation in the mélange of his mother's fried buffalo fish, the Darbys' boiled crawdads, and the McMahons' sausages and baked beans – adumbrates the emergence of 1960s-era collective Black consciousness, no less in relation to culinary practices than to properly political ideas and activities.

* * *

One way of glossing the situation recounted above is to say that soul food discourse is a story that U.S. Blacks tell themselves about themselves, in the service of constituting themselves as a recognizable people. At the same time, inasmuch as it is typically focused "on the practicalities and problems faced daily in the … small-community context" – as Roger Abrahams has argued – African American storytelling also potentially helps constitute responsible *persons* who are consequently fit to be members of a given social cohort.[35] As a *Bildungsroman* explicitly focused on the ethical training of its child protagonist, *Such Sweet Thunder* at times presents a strikingly direct approach to such moral education, as we see in an episode that occurs in the immediate aftermath of Miss Myrt's dance performance, cited above. The Joneses and their neighbors remain arrayed on their respective porches after "Mr. Geetar Man" has passed out of sight and as the evening settles. Presently, we are told:

> Two figures appeared upon the very dim horizon, a man and a woman. They made their way slowly down the alley. The woman carried a basket on her left arm and linked her right arm in the left arm of the man. Every few yards she would halt and take something from her basket and toss it with a wide sweeping theatrical gesture to the left and to the right, bowing gracefully, touching her lips with the tips of her fingers and blowing kisses to the people on the porches.
>
> Here and there someone sniggered, but not loudly, while most of the people looked on with a sort of respectful awe.[36]

It isn't long before we learn the identities of this eccentric pair, as upon seeing them, Rutherford exclaims, "Aunt Tish and Gloomy Gus!" He continues:

> "But that ain' his real name. ... His real name is – do you remember what Pr'fessor Bowles said it was that time, Babe?"
>
> "Naw, I don'," said Viola, "Worthington? That ain' it, but it was somethin' like that. I think, anyway."
>
> "They ain' quite right in the head, Amerigo," said Rutherford softly. "I been seein' 'um ever since I kin remember. But they're nice people, though. They don' bother *nobody* unless you bother them. Don' *never* fool with that old man! Naw sir!"[37]

It turns out that "that time" to which Rutherford refers was a moment when the young Rutherford and Viola, along with other friends and classmates, had committed their own offense against the peculiar couple and were called to account for it by their school principal. Amerigo listens as his mother picks up the story, ticking off the names of childhood friends as she proceeds:

> "They usta live down in Belvedere Holla," Viola was saying, "in a ol' tin shack patched up with cardboard. We usta pass by there every mornin' on the way to school, me an' your daddy, an' T. C., an' Ada, an' Dee Dee, an' Zoo – an' a whole bunch of us. Rutherford an' T. C. an' the rest of them little ragamuffins usta throw rocks at the house an' run!"
>
> "Aw Babe!"
>
> "Well, we did! An' hide behind the trees an' peep out to see what they'd do. An' we all laughed to beat the band when they couldn' catch us. We was just kids. We didn' mean no real harm, I guess"....
>
> "Somebody told Principal Bowles ... They had a assembly in the main auditorium that mornin'."

At this point, Rutherford and Viola together slip into a reverie of remembrance through which they recapitulate what Professor Bowles told the group: "'How's it go?' said Rutherford softly, as though he were speaking to himself"; and then, quoting Principal Bowles: "I want to tell you a story – that's how he started! An' man, he really told it, too, I'm tellin' you! He had all 'um little niggahs cryin' an' red-eyed!" Viola takes up the thread:

> "Once there was a beautiful young girl …, she was petite an' quiet, an' very intelligent an' refined. But that didn' mean she was stuck up. She could be a lot a fun. Most of all she liked to dance."
>
> "'Cause she was so smart she went to college," Rutherford continued. "There she fell in love with a bright han'some young man. He fell in love with her, too."[38]

Rutherford goes on in this vein, ventriloquizing Professor Bowles and every once in a while slipping into the educator's elevated diction, explaining to Amerigo that, at one point, after they had finished college, married, and had two children – Michael and Rosamond – the couple attended an evening piano recital while their son and daughter remained at home, asleep. They returned to their house to find it ablaze, and, as Rutherford puts it, "they had to watch their children burn up in that fire – alive!" Rutherford then wraps up the tale and provides the tacit moral:

> They wasn' never no more the same after that … They got old. They forgot things all the time – to eat, to sleep. People usta see 'um runnin' an' hollerin' through the streets at night. That was long ago, the old man said, kinda quiet-like, but that beautiful woman and handsome man are still alive and together. They live alone, in a old shack in Belevedere Holla. They live as good as they kin. They don' do no harm to nobody. They talk to theyself a lot, an' people think that 'cause they do that they crazy. The man has a sad an' sometimes troubled look on his face, an' he has to wear old worn-out clothes, that's why the people nicknamed 'im Gloomy Gus. The woman's called Aunt Tish 'cause she usta take scraps of colored tissue paper an' make all kinds a flowers and ribbons an' stick 'um in her hair.
>
> Children often throw rocks at 'um, but I suppose God'll forgive 'um both, the young an' the old people, 'cause they just don' understand. Just like I'm sure that God'll forgive Aunt Tish an' Gloomy Gus for bein' the devoted parents of Mike an' Rosamond.[39]

With its reference to those benighted souls who "just don' understand," its positing of the youthful Viola and Rutherford as themselves examples in this regard, and its explicit injunction – issued by Rutherford – to "*never* fool with that old man," this story serves a function whose socializational import is quite clear, and it has analogs in this respect among the archive of nonfictional tales gathered within African American

communities during the period when Carter was shopping his manuscript to publishers.

To cite one example, practically at random: in a footnote to his classic
1967 study *Tally's Corner* – which has been lauded and censured in equal
measure[40] – Elliot Liebow relates a story told to a casually assembled group
by one of the Washington, DC, "Negro streetcorner men" on whom
Liebow focused his ethnographic research from 1962 to 1963, in which a
drunken man "force[s] his wife to perform an 'unnatural act'" (i.e., either
anal or oral sex), and she, in turn, "burie[s an] axe in the middle of his
forehead" after he has fallen asleep: "Screaming, she ran from the house
and told her story to the people in the town. She didn't ever come to trial,
said Stanton [Liebow's informant], concluding his story. 'They didn't even
carry her to court.' Tonk, Boley, and everyone else [i.e., the others among
Liebow's subjects who are present for the recounting of the tale] agreed that
justice had been done." Indeed, underlying that agreement, according to
Liebow, is the conviction shared by the study's subjects that all sexual
practices other than "simple and direct coitus" "stand in clear violation of
the heterosexual relationship" as it is idealized within the community
under examination.[41]

As much as it differs in tone and tenor, then, Stanton's tale serves the
same sort of normative purpose as the story of Gloomy Gus and Aunt
Tish that is related to Amerigo by his parents, inasmuch as it establishes
the terms of proper behavior within the community in which it is
recounted. Socialization need not go forward in such a moralistic or
didactic fashion, however. Indeed, focused as he is on the African
American folktale, Abrahams himself identifies the process with the
trickster narratives that loom so prominently on the folkloric landscape,
which bear relatively little pedagogical import beyond serving "as a direct
reminder of how careful people should be in life."[42] While there is no
trickster per se in *Such Sweet Thunder*, there are numerous instances in
which a hapless rascal unwittingly puts himself in harm's way "for the
sheer joy of taking on the challenge," as Abrahams characterizes the
attitude with which the trickster customarily forwards his shenanigans.[43]
Not only is this personage typically male in Carter's novel, as my wording
above suggests; often as not, he is Amerigo's own father, Rutherford,
conjured in his juvenile form in stories related to Amerigo by his parents
and their friends. Central among those friends is the aforecited T. C. –
Thomas Corning Belcher – a childhood schoolmate of Rutherford's and
Viola's whose continued closeness to the family substantiates his informal
status as Amerigo's "Uncle T. C."[44]

To be sure, Viola and Rutherford themselves regale Amerigo with tales from their youth in which T. C. is the butt of the joke – an overgrown underachiever at once lovable and loyal: as Viola tells Amerigo at one point, "her voice trembling with laughter, 'he was in the *seventh grade*, fixin' to *graduate*, an' didn' even know his ABCs!'" When Amerigo accordingly observes that T. C. "sure was dumb!" Rutherford swiftly corrects him:

> "Naw he wasn', Amerigo! ... Naw he wasn', that niggah was *smart!* He knew all about fishin' an' huntin', an' hosses. An' he knew e-v-e-r'-b-o-d-y's first, middle, an' last name, an' they brothers' and sisters' names, an' when was they birthday an' when they was sick an' what they *had* – an' not only this year, but *last* year – an' the year before that, too! He knew what you liked an' what you didn' like, an' he would give it to you, too, if he could. If you could catch him in one place long enough. T. C. had a heart a gold! A-l-l the gals was *crazy* about that niggah! *Nice* girls, too! An'-an' a-l-l the teachers, an' even Pr'fessor Bowles. He never did nobody no harm, except maybe hisself, but then he had so much fun doin' whatever he did that it didn' make you feel bad, even if it was against hisself. Naw-naw, that joker wasn' dumb, Amerigo, that cat was lazy!"
>
> "I don' even think he was lazy," said Viola tenderly. A feeling of shame rose to Amerigo's throat.
>
> "Naw. That's right, Babe," said Rutherford thoughtfully. "He was just bigger than the rest of us, tall an' powerfully built for his age. He just flunked out all the time 'cause he never came to school, 'cause he was ashamed to have to sit with all us little kids. So he'd just goof off."[45]

Then, having chortled with Viola over a remembered episode in which T. C. disrupted the school day by bringing an "old nag" onto the grounds and was warned by the principal, "If you ever bring that beast on school property again, I'll have you expelled from school," Rutherford reflects: "Yessir . . ., ol' T. C. was a lot a fun, Amerigo. An' nobody better *not* bother me an' Viola! He'd run them li'l niggahs wild! An' they was some tough jokers, too, Amerigo, m-e-a-n li'l niggahs, with knives, an' they'd use 'um, too!"[46]

His devotion and good-naturedness thus established, T. C. is now ready to make his own entrance onto the scene, first as a "tall handsome figure" that Amerigo calls to mind as he listens to his father reminisce about the days of their youth,[47] and then as a voluble raconteur who takes up the role of storyteller that Viola and, especially, Rutherford have inaugurated. The first instance of his functioning in this manner occurs within a complicated flashback sequence that ensues as Viola ushers Amerigo through the streets of their extended neighborhood to drop him off for his very first day of

school. The various landmarks they pass elicit memories from Amerigo's
mother:

> "Here's Troost Hill!" Viola declared excitedly. "It's been a long time since I
> been down here. Your daddy an' me, an' T. C., an' a whole bunch a us usta
> slide down this hill in the winter. You see how steep it is? We usta start at the
> boulevard an' cross the avenue, here! An' coast on down past the holla, an' –
> you might think I'm lyin' – a-l-l the way down to Garrison Square!" [48]

This reflection triggers Amerigo's own memory of hearing T. C. himself
describe his, Viola's, and Rutherford's sledding adventures during their
childhood:

> "Boy, your daddy an' me could really *do* that thing!" he heard T. C. saying.
> "Him an' your momma an' me we sure usta cut 'um! We'd build a fire at the
> top, see, an' one at the bottom. Some a them jokers would even take off from
> Tenth Street an' cut across the traffic at the Boulevard. Troost Hill was enough
> for me, Jackson – an' your daddy, too! Ask 'im how he got that scar on his
> ankle. Ha! ha! ha! That little darkie like to got us both killed. M-a-n he took off
> from the boulevard, see? An' me, like a fool, right behind 'im – at night! Zoom!
> Like a bat out a hell! Down Troost Hill. An' c-o-l-d! Aw man! that north wind
> made you wish you was down home. Well, old Rutherford hit the avenue, see,
> sort a narrow-like, close to the curb. The wind was blowin' in that little joker's
> face so hard he didn' see the streetcar comin' till it was damned near on top of
> 'im. M-a-n you shoulda seen that little joker hustle, scootin' that old raggedy
> sled a his around an' draggin' his feet. The streetcar conductor was a clangin'
> and a clangin'! I thought he was gonna kick that bell to death!"
>
>   "'Fall off an' roll!' I hollered. 'Fall off an' roll!' But that little monkey was
> so scaired he wouldn' let go. He flattened out like a pancake an' ran –
> Amerigo if I'm lyin' I'm dyin' – u-n-d-e-r the streetcar like a express train!
> The streetcar conductor slammed on the brakes an' sparks flew ever'
> whichaway! The wheels was slippin' on the ice between the tracks. Whew!
> I hope I never see nothin' like that no more as long as I live! Am I lyin',
> Rutherford?"
>
>   "I sure was hittin' 'um, all right," he answered.
>
>   "The conductor pulled 'is cap down over 'is eyes. He gave that cat up for
> dead! I shot around the streetcar an' just did miss the fireplug by the skin a
> my teeth. M-a-n – I was really goin'. I was headin' down the hill, see, an'
> when I looked up I couldn' see Rutherford *nowhere!* Lord! They done killed
> that joker, sure, I thought. An' when I got to the bottom of the hill, there
> was your daddy, Amerigo, tremblin' like a leaf! C-r-y-i-n'! 'Cause he lost his
> shoe! Ah – ha! ha! An' then – you know what?"
>
>   "What?" watching the morning sunlight slant down the hill, throwing
> elongated shadows from the trees just above the flower shop on the opposite
> corner....

"He had a gash in his ankle that long!" doubling his fist, extending his forefinger and intercepting the axis of his wrist in order to indicate a length of about six inches.

"Every time you tell that lie," Viola exclaimed, "that cut gits bigger!"

"They took *nine* stitches in it! Well, anyway, we tied that li'l cat's ankle up, it was deep, too, an' got warmed up an' then – we *did it agin!* When he got home his ol' lady like to beat 'im to death for losin' that shoe! Ah – ha! ha!"[49]

Only such a full-length excerpt can convey the quality of T. C.'s narration, though the nature and extent of the risk to which the young Rutherford was routinely subjected are just as effectively illustrated by a summary of another story T. C. tells about their childhood, in which Rutherford, generally an expert in the water, develops a cramp while he and T. C. are swimming in the local Missouri River. When T. C. tries to come to his aid, Rutherford panics and starts to fight him off. "Well," T. C. tells Amerigo, "he like to got us *both* drowned. I got away from that cat. Started to treadin' the water, Jack. Prancin'-like. An' then I squared off on that joker. Haw! haw! I hit 'im with a c-l-e-a-n right cross. Right on the button! An' that cat saw stars!" Having next been pulled from the water and had "half the river" pumped out of him by T. C., Rutherford then, according to T. C., "rolled his bloodshot eyes an' said – you know what he said?" When Viola and Amerigo both indicate that they have no idea what Rutherford said, T. C. repeats the words for them verbatim: "Niggah – what you come hittin' me for? Ah-ha! ha! Ain' that a killer?"[50]

For all their depiction of roguish mischief-making, bona-fide trickster tales rarely offer any practical lesson. Indeed, according to Abrahams: "If there is any advice for real-life behavior in the stories, it is to remind us to be on guard constantly for others' tricks" – a warning that the trickster himself would do well to heed, inasmuch as "even when he seems to win, there is no 'living happily ever after' ending to his stories. Instead," Abrahams contends, "there is a 'to be continued' feeling at the conclusion; for, as in the adventures of European scamps like Reynard the Fox and Till Eulenspiegel, we know that Trickster will simply go from one predicament of his own making to another."[51] Of course, this is not entirely true of Rutherford in *Such Sweet Thunder*, who, after all, grows up, and thus evidently *out of* his predilection for mishap, while the novel itself by no means constitutes an instance of folklore. Nevertheless, for Amerigo to hear stories of a time when his father seemingly *was* prone to repeated misadventure is for him to gain a greater understanding of his ancestral past, and thus to solidify his sense of belonging within the community of which his family is an integral part.

Such community-building is fostered by storytelling of whatever sort, whose function in this regard in a late 1960s African American context is demonstrated by an anecdote from Carol Stack's landmark 1974 study, *All Our Kin*, for which Stack installed herself among poor Black families originally from rural Arkansas and Mississippi who had migrated to the Midwest urban neighborhood designated by Stack as "The Flats."[52] Young and white, Stack, like the nineteen-year-old daughter of two of her research subjects, was six-months pregnant when she began the project. While this fact evidently eased her entrée among the female members of the Jackson family, including the mother, Viola, and Verna, the pregnant daughter, Viola's husband, Leo, and his brother remained wary of Stack's presence in the household. Finally, as Stack tells it:

> One incident eased my communication with Viola's husband and his brother. Late one evening I was at the Jacksons' home, still pregnant, my cumbersome silhouette similar to Verna's. I was wearing dark tights and the rooms were poorly lighted, with the television providing the brightest rays. Leo, slumped down in his chair, called out to me, "Hey, Verna, get your baby his bottle so he'll stop his crying." Leo had confused me with Verna. He laughed so hard it was difficult to stop. From then on, when any relative or friend dropped by, Leo recounted this story. All their kin in The Flats – more than seventy people – heard it sooner or later.[53]

This last sentence is more telling than it may appear at first glance, inasmuch as one of Stack's primary objectives is to demonstrate "how people are *recruited* to kin networks"[54] – a process whereby, for Stack's subjects, and as the foregoing wording suggests, "Friends may be incorporated into one's domestic circle: if they satisfy one another's expectations, they may be called kin – cousins, sisters, brothers, daddies."[55] What this observation implies, of course, is that the audience for Leo Jackson's story about his mistaking Carol Stack for Verna Jackson did not consist only of blood relations societally recognized as his natural kin, but rather that his very telling of the story helped to consolidate his effective kinship with blood relations and friends *alike* – Stack herself potentially among them.

* * *

This latter prospect suggests that African American community is always liable to be more extensive, capacious, and contingent than the term itself might seem to imply – arguably an inevitable situation insofar as community is constructed through the kinds of quotidian, domestically oriented practices under discussion here, whose fluidity renders them permeable by whoever happens into the domestic milieu. That expansiveness does not necessarily render the community in question any less *Black*, however, since it is the practices themselves that constitute that Blackness, albeit in complex relation with the subjects who forward them, and all the various social identities those subjects bear. If domestic, familial, and neighborly configurations are precisely the contexts in which such complex relationality is most thoroughly worked and reworked, then it makes sense that we would look to them as sites where Blackness is produced in the forms that are most meaningful to those who are living it. This is as true of the 1960s manifestations of such sites as it is of their present-day incarnations, and if readers of Vincent Carter's manuscript failed to perceive such venues as crucibles of a rich and supple cultural Blackness (a questionable notion in any event), there is no reason for us to repeat the error. Indeed, the novel alerts us to the myriad and complicated ways in which Blackness and Black belonging were generated among African Americans, not only during the period in which the story is set, but also during the decade in which the book was completed – and emphatically, insistently, repeatedly not published.

Notes

1. Bledsoe (2003). The story of the manuscript's multiple rejections was first reported by Herbert Lottman, cited below.
2. Lottman (1973 [1970]), ix for the quotation.
3. The publisher in question is Chip Fleischer, who just prior to the book's March 2003 release surmised in print that Carter's lack of success in selling the novel during his lifetime "probably had to do with the times and what publishers were looking for in the way of 'Negro literature'" (Fleischer 2003, 29). By the time the novel was issued, Fleischer had become more resolute in his judgment about the preferences of publishers during the 1960s, and his contentions in this regard were adopted and further circulated by such journalists and reviewers as Margaret Stafford (2003), who flatly asserted that "Black writers in the 1960s were encouraged to write about Black rage [and] civil rights," and Erik Bledsoe (2003).
4. Lottman here is speaking specifically of *The Bern Book*. See his foreword to *Such Sweet Thunder*, unedited hardcover edition (Lottman 2003), vii for the quotation.
5. Fleischer, quoted in Stafford (2003); Bush (2003), 1376; and Graham (2003), 3rd ed., B8.

6. Lottman (1973), x.

7. Fleischer (2006), 427.

8. Regarding the critical limits of realist aesthetics in African American literature, see Harper (2015).

9. Clarke (2003), SP8.

10. Carter (2006), 175. All future references will be keyed to this paperback
edition of the novel.

11. Ibid., 127–28.

12. Ibid., 231.

13. Ibid., 77.

14. Ibid., 79–81.

15. Contextual cues in the novel suggest that this scene is set around 1929 or 1930, and
while the Charleston is generally understood to have become "an international
dance craze" around 1925 (see Knowles 2009, 145), according to Marshall and Jean
Stearns, characterizations of it as "already out of fashion" were circulating among
savvy African American constituencies as early as 1919 (Stearns and Stearns 1994,
110–11).

16. Regarding James Brown's 1959 recording of "(Do the) Mashed Potatoes," credited to Nat Kendrick and the Swans, see Guralnick (1999 [1986]), 232. On "(Do
the) Mashed Potatoes" and Brown's 1962 "Mashed Potatoes U.S.A.," see Wolk
(2004), 13, 46, 98. On the 1962 recordings of "Mashed Potato Time" and "Gravy
(for my Mashed Potatoes)" by Dee Dee Sharp, see (Jackson 2004), 34, 265, 268.
On the origins of the mashed potatoes in the Charleston, see Stearns and Stearns
(1994), 4; and Hazzard-Gordon (1990), 87.

17. See Hazzard-Gordon (1990), 156–59.

18. Hare (1970), 87.

19. Ibid., especially 34–35.

20. See Hazzard-Gordon (1990), chapter 2 (especially 81–84) and 122.

21. Carter (2006), 126.

22. Ibid., 65–66.

23. With approximately 35 species thickly distributed across all 114 of its counties,
Missouri boasts an abundance of crayfish that is "greater than almost anywhere else in the world." Indeed, in 2007 the crayfish was designated as the
state's "official invertebrate." See the "Crayfish Facts" provided by the
Missouri Department of Conservation, and the "State Symbols of
Missouri" listed by the Missouri Secretary of State, available respectively at
https://mdc.mo.gov/wildlife/wildlife-facts/aquatic-invertebrate-facts/cray
fish-facts and www.sos.mo.gov/symbol/invertebrate [accessed September 23,
2021].

24. See Broomfield (2016), 92; Crouch (2013), 188. According to Broomfield, the
neighborhood in question "was bounded on the north by Independence
Avenue, Troost on the west, Twenty-Seventh on the south, and Benton
Boulevard on the east" (92), while the textual evidence suggests that the
Joneses live in the extreme northwesterly portion of this area, delimited by
Independence and Troost Avenues on the north and west, and by Twelfth

Street and the Paseo on the south and east. The novel explicitly names "Eighteenth an' Vine" as the location of the dance that Amerigo's parents attend before Rutherford violently assaults Viola (Carter 2006, 168).
25. Broomfield (2016), 93.
26. Carter (2006), 72–74.
27. Broomfield (2016), 93.
28. Miller (2013), 29–30.
29. Ibid., 29.
30. Carter (2006), 63.
31. This passage is presented as it appeared in "Excerpts from Paper on Which the 'Black Power' Philosophy Is Based" (1966), 10 – a source that Miller himself consulted. Somewhat ironically, the more canonical edition of the paper at this point is the reissued version constituting the pamphlet "Black Power: A Reprint of a Position Paper for the SNCC Vine City Project," published in 1966 by the United States National Student Association and available at www.freedomarchives.org/Documents/Finder/DOC513_scans/SNCC/513.SNCC.black.power.summer.1966.pdf [accessed September 23, 2021]. Vine City was the Atlanta neighborhood in which the Atlanta Project primarily focused its organizing efforts (see Carson 1995, 192–93).
32. Miller (2013), 45. According to Carson, not only was Carmichael not yet the chair of SNCC when the dissident Atlanta Project members issued their paper – as a *rebuke* to the SNCC staff – in March 1966; he also "joined [with other SNCC leaders] in opposing the Atlanta separatists," whose statement argued for the expulsion of whites from the organization. That said, Carson asserts that Carmichael was nevertheless sufficiently "affected by the ideas expressed in the position paper" to challenge John Lewis for the post of SNCC chair, which he assumed in May 1966. The statement's key ideological arguments, Carson attests, were authored by Bill Ware, Donald Stone, and Roland Snellings. See Carson (1995), 191–203, especially 196, 199–200.

   Miller himself seems to have recognized that he ought not identify Carmichael too closely with the 1966 Black Power position paper. While in the edition of *Soul Food* that I cite above Miller indicates that the paper was drafted by a "Carmichael-inspired" SNCC (2013, 45), a presumably earlier online electronic edition, issued by ProQuest's Alexander Street publishing platform, explicitly claims that Carmichael himself personally *wrote* what was actually the Atlanta Project's statement (see *Soul Food*, 44–45, as it appears at https://alexanderstreet.com/). The error likely derives from the suggestion – promulgated soon after Carmichael took over as chair of SNCC in the very issue of the *New York Times* that Miller references – that Carmichael "played a leading role in the preparation of a position paper on the new black philosophy, which was used to reverse the committee's policy on whites" ("Black Power Prophet: Stokely Carmichael," 1966, late city edition, 10).
33. Miller (2013), 46.

34. Ibid., 45, 46.
35. Abrahams (1985), xix.
36. Carter (2006), 83.
37. Ibid., 84.
38. Ibid., 85.
39. Ibid., 86.
40. For a concise review of the positive and negative responses generated by Liebow's book, see Embrick (2008), 263–65.
41. Liebow (2003), 93n.4. Liebow adopts the phrase "simple and direct coitus" from Alfred C. Kinsey, Wardell B. Pomeroy, and Clyde E. Martin; see their landmark 1948 study, *Sexual Behavior in the Human Male* (1975), 379.
42. Abrahams (1985), 8.
43. Ibid., 3.
44. Carter (2006), 23, 25.
45. Ibid., 22–23.
46. Ibid., 23–24.
47. Ibid., 25.
48. Ibid., 100.
49. Ibid., 100–1.
50. Ibid., 246.
51. Abrahams (1985), 20, 3.
52. If *Tally's Corner* has been both faulted for furthering the idea that dispossessed urban Blacks participate in a self-perpetuating "culture of poverty" and praised for countering that notion, Stack's book has been consistently cited for repudiating such "blame-the-victim" theorizations of social marginality from the moment of its publication. See, for example, Frank Munger's 2002 assessment of Stack's achievement in this vein, which Munger considers to be shared in both by *Tally's Corner* and by Joyce Ladner's 1971 *Tomorrow's Tomorrow* (Munger 2007, 1–25, especially 8–10).
53. Stack (1997 [1974]), 9. Stack says that she began her study "in the mid-sixties" (x), and contextual information provided elsewhere in her book suggests that she first met the Jacksons in 1967 (9, 10).
54. Ibid., xii; emphasis added.
55. Ibid., 29–30.

References

Abrahams, R. D. 1985. *Afro-American Folktales: Stories from Black Traditions in the New World*. New York: Pantheon Books.
"Black Power: A Reprint of a Position Paper for the SNCC Vine City Project." 1966. United States National Student Association. http://freedomarchives.o rg/Documents/Finder/DOC513_scans/SNCC/513.SNCC.black.power.sum mer.1966.pdf [last accessed September 23, 2021].

"Black Power Prophet: Stokely Carmichael." 1966, August 5. *New York Times*, late city edition.

Bledsoe, E. 2003, April 15. "Review of *Such Sweet Thunder*, by V. O. Carter." Foreword Reviews. www.forewordreviews.com/reviews/such-sweet-thun der/ [last accessed September 23, 2021].

Broomfield, A. 2016. *Kansas City: A Food Biography*. Lanham, MD: Rowman & Littlefield.

Bush, V. 2003, April 1. "Review of *Such Sweet Thunder*, by V. O. Carter." *Booklist.*, 1376.

Carson, C. 1995. *In Struggle: SNCC and the Black Awakening of the 1960s*, 2nd ed. Cambridge, MA: Harvard University Press.

Carter, V. O. 2003. *Such Sweet Thunder*, unedited hardcover edition, foreword by H. Lottman. South Royalton, VT: Steerforth Press.

    2006. *Such Sweet Thunder*, paperback edition, afterword by C. Fleischer. Hanover, NH: Zoland/Steerforth.

Clarke, G. E. 2003, May 17. "A South You Haven't Seen." *National Post* (Toronto, Canada).

Crouch, S. 2013. *Kansas City Lightning: The Rise and Times of Charlie Parker*. New York: HarperCollins.

Embrick, D. G. 2008. "Tally's Corner." In *International Encyclopedia of the Social Sciences*. 2nd ed. Vol. 8, ed. W. A. Darity, Jr., 263–65. Detroit, MI: Macmillan Reference USA.

Fleischer, C. 2003. "On Rediscovering Vincent O. Carter." *New Letters* 69.2&3 (Winter/Spring): 27–31.

    2006. "Afterword." In *Such Sweet Thunder*, by V. O. Carter, paperback edition. Hanover, NH: Zoland/Steerforth.

"Excerpts from Paper on Which the 'Black Power' Philosophy Is Based." 1966, August 5. *New York Times*, late city edition.

Graham, R. 2003, May 8. "Weathering Decades, 'Sweet Thunder' Resounds with Jazzy Style." *Boston Globe*, 3rd edition.

Guralnick, P. 1999 [1986]. *Sweet Soul Music: Rhythm and Blues and the Southern Dream of Freedom*. New York: Back Bay Books.

Hare, N. 1970 [1965]. *The Black Anglo-Saxons*. New York: Collier.

Harper, P. B. 2015. *Abstractionist Aesthetics: Artistic Form and Social Critique in African American Culture*. New York University Press.

Hazzard-Gordon, K. 1990. *Jookin': The Rise of Social Dance Formations in African-American Culture*. Philadelphia, PA: Temple University Press.

Jackson, J. A. 2004. *A House on Fire: The Rise and Fall of Philadelphia Soul*. New York: Oxford University Press.

Kinsey, A. C., W. B. Pomeroy, and C. E. Martin. 1975 [1948]. *Sexual Behavior in the Human Male*. Bloomington: Indiana University Press.

Knowles, M. 2009. *The Wicked Waltz and Other Scandalous Dances: Outrage at Couple Dancing in the 19th and Early 20th Centuries*. Jefferson, NC: McFarland.

Liebow, E. 2003 [1967]. *Tally's Corner: A Study of Negro Streetcorner Men*. Lanham, MD: Rowman & Littlefield.

Lottman, H. 1973 [1970]. "The Invisible Writer." In *The Bern Book: A Record of a Voyage of the Mind*, by V. O. Carter, v–xi. New York: John Day.

——— 2003. "Foreword." In *Such Sweet Thunder*, by V. O. Carter, unedited hardcover edition, vii–x. South Royalton, VT: Steerforth Press.

Miller, A. 2013. *Soul Food: The Surprising Story of an American Cuisine, One Plate at a Time*. Chapel Hill: University of North Carolina Press.

Munger, F. 2007 [2002]. "Identity as a Weapon in the Moral Politics of Work and Poverty." In *Laboring Below the Line: The New Ethnography of Poverty, Low-Wage Work, and Survival in the Global Economy*, ed. F. Munger, 1–25. New York: Russell Sage.

Stack, C. B. 1997 [1974]. *All Our Kin: Strategies for Survival in a Black Community*. New York: Basic Books.

Stafford, M. 2003, March 1. "Kansas City Author Gets Another Chance, 20 Years after His Death." Associated Press Newswires.

Stearns, M., and J. Stearns. 1994 [1968]. *Jazz Dance: The Story of American Vernacular Dance*. New York: Da Capo.

Wolk, D. 2004. *James Brown's* Live at the Apollo. New York: Continuum.

CHAPTER 10

Radio Free Dixie, *Black Arts Radio, and African American Women's Activism*

Cheryl Higashida

Introduction*

On August 26, 1963, U.S. listener Clark Nobil wrote the following to *Radio Free Dixie*, the Black revolutionary English-language program of music, news, and commentary broadcast weekly from Havana, Cuba:

> Armed with twisted facts and false imputations, you fulminate honest and sincere lawmakers. You blatantly make scurrilous accusations upon the society in which I live. You militate in favor of widespread revolt by the Negro against the white. You refute the irrefutable. You change the immutable.
>
> Furthermore, I am sorry to say we have such a formidable enemy, the radio. Your 50,000 watts reaches out and spreads your venomous lies all along the Atlantic coast line.[1]

While engaging in paranoiac hyperbole, Mr. Nobil's letter dramatizes the power of radio in the service of Black liberation – the medium's potential to "refute the irrefutable," to "change the immutable" – "all along the Atlantic coast line" in the 1960s, as African American activists sought to build on the gains of the Civil Rights Movement. From July 1962 to March 1966, exiled African American freedom fighters Robert and Mabel Williams wrote, produced, and hosted *Radio Free Dixie* from revolutionary Cuba in order to inform and politicize African Americans, and to foster international support for Black liberation.[2] Initially broadcast from Havana's 11,000-watt English-language station CMCA, and then its 50,000-watt cultural station Radio Progreso, *Radio Free Dixie* could be heard in the West Indies, throughout the United States (with the aid of rebroadcasts of shows recorded on tape), and as far north as Saskatchewan, Canada.[3] A dialectic of exile and empowerment materialized through the medium of radio: the invisibility of the Williamses' voices reminded listeners of their enforced physical absence from U.S. sites of struggle,

253

while their audibility spoke to their transformed presence throughout the decolonizing West Indies and settler states of North America.

Scholars have focused on the archive of Robert's printed or transcribed editorials – one could say, the "meat" of the show.[4] Indeed, the extent to which the show is equated wholly with Robert is evident in Timothy Tyson's decision to title his groundbreaking monograph *Radio Free Dixie: Robert F. Williams and the Roots of Black Power* (1999), despite the fact that Tyson only cursorily discusses the show, in keeping with his general dismissal of Robert's activism beyond the United States.[5] I argue that *Radio Free Dixie*'s aural arts and "secondary orality" are essential to understanding the show's Black internationalism, to recovering Black women's activism, and to reflecting on how the media work of women of color requires different approaches to the archive. In particular, we need to hear Robert's voice in dialogue with *Radio Free Dixie*'s seemingly minor components – the newscasts, storytelling, and commentary – that were presented and performed by women. This in turn impacts our understanding of how *Radio Free Dixie* contributes to debates over historical, political, and intellectual distinctions between the Civil Rights and Black Power phases of the Black Liberation Movement in the United States, debates that have crystallized around the concept of a "long civil rights movement" spanning the twentieth century through the present.[6]

Due to its ephemerality, radio has presented greater challenges to scholars than phonograph records or television: radio, especially in its early years, was not recorded as print literature, film, or music albums were. While accessible sound recordings of *Radio Free Dixie* are few, full transcripts of all the shows are available through the ProQuest History Vault database as well as Robert Williams' papers at the Bentley Historical Library of the University of Michigan. Although radio scholars have considered written archives to be inferior to sound recordings, media historian Josephine Dolan contends that talking and listening are "constituted in relation to a range of cultural competencies that are produced at the interface of written, photographic, and aural texts."[7]

Radio Free Dixie's voices emerge at this interface of the written, the visual, and the aural. They are not just transcribed perspectives or idioms, but accented, inflected speech and sound that were performed for audiences across the Americas. As aware as they were of the impact of mass communications and propaganda on Black struggles for civil rights and self-determination, Robert and Mabel keenly appreciated the power of radio as medium and art: they maximized radio's complementarity with Black traditions of storytelling, music, and the Church. When Mabel read

Langston Hughes' Simple stories, this re-created the art of storytelling along with the vernacular quality of the stories themselves, which Mabel pointed out were "based on conversations heard or overheard in bars and on the street corners of Harlem."[8] Meanwhile, jazz was for Robert Williams "a new psychological concept of propaganda" that "people could feel, that would motivate them."[9] With *Radio Free Dixie* he was striving for "something similar to what is used in the churches – the 'sanctified church,' there is a certain emotion that people reach."[10] The show thus exemplifies what Walter Ong refers to as the "secondary orality" of electronic media like radio, television, and the telephone, which reiterate and transform oral culture's "participatory mystique, its fostering of a communal sense, its concentration on the present moment, and even its use of formulas."[11]

Radio Free Dixie's Black internationalism was expressed not only through its vocality but also its polyvocality: Robert's voice in dialogue with music as well as news reports, folklore, and political statements that were read primarily by Mabel Williams and Jo Salas, a Cuban woman who had spent several years in the U.S. Mabel's and Jo's readings of statements and news stories could be dismissed as ventriloquizing or parroting the words of others rather than them speaking their own minds. But in attending to both the textual and performative dimensions of *Radio Free Dixie* – the archive and the repertoire – I argue that Mabel's, Jo's, and Robert's readings comprise, in Diana Taylor's words, a "repertoire of embodied practices as an important system of knowing and transmitting knowledge."[12] Examining Robert's commentary and analysis as one (albeit crucial) part of the show alongside others, enables us to apprehend the ways in which the show worked within, but also critically challenged, traditional gender roles in the Black Liberation Movement.

Voices of the South

In late summer 1961, Robert Williams, comrades Mabel Williams and Mae Mallory, and Robert and Mabel's two young sons went into hiding after a violent confrontation with white vigilantes and the state. As president of the National Association for the Advancement of Colored People (NAACP)'s Monroe, North Carolina chapter, Williams had established an international reputation through advocating armed self-defense for African Americans, leading a successful community campaign that drew the world's attention to the horrors of Jim Crow (the 1958 "Kissing Case"), and publishing *The Crusader* weekly newsletter, which linked African American history and struggles to Third World anticolonialism. By 1961, Martin Luther King, Jr., had found it necessary to defend his philosophy of nonviolence against Williams, and Williams had visited revolutionary Cuba twice, the second time at Castro's invitation.

In August 1961, Monroe citizens and Freedom Riders were demonstrating for racial equality in the hometown that Williams "shared" with the segregationist, anti-communist future U.S. senator – and popular radio and TV commentator – Jesse Helms. White mobs sparked a riot that badly injured many demonstrators including Student Nonviolent Coordinating Committee (SNCC) leader James Forman. As Robert, Mabel, and their supporters prepared to defend themselves at the Williamses' house, vigilantes shot at them throughout the night, and word of the National Guard's approach came their way. Robert, Mabel, their sons, and Mae Mallory had to flee for their lives. Wanted by the FBI on trumped-up charges of kidnapping a white couple, it would be eight years before the Williamses set foot in the United States again.[13] Aided by a network of allies, they escaped to Canada, where they were sheltered for six weeks by Anne and Vernel Olsen.[14] From there they eventually made their way to Cuba, the site of their next phase of struggle.

An acute propagandist as well as a skilled organizer, Robert wasted no time in reestablishing *The Crusader* in Cuba and negotiating with Castro to broadcast a radio show from Havana's CMCA, and then Radio Progreso.[15] In the first issue of *The Crusader in Exile*, Robert declared: "the racists of Monroe have not triumphed. They have merely forced me to a more extensive field of struggle. Unwittingly they have maneuvered our forces into a position that affords us the most powerful and effective weapon ever to fall in our hands."[16] This weapon was *Radio Free Dixie*, first broadcast on July 27, 1962, nearly a year after the Williamses' flight from Monroe. Shortly before the first show aired, the Williamses' comrades, supporters, and foes heard a familiar voice announcing:

> This is Robert F. Williams, freedom fighter refugee from racial oppression in the U.S.A., speaking to you from Havana, Cuba, Free territory of the Americas ... I invite you to listen to Jazz, Afro-American folklore, news, interviews and commentary over Radio Free Dixie. Our new program is dedicated to a better understanding of the Afro-American struggle in North America. We shall be on the air every Friday night from 11 'til midnight, 690 on your dial. Don't forget to listen weekly to Radio Free Dixie – the free voice of the South.[17]

Robert's opening words on the inaugural show made manifest that the medium of radio, the station's revolutionary situation, and the program's aims and content conjointly produced "our new voice of freedom." This collective voice, while first and foremost African American, merged with that of the Cuban people whose revolution was "a spirit for all of the oppressed peoples of the world," and whose infrastructure amplified revolutionary internationalism.[18]

Radio was an ideal medium to convey and foster internationalism among nations and people fighting for self-determination. On the one hand, as Michelle Hilmes has argued, radio as much as print media fostered national "imagined communities" with its "power not only to assert actively the unifying power of simultaneous experience but to communicate meanings about the nature of that unifying experience."[19] Of all mass media, radio was especially important in informing, engaging, and shaping the imagined community of Black America in the second half of the twentieth century.[20] In the 1940s, the Federal Communications Commission broke network monopolies on radio, and then television usurped radio's role as the primary medium of mass entertainment, giving radio producers more freedom to experiment with different formats now that corporate attention was focused elsewhere. As these developments fueled the growth of Black-oriented radio programing entirely for African Americans (but not necessarily *by* them),[21] radio became the most important source of news, entertainment, and education for African Americans in the South.

On the other hand, there were tremendous obstacles to informing listeners about freedom struggles over the radio in the U.S. Stations in the South faced economic and social pressure, if not outright violence, if they broached integration or civil rights. In the 1950s and early 1960s, only a few southern stations – such as WERD and WAOK in Atlanta, WENN in Birmingham, and WGIV in Charlotte – either covered developments in the movement, provided airtime to civil rights groups and leaders, or materially supported desegregation and voting rights efforts. Outside the South, it was possible for Black-oriented and independent radio to apprise Black and white audiences of struggles for racial justice and freedom in Dixie, along with fundraising and giving airtime to the Southern Christian Leadership Conference (SCLC), the SNCC, and the Congress of Racial Equality (CORE).

Even for these listeners, however, *Radio Free Dixie*'s radical, eventually revolutionary, Black internationalism represented something completely different from and at odds with Cold War liberalism and the predominantly nonviolent direct-action tactics of the Civil Rights Movement. As the program's press release put it, *Radio Free Dixie* offered "the first completely free radio voice that the Negro people have had to air their case against brutal racial oppression."[22] Given the strictures on radical Black critique in the United States, Cuban radio was an ideal medium for Robert's and Mabel's show, since its signals could be transmitted and received more quickly and discreetly than print, especially with the proliferation of portable transistor radios.

Moreover, the show's transnational operations made it a vehicle for imagining Black nationhood in relation to other revolutionary nationalisms. The fact that *Radio Free Dixie* emanated from Havana was a constant reminder of the history of African American and Cuban solidarity.[23] As Robert came to espouse the violent overthrow of the United States, urging African Americans to engage in urban guerrilla warfare within a framework of "domestic colonialism," he implicitly positioned *Radio Free Dixie* in the revolutionary tradition of radio in Cuba and Algeria.[24] Indeed, Robert's own realization of the power of radio emerged not only from its domestic popularity in the United States, but from its transgression of national borders and ability to bring "Cuba" into his home. As a child he had been impressed by how his father, listening to radio at night, occasionally picked up Spanish speech and song. At the time, Williams thought that the broadcast came from Mexico, but he later asserted that it must have originated from Havana. When he tuned into Radio Havana from Monroe one night in 1960, as a Fair Play for Cuba Committee member, Williams realized that "if the Cubans were to use some English in their long-wave programs, they'd be able to get through to millions of listeners in the United States."[25]

Consequently, the Williamses' access to the airwaves presented a notable strike within Cold War media wars, as CIA-supported Radio Swan blanketed the Caribbean with counterrevolutionary propaganda aimed at Cuba.[26] Numerous U.S. newspapers reported with alarm on Robert's "inflammatory" show, and one FBI informant asserted that "probably one of the most dangerous weapons being utilized by the CASTRO regime against the United States is the radio program called Radio Free Dixie."[27] Robert himself saw *Radio Free Dixie* going up against Washington, DC's Voice of America broadcasts, which in his words would "beam Kennedy's propaganda around the World, especially to the Afro-asian [sic] World."[28]

Within both *Radio Free Dixie* and *The Crusader* newsletter, the centerpiece would seem to be Robert's editorial: Robert's commentaries appeared on the first page of each issue of *The Crusader*, usually without any other story, and the newspaper continued to publish Robert's on-air commentaries, reinforcing their primacy. It has thus made sense to focus on Robert's words, and to treat his *Radio Free Dixie* commentary as text divorced from speech since it regularly appeared in print. Nonetheless, by tuning in to the aural properties of *Radio Free Dixie*, we can better appreciate how it articulated and redefined Black internationalism by putting Robert's editorial in conversation with the show's "other" voices.

While recognizing the Eurocentrism and ahistoricism of Walter Ong's thought, his concept of secondary orality is useful for apprehending the radio arts and women's voicings of Black internationalism. Secondary orality refers to "a more deliberate and self-conscious orality, based permanently on the use of writing and print in particular."[29] Robert's commentaries in jive talk vividly demonstrate the show's self-aware navigation of oral culture. What I believe is the first *Radio Free Dixie* commentary in jive (on October 18, 1962, almost three months into the show) begins more casually than usual, yet still strikes the formal oratorical style that was Robert's wont:

> Greetings My Friends:
>   Tonight I want to have a plain down home talk with you. Yes, I want to speak to you about something that I saw Tuesday, that I wish you all could have seen.

However, Robert's invocation of Franklin D. Roosevelt's fireside chats ("I want to talk for a few minutes with the people of the United States about banking") quickly gives way to something quite different: "Man, as the cats say down home, it was a sight for sore eyes to see our boys Fidel and [Algerian revolutionary] Ben Bella."[30] This jive talk was obviously pitched at youth who tuned in to the postwar generation of African American deejays popular for their verbal dexterity and vernacular style. But the *planned* spontaneity of Robert's speech, which he had written for the show and read from a script,[31] exemplifies its secondary orality:

> where primary orality promotes spontaneity because the analytic reflectiveness implemented by writing is unavailable, secondary orality promotes spontaneity because through analytic reflection we have decided that spontaneity is a good thing.[32]

Self-consciously marking his transition to "plain down home talk," Robert alludes to the fact that he speaks as if directly addressing his community in a manner that is remarkably like primary orality, while he in fact integrates distant and diverse listeners and topics in a fashion remarkably unlike primary orality. As a result, he renders familiar "our boys Fidel and Ben

Bella," figures who would be distinctly foreign and even suspect to many of his listeners.

It was not solely Robert's voice that expressed Black internationalism so powerfully, however, but its call-and-response with music and multiple voices, many of which were the voices of women of color, of whom the *Radio Free Dixie* transcripts suggest that listeners heard as much if not more so than Robert. In *The Crusader*, Robert's editorial was often accompanied by Mabel's cartoon art, which occupies its own center space and has its own voice (Fig. 10.1).[33]

Columns by Mabel and Ethel Azalea Johnson ("Asa Lee"), news, poetry, book reviews, and letters from readers filled the subsequent pages. On *Radio Free Dixie*, Robert's editorial was in dialogue with news stories and other commentaries that situated U.S. events like the 1965 Watts uprising in a global context. Furthermore, Mabel's reading of a featured story roughly one-third of the way into the program balances Robert's editorial at the two-thirds mark.

In contrast to Robert's self-penned editorials, Mabel and Jo read the words of others: Langston Hughes' stories; declarations by draft resisters; statements by organizations like the Afro-Asian Writers' Conference; or editorials and reports from newspapers. This division of labor was certainly a sexual one, with Mabel and Jo in a lesser, passive, "feminine" position of ventriloquizing the words of others, in contrast to Robert's dominant, active, "masculine" role in writing and broadcasting his own editorials. This was in keeping with traditional gender roles that Mabel occupied in the production of *The Crusader* (e.g., sustaining the paper while Robert went on speaking tours; drawing attention to herself in her essays as a mother and wife in the struggle).[34] However, drawing on Diana Taylor's theorization of the archive and the repertoire, I propose that Mabel's and Jo's readings and newscasts should be understood as performances enacting female agency and embodied memory. It is through nonverbal as well as verbal performance – intonation and attitude; the speakers' socially constructed voices, bodies, and embodiments; and the tensions between their embodied identities and those of the people and characters to whom they give voice – that women's histories and articulations of Black internationalism emerge.[35]

An example of such performance is Mabel's readings of Langston Hughes' Simple stories about Harlemite everyman Jessie B. Semple ("Simple"), a regular feature of *Radio Free Dixie* in its first few weeks. Taking the form of Simple's conversations with an unnamed narrator, the

THE CRUSADER
WEEKLY NEWSLETTER

VOL. 2 - NO. 16   NOVEMBER 5, 1960   MONROE, N. C.   PRICE 10¢

HIS MASTER'S VOICE

The average American mentality is the product of a conglomeration of slanted facts, half truths and outright lies constantly fed by mass communication media sponsored by big business. America today is a victim of herd instinct motivation. Clear thinking minds, uninfected by propaganda and traditional prejudice, are as scarce as American honesty.

fro-Americans must stop blindly taking direction from white slave masters. Afro-Americans must cease believing that a self-acclaimed master race can be interested in universal social justice.

As a race we must never forget that the American slave master and his American "democratic" slavery was the most barbaric in the annals of history. It stretches over a period of 300 years

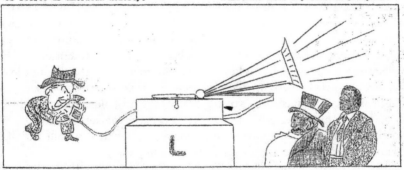

"DE MASTER'S VOICE."

What a magic spell the mass media holds the people under. Mass media is quite capable of showing danger where there is none, of hiding it where it truly exists. It is capable of creating enemies where there should only be peace and friendship. It has a wanton disregard for truth unless the truth coincides with the sponson's vested interest.

Afro-Americans are the most lied to factions of all the national ethnic groups. They seem more susceptible to brainwashing by the white masters. Af-

with a sundry record of murder, plunder, rape, bastardry, incest, exploitation, segregation, kangaroo law and Jim Crow. We must remember that there are people in this democratic land of ours who can still remember slavery and the Christian gentlemen who dealt in the profitable transaction of human bondage. We must remember that the white masters we trust so much today and sometimes worship, are not God, but direct descendents through blood and mores of UnGodly and inhumane slave holders.

(continued next page.)

Figure 10.1 *The Crusader* newsletter with Mabel Williams' political cartoon, November 5, 1960.

stories themselves are an archive of performance as fictionalizations of "conversations heard or overheard in bars and on the street corners of Harlem," as Mabel described them for her listeners.[36] References on *Radio Free Dixie* to the Simple stories as folklore further emphasized their affiliation with African American oral traditions,[37] although they were in fact first published as a column in *The Chicago Defender* and then collected in a book. Further meshing orality, aurality, performance, and literature, Hughes had originally planned the Simple stories to be a radio play. The Williamses' decision to feature Simple from their very first show demonstrated their attunement to popular Black art that was suited for radio broadcast.[38]

As one would expect, the Williamses selected carefully from the archive of Simple stories in order to present those that best complemented the show's message. On the first broadcast of *Radio Free Dixie*, Mabel read "When a Man Sees Red," in which Simple contests assumptions that he is under foreign communist influence for standing up for his rights: "I was born in America, I live in America, and long as I have been black, I been an American."[39] The Williamses wanted the same to be known about them, now that their exile in Cuba would fuel efforts to delegitimize their political struggle through associating it with communism. By voicing Simple's words, "long as I have been black, I been an American," Mabel harnessed the power of the African American vernacular to express the national-popular in a speech act that reclaimed American identity for Black revolutionaries.

Mabel's performance of the Simple story "Income Tax" affirmed internationalism through the special properties of radio. Along with depicting the armed self-defense and direct action that the Williamses advocated – a Black soldier takes a gun with him to hold a sit-in on the army's Jim Crow toilets – the story culminates with an Irish policeman supporting the refusal of the soldier, now a taxi driver, to serve a white southerner. Integral to the depiction of international and interracial solidarity between the Irish policeman and the Black soldier/cabbie are their voices. Mabel's awareness of their dramatic power over the radio is indicated by the accent marks on the transcript to aid her with intonation, pitch, and emphasis:

"Down En Mississippi a colored soldier has to have a <u>gun even to go to the toilet</u>!"[40]

Similarly, the Irish policeman's support of the Black soldier's refusal to drive the white southerner is heightened through dialect:

> Of course, I understand. Be jeezus! It's like that exactly that the damned English did the Irish. Faith, you do not have to haul him . . . Stranger, get yerself another cab.[41]

If, as Janet Neigh argues, radio helped Hughes develop a diasporic poetics, "Income Tax" shows that Hughes' Black Atlantic intersected with the Irish diaspora.[42] Hughes' interracial internationalism was amplified through Mabel's performance of Black and Irish voices in dialogue: an African American woman performing as an Irish American man suggests the cultural cross-fertilization that Marshall McLuhan imagined would arise from the decentralized sociopolitical formations (his "global village" or "ministates") that were spurred by electronic media.[43] In a similar vein, Mabel's and Jo's news reportage enacted international solidarity: U.S.-born Mabel read reports pertaining to Cuba and other countries (e.g., a story about representatives from sixty-three countries expressing solidarity against "Yankee imperialists" during a May Day celebration in Havana), while Cuban-born Jo Salas read the news about African Americans (Malcolm X's Organization of Afro-American Unity; the jailing of two Black youths in Mississippi for attempting a sit-in at an ice show).[44]

Correspondence indicates that *Radio Free Dixie* indeed facilitated internationalist and interracial affiliations. Noel Bailey in Kingston, Jamaica, wrote that he and his neighbors listened regularly to the show, while a letter from the international liaison of China's broadcasting administration stated that they had incorporated the recordings of "Negro songs and music" that Robert and Mabel had presented them, and in return they were sending "a set of eight Chinese records entitled 'Peking in Melody.'"[45] But the greatest subset of listener correspondence by far came from white male liberals and progressives in the United States, including amateur radio operators who happened upon the show and were drawn to the music and/ or the message. For example, Frank Merrill of the Newark News Radio Club wrote in his report of reception: "I also think racial discrimination should be stopped because it isn't their fault they are black. If there was a demonstration against discrimination here, I would be in it." Alan O. Campbell of the same club wrote: "I found the program most interesting and the signal was good enough so that it should be possible for me to tune in quite often. The music played was very good."[46] Ensign Thomas Parker, "a young American with a rather good liberal education," objected to Robert's contribution to efforts "to increase strife and discontent in America, using the Negro to achieve this." But, he added:

> Rest assured that I don't question the convictions of most of your announcers and help, however the total effect is too obviously an extension of Communist subversive policy. I would have thought Cuban propaganda would be a little more subtle and difficult to analyze. Well, keep up your excellent jazz.[47]

A letter from Clifton Bryant, a white West Virginian, provides some insight into why African American working-class correspondence is lacking. Bryant explained that as a poor man with a disability and a family of five to support: "I cannot write you as much as I would like because the postal cost is so high."[48] This indicates the economic difficulties that many of the show's listeners faced in contacting Robert, on top of the threat of political persecution should they be found writing to him in Havana. That said, the amount of white-authored correspondence to Robert suggests the reach of even revolutionary Black radio across color lines. And while white liberal support was ancillary to Robert's goals of social justice and self-determination for African Americans, he took his white listeners seriously enough to write back to them, symptomatic of his open approach to fostering alliances.

Just as importantly, *Radio Free Dixie* gave listeners a radical alternative to Cold War womanhood predicated on middle-class domesticity, an ideal that imbued Black as well as white appeals to citizenship. Brian Ward suggests that the proliferation in the 1940s through the 1960s of African American homemaking radio shows, where many – although not all – of radio's Black female voices could be found, was symptomatic of the politics of respectability and Black consumerism through which civil rights were often advanced.[49] Mabel worked to some extent within this discourse, indexing citizenship and human rights to heterosexual domesticity. For example, an on-air effort to raise support for imprisoned Monroe freedom fighter Mae Mallory relied on sentimental tropes of mothers and children:

> Tonight in the so-called free world, a mother of two children languishes in a dismal jail. She has been deprived of the right and joy to give companionship and guidance to her teenage daughters . . . Only a mother could know the torment of being denied the divine happiness of fulfilling the sacred obligations of mother-hood.[50]

By contrast, Mallory espoused a Black militant proto-feminist stance in reflecting on her situation in a letter that appeared in *The Crusader* the previous year. Along with insisting that she "knew what [she] was doing when [she] came to Monroe" to support Robert and had "no regrets," she proclaimed that "the masses can choose their own leader and carry on in his absence." She ended on a note of Black women's solidarity, praising "the women from Buffalo, New York [who] have been coming down to Cleveland to see me often," including Black left civil rights leader Queen Mother Audley Moore.[51]

In other ways, however, Mabel's reportage enacted a militant Black motherhood that challenged liberal capitalist gender roles and racist hierarchies. On June 7, 1963, following the chords of "We Shall Overcome," Mabel read in its entirety a *Pittsburgh Courier* story about Annie Pearl Fairfax, a disappeared Black mother who had been sentenced to a one-month jail term "for daring to defend herself against unspeakable police brutality," and who had not been seen since. Although the reading of a news story might not register as performance, a performance studies approach (as defined by Taylor) illuminates important elements of Mabel's reading that go unheard and unseen through a narrow focus on the verbal meaning of the written archive. For one, it is possible that Mabel brought the *Courier*'s article to life through her particular inflections and emphases, similar to how she performed the voices of the Simple stories. For another, performance draws our attention to "the embodiment of the social actors" and "the social construction of bodies in particular contexts," which play crucial roles in the storage and transmission of knowledge.[52] In this light, Mabel does not relay Fairfax's story as an "objective" or "neutral" reporter. Rather, the story is mediated by Mabel's embodied act of reading as a Black mother who had similarly met banishment from her home and children for resisting the police.

Quoting the *Courier*, Mabel informed her listeners that "Mrs. Fairfax administered a thorough beating to the abusive cop" who had "'jumped on' Mrs. Fairfax, and that she 'whipped him.'" Mabel concluded (still by way of the *Courier*) by connecting Fairfax's likely murder to racial terror dating back to slavery, as well as to the well-known case of Rosa Ingram, another African American mother who had been jailed for defying a white man: "She [Ingram] shot her oppressor. Mrs. Fairfax merely trounced hers." Mabel's embodied reading as a Black mother who herself stood up to state repression powerfully reiterates the point that Fairfax's fate was not an isolated anecdote, but part of a series of racist police violence against African American women including Ingram, Mabel, and potentially her listeners.[53]

In an especially striking performance of militant Black womanhood on *Radio Free Dixie*, Mabel represented a version of her own resistance on the air as the Civil Rights Movement was transitioning to Black Power. On April 9, 1965, just two months before the Watts uprising, Mabel read a story from *The Militant*, the paper of the Socialist Workers Party, about the production of Frank Greenwood's dramatization of the Monroe armed self-defense movement, *If We Must Live*.[54] A former communist turned Black nationalist, Greenwood had been so moved by Robert's 1962 book, *Negroes with Guns*, that he wrote his play to spread the word about the Monroe movement.[55] *If We Must Live* debuted in Los Angeles in spring 1965, its run coinciding with the Watts uprising; Greenwood put on a free show for the youth of Watts. Many of these young African Americans were likely unaware of Robert Williams – according to the Black radical journalist Richard Gibson, Robert and the Monroe self-defense movement were not being invoked in conjunction with Watts – but they enthusiastically embraced the play's heroes.[56] *If We Must Live* thus helped keep alive the history of the Monroe movement as the Black freedom struggle transitioned from predominantly nonviolent direct action, aimed at reforming and integrating the U.S. social order, to being a movement rooted in multiple forms of nationalism and revolutionary internationalism.[57] In this context, it is significant that Greenwood foregrounded Black women's militancy, something that interested *The Militant*'s Della Rossa (who in the following months would write the pamphlet *Why Watts Exploded: How the Ghetto Fought Back*). Rossa called attention to

> the scene where Wilson's wife [Greenwood changed "Williams" to "Wilson"] grabs a rifle and scares the white cop out of her house. In the play, it is Wilson's wife who makes the famous statement for which Rob Williams was suspended from the NAACP – "We must meet violence with violence."[58]

Having Mabel's character fight the police and voice Robert's signature statement suggests that the cultural memory of Monroe was open to reenactments by different participants, activating new meanings for the present and future. Mabel's performance of her character's support of armed self-defense in the course of reading Rossa's review on *Radio Free Dixie*, spoke to and amplified the ways that she and other Black women like Mae Mallory, Rosa Ingram, Annie Pearl Fairfax, and Queen Mother Audley Moore were major figures in the Black liberation struggle. This rearticulated the masculinist rhetoric of self-defense, which persistently invoked Black men protecting Black women and children while demeaning femininity by associating it with subordination to male leadership, or with acquiescence to white supremacy.[59]

Conclusion

Robert's political evolution, along with Timothy Tyson's definitive monograph on Robert, has been a flashpoint in debates over "the long civil rights movement." The long movement framework proposed by Jacquelyn Dowd Hall, Jeanne Theoharis, and Komozi Woodard, among others, departs from traditional periodizations of the "classical" Civil Rights Movement from 1954 through 1965, followed by its decline due to the Black Power Movement. Instead, the long movement posits historical continuities between Black-labor-left coalitions of the Depression/Popular Front era and the modern Civil Rights and Black Power movements. According to Hall, this has several major implications: it challenges assumptions that U.S. racism was localized solely or primarily in the South; it illuminates the connections between movements for labor rights and civil rights; it draws attention to women's activism; it contests the narrative of declension and demonization of Black Power; and it presents a deeper history of the Reagan/Bush-era neoconservative/neoliberal backlash. Tyson's study of Robert exemplifies the long movement thesis, as he asserts that Robert's life "illustrates that 'the civil rights movement' and 'the Black Power movement' emerged from the same soil, confronted the same predicaments, and reflected the same quest for African American freedom."[60] For Sundiata Cha-Jua and Clarence Lang, however, Tyson's claim *"more than any other* justifies [their] deployment of the vampire analogy" with the long movement thesis. The long movement's ahistoricism and lack of specificity, according to Cha-Jua and Lang, render it like the vampire, "outside of time and history, beyond the processes of life and death, and change and development."[61] On the other hand, Black Power scholar Peniel Joseph extols Tyson's study for demonstrating that "elements of civil rights activism and black power militancy coexisted in complex, combative, and novel ways," and for complicating the hierarchical opposition of the "good" (nonviolent, racially inclusive) Civil Rights Movement to the "bad" (violent, exclusionary) Black Power Movement.

With its time frame of 1962 to 1966 straddling the classically defined transition from Civil Rights to Black Power, *Radio Free Dixie* exemplifies the continuities and discontinuities between Civil Rights activism and Black Power militancy: the show's report on *If We Must Die* re-articulates the militant Civil Rights activism of the Monroe armed self-defense movement for the Black Power era. However, *Radio Free Dixie* is especially telling in this regard as a collective project in which women played significant and distinct roles. Despite persistent assumptions then and now that *Radio Free Dixie* was Robert's show, I have argued that it shifts away from the "great man" approach to history privileging a single individual. To be sure, Robert deserves continued study. However, a narrow focus on Robert prevents us from apprehending the more complex milieu that gave rise to and shaped his work, including the activism and cultural work of Black women who are obscured by a methodological focus on individual men. Consigned to "lesser" roles of reporting news and reading stories, Mabel Williams' and Jo Salas' work can appear superfluous in relation to Robert Williams' self-authored editorials. Yet the nonverbal and verbal elements of performance in *Radio Free Dixie*'s archive indicate that newscasting and hosting enabled radical women of color to have agency in the nexus of oral performance, print culture, radio transmission, and reception across the Americas. By amplifying the activism and everyday resistance of Black women such as Mae Mallory, Asa Lee, Audley Moore, Rosa Guy, and Annie Pearl Fairfax, Mabel challenged masculinism and patriarchy in the Black Liberation Movement as Black Power was emerging.

   Radio Free Dixie thus exemplifies what Rayvon Fouché calls Black vernacular technology creativity, or "black technological utterances rooted within black cultures, black communities, and black existences."[62] The Williamses' engagement with the revolutionary potential of radio contests the cultural narratives of declension via mass media posited by Theodor Adorno and Jean-Paul Sartre, who saw radio to be a vehicle for producing passive consumers. Focusing on commercial and state radio, Sartre saw its listeners as a fundamentally "impotent" serial collective vis-à-vis the determining univocality of the broadcaster's voice. However, radio in the service of counter-hegemonic or revolutionary struggle contributed to the dynamic ebb and flow of self-conscious groups engaged in collective action: Black-oriented radio in the United States helped mobilize the Civil Rights Movement; the station of Algeria's National Liberation Front drew listeners who collectively reconstructed and in effect created the FLN's jammed broadcasts.[63]

   In this vein, *Radio Free Dixie* created possibilities for its audience to make the leap from passive serial collectivity to active identification with Black struggle. Listeners and supporters wrote in from the very first show; they sent newspaper clippings and announcements to be read on air; they responded to requests for "jazz, Dixieland, folk music and recordings of the current protest movement in the South"; they visited Robert in Havana and sat in on the show.[64] This desire to contribute to *Radio Free Dixie* and *The Crusader in Exile* spoke to the way that Black revolutionary media were not simply objects of consumption but collective projects that drew on the talents and ambitions of women and men across national boundaries. In particular, *Radio Free Dixie* exemplifies the obscured yet ongoing adaptation and appropriation of technology by women of color to record and make history.

Notes

* I thank John Munro, Steven Belletto, and Shu-Ling Chen Berggreen for enlightening conversations and opportunities to present versions of this work at St. Mary's University, Lafayette College, and the Media Research and Practice Colloquium at the University of Colorado at Boulder. My research has also benefited from presenting at conferences of the American Studies Association and, thanks to Owen Walsh, the African American Intellectual History Society. The Bentley Historical Library staff assisted my research of *Radio Free Dixie* transcripts. I am especially indebted to the Freedom Archives and its directors Claude Marks and Nathaniel Moore for their insights, research, and resources, which are indispensable to the study of *Radio Free Dixie*, Robert and Mabel Williams, and social movement history and media.

1. Nobil (1963).
2. I hereafter refer to Robert and Mabel Williams as "Robert" and "Mabel" rather than by their surnames, to distinguish them clearly and concisely. I mean no disrespect whatsoever to these important historical figures and freedom fighters.
3. Williams quoted in Tyson (1999), 287. Listener correspondence from the United States South, Southwest, and Midwest further indicates the range of *Radio Free Dixie*'s reach.
4. Rucker (2006), Mislan (2015).
5. Robeson Taj Frazier (2014) importantly breaks with the androcentric focus on Robert, as well as U.S.-centric study of the Williamses.
6. I follow Sundiata Keita Cha-Jua and Clarence Lang's terminology of the "Black Liberation Movement" to refer to twentieth- and twenty-first-century U.S.-based Black freedom movements. Cha-Jua and Lang (2007) use this term to register the historical and scholarly distinctions between the Civil Rights and Black Power movements that are denied by the idea of the "long civil rights movement." While I agree that these movements are distinct, I also build on the work of long movement scholars, who excavate key continuities between Civil Rights, Black Power, and other movements like the Old and New Left.
7. Dolan (2003), 70.
8. Williams and Williams (1962a).

9. Quoted in Tyson (1999), 288.
10. Ibid.
11. Ong (1982), 133–34.
12. Taylor (2003), 26.
13. See Tyson (1999), 262–86.
14. Wright and Wylie (2009).
15. Williams quoted in Tyson (1999), 287. A great deal of listener correspondence with radio club members indicates the range of *Radio Free Dixie*'s reach as well as its limitations. Replying to one listener, Williams wrote: "People have reported hearing us from as far away as New York, Chicago and Detroit" (Williams 1963).
16. Williams (1962a).
17. Williams (1962b).
18. Williams and Williams (1962a).
19. Hilmes (2012), 352.
20. Black-oriented radio with programing entirely by and for African Americans mushroomed in the United States after World War II, as did the number of African American households with radios. In North Carolina, according to Brian Ward: "the proportion of African American families with radio sets leapt from 1 percent in 1930 to 33 percent just over a decade later"; in the rural South as a whole, "black radio ownership levels had reached 75–85 percent by the late 1950s" (Ward 2004, 7).
21. William Barlow notes: "The first two black-owned stations in the country were established in 1949, but the number did not grow decisively or steadily" (Barlow 1999, 245). Indeed, due to economic pressure and threats of violence, Black-owned stations, especially in the South, were not necessarily more reflective than white-owned stations of African American interests.
22. *Radio Free Dixie* press release (1962).
23. On African American and Cuban solidarities and alliances, see Guridy (2010) and Young (2006).
24. Robert Williams, quoted in Rucker (2006), 29.
25. Cohen (1972), 225.
26. Barlow (1990), 126.
27. Szulc (1964), 13.
28. Williams and Williams (1963). For Robert, radio provided a greater sphere of influence than that of print, as he expressed to a student radio station staff member: "Formerly, I could reach only a few people while living in the 'Free World' with my Newsletter, THE CRUSADER and public speaking. From here, I am reaching the whole world, so the racists have done their cause and their country's cause a great disservice" (Williams 1964b).
29. Ong (1982), 134.
30. Williams and Williams (1962c), 15.
31. The script for the show has a cover page stating: "To be taped October 18, 1962" (ibid.).
32. Ong (1982), 134.

33. M. Williams (1960), 1.
34. Robert himself understood Mabel's work in traditional, patriarchal terms: "My wife works as my secretary," he wrote in one letter. Even here, however, Robert's very next sentences suggest how Mabel navigated Cuba on her own terms: "She has completed a course in Spanish. I haven't had time yet, therefore, I still have a language handicap" (Williams 1964c).
35. It might seem problematic to apply the term "performance," which Taylor defines as ritualized, formalized, or reiterative behavior, to on-air readings of written stories and statements. These are far afield from dance, religious rites, and other collective, participatory, and – crucially – live acts that Taylor calls performance. However, this is where *Radio Free Dixie*'s secondary orality comes into play: if acts of primary orality correlate with performance, we can think of *Radio Free Dixie*'s secondary orality as those performances transformed through their reliance on print culture. In fact, Taylor stresses that the (written and material) archive and the repertoire (of performances) generally work in tandem, belying binaries of the unmediated, modern, truthful archive vs. the mediated, primitive, false or unverifiable repertoire (Taylor 2003), 21.
36. Williams and Williams (1962a), 2.
37. Ibid.
38. Indeed, Janet Neigh contends that Hughes' 1940s poems like "Montage of a Dream Deferred," drawing on his experiences with radio journalism, exhibit a diasporic "radio connectivity" that "imagine possibilities for the technology of radio to bring about cross-cultural social relationships that exceed white control" (Neigh 2013, 273). In this sense too, *Radio Free Dixie* builds on the political imagination of its Black internationalist predecessors.
39. Hughes (2000), 85.
40. Williams and Williams (1962b), 6.
41. Ibid., 7.
42. Hughes suggests that African and Irish Americans share a history of colonialism in a section of "Income Tax" that Mabel did not read. After hearing about the Irish policeman's support for the Black taxi driver, Simple says that he would have asked the officer: "Well, before you-all got free – kicked around as you was – did you still have to pay taxes to the British?" The narrator responds, "Of course, the Irish had to pay taxes. All colonial peoples have to pay taxes to their rulers." Simple's resistance to paying taxes when he "can't even vote down home" is thus linked to colonial subjugation (Hughes 2002, 101).
43. McLuhan (1995), 257.
44. That Mabel and Jo deliberately presented particular stories is suggested by the fact that they did not simply alternate with each other (Williams and Williams 1964, 6–8).
45. Williams (1964a), Chiung (1964).
46. Merrill (1963).
47. Parker (n.d.).
48. Bryant (1963).

49. Ward (2004), 91. According to William Barlow, African American women "made significant gains in the field of broadcasting" as Black-oriented radio grew in the post-World War II period. Outside of secretarial work, their options were primarily to be radio entertainers or hosts of the homemaker shows. But these could lead to full-time deejay positions (Barlow 1999, 147).
50. Williams and Williams (1962d), 1.
51. Mallory (1961), 3.
52. Taylor (2003), 29.
53. Another example of *Radio Free Dixie*'s serialization of Black female militant resistance to the police is Mabel's reading of a news report from the March 5, 1965 issue of *Muhammad Speaks*, "West Coast Blasts Brutal Bay Area Beating of Women Tenants," describing two sisters who were beaten by police for speaking out against a white slumlord, and who proceeded to file suits against the police (Williams and Williams 1965, 1–2).
54. *The Militant* and the SWP as a whole staunchly supported Black self-defense and nationalism. *The Militant* regularly printed Malcolm X's speeches, and Julian Mayfield had covered the Monroe self-defense movement for the paper. However, when she read *The Militant*'s coverage of *If We Must Live*, Mabel chose not to identify the paper, presumably in an effort to avoid identification with particular left parties.
55. Greenwood (1965). Among his accomplishments, Greenwood helped pioneer Black studies, as co-founder of the African American Cultural Association.
56. Gibson (1965).
57. Indeed, the Watts production spurred interest in producing *If We Must Live* in the South, after Gil Moses of the Free Southern Theater caught that performance. Greenwood had also received a request from China for the script.
58. Rossa (1965), 5.
59. Robert regularly spoke of armed self-defense in this way, but numerous other examples of this pervasive discourse can be found, such as Deacon for Defense and Justice spokesman Charles Sims' statement that: "We had to arm ourselves because we got tired of the women, the children being harassed by white night-riders" (quoted in Tyson 1999, 291). This element of patriarchal Black militancy was also played up in the *Los Angeles Times* review of the play, which lauded a scene in which "with fiery logic the wife demands her husband stop his dangerous activities, culminating her tirade with a spat-out: 'Guts don't get no grits!'" Nonetheless, this review captures the way that the play's form and subject matter engendered an interactive community theater "as emotional as a revival meeting, with the audience brought to the brink of booing the many villains and cheering the hero" (Thomas 1965, B9).
60. Cha-Jua and Lang (2007), 275.
61. Ibid., 265.
62. Fouché (2006), 639–40.
63. Fanon (2012). See also Baucom (2001).

64. Clyde Appleton wrote: "You mentioned that you need news from the South. If you wish me to, I'll be glad to clip things from the local press that I think you might be able to use. The enclosures in this letter are from the past few days papers" (Appleton 1963). While exile in Cuba gave the Williamses the opportunity to broadcast, they lacked access to recordings of U.S. American popular music. For an example of Robert's urgent request for music, see "S.O. S." (1962), 6.

References

Appleton, C. 1963, May 6. Letter to Robert Williams. Robert F. Williams Papers (Box 1). Bentley Historical Library, University of Michigan.

Barlow, W. 1990. "Rebel Airways: Radio and Revolution in Latin America." *Howard Journal of Communications* 2.2: 123–34.

1999. *Voice Over: The Making of Black Radio*. Philadelphia, PA: Temple University Press.

Baucom, I. 2001. "Frantz Fanon's Radio: Solidarity, Diaspora, and the Tactics of Listening." *Contemporary Literature* 42.1: 15–49.

Bryant, C. E. 1963, May 7. Letter to Robert Williams. Robert F. Williams Papers (Box 1 Correspondence). Bentley Historical Library, University of Michigan.

Cha-Jua, S. K., and C. Lang. 2007. "The 'Long Movement' as Vampire: Temporal and Spatial Fallacies in Recent Black Freedom Studies." *Journal of African American History* 92.2: 265–88.

Chiung, F. 1964, October 6. Letter to Robert Williams. Robert F. Williams Papers (Box 1 Correspondence). Bentley Historical Library, University of Michigan.

Cohen, R. C. 1972. *Black Crusader: A Biography of Robert Franklin Williams*. New York: Lyle Stuart, Inc.

Dolan, J. 2003. "The Voice that Cannot Be Heard: Radio/Broadcasting and 'the Archive.'" *Radio Journal: International Studies in Broadcast and Audio Media* 1.1: 63–72.

Fanon, F. 2012. "This Is the Voice of Algeria." In *The Sound Studies Reader*, ed. J. Sterne, 329–35. New York: Routledge.

Fouché, R. 2006. "Say it Loud, I'm Black and I'm Proud: African Americans, American Artifactual Culture, and Black Vernacular Technology Creativity." *American Quarterly* 58.3: 639–61.

Frazier, R. T. 2014. *The East Is Black: Cold War China in the Black Radical Imagination*. Durham, NC: Duke University Press.

Gibson, R. 1965, August 16. Letter to Robert Williams. Robert F. Williams Papers (Box 1 Correspondence). Bentley Historical Library, University of Michigan.

Greenwood, F. 1965, April 30. Letter to Robert Williams. Robert F. Williams Papers (Box 1 Correspondence). Bentley Historical Library, University of Michigan.

Guridy, F. A. 2010. *Forging Diaspora: Afro-Cubans and African Americans in a World Empire and Jim Crow.* Chapel Hill: University of North Carolina Press.

Hilmes, M. 2012. "Radio and the Imagined Community." In *The Sound Studies Reader*, ed. J. Sterne, 351–62. New York: Routledge.

Hughes, L. 2000. "When a Man Sees Red." In *The Return of Simple*, ed. A. S. Harper, 83–86. New York: Hill & Wang.

2002. "Income Tax." In *The Collected Works of Langston Hughes*, Vol. 7, ed. A. S. Harper, 98–101. Columbia: University of Missouri Press.

Mallory, M. 1961, December 2. "A Letter from Mae." *The Crusader*, 3.

McLuhan, E. 1995. "Playboy Interview: Marshall McLuhan – A Candid Conversation with the High Priest of Popcult and Metaphysician of Media." In *Essential McLuhan*, ed. E. McLuhan and F. Zingrone, 233–69. New York: Basic Books.

Merrill, R. 1963, April 15. Report of reception; Campbell, A. O. (1964, October 5). Report of reception. Robert F. Williams Papers (Box 1 Correspondence). Bentley Historical Library, University of Michigan.

Mislan, C. 2015. "'In the Spirit of '76 Venceremos!': Nationalizing and Transnationalizing Self-defense on *Radio Free Dixie*." *American Journalism* 32.4: 434–52.

Neigh, J. 2013. "The Transnational Frequency of Radio Connectivity in Langston Hughes's 1940s Poetics." *Modernism/Modernity* 20.2: 265–85.

Nobil, C. M. 1963, August 26. Letter to Robert Williams. Robert F. Williams Papers (Box 1 Correspondence). Bentley Historical Library, University of Michigan.

Ong, W. 1982. *Orality and Literacy.* New York: Routledge.

Parker, T. N.d. Letter to Robert Williams. Robert F. Williams Papers (Box 1 Correspondence). Bentley Historical Library, University of Michigan.

Radio Free Dixie press release. 1962, July 27. *Radio Free Dixie* broadcast transcripts, Folder: 09051–011–0490, Black Power Movement, Part 2: The Papers of Robert F. Williams, ProQuest History Vault.

Rossa, D. 1965, March 15. "Los Angeles Theater Group Presents the Monroe Story." *The Militant*, 5.

Rucker, W. 2006. "Crusader in Exile: Robert F. Williams and the International Struggle for Black Freedom in America." *The Black Scholar* 3.2–3: 19–34.

"S.O.S." 1962, September. *The Crusader*, 6.

Szulc, T. 1964, July 28. "Expatriate, on Cuban Radio, Calls on U.S. Negroes to Meet Violence with Violence." *The New York Times*, 13.

Taylor, D. 2003. *The Archive and the Repertoire: Performing Cultural Memory in the Americas.* Durham, NC: Duke University Press.

Thomas, K. 1965, April 24. "'If We Must Live' Blasts Away, Ringing with Truth." *Los Angeles Times*, B9.

Tyson, T. 1999. *Radio Free Dixie: Robert F. Williams and the Roots of Black Power.* Chapel Hill: University of North Carolina Press.

Ward, B. 2004. *Radio and the Struggle for Civil Rights in the South.* Gainesville: University Press of Florida.

Williams, M. 1960, November 5. "De Master's Voice." *The Crusader*, 1.

Williams, R. 1962a, April. "Truth Crushed to Earth Shall Rise Again." *The Crusader* 3.8: 3.

    1962b, 27 July. "First Announcement, Negro Press, Radio Progresso [sic]." *Radio Free Dixie* broadcast transcripts, Folder: 09051–011–0490, Black Power Movement, Part 2: The Papers of Robert F. Williams, ProQuest History Vault.

    1963, April 24. Letter to Clyde Appleton. Robert F. Williams Papers (Box 1). Bentley Historical Library, University of Michigan.

    1964a, January 30. Letter to Noel Bailey. Robert F. Williams Papers (Box 1 Correspondence). Bentley Historical Library, University of Michigan.

    1964b, January 30. Letter to J. A. Lumpp. Robert F. Williams Papers (Box 1 Correspondence). Bentley Historical Library, University of Michigan.

    1964c, March 30. Letter to Dick Bayer. Robert F. Williams Papers (Box 1 Correspondence). Bentley Historical Library, University of Michigan.

Williams, R., and M. Williams. 1962a, July 27. *Radio Free Dixie* transcript. Robert F. Williams Papers (Box 10). Bentley Historical Library, University of Michigan.

    1962b, August 17. *Radio Free Dixie* transcript, 6. Robert F. Williams Papers (Box 10). Bentley Historical Library, University of Michigan.

    1962c, October 18. *Radio Free Dixie* transcript, 15. Robert F. Williams Papers (Box 10). Bentley Historical Library, University of Michigan.

    1962d, November 2. *Radio Free Dixie* transcript, 1. Robert F. Williams Papers (Box 10). Bentley Historical Library, University of Michigan.

    1963, February 22. *Radio Free Dixie* transcript. Robert F. Williams Papers (Box 10). Bentley Historical Library, University of Michigan.

    1964, May 1. *Radio Free Dixie* transcript, 6–8. Robert F. Williams Papers (Box 10). Bentley Historical Library, University of Michigan.

    1965, April 16. *Radio Free Dixie* transcript, 1–2. Robert F. Williams Papers (Box 10). Bentley Historical Library, University of Michigan.

Wright, R., and L. Wylie. 2009. *Our Place in the Sun: Canada and Cuba in the Castro Era.* University of Toronto Press.

Young, C. 2006. *Soul Power: Culture, Radicalism, and the Making of a U.S. Third World Left.* Durham, NC: Duke University Press.

Index